THE RICHES OF ANCIENT AUSTRALIA

Dr Josephine Flood was born in Yorkshire, England. She attended Cambridge University where she gained her BA degree. In 1963 she moved to Australia to live, and became a lecturer in archaeology at the Australian National University, where she later gained an MA degree and a PhD. In 1978 Dr Flood was appointed Senior Conservation Officer with the Australian Heritage Commission in Canberra, and in 1984 she became an Assistant Director as head of the Aboriginal Environment Section. In 1991 she was elected a Fellow of the Australian Academy of the Humanities.

Dr Flood has travelled extensively. She joined two women's mountaineering expeditions in the Himalayas, and participated in fieldwork in Australia, most recently in an expedition near Katherine in the Northern Territory. She is the author of numerous articles and papers on Australian prehistory, and three books: *Four Miles High* (1966), *The Moth Hunters* (1980) and *Archaeology of the Dreamtime* (1983, new edition 1989).

By the same author

Four Miles High
The Moth Hunters
Archaeology of the Dreamtime

THE RICHES OF ANCIENT AUSTRALIA

AN INDISPENSABLE GUIDE FOR EXPLORING PREHISTORIC AUSTRALIA

JOSEPHINE FLOOD

University of Queensland Press

First published 1990 by University of Queensland Press
Box 42, St Lucia, Queensland 4067 Australia
Reprinted 1993

Typeset by University of Queensland Press
Printed in Australia by Globe Press, Melbourne

Distributed in the USA and Canada by
International Specialized Book Services, Inc.,
5602 N.E. Hassalo Street, Portland, Oregon 97213-3640

AUSTRALIAN HERITAGE COMMISSION

Australia's Heritage
The University of Queensland Press
acknowledges the support and encouragement
of the Australian Heritage Commission

Cataloguing in Publication Data

National Library of Australia

Flood, Josephine.
   The riches of ancient Australia.

   Bibliography.
   Includes index.

   1. Historic sites – Australia – Guide-books.
   2. Australia – Antiquities – Guide-books.
   [3]. Aborigines, Australian – Antiquities
   – Guide-books. 4. Petroglyphs – Australia
   – Guide-books. 5. Rock paintings – Australia
   – Guide-books. 6. Australia – Description
   and travel – 1976 –   – Guide-books. I. Title.

919.40463

ISBN 0 7022 2259 3

This book is dedicated to the traditional owners and custodians of this heritage, the Aboriginal people of Australia.

Contents

Illustrations

Table

Plates

Figures

Foreword

This first comprehensive guide to Australia's prehistoric heritage, *The Riches of Ancient Australia: A Journey into Prehistory,* has been written to meet expressed community demands – for people wishing to know more about Australia's prehistoric heritage without having to grapple with technical terms, and to help people recognise, appreciate and visit important prehistoric places throughout Australia. It also aims to ensure that people who visit these places treat them with respect.

The book is directed to a wide audience. Aboriginal communities, academics, educators, public servants, members of the conservation movement, politicians, members of the tourist industry, developers, members of the mining and agriculture industries and students will all benefit from this book. At the same time it makes excellent reading for anyone who wants to make an armchair tour of ancient places. International visitors will find the book more than useful. Australia, at last, can take its rightful place among the nations which possess some of the riches of the world's human and natural heritage.

Josephine Flood, a professional archaeologist, produced *The Riches of Ancient Australia* while working as the full-time head of the Aboriginal Section at the Australian Heritage Commission. It is part of her personal out-of-hours activities as a professional archaeologist, as an author, researcher and mother of three. It suffers not in the slightest because of this. The book is another first for Dr Flood. She was the first researcher to write comprehensively about the Aboriginal prehistory of the Australian Alps in her book, *The Moth Hunters: Aboriginal Prehistory of the Australian Alps.* The choice of the south-eastern highlands as the focus of Josephine Flood's PhD thesis reflects her long interest in mountains and mountaineering. Her first book *Four Miles High* told the story of her journeys to Afghanistan, India and Nepal to scale previously unclimbed peaks. The two expeditions which she joined consisted solely of women. Her first job after completing her bachelor's degree at Cambridge University was as a rock-climbing instructor in North Wales. She has also climbed in Europe and New Zealand, skied in Australia and elsewhere and in 1986 rafted down the Franklin River in south-west Tasmania to view the World Heritage Area at close quarters.

Josephine Flood's most recent book is the popular *Archaeology of the Dreamtime,* a highly readable, authoritative account of the story of prehistoric Australia and her people. It was first published in 1983 and a new edition appeared in 1989. Dr Flood has made and continues to make a considerable contribution to Australian prehistory and to the work of the Australian Heritage Commission. She is a committed, dedicated and highly respected professional and one of the longest-serving staff members at the Commission.

The Riches of Ancient Australia is being published at a time when the Australian Heritage Commission is raising public awareness about the Register of the National Estate – the inventory of all those places that Australians want to keep – and is stimulating nominations of Aboriginal places to the Register. This book is not only a very important contribution to the growing awareness amongst Australians that our heritage must be protected, but it is another fine example of Dr Flood's ability to pioneer areas in her field. It was a brave step to go ahead with this project in the face of possible opposition from people who believe that the only way to protect Aboriginal sites is not to let anyone know where they are located. However, a policy of protection through anonymity can lead to accidental damage or destruction of sites by people who do not realise their significance, or even existence. Instead, this book focuses on sites which have been opened and interpreted to the public in accordance with the widely accepted principles of visitor management and site protection described in a Commission publication *Tourists and the National Estate,* by Professor Fay Gale and Jane Jacobs.

Thousands of Australians and people from overseas visit prehistoric Aboriginal sites every year. The best way to protect them is by educating the public to their significance and thus minimising or preventing the possibility of damage. This book urges people to "Do the right thing". My hope is that readers will all heed Dr Flood's suggestions. Such heritage conservation is extremely important if we are to ensure that our heritage is passed on to future generations of Australians who accept, appreciate and understand that humans have lived on this unique continent for more than fifty thousand years. Much damage has been done to Aboriginal Australia since 1788 and this is another work which aids the reconciliation process, involving acceptance that the Aboriginal heritage is a vital part of the national estate and must be protected. It should be emphasised that there has been extensive consultation over a two-year period with Aboriginal organisations, State and Territory sites and heritage authorities, and others about the contents of the book.

The Commission is proud to have been able to support the University of Queensland Press with another excellent book in its Australia's heritage series.

P.J. Galvin, Chairman
Australian Heritage Commission

Preface

This book is for Aboriginal people and others who wish to know more about Australia's prehistoric heritage, and to visit some of the continent's outstanding sites. It has been written to help people appreciate and see some of Australia's prehistoric heritage places. There is a clear demand by both Aboriginal people, whose cultural heritage it is, and by non-Aborigines for information on Australian prehistory. One of the questions frequently asked by Aboriginal and other Australians and by visitors from overseas is: "Where can I see something of the Aboriginal heritage of Australia?" This book gives a general introduction to the prehistory of each state and territory and then a detailed account of some selected prehistoric sites which are open to the public.

In view of the Aboriginal cultural revival of the last few years and the increasing demand for cultural tourism, most site managers now consider that at least a small selection of sites should be open to visitors, so the present generation may have the pleasurable, educational and uplifting experience of seeing some of the material evidence of this complex, age-old culture.

With careful management and presentation, the opening of sites to visitors can have a positive rather than a negative effect on both visitor appreciation and site conservation. This has been well documented by Professor Fay Gale and Jane Jacobs of Adelaide University in their book *Tourists and the National Estate: Procedures to Protect Australia's Heritage* (published by the Australian Heritage Commission in 1987), which is a study of visitor management at some of the Aboriginal rock art sites of Kakadu and Uluru National Parks.

It must be strongly emphasised that all Aboriginal sites mentioned in this book are legally protected under state/territory and/or federal legislation. Any damage to such sites or removal of artefacts is against the law and is a serious offence, punishable with heavy penalties.

Three categories of sites are included. Firstly, there are those which are open to the public; some are described in detail at the end of each regional chapter. Second, there are sites which may be visited only by special arrangement, where permission for access must be sought from Aboriginal custodians, landowners or state sites authorities, as indicated in the text. Third, there are sites to which there is absolutely no public access — general reference is made to these sites because of their importance in the story of Australian prehistory.

Information, advice and permission where necessary should be sought from the relevant state/territory sites authorities (listed on pages 361–63). It is recommended that travellers seek advice before visiting any Aboriginal site except those open to the public within national parks, because the management of Aboriginal sites is a dynamic process and the situation regarding visits may have changed since this book was written.

In addition to prehistoric cultural sites, some non-cultural sites are included, such as extinct volcanoes, animal fossil sites and limestone cave formations. This choice reflects my own interests, not only in the human story but in trying to understand the land in which we live. It also seems a shame for visitors to travel long distances to see a particular prehistoric Aboriginal site and miss visiting an outstanding natural phenomenon in the same region because they are unaware of its existence. In any case, a sharp division cannot be made between the cultural and the natural environment. Rather, like Aboriginal people, who hold the concept that "We belong to the land and the land belongs to us", readers from all backgrounds should recognise the strong relationships between human beings and nature.

The focus is on *prehistoric* sites rather than on places from the historic period, defined in Australia as post-1788. Historic Aboriginal sites are of prime importance to Aboriginal people, but have already received considerable attention from both Aboriginal and non-Aboriginal writers, most recently from Professor John Mulvaney in his book *Encounters in Place: Outsiders and Aboriginal Australians 1606-1985*. Nevertheless, there is not always a sharp division between the historic and the prehistoric. Many campsites, for instance, contain evidence of occupation from both periods, and in the case of rock paintings it is often difficult to ascertain their age. My rule of thumb has therefore been to exclude any wholly historic sites, but when a site is likely to be at least in part prehistoric, to include it, as part of a living, on-going culture

The places chosen for detailed description are important prehistoric sites which are in the Register of the National Estate and which are accessible to the general public. The Register is the Australian Heritage Commission's inventory of "those places, being components of the natural environment of Australia or the cultural environment of Australia, that have aesthetic, historic, scientific or social significance or other special value for future generations as well as for the present community".

Sites excluded are particularly sensitive ones like prehistoric burials or those with nothing to see, such as sites whose artefacts have been removed to museums. Museums, especially those in capital cities, are excellent starting points for the visitor, and some information about them is included here. The manuscript has been checked by the relevant state/territory Aboriginal and government authorities, and modified in the light of their comments.

Efforts have been made to consult relevant Aboriginal land councils and communities on the text and illustrations for their region. Only two requests for changes were received, and photographs of rock art at Emily Gap and Uluru in the Northern Territory were withdrawn at traditional owners' request.

Other sites not generally included here are Aboriginal sacred sites, also known as Dreaming places or living, story, ethnographic or mythological sites. Sacred sites are omitted for several reasons: information about them is often confidential and access restricted; it is more appropriate for an Aborigine rather than a non-Aborigine to describe them; and visiting such sites is rarely a meaningful experience without a local Aboriginal guide to interpret the site. Occasionally such sites have been included if the Aboriginal custodians encourage public visits, or if heritage trails follow Dreaming tracks, or if they have other elements of significance such as rock paintings.

Detailed descriptions of Aboriginal lifeways in different regions were reluctantly omitted, as being beyond the scope of this book, so I was delighted to see the publication recently of *Burnum Burnum's Aboriginal Australia: A Traveller's Guide.* This describes through Aboriginal eyes the lifestyles, history, art and lore of the original Australians. It is thus directly complementary to the present work, which continues the story of this island continent further back in time.

Three introductory chapters precede chapters on seventeen different regions. The introductory chapters set the scene on a continent-wide basis and explain themes recurring in later chapters. They give only a brief general account of Australian prehistory and rock art, for which readers are referred to works listed in the Further Reading section. There is a Glossary, and chapter End Notes, given at the back of the book, refer to some of the key materials which readers may wish to follow up. Usually references are given to only the most up-to-date, comprehensive, published books, articles or monographs, since reference to generally unavailable, unpublished reports and theses only leads to frustration.

The regional chapters are arranged to take the reader round Australia in a snake-like, anti-clockwise journey, starting in Western Australia and finishing in Tasmania (Figure 0.1).

Acknowledgments

Thanks go to the following individuals and organisations for their helpful comments on the manuscript, and assistance with Aboriginal consultation in some cases:

Aboriginal Heritage Section, Department of Environment and Planning, South Australia (Mr Bob Ware, Mr Neale Draper and Ms Jo Bramley)   (Chs. 12 and 13)

Aboriginal Sacred Sites Protection Authority, Darwin (Mr David Cooper and Mr Peter Blackwood)   (Chs. 8 and 11)

Dr Michael Archer, University of New South Wales   (Ch.9)

Australian National Parks and Wildlife Service (Ms Hilary Sullivan)   (Chs. 8 and 11)

Mr Alex Barlow, Education Officer, Australian Institute of Aboriginal and Torres Strait Islander Studies *(passim)*

Mr Robert Bednarik, Editor *Rock Art Research*   (Chs. 3, 6, 12 and 13)

Conservation Commission of the Northern Territory (Mr Pat Somers)   (Chs.8 and 11)

Mr Richard Cosgrove, La Trobe University   (Ch.20)

Mr Howard Creamer, National Parks and Wildlife Service, NSW   (Ch. 17)

Department of Conservation and Land Management, Western Australia (Mr H. Chevis and Mr C. Done)   (Chs. 4, 5, 6 and 7)

Department of Parks, Wildlife and Heritage, Tasmania (Mr Steve Brown and Mr Greg Middleton)   (Ch. 20)

Mr John Feint, Heritage Unit, ACT Department of Environment, Land and Planning (Ch. 19)

Gagadju Association, Kakadu National Park   (Ch. 8)

Professor Fay Gale, University of Western Australia   (Chs. 12 and 13)

Mr R.G. Gunn, rock art consultant   (Chs. 8, 13 and 14)

Associate Professor Sylvia Hallam, University of Western Australia   *(passim)*

Dr Jeannette Hope, National Parks and Wildlife Service, NSW   (Ch. 16)

Dr Rhys Jones, Australian National University   (Chs. 8 and 20)

Mr Bernie Joyce, Department of Geology, Universityof Melbourne   *(passim)*

Mr Dick Kimber, Alice Springs   (Ch. 11)

Mr David Lambert, National Parks and Wildlife Service, NSW   (Ch. 18)

Dr Ronald Lampert, Australian Museum   (Chs. 13, 16, 17 and 18)

Ms Jane Lennon, Department of Conservation, Forests and Lands, Victoria (Chs. 14 and 15)

Professor Isabel McBryde, Australian National University   (Chs. 16, 17 and 18)

Ms Jo Macdonald, Australian National University   (Ch. 18)

Ms Mireille Mardaga-Campbell, James Cook University   (Ch. 9)

Dr Michael Morwood, University of New England   (Chs. 1, 3, 9 and 10)

Mutitjulu Community, Uluru National Park   (Ch. 11)

New South Wales National Parks and Wildlife Service   (Chs. 16, 17 and 18)

Mrs Margaret Nobbs, rock art specialist, Adelaide   (Chs. 12 and 13)

Mr Michael Pickering, Northern Land Council   (Ch. 8)

Dr Rosemary Purdie, Australian Heritage Commission   *(passim)*

Mr Richard Robins, Queensland Museum   (Chs. 9 and 10)

Dr Andree Rosenfeld, Australian National University   (Ch. 3)

Mr Michael Rowland, Cultural Heritage Branch, Department of Environment and Heritage, Qld   (Chs. 9 and 10)

Dr Michael Smith, Australian National University   (Chs. 8, 11, 12 and 13)

Tasmanian Aboriginal Centre   (Ch. 20)

Dr Gerry Van Tets, CSIRO   (Ch. 2)

Victoria Archaeological Survey (Mr Michael McIntyre and Mr Don Hough) (Chs. 14 and 15)

Mr Grahame Walsh, Queensland National Parks and Wildlife Service   (Chs. 9 and 10)

Western Australian Heritage Committee (Mr David Colvin and Dr Averill O'Brien)   (Chs. 4, 5, 6 and 7)

Western Australian Museum (Ms Elizabeth Bradshaw, Mr Ken McNamara, Mr Michael Robinson)   (Chs. 4, 5, 6 and 7)

Maps and figures are by Irene Jarvin, to whom I am grateful for her meticulous and painstaking work. I took the photographs unless stated otherwise, and I much appreciate the generous provision of photographs by those people acknowledged in the captions. Final editing of the manuscript was carried out by Clare Hoey, and Jane Morrison of the Australian Heritage Commission also assisted. My thanks to both of them for their helpfulness in coping with my inconsistencies.

I would also like to thank Dr Craig Munro and Ms Rosanne Fitzgibbons of University of Queensland Press for their faith, encouragement and confidence throughout what proved to be a lengthy and challenging assignment.

On a personal note, my heartfelt thanks go to my children, Adrian, Michael and Nadine, for their support and understanding while I was going through the difficult task of fitting the writing of this book into evenings and weekends between April 1986 and January 1990.

It should be mentioned that site coverage in this book is deliberately uneven. The varying degree of detail given in site descriptions reflects the varying amount of information available locally to the visitor at the time of writing. This ranges from full information in visitors' centres, leaflets and interpretive signs to absolutely nothing. Where there is little or no information, my coverage is necessarily much fuller than elsewhere, since the object of this book is to enhance visitor experience and appreciation of the Aboriginal cultural heritage.

The book has been partially revised and up-dated for a new edition in early 1993, and mention made of some of the latest archaeological discoveries. These additions are included in the index, and pagination remains the same. All dates on sites are quoted as published, but current opinion among the dating laboratories is that radiocarbon dates on sites older than 30,000 years are likely to be older than stated. This is because they are nearing the limit (40,000 years) to which this dating method can be applied.

Finally, there is an element of trust in the reader's goodwill towards Australia's heritage in producing a book such as this. I am confident that that trust will not be betrayed; that you will take nothing away but your memories and leave nothing behind but your footprints.

Josephine Flood
Canberra, January 1990.
Revised September 1992.
Fyfnhon Bedr,
Llanbedr-y-Cennin,
Conwy, Gwynedd.
UK LL32 8YZ

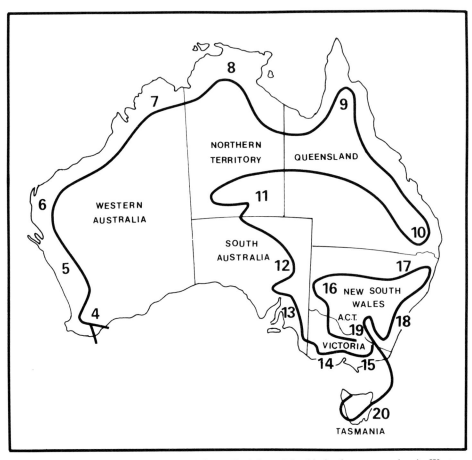

Figure 0.1 The snake-like route around Australia followed in this book, commencing in Western Australia and finishing in Tasmania. The numbers refer to chapters treating each region.

CHAPTER ONE

Do the Right Thing!

This book has been written to help people recognise, appreciate and visit some of Australia's important prehistoric places, but first attention must be drawn to the obligations and responsibilities all visitors share in the conservation of this unique heritage.

These places are vulnerable to accidental damage from even the most well-intentioned visitor. While this chapter focuses on the dos and don'ts of visiting Aboriginal sites, much of the advice will also be relevent to other types of heritage places. (A site is a place where past human activity is identifiable.)

First, virtually all these heritage sites and "relics", "objects" or "artefacts" are the property of the Crown and are protected under state, territory and/or federal legislation. (An Aboriginal artefact is any object made or modified by Aborigines but excluding those made in recent times for sale.) Under most state legislation, Aboriginal "relics" are protected as a class; they need not be specially declared or registered. "Relics" are defined in the National Parks and Wildlife Act 1974 of New South Wales as "any deposit, object or material evidence (not being a handicraft made for sale) relating to indigenous and non-European habitation of the area . . .".

One gap in present legal protection of Aboriginal sites is that natural features such as a distinctively shaped boulder, a waterhole or a mountain top may well be sacred sites of great significance to an Aboriginal community, but may contain no evidence of past Aboriginal activity. Such natural sacred sites, also termed Dreaming, mythological, traditional, ethnographic or living sites, are not generally recognised or protected, unless specially declared under the relevant law. At present the existence of sacred sites is not recognised under either Queensland or Tasmanian legislation, and in most other regions they have to be specifically registered before they can be protected. Only in Western Australia and South Australia do sacred natural features receive the same "blanket" protection as a class as the "relics" sites and objects. In a recent piece of legislation enacted, the South Australian Aboriginal Heritage Act 1987, any Aboriginal site or object is protected which is of traditional significance to Aboriginal people, or of archaeological or anthropological significance.

Three pieces of federal legislation relevant to the Aboriginal heritage are in force. The first is the Australian Heritage Commission Act 1975, which provides for the development of the Register of the National Estate, an inventory of heritage places. There are now some 8,000 heritage places, including over 6,000 individual Aboriginal sites, in the Register. Virtually all sites mentioned in this book, whether Aboriginal or natural environment places, are in the Register of the National Estate.

Two other pieces of federal legislation are relevant: the Protection of Movable Cultural Heritage Act 1986, which governs the export and import of artefacts, and the Aboriginal and Torres Strait Islander Heritage Protection Act of 1984. This allows Aboriginal groups to apply for protection for significant sites and objects under threat, and is a useful weapon with which to protect endangered sites and artefacts.

The question is sometimes asked, "Why is it necessary to protect ALL these Aboriginal sites? Why not just a small sample of the most significant ones?" The answer is that each Aboriginal site is a unique manifestation of Aboriginal society; no two sites exactly replicate each other. They are all part of the Aboriginal heritage of Australia, which is of great significance to Aborigines and non-Aborigines alike. Therefore Australians should try to conserve all Aboriginal sites, but at the same time accept that some will be lost through natural agency and others which stand in the way of development projects may have to be sacrificed after salvage archaeology has been carried out.

The various pieces of state legislation vary in detail, but in general contain the following provisions for protection of Aboriginal heritage sites and objects, with heavy penalties for any contravention:

1. It is against the law to disturb or damage any Aboriginal site or object.
2. It is against the law to destroy any Aboriginal site or object.
3. It is against the law to deface or cover up any Aboriginal site or object.
4. It is against the law to desecrate any Aboriginal site or object.
5. It is against the law to remove or collect any Aboriginal object (not made for sale).
6. It is against the law to excavate any Aboriginal site or object without permission from the relevant authority.

In case any of these prohibitions seem unnecessary to visitors, they are all based on problems which have arisen from time to time. Regarding number 3, the words "cover up" were included after a landholder in Queensland bulldozed earth over a set of Aboriginal axe-grinding grooves while carrying out construction work. Other people have removed artefacts and souvenired skulls from burials, or sold them to anatomy students (figure 1.1).

Even those visitors who take every care to obey the law can accidentally cause damage to sites, for instance by stirring up dust with their feet or inadvertently brushing up against rock paintings. It is important to move carefully to avoid touching rock paintings or other vulnerable sites, or trampling on rock engravings, stone arrangements, middens or other remains (figure 1.2).

Visitors may come across sites whose existence seems to be unknown; in this case they should take photographs and collect as much information as possible on where and what the site is, and pass it on to the state sites authority and other appropriate people. (It is possible to obtain blank site-recording forms from the state sites authority for this purpose.) It is also worth notifying the sites

Figure 1.1 Did you know that it is against the law to remove or sell relics? You can be taken to court and fined heavily. (D. Parsons, Victoria Archaeological Survey)

authorities of problems at a site, such as recent vandalism or a missing visitors' book.

Visitors' books have been placed in weatherproof boxes at many sites for visitors to record their names and comments; this is a useful way for site managers to know visitor numbers and monitor their impact on the site, and to provide somewhere for them to record their visit apart from on the rock itself.

Figure 1.2 Even people going about their everyday work might be breaking the law. All Aboriginal sites are protected by law, but many have been accidentally destroyed. (D. Parsons, Victoria Archaeological Survey)

Visitors' books are usually made of paper but there is even one of rock! This is at Chambers Pillar in the Northern Territory, where an artificial stone column has been erected for visitors to inscribe their names to keep graffiti off the actual pillar.

The rest of this chapter is devoted to describing the wide range of Aboriginal heritage places included in this book, and to suggesting appropriate visitor behaviour.

There are more than 60,000 Aboriginal sites on record in Australia, and they are found all over the continent. Site distribution maps give the impression that the largest numbers of sites are in south-eastern Australia, but this is just the result of the greater amount of surveying done in areas close to big cities such as Sydney where much development is taking place. Everywhere that archaeologists have looked for sites, they have found them, from the Simpson Desert to the Snowy Mountains, from the Great Barrier Reef Islands to apparently uninhabited south-west Tasmania. Indeed, some would say that Australia is one continuous Aboriginal site!

Economic sites predominate, including camping places, quarries, axe grinding grooves, wells and scarred trees. The vast majority are old campsites, in the same way that the vast majority of historic structures in Australia are houses, the places where people lived. These occupation sites are of scientific importance because to varying degrees they contain information about Aboriginal prehistoric material culture. They can tell visitors about past environments and how people lived, what food they ate, how they utilised the land and its resources, the type of tools they used and how they made them, and the season and size of the group occupying a particular site. Occupation sites take various forms, and may be divided into two large classes: economic sites, and religious, ceremonial and burial sites.

Economic sites

Open campsites

Open or surface campsites are areas in the open air showing a concentration of debris associated with human occupation. Stone artefacts are the most common indicators of past Aboriginal presence, but charcoal, food remains, baked clay, and fire-blackened and cracked stones may also be found. Campsites vary tremendously in size, from hundreds or even thousands of artefacts scattered over several hectares to two or three stone artefacts, often termed a "lithic scatter", or even the findspot of a single manuport. (A "manuport" is an object unmodified by human hand but occurring out of context, because it has been transported by human agency; the name is derived from Latin, meaning "carried by hand".) Artefacts, on the other hand, are objects modified by humans. If they have clearly been used or manufactured for use, they are described as tools, but waste flakes produced in the course of manufacturing a stone tool are simply termed stone artefacts.

Some open campsites are stratified; that is, they consist of successive layers or horizons of occupational debris and/or sediments. The layers may be dated by obtaining radiocarbon dates on organic material such as charcoal in the various layers. Much information can be gained by archaeologists who carefully study the nature and distribution of artefacts on such campsites, but any collecting, besides being against the law and a punishable offence, destroys the integrity of the site.

Occupational deposits in rockshelters and caves

In caves and rockshelters (naturally formed rock overhangs in a cliff, outcrop or boulder sheltering a floor area) there are frequently occupational deposits of debris from past camping there (plate 1.1). These are important archaeologically, because they often contain clearly stratified material in a good state of preservation. Examination by qualified researchers can give valuable insights into the nature and duration of prehistoric use of the site. If an occupational deposit is disturbed, even by excessive trampling, its scientific value is easily destroyed. Any activity which causes erosion or disturbs the site should be avoided, and of course it is illegal to collect any artefacts or dig into the deposit (figure 1.3).

Middens

Middens are deposits or refuse heaps, usually consisting mainly of shells. They are the most common and visible type of Aboriginal site on the coast, and middens of estuarine and freshwater shells also occur beside rivers and inland lakes. Essentially, middens are the remains of numerous Aboriginal meals of shellfish. They can be distinguished from natural deposits of shell because Aboriginal

Figure 1.3 Just because you like digging doesn't mean you are allowed to excavate relics. Excavation permits are given only to people with professional archaeological qualifications. (D. Parsons, Victoria Archaeological Survey)

Plate 1.1   The stratified occupational deposit in Fromms Landing shelter 6, which was excavated by D.J. Mulvaney in 1963. (D.J. Mulvaney)

people were selective, eating mainly mature specimens of edible species, whereas a natural shell deposit will contain also immature and inedible species.

Some middens are stratified and also contain stone and bone artefacts and charcoal. Middens going back in time more than 30,000 years have been found at Mungo in Western New South Wales. They vary from shallow, surface scatters of shell, heavily eroded by wind and water action, to plant-covered, stable deposits several metres thick. It is not always the largest or most impressive middens which prove to have the highest scientific potential, so like other types of Aboriginal sites, they should be conserved on principle. In fact, many have been destroyed over the years in the course of coastal development, but now protective environmental legislation is in place, further destruction should not take place except when unavoidable and after comprehensive survey, recording and salvage archaeology has been carried out.

Mounds

Mounds are artificial elevations created by the deliberate heaping up of earth above the level of the surrounding country. Many such mounds have occupational debris in the surface layers and evidence that wooden huts were formerly built on top of them. Some of them were oven or cooking mounds, and contain debris from earth cooking ovens, including ash, charcoal, heat discoloration and possibly hearth stones, burnt clay or termite mound as heat retainers. Repeated use of the site created large heaps of refuse. These are particularly common along major rivers such as the Murray in Victoria, where the mounds are known as kitchen middens, oven mounds or mirr'n-yong heaps, mirr'n-yong being the Aboriginal name for a type of vegetable tuber.

Quarries

Both stone and ochre quarries are found, but ochre quarries are relatively rare. A stone quarry can usually be recognised by the large amount of flaking and battering of exposed rock surfaces, and the presence of partly shaped artefacts and manufacturing debris such as waste flakes and utilised cores. (A core is a lump or nodule of stone from which flakes have been removed by striking it with another stone.) Igneous rock such as basalt and greenstone was prized for making stone axeheads because of its hardness and fine grain. In axe quarries axe "blanks" may be found; these are pieces of igneous rock roughed out to the size and shape of an axehead but without the chisel-like, ground cutting edge of the finished tool. (These are artefacts and should be left *in situ*.)

In other quarries sandstone was extensively exploited to make grinding or ceremonial stones. Elsewhere ochre was the prized resource, and high quality ochre was traded over hundreds of kilometres. Quarries, whether stone or ochre, provide valuable information on Aboriginal technology and exchange networks. Detailed scientific comparison of the rock types in Aboriginal quarries with the material of axes in museum collections has revealed the existence of a vast exchange network. Axeheads were traded as far as 800 kilometres from their source quarry. Some of this trade or exchange was the result of a desire for raw material or exotic goods not available locally, but there was also a complex system of reciprocal gift-giving and social and ritual links.

Grinding grooves and patches

Artefact sharpening grooves are a by-product of manual rubbing of an artefact to and fro to grind its surface. They are found on generally flat areas of soft rock, particularly sandstone, near creek beds or other sources of water used during the manufacturing or resharpening process. Axe grinding grooves are most common and are typically broad and shallow, whereas long narrow grooves were more probably caused by grinding bone tools or wooden spear shafts.

Grinding patches are rock pavements or slabs worn smooth by Aborigines grinding on their surface. They are most commonly found in arid regions, where Aboriginal people, especially women, carried out seed grinding.

Scarred trees

Scarred trees show scars caused by the removal of bark to make various artefacts, such as canoes, shields, boomerangs or coolamons (carrying dishes). When first cut, the scars in the bark would have been sharp and quite shallow, but since then the trees have grown many layers of bark so that the regrowth on the margins of the scars is now rounded and deep. Scarred trees used to be extremely common all over Australia, but are becoming increasingly rare due to loss through natural decay, bush fires, clearing and timber harvesting.

Wells

In the more arid parts of Australia there are wells of various types; natural wells in a rock surface, rock wells that have been manufactured by deepening natural pits, and earth wells. The surface was usually covered with a flat slab of stone or bark to prevent evaporation. Such wells, known as gnamma holes in South and Western Australia, were usually some distance from a natural water supply. Mapping the location of these waterholes and their associated campsites builds up a picture of lines of movement of prehistoric people in an arid environment.

Fish traps

A number of fish traps are scattered around the coast of Australia, particularly in the tropics, and some of these are still used by local Aboriginal communities. They consist of barriers formed by dry stone walls, often surmounted by wood or reed fences, which form small enclosures or pens within a tidal area to trap fish as the waters recede. They work on the basic principle that fish swim into them at high tide and then become trapped as the water level goes down when they can be easily caught. A few traps also remain on inland creeks and rivers, such as those at Brewarrina. Others like the Lake Condah examples were part of a complex piece of "hydraulic engineering" devised to produce regular large catches of eels.

Religious, ceremonial and burial sites

The sites described above can all be termed economic sites, but the sites of greatest importance to Aboriginal people are burial, religious and ceremonial sites. Burial sites are of particular concern, and Aboriginal people feel very strongly that the remains of their ancestors should not be disturbed. There are severe penalties for interfering with human remains in any way. Human remains which do come to light through the processes of natural erosion or in the course of development works are usually removed by the state sites authority, and given to the Aboriginal community for immediate re-burial.

No burial sites are open for public visitation, and no Aboriginal skeletal remains are displayed in any museum. Anyone coming across a prehistoric burial site should not disturb the remains, but immediately report them to the local Aboriginal community and the state sites authority (figure 1.4).

Figure 1.4   It is against the law to dig up or collect any human remains, your grandmother's or anyone else's! (D. Parsons, Victoria Archaeological Survey)

Ceremonial sites

These sites tend to be stone arrangements or ceremonial grounds, which are known in New South Wales and south-east Queensland as bora grounds. Bora grounds usually consist of two rings and a connecting pathway. The round or oval rings are surrounded by an earth bank, which was often topped by a brushwood fence when ceremonies were being held. A few examples survive, but such earth constructions are vulnerable to the plough and bulldozer, and many have been destroyed by accident. They are one of the very few types of Aboriginal site which can be identified on air photographs. Either the low banks cast a shadow if photographed when shadows are long, or the differing depth of soil produces "soil marks". (The earth banks tend to produce lusher, green grass because of the greater depth of soil.)

Stone arrangements were also associated with ceremonies, and sometimes were constructed in conjunction with bora grounds. They vary widely in form, ranging from simple cairns, or piles of stones, to complex groupings of stone circles, single lines, corridors or other designs. They are usually found close to water and ochre sources, but also occur in remote and relatively inaccessible places such as the tops of mountains or outcrops, where they were often associated with initiation ceremonies.

They are among the most fragile Aboriginal sites, and should not be interfered with in any way. Do not move the stones, even if they appear to be out of position, or make additions to the site. In most cases, even if traditional knowledge about them has not survived, they are sacred places, akin to the cathedrals and churches of European culture.

Natural sacred sites

There are many thousands of natural features in Australia which, although they contain no material evidence of Aboriginal ownership and use, are of considerable traditional significance to Aboriginal people. These sacred sites or Dreaming places, whether a rock formation, waterhole, cave or other natural feature, represent a direct link between contemporary Aboriginal custodians and their traditional culture. Central to Aboriginal beliefs is the conviction that the whole world — the sea, land, all living things and human beings — originated in the deeds of spirit ancestors in the Dreamtime, the era of creation.

The landscape is a visible imprint and physical proof of the Dreaming's spiritual energies, as the great ancestral spirits travelled across the country. Geographical features (not always impressive to non-Aboriginal eyes) mark episodes in these stories. Places where they created a landform, left an object behind or transformed themselves into a physical feature, plant or animal are sacred sites. Stories, songs, dances, rituals and sacred objects were ordained in the Dreamtime and are associated with each site. Songs follow the paths of the ancestral beings whose deeds they tell; they are linked together in a Dreaming track or songline. The spirit ancestors' songs are like maps, charting a "road" linking places where food and water can be found and where rituals must be performed.

Some of these Dreaming tracks are being presented and interpreted to the public by means of heritage trails. The story given out for visitors is a general public version; the deeper levels of meaning are restricted to senior traditional owners.

Rock art

There are more rock art sites open to visitors than any other type of Aboriginal site, and more than half the Aboriginal sites in the Register of the National Estate are rock paintings or engravings. Rock art sites therefore inevitably feature strongly in this book, and the antiquity, development, variety and techniques of rock art are described in chapter 3. Rock art is readily appreciated by the visitor, but also, with the best will in the world, easily inadvertently damaged. The main problems are caused by touching or by stirring up dust. The first cardinal rule is not to touch the art, nor let any part of yourself or your clothing come into contact with the rock surface. This includes your feet — do not walk on or close to painted or engraved surfaces! Engravings appear to be much more robust than ochred art, but engravings are also vulnerable to damage.

The second cardinal rule is not to alter the rock art in any way. This means not scratching or chalking round figures to make them stand out better in photographs, nor spraying water on paintings "to bring up the colours". A visitor to Split Rock near Laura threw a bucket of water on rock art; the effect was not to brighten the paintings up but only to wash the pigment away down the wall.

The third rule is not to change the environment of a site, by stirring up dust with your feet, driving your vehicle too close, lighting a campfire in the rockshelter or other similar activities.

Rock art is deteriorating at an alarming rate through natural agencies. Termites are building their tracks across the paintings, mud-daubing wasps and swallows construct nests in the rockshelters, cattle and other animals rub against the walls, water runs down and washes ochred art off, bushfires, erosion and exfoliation cause the rock surface to crack and crumble. Comparison of photographs of a site taken 20 years ago with the same site today is a sobering experience; whole figures and even whole panels of art have completely disappeared.

It may well be that there will be little ochred art left in another 50 years, now that it is no longer being regularly retouched as part of a living culture. It is therefore essential both to make a first-class archival record now and to enlist sympathy and support for the cause of rock art conservation by bringing the problems to the public's attention. Site managers have finally come to realise that this cannot be done if all sites are kept closed and "anonymous"; at least a small sample of rock art sites in each state need to be open to visitors. The Australian rock art sites which are open to the public comprise less than 0.1 per cent of the total number of sites.

A few rock art sites are sacred and open only to certain groups; these are both men's and women's sites. Others are secular and were used by whole family groups as camping places in the wet season. The particular value of rock art sites, for Aboriginal and non-Aboriginal people alike, is the way in which they illustrate the richness and complexity of the Aboriginal artistic and cultural tradition. This artistic legacy continues to be demonstrated in bark paintings and other mediums, but Australia's rock art has the distinction of being the longest surviving continuous cultural tradition in the world.

CHAPTER TWO

Introduction to Australian Prehistory

The story of Australia does not begin 40,000 years ago or even 100,000 years ago, but at the beginning of time. The rocks which make up Australia began to form about four and a half billion (4,500,000,000) years ago (see the geological time chart in figure 2.1).[1] This period, comprising the Precambrian and Palaeozoic eras, witnessed the creation of most of Australia's rocks: igneous rocks which solidified from molten material in and below the earth's crust, sedimentary rocks laid down from material eroded from older rocks by wind, water or ice, and metamorphic rocks derived from the previous kinds through alteration by heat and pressure. The older rocks were covered over by more recent rocks, but here and there erosion has exposed them to view. One of the oldest, most weathered landscapes is the Pilbara, where there are rocks between 2,600 million and 3,100 million years old.

In Australia one of the earliest forms of life on this planet has been found not only in fossil form, but also alive and well today. Three and a half billion years ago in shallow waters around volcanic islands, energy from the sun's radiation linked carbohydrates, phosphates and nitrogen to form nucleic acids, proteins and amino acids — life's building blocks. The first living organisms were single-celled bacteria. Sheets of cyanobacteria, tiny single-celled organisms, lived in shallow water, covering underwater surfaces and trapping particles of mud or silt to form growing mound-like structures called stromatolites. A stromatolite is "an organo-sedimentary structure produced by the sediment-trapping, binding and precipitation of micro-organisms" or more simply "a mound produced by cyanobacteria".[2] The mounds are constructed by complex communities of many different species of microbes, which have developed the ability to build. In the Pilbara fossilised stromatolites have been found in rocks between 3,450 and 3,550 million years old; this is the oldest firmly established evidence for life on earth. Other stromatolites are still growing today in lakes and embayments in Western Australia such as Shark Bay (see chapter 5). They resemble cauliflowers and appear to be lifeless rocks, but they are living organisms with a soft and spongy surface.

From about 2,500 to 570 million years ago stromatolites were the dominant form of life on earth and were widespread on the shorelines of Australian lakes

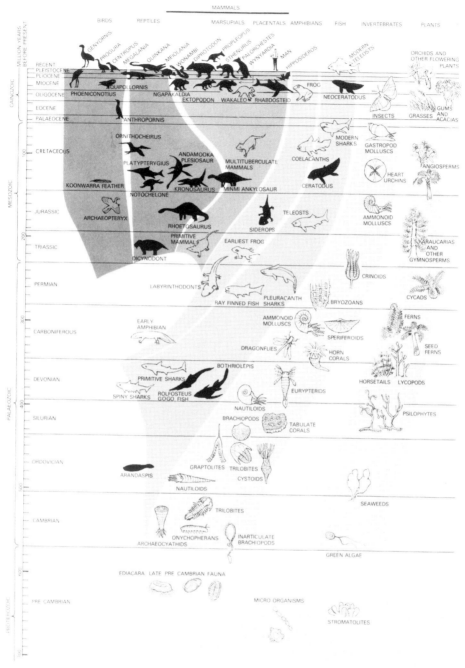

Figure 2.1 The changing Australian flora and fauna throughout geological time. (After E.M. Truswell and G.E. Wilford, Bureau of Mineral Resources, in *Kadimakara: Extinct Vertebrates of Australia*, eds P.V. Rich, G.F. van Tets and F. Knight, Pioneer Design Studio 1985, p.58)

and seas. About 1,400 million years ago the first green algae evolved, and for the next 400 million years bacteria and simple algae were the only life forms on earth (figure 2.1). Between about 1,000 and 570 million years ago life diversified. The

Plate 2.1   Fossil flat sea worm *(Dickinsonia)* from Ediacara, estimated at 600 million years old. (B. Macdonald, courtesy SA Museum)

first communities of multi-celled soft-bodied organisms evolved, and jellyfish, primitive worms and sponges joined simpler, single-celled organisms in the oceans and tidal flats.

Stromatolite numbers then declined drastically, but this ancient life form did not altogether disappear. In a very few places in the world living representatives still exist. One such place is the west coast of Western Australia, where at Shark Bay and in coastal lakes, stromatolites can be seen growing today. With an ancestry going back 3.5 billion years, they have been termed "the ultimate living fossils"!

Very early fossils are also found in the Flinders Ranges in South Australia, ranging from microscopic plant remains at least 1,000 million years old, to the jellyfish, segmented worms and soft coral of the Ediacara sandstone, dated to some 650 million years ago and probably the oldest, well-preserved fossil fauna in the world (plate 2.1).

There was a dramatic evolutionary explosion of life in the oceans about 570 million years ago at the beginning of the Cambrian era. Most of eastern Australia was covered by seas deepening to the east and populated by sea anemones, jellyfish, worm-like creatures and trilobites, segmented marine animals between 2 and 50 centimetres long which included swimmers, burrowers and bottom-dwellers. Great reefs were formed by Archaeocyathids, sponge-like filter-feeders from 8 to 10 centimetres tall.

Jawless fish, the first vertebrate creatures (animals with a backbone), appeared during the succeeding Ordovician period, between 500 and 435 million years ago. Then during Silurian times, life began on land. Land plants evolved from seaweeds, shorelines were colonised by plants and the first fish with jaws developed.

By 395 million years ago, at the beginning of the Devonian period, plants were spreading from the water margins to form thick vegetation in swampy areas, dominated by tree-like club mosses and "horsetails". Still much of Australia was covered by sea, and in the Kimberley there are Devonian ranges of fossilised limestone reefs some 360 million years old.

At this time Australia was still united with all the world's continents in the single landmass of Pangaea, but then this broke into two, and the southern landmass called Gondwana drifted southwards towards the South Pole. As part of Gondwana, Australia drifted through a series of different climatic zones. In Carboniferous times, between about 345 and 280 million years ago, glaciers developed and covered much of Australia, and hardy seed ferns grew in a cold, dry environment.

During the Permian epoch, some 250 million years ago, great ice sheets still occupied much of the land, and in South Australia rock slabs scratched and rounded by the passage of Permian glaciers can be seen at Hallett Cove (see chapter 13). There were no reptiles in Australia and trilobites and primitive corals died out, but large primitive amphibians, labyrinthodonts such as *Trucheosaurus* and *Bothriceps*, were plentiful, together with insects and fish. Ferns and horsetails abounded, and palm-like cycads, early conifers and ginkgoes occurred for the first time.

In Triassic times, about 225 to 195 million years ago, Australia was gradually reduced to a land of low relief. The climate became warmer and drier, ferns and insects were abundant and the first Australian reptiles appeared.

The age of dinosaurs followed in the Jurassic period, between 195 and 135 million years ago. The climate was warm and wet, fish resembling modern kinds and large aquatic reptiles inhabited the water while huge herbivorous dinosaurs browsed amid lush vegetation. By Cretaceous times, 135 to 65 million years ago, a shallow sea had invaded much of the continent, especially the interior lowlands of the Murray, Darling and Cooper River basins. Australia's first birds and a mammal — a platypus-like creature — appeared, together with flowering plants. Conifers and cycads declined, and dinosaurs and the giant aquatic reptiles were extinct by 65 million years ago.

During all these aeons Australia had been part of the great southern super-continent, Gondwana, along with Antarctica, southern India, most of Africa, Madagascar, much of South America and the nucleus of New Zealand; but around 120 million years ago Gondwana began to break up. By about 55 million years the crustal plate which makes up Australia had broken away from Antarctica, and the long drift northwards had begun. Australia drifted some 3,000 kilometres northward, and indeed is still drifting, at the rate of about eight centimetres per year.

From the beginning of separation until about fifteen million years ago the climate was much warmer and wetter, and fossils show that much of Gondwana was covered with temperate and subtropical rainforest, rich in ferns, conifers and the ancestors of the present Australian flowering plants. So the piece of Gondwana which drifted north to become *Terra Australis*, the south land, was a rocky raft loaded down with rainforest, cycads, southern beech and broadleaf forest, monotremes (the unique egg-laying mammals — the platypus and echidna), primitive three metre long lungfish, flightless birds and marsupials.

Australia is rich in vertebrate fossil animal remains, which range from extinct marsupials to dinosaurs, and dinosaurs' footprints left in mud which turned to stone near Winton, Queensland. The arid regions of South Australia and Queensland are particularly rich in such vertebrate remains of extinct animals, but the bones are usually better seen in museums than on site (plate 2.2). Museums particularly worth a visit for the fossil enthusiast are the Australian Museum, Sydney, the Museum of Victoria, Melbourne, the Queensland Museum, Brisbane, the South Australian Museum, Adelaide and the Western Australian Museum, Perth.

The period between about 65 and 23 million years is known as the Early Tertiary, and was followed by the Late Tertiary or Miocene epoch, lasting till the Pleistocene or ice age commenced about two million years ago. In the early Miocene period some 20 to 15 million years ago freshwater lakes dotted central Australia. Now dry lakes such as Lake Eyre were surrounded by subtropical rainforest and teemed with freshwater dolphins, lungfish, turtles, crocodiles and platypuses. This is also the time of the remarkable Riversleigh fossil fauna deposit in Queensland (see chapter 9). But during the late Miocene, about fifteen million years ago, the climate began to cool and dryness fanned out from the southern central part of the continent. Eucalypts, wattles (acacias) and grasslands spread, and bats, monitor lizards and rodents crossed the narrowing water barriers to reach Australia from south-east Asia.

During the last two million years, known as the Quaternary, the climate oscillated strongly, causing extensive modification of the environment. In dry periods desert dunes came into being, whereas in cooler periods with less evaporation lakes formed or grew in size, and rivers like the Murray and the Murrumbidgee enlarged their courses. This was the ice age or Pleistocene period (usually dated between 2,000,000 and 10,000 years ago), although Tasmania was the only part of Australia which was heavily glaciated and the ice age seems to have ended earlier in Australia than elsewhere. During the final cold period some 25,000 to 15,000 years ago there were also small glaciers in the Snowy Mountains of New South Wales.

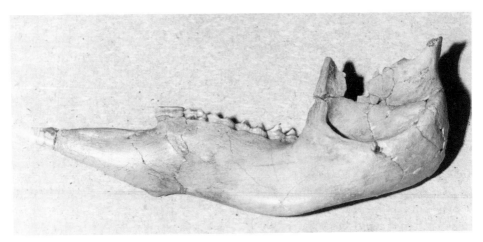

Plate 2.2 Lower jaw of an extinct kangaroo, *Troposodon*, 2 to 3 million years old, SA. (B. Macdonald, courtesy SA Museum)

Table 2.1   The human story in Australasia

Years ago	In Australia	In rest of world
1.2 million		*Homo erectus* in Java
500,000–300,000	*Homo erectus* in Zhoukoudian, China	
c.100,000		Early *Homo sapiens* in Java
c. 50,000	Humans reach Australia Humans in Arnhem Land, using ochre	
c. 44,000?	Engravings executed in the Olary region of South Australia	
c. 40,000	Humans at Lake Mungo in western New South Wales	Humans at Huon in New Guinea Humans in Lang Rongrien Cave in peninsular Thailand
c. 38,000	Humans have reached south-west Western Australia, and camp on the Upper Swan River (near Perth)	Humans in Leang Burung 2 in Sulawesi
c. 37,000	Occupation at Nurrabullgin Cave, Mount Mulligan, north Queensland	
c. 35,000	Humans have moved into Tasmania at a time of low sea level and are camping in caves in the south-west (Warreen Cave on Maxwell River)	
c. 32,000	Engravings made in Sandy Creek rockshelter, Cape York Peninsula	Humans in islands of New Britain and in Matenkupkum Cave in New Ireland
c. 30,000	Funerary rites are used at Lake Mungo	
c. 25,000	A young woman is cremated at Lake Mungo	
c. 20,000	People are living all over Australia, in every type of environment. Megafauna still present	
c. 18,000	Height of the last glaciation. Small glaciers on the Snowy Mountains and in Tasmania; sea level is about 150 metres below present level	
c. 13,000	Australia's oldest ornaments, bone beads, are made (Devils Lair, WA)	The ice age ends
c. 10,000	The world's oldest returning boomerangs are in use at Wyrie Swamp, SA	Agriculture is practised in the New Guinea highlands
c. 8,000	New Guinea and Tasmania are both finally separated from Australia by rising seas	People in Asia begin using metals
c. 4,680		Great pyramids built in Egypt
c. 4,000	Dingo reaches Australia. New, specialised small tools in use	
c. 3,000		Iron tools in use
c. 2,000	Australians fishing with hooks and lines	
		Jesus Christ is born
c. 800	Aborigines in west Victoria build stone houses in semi-permanent villages	
496	Macassans pay annual visits to northern Australia from Indonesia for trepang fishing	Columbus "discovers" America
218	Captain Cook sails up east coast of Australia	
200	First white settlers arrive in Sydney Cove	

The ice age, however, had a profound effect on sea level, for massive ice sheets in other parts of the world locked up so much water on land that the ocean level fell as much as 150 metres. Although this never created a complete land bridge between south-east Asia and Australia, it did create a great deal more dry land between Australia and her Asian neighbours. It was at this stage that humans came onto the Australian stage (table 2.1).

The earliest evidence of human presence in mainland Australia currently comes from rockshelters in Kakadu with 50,000-year-old occupation, and campsites with

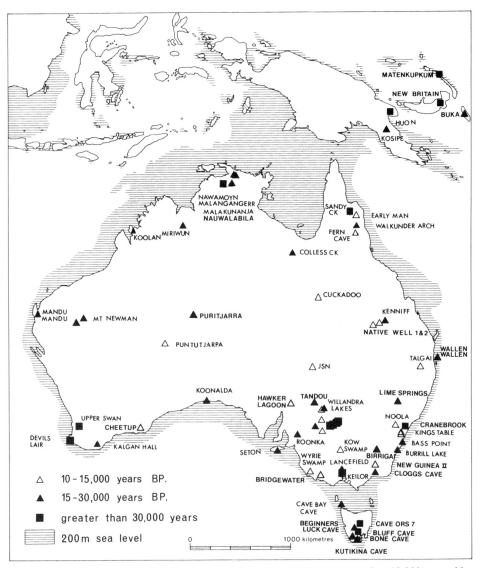

Figure 2.2   Greater Australia, showing the archaeological sites which are more than 10,000 years old.

stone tools and with charcoal radiocarbon-dated from 45,000 to 38,000 years old at Mungo in the Willandra Lakes region and the Upper Swan site (figure 2.2). Over a dozen other sites date to more than 30,000 years, and the great antiquity of Aboriginal culture is undisputed.

There has been considerable debate on the other hand about claims for cultural sites 60 or 80 or 100 thousand years old. In particular at Lake George near Canberra a 350,000-year-long pollen sequence obtained by Dr Gurdip Singh[3] of the Australian National University demonstrated a huge increase in the amount of charcoal present during the last interglacial period, about 120,000 years ago. This is evidence of a much higher incidence of fires than before, and an abrupt change to fire-tolerant vegetation dominated by *Eucalyptus* trees. These changes, according to Singh, are due to the arrival of Aboriginal people with their practice of regular burning as an aid in hunting, but others have disputed both the interpretation and the dating of this evidence. While early cultural sites may well come to light in the future, at present there is no solid evidence to prove the presence of humans in Australia much before 40,000 years ago.

Since the earliest sites found so far are in the south of the continent, archaeologists have suggested that people first set foot in the continent some time before 40,000 years ago. Aborigines on the other hand see themselves as indigenous rather than as Australia's earliest migrants, in the sense that they have no other race history except that associated with the country where they live.

Much Aboriginal history, even from the extremely distant past, is preserved in oral traditions and stories about the Dreamtime, the era of creation. While some traditions tell of the creation heroes arising from the land, the sky or the sea, others suggest an overseas origin. For example Aboriginal elder, Wandjuk Marika, recounted the origins of his own people in Arnhem Land:

> The truth is, of course, that my own people, the Riratjingu, are descended from the great Djankawu who came from the island of Baralku far across the sea. Our spirits return to Baralku when we die. Djankawu came in his canoe with his two sisters, following the morning star which guided them to the shores of Yelangbara on the eastern coast of Arnhem Land. They walked far across the country following the rain clouds. When they wanted water they plunged their digging stick into the ground and fresh water flowed. From them we learnt the names of all creatures on the land and they taught us all our Law.[4]

The reason why scientists believe in an overseas origin for Australia's first people is that there is nothing in the Australian fauna, past or present, from which humans could have evolved. There are no anthropoid or pongid (ape-like) ancestors in Australia from whom they could be independently descended. If Aborigines had evolved in isolation from the rest of humanity, they would be a separate species, unable to interbreed with other humans and produce fertile offspring. This is not the case; all human beings in the world today belong to a single species of *Homo sapiens* and can interbreed.

Humans have been in south-east Asia for just over one million years, but for more than three million years there has always been a water barrier at least 50 kilometres wide between Australia and her nearest neighbours. This prevented all Asian animals from making the crossing, except for birds, bats, rats, mice and the dingo, thought to have been brought to Australia by seafarers about 4,000 years ago.[5]

It is evident that the ancestors of today's Australian Aborigines managed to cross this ocean barrier sometime before 40,000 years ago. During this Pleistocene period the sea level fluctuated dramatically. At times of low sea level the continental shelf was exposed and the area of habitable land around Australia was much larger than today. Torres Strait and Bass Strait dried up, making Papua New Guinea, Tasmania and many other islands part of "Greater Australia" (see figure 2.2).

The most likely times of entry were during periods of low sea level, perhaps about 52,000 or 70,000 years ago when the sea dropped to around minus 120 metres below present level, although if appropriate watercraft were available, the crossings could have taken place at any time. There was probably a series of water crossings to reach Greater Australia, the Bismarck and Solomon Islands and elsewhere, showing a long-standing and competent water-crossing ability. Whether the arrivals were accidental castaways or the world's first ocean voyagers sailing bamboo rafts, researchers will probably never know. Likewise what brought the first people to Australia will remain a mystery. Was it the shrinking of their Asian territory as the ocean rose after a period of low sea level? Or was it a period of particularly violent volcanic eruptions in the Pacific "rim of fire"? Or was it the smoke from bushfires started by lightning in northern Australia which people could see in the far distance from their Indonesian homeland? Or birds migrating south at the end of the northern hemisphere summer and the southern winter?

The first Australians were ancestors of the Aboriginal people of today, although they differed from them physically in a number of ways. All prehistoric human skeletal remains found in Australia belong to the youngest form of the human race, *Homo sapiens*, but there is a considerable range of variation within this Australoid physical type. More than 100 fossil human remains older than 6,000 years have been found in Australia, but only one complete skeleton older than 20,000 years. This is from a 30,000-year-old burial of a man at Lake Mungo in western New South Wales, named Mungo III. There are also the cremated and broken-up bones of a young woman, Mungo I, dated to about 25,000 years. Surprisingly, some of these ancient people were far more lightly built, or "gracile", than modern Aborigines. They had delicate bones and small, thin skulls, with small jaws and teeth and no brow ridges. Other later remains indicate that anatomically similar people were still living in south-eastern Australia between 15,000 and 6,000 years ago.

In contrast, a group of heavily built, "robust", early Australians have come to light at Kow Swamp in the Murray River Valley in Victoria, in a burial site radiocarbon-dated between 13,000 and 9,000 years ago. This robust group were large, thick-boned and heavy, with massive teeth and jaws, pronounced brow ridges and long, receding foreheads. More than 40 individuals were excavated by Alan Thorne; they included men, women, juveniles and infants. This burial complex is the largest single population from the Late Pleistocene excavated in one locality anywhere in the world, and is of supreme significance in the global study of human physical development.

People with similar robust features were scattered throughout south-eastern Australia between 15,000 and 6,000 years ago or later, and have also been found as far afield as Cossack in Western Australia. These robust people, while definitely *Homo sapiens*, have certain archaic features generally considered to belong to their predecessors, *Homo erectus*. An extremely archaic, robust skull, Willandra Lakes Hominid 50, has been found in the Mungo region; Thorne says that this skull is so robust it makes the Kow Swamp ones look gracile! While clear archaeological evidence of the earlier presence of the robust group remains elusive, it seems most likely that the people with more archaic features appeared earlier than those of fully-developed modern type.

A relict group of early people probably entered the continent before 50,000 years ago from the Indonesian region, for there are similarities with Solo Man who lived on the banks of the Solo River in Java some 100,000 years ago. Others more closely resemble humans in southern China, and it may be that there was migration from there by way of the island chain of the Philippines.

There is considerable disagreement among physical anthropologists about whether the two contrasting physiques found in early Australia do represent two distinct groups of people, as maintained by Thorne and Webb,[6] or are simply the two ends of a continuum of physical variation, as Brown believes.[7] While there is marked regional variation among the modern Aboriginal population, there is also a basic unity and long continuity in the Australoid physical form. Further archaeological data are needed to try to resolve this question. If there were more than one group of migrants, they eventually intermarried and evolved into the modern Aboriginal population. This merging seems to have taken place by about 6,000 years ago, when it is thought that the Aboriginal population increased and greater social interaction developed between groups who may have led entirely separate lives before.

Modern Australians will never know when the first human footprint was made on an Australian beach nor whose it was, but it is clear that when the first arrivals moved inland, they would have found a totally strange environment. Even 50,000 years ago the centre would hve been far more arid than anywhere in south-east Asia. Marsupials would have been unfamiliar, except for those encountered in what is now Papua New Guinea but was then part of the Greater Australian continent.

Marsupials included giant extinct species, the megafauna, such as three metre high kangaroos and the *Diprotodon* of wombat-like form but rhinoceros size. Fortunately most of these unfamiliar animals were gentle herbivores, which posed no threat and would have fallen easy prey to the hunters. Nevertheless, others may have been fierce predators. There was the giant bird, *Genyornis,* armed with sharp beak and legs with a lethal kick, the land crocodile, *Quinkana,* the giant carnivorous goanna, *Megalania,* which was several orders of magnitude bigger than the largest goanna nowadays, the marsupial ''lion'', *Thylacoleo,* probably resembling the North American mountain lion of today, and the massive python, *Wonambi naracoortensis,* estimated to have been five metres long.

Humans and megafauna coexisted in Australia for at least 30,000 years, and the bones of giant extinct animals have been found associated with stone tools and other debris of Aboriginal occupation at a few archaeological sites, for instance Lime Springs on the Wellington Plains of New South Wales.[8] The megafauna's final extinction was probably due to a combination of factors. Aboriginal hunting no doubt played its part, but there was also stress in the Late Pleistocene from increasing heat and evaporation and consequent drying up of surface water in the inland lakes.

Aboriginal oral traditions about the bunyip or yowie and other giant beasts have probably been handed down from the time when such monstrous creatures still roamed the landscape. In Central Australia these extinct, gargantuan animals were called Kadimakara, or Dreamtime animals which no longer exist. The presence of gigantic bones on the surface of salt lakes like Lake Eyre and Callabonna was explained by the Dieri Aborigines thus:

> The deserts of Central Australia were once fertile, well-watered plains. Instead of the present brazen sky, the heavens were covered with a vault of clouds, so dense that it appeared solid; where today the only vegetation is a thin scrub, there were once giant

gum-trees, which formed pillars to support the sky; the air, now laden with blinding, salt coated dust, was washed by soft, cooling rains, and the present deserts around Lake Eyre were once a continuous garden.

The rich soil of the country, watered by abundant rain, supported a luxuriant vegetation, which spread from the lake shores and the river-banks far out across the plains. The trunks of lofty gum trees rose through the dense undergrowth, and upheld a canopy of vegetation, that protected the country beneath from the direct rays of the sun. In this roof of vegetation dwelt the strange monsters known as the "Kadimarkara".

Now and again the scent of the succulent herbage rose to the roof-land, and tempted its inhabitants to climb down the gum trees to the pastures below. Once, while many Kadimakara were revelling in the rich foods of the lower world, their retreat was cut off by the destruction of the three gum-trees, which were the pillars of the sky. They were thus obliged to roam on earth, and wallow in the marshes of Lake Eyre, till they died, and to this day their bones lie where they fell. After the destruction of the gum trees, the small holes in the forest-roof increased in number and size, until they touched one another, and all the sky became one continuous hole; wherefore the sky is called "Puri Wilpanina", which means the "Great Hole".[9]

This oral tradition bears an uncanny resemblance to the theories scientists accept today about the changing environment in Central Australia and the increasing aridity which contributed to the demise of the megafauna. The Lake Eyre region was once much more well-watered and greener, supporting a wide array of plant-eating marsupials, dolphins, flamingoes and giant lungfish. This was in the Miocene epoch, some fifteen million years ago, but elements of this early fauna survived into the late Pleistocene. The first Australians would certainly have been familiar with *Diprotodon*, one of the common marsupials of the late Pleistocene, but the *Diprotodon* whose bones are eroding out of the saltpans of Lake Callabonna died 70,000 years ago, becoming bogged in the marshes or dying of thirst when the lakes dried up.

Aboriginal "myths" have survived in various parts of Australia giving detailed and specific accounts of events which happened many thousands of years ago; for example, the separation of Kangaroo Island from the mainland of South Australia by the rising, post-glacial sea and the eruption of volcanoes on the Atherton Tableland in Queensland; both happened more than 10,000 years ago. It is not surprising that dramatic events of such magnitude left their mark in the rich body of oral tradition which has been handed down from each Aboriginal generation to the next. What is tragic is that so much of this traditional knowledge has been lost over the last 200 years.

The pattern of the first peopling of Australia is still unclear, although new, tantalising clues are being found year by year. It used to be thought that the coasts were colonised earlier than the centre of the continent, by people whose economy and technology were adapted to life by the sea. Two of the oldest human occupation sites currently known in Australia are both in the coastal zone, and the Willandra Lakes region could be easily reached from the coast by following large rivers inland. However, in 1987 the first Pleistocene site was found in Central Australia, the Puritjarra rockshelter west of Alice Springs which was inhabited well before 25,000 years ago. More recently still, some rock engravings in the arid Olary region of South Australia have been found to be 32,000 years old, if the new scientific method used to date the desert varnish which covers them proves to be valid. And in the Kakadu region in Arnhem Land Rhys Jones has discovered stone tools more than 50,000 years old at the bottom of a three metre deep occupational deposit in the rockshelter of Malakunanja site 2.[10] Even more excitingly, "crayons" of high grade ochre or haematite were in the same layer, indicating that some form of art was being practised by Australia's first inhabitants. Below there was nothing but sterile sand, suggesting that the basal layer in this site in the extreme north of the continent may well be our earliest known traces of human arrival in Australia.

It therefore now seems likely that the centre of Australia was inhabited as early as the coasts. The centre would have been a much more hospitable environment during the glacial period, when a cooler climate, with a drop in annual average temperature of about seven degrees Celsius, would have resulted in far less evaporation and consequently far more surface water. The so-called "lakes", in reality dried-up saltpans, which now dot the map of Central Australia would then have been real freshwater lakes teeming with fish and other creatures. The country would have been much greener; a visit to Palm Valley west of Alice Springs gives an idea of what the heart of Australia may have looked like then. The gradual transformation of this prehistoric "Garden of Eden" into the Red Centre was completed by about 15,000 years ago, and although Aboriginal people appear to have inhabited the centre throughout the Holocene period, traditional population in the desert country was extremely low.

The pattern of settlement which is emerging is that by about 20,000 years ago Aboriginal people were inhabiting a wide range of different environments all over Australia, from the tropics to the snows. They were in the arid core, on the coasts round most of the continent, in the Blue Mountains and the foothills of the Snowy Mountains, and hunting wallabies within sight of glaciers in south-west Tasmania. They were mining flint and marking symbols on the soft limestone walls of caves deep below the ground, lit only by brush torches; they were making stone and bone tools and wearing ornaments and skin cloaks.

Glimpses of Pleistocene Aboriginal culture have come from a number of sites, notably Devils Lair in Western Australia, Cloggs Cave in Victoria, a series of rockshelters in Kakadu National Park in the Northern Territory, Kenniff Cave in Queensland, Mungo and other sites in New South Wales and several caves in Tasmania. Most of the evidence is in the form of stone tools, but microscopic analysis of use-wear and residues on the working edge can give a surprising amount of information about the tool's function, whether it be chopping down trees, cutting up animal corpses, scraping or smoothing animal skins to wear, grinding grass seeds into flour or pounding up the starchy rhizomes of bracken fern roots for food, arming weapons of war or the chase, or manufacturing or engraving wooden artefacts.

The earliest stone toolkit in Australia is known as the Australian core tool and scraper tradition. This industry was first identified and described at Mungo, which has become the "type site" or benchmark, with which assemblages or sets of stone tools from other sites are compared. This technological tradition is characterised by hand-held tools, although a few hafted axes have been found in Pleistocene deposits in northern Australia. Chopping was done with large, heavy choppers made from cores with steeply flaked edges; some are termed horsehoof cores because their overhanging edges and domed shape resembled a horse's hoof. For scraping, planing and cutting sharp-edged flakes and steep-edged scrapers made of thick flakes were used. Many tools were "maintenance tools";

they were stone tools used to fashion other tools of wood, bone, shell or stone, in other words, tools to make tools.

What is visible at Mungo is the contents of a Pleistocene craftsman's toolkit, the prehistoric equivalents of the modern hammer, chisel, plane, kitchen knife and penknife. It is not surprising, therefore, that the same basic stone toolkit remained in use from the earliest occupation until the last few thousand years. There are regional variations, in some cases occasioned by different raw material. For example, the early chopping tools in highland country were usually made from large rounded cobbles collected from fast-flowing mountain rivers.

There was also a gradual progression over time towards less massive but more efficient and specialised stone tools. Later Pleistocene campsites have fewer core tools, smaller scrapers and a wider range of tool types. No doubt stone tools were a relatively small part of the equipment of these early Australians. Like later Aborigines, they probably used wooden spears, digging sticks and carrying dishes together with woven "dilly bags" and baskets. Such organic items very rarely survive in archaeological sites, so what is preserved is only a tiny fragment of the whole material culture.

Bone tends to be preserved in limestone caves, and bone tools have been found in sites such as Devils Lair in Western Australia, Cloggs Cave in Victoria and Kutikina Cave in Tasmania. Most common are sturdy bone points made from the fibula (small leg bone) of a macropod (wallaby or kangaroo). A glossy sheen is detectable on the tips of most of these, suggesting that they were used to make holes through animal skins or bark. Rounded river cobbles bearing a polish from burnishing some soft material have been associated with bone points, which most archaeologists believe were awls used for piercing holes in skins to make cloaks or rugs. Similar bone awls and burnishing stones were used in the nineteenth century to make skin cloaks by Aborigines living in the colder southern part of mainland Australia.

Wooden artefacts have been found so far in only one early site, Wyrie Swamp, a peat bog in the south-east of South Australia. The excavation of this site resulted from a fortunate chance encounter in a hospital. When archaeologist Roger Luebbers was recovering from a slipped disc, he found that the man in the next hospital bed had a peat bog on his land and had found wooden artefacts deep within it. Preservation conditions in peat bogs are excellent, and Wyrie Swamp yielded 25 digging sticks, spears and boomerangs in a layer dated to 10,000 years. These represent the traditional equipment of Aboriginal Australians. Women were equipped with digging sticks, men with spears and, in most regions, boomerangs.

An unexpected refinement among these 10,000-year-old artefacts was the presence of javelin-type spears with carved wooden barbs. These would have been effective in hunting kangaroos and other large game, for barbed spears are difficult to dislodge from a wound, and can cause death through loss of blood.

Even more surprising were returning boomerangs. Their lateral twist and curvature are the classic properties of a well-designed aerodynamic missile, and the two wings are oriented in different aerodynamic planes. The returning boomerang is an extremely sophisticated piece of technology, invented in Australia more than 10,000 years ago. These are the world's oldest returning boomerangs; the so-called boomerangs found elsewhere, as in Florida and Egypt, are not true boomerangs but throwing sticks.

Australia was the only inhabited continent where the end of the Pleistocene was not marked by major cultural changes such as the development of agriculture and urbanisation. The well-established hunter-gatherer way of life continued, whereas most people in the rest of the world, including the inhabitants of Papua New Guinea, became farmers, horticulturalists or herdsmen. Nor did pottery, the use of metals, the bow and arrow or urbanisation develop.

The reasons for this cultural stability and continuity in Aboriginal Australia probably lie in the nature of the Australian environment. The hunter-gatherer way of life was admirably suited to this driest of inhabited continents. Aboriginal people lived, and lived well, in a variety of harsh environments where European farming was later to flounder miserably. A particular food resource might be a temporary staple while seasonably abundant, but a wide range of foods was exploited. Such a broad-based foraging system minimises risks and overcomes a shortage of any particular food much more effectively than an agricultural community relying on more restricted food resources. Aboriginal Australia was never vulnerable due to the failure of one crop.

Population numbers were affected by the available food, which in turn was related to water resources. Areas of higher rainfall were generally richer in food, and therefore supported a higher number of people. Population was kept in equilibrium with the environment and below the country's carrying capacity, the level it could support. Temporary, seasonal abundances tended to be used to increase the amount of leisure for religious and social life, and to hold great ceremonial gatherings. Effort was channelled into providing sufficient leisure for a rich religious and artistic life.

In general traditional Aboriginal people had more leisure than the average farmer or office worker, and ate well, indeed better than many white people do today. There was therefore no incentive to try to increase the food supply by horticulture or farming, unless major environmental or population stresses were experienced. There were also virtually no plants or animals which could have been domesticated, none of the sheep, cows, pigs, goats, chickens or horses of other continents.

The main change requiring adaptation was the rise in sea level at the end of the ice age, about 12,000 years ago, which flooded some two and a half million square kilometres, or about one-seventh of Greater Australia. This drastic loss of land seems to have pushed occupation into more marginal environments, which had previously been uninhabited or only rarely visited. In a continent the size of Australia people could respond to regional environmental changes by moving elsewhere rather than by major cultural adaptation.

Although the rising sea inundated large tracts of land, the new coastline gave richer opportunities for human settlement. Stabilisation of sea level extended tidal reefs and estuaries, the zones of the shore most productive of accessible fish and shellfish for Aboriginal foragers. At the mouths of rivers sandy barriers formed lagoons. Many food-rich small bays and inlets also developed in drowned river valleys. In this way some regions, especially those on the coast, became more suitable for human exploitation.

While cultural changes did occur, most were relatively minor. In Central

Australia in response to the drying up of Pleistocene lakes, Aborigines changed their staple foods from freshwater aquatic foods like fish and shellfish to flour made from wild grass seed. The extensive collecting, grinding, winnowing and baking of grass seeds as food was a significant technological step forward. There was no wheat, barley or corn in prehistoric Australia, but there was a native millet, *Panicum decompositum*. This was exploited throughout the arid lands. The grass was gathered when the seed was full and contained maximum amounts of protein and vitamins and the grass was still green. It was stacked in heaps and the seeds left to dry and ripen, whereupon they were threshed so that the seeds fell to the ground in one spot. In south-west Queensland stone knives were used for reaping — important evidence of semi-agricultural practices in Australia. Large flat upper and lower millstones were used to grind the hard seeds into flour to make bread.

The exploitation of wild millet by the people of the inland riverine plains has been called "incipient agriculture" and it provided about 30 per cent of their diet, but they did not take the final steps of tilling the soil, planting seeds and storing the surplus food produced. Instead they ensured a maximum return of food by foraging a wide variety of resources and using an array of specialised techniques. Sophisticated methods for detoxifying otherwise poisonous cycads such as *Macrozamia* nuts were developed in Queensland, and complex systems of waterways and traps were constructed at Lake Condah and elsewhere in western Victoria to harvest eels and fish.

Other changes accompanied this intensification of foraging techniques. "Intensification" is a term which generally refers to increases in both productivity and production, and there is evidence in prehistoric Australia since about 4,000 years ago of increases in the complexity of social relations and economic growth, semi-sedentism and, by inference, population sizes. Throughout Australia from about 4,000 years ago there was a remarkable upsurge in the rate of establishment of new occupation sites and the intensity of site usage. The prehistoric economy became more complex, with an increase in the number of resources exploited, improvement in harvesting and capturing techniques, and greater use of marginal environments such as arid, montane, rainforest or swampland areas. A trend towards a less nomadic, semi-sedentary way of life is exemplified by longer-term base camps. Inter-group relations became more intensive, with an increase in group mobility, ceremonies and exchange/trade of goods. Ceremonial gift exchange systems spread across vast distances.

The last 4,000 years have witnessed many innovations in Aboriginal Australia. It is uncertain as yet whether these innovations diffused into the continent from Asia or were the result of independent invention within Australia. One element, the dingo, certainly was introduced from outside Australia. Its bones first occur in southern archaeological sites of about 4,000 years, and it is thought to have entered the continent more than 4,000 years ago. The dingo's closest relative seems to be the Thai dog[11] of south-east Asia, but how the dingo reached Australia is not known.

Other items which may have diffused into Australia were new specialised small tools such as spear points, but these could equally well be of local origin. Stone tools generally became smaller and more standardised, and were hafted or bound to a handle with resin as glue. These specialised composite artefacts were added to the toolkit between 5,000 and 4,000 years ago, and are known as the small tool

Figure 2.3 Pleistocene Australia. (Peter Murray, *Australian Prehistoric Animals*, Methuen, 1984: frontispiece)

tradition. Their outstanding characteristics are the symmetry and delicate trimming or pressure-flaking of tiny, slender blades made from fine-grained rock, hafted onto a wooden handle to make a light, very effective tool. These composite tools of two or even three parts include spear-throwers with a small stone adze hafted onto one end, and stone-tipped spears.

The spear-thrower or woomera seems to have been an independent invention in Australia in the mid-Holocene. It increased the distance over which a spear could be thrown to more than 100 metres, making the Australian spear a deadly weapon of war or the chase. Spears were probably Australia's first export goods, for they were much sought after by Torres Strait Islanders, either for fishing or fighting, or for use with the spear-thrower in hunting dugong.

Other new weapons included the "death spear", which was a long wooden spear armed with as many as 12 stone barbs set with resin into a groove down each side of the shaft. These stone barbs were set in such a way that when a spear penetrated flesh, it would not easily fall out, and the hunted animal would tend to die from loss of blood if it had not been killed outright. The barbs were plain small pieces of sharp stone such as quartz, or carefully fashioned "backed blades".

Backed blades are long, slim pieces of stone blunted or backed by chipping across one edge. They first appeared about 5,000 years ago. The most common are Bondi points (named after the Sydney beach where they were first found), which are slender, asymmetrical blades with a thick, blunted back, resembling a tiny penknife. Another type is the geometric microlith, which is also a backed blade but is much broader in proportion to its length and is usually geometric in shape, crescentic, triangular or trapezoidal.

There is a trend towards greater complexity and regional diversity throughout the late Holocene. This intensification in Australia is similar to cultural processes in other countries, such as the Mesolithic of Europe, and is probably a natural evolutionary step towards more intensive levels of hunting and gathering and more complex social relationships. These developments, however, were drastically disrupted by the near-fatal impact of European settlement in 1788.

CHAPTER THREE

Introduction to Australian Rock Art

Many of the riches of ancient Australia are sites containing pictures painted, drawn, stencilled, imprinted or engraved on stone. Such pictures or marks are usually known as rock art, and this term will also be used in this book without implying that Australian Aboriginal art was ever "art for art's sake". There were no professional artists in Aboriginal society, but significant pictures were made by particularly skilled individuals as part of religious life. Painting was, and still is in certain regions, a vital, traditional accompaniment to rituals and ceremonies. Rock art is part of the Aboriginal expression of life's meaning, and a manifestation of spiritual beliefs. At the same time, casual, secular pictures were and still are made. Stencils of children's hands may record their visit to a site, or small, stick-like figures or "doodles" painted low on the wall of a rockshelter mark its use as a camping place by a family group.

Most of Australia's rock art is prehistoric, which means that there is no record of its meaning available, but in certain regions rock art is part of a living tradition, and can be explained by Aboriginal traditional owners. Few such sites are open to the public, but where they are, a "public" version of the stories behind the art may be given to visitors. Such sites are Dreamings, places where ancestral creator powers made things the way they are. These mythic, shape-changing beings travelled the country, creating the form of the landscape. A series of sites are often linked together as a "dreaming track" or "songline", places on the journey of an ancestral being. It is possible to follow such dreaming tracks on some of the heritage trails recently set up in states such as Western Australia and South Australia.

Rock art embraces many different techniques and styles of pictures. There are two major groups, pigmented and engraved. Pigmented styles or pictographs comprise all pictures in which pigment has been added to the rock surface, and include paintings, drawings, stencils and prints. Engravings or petroglyphs on the other hand are the product of a subtractive process, in which the engraver has removed some of the rock surface by pecking, pounding, abrading or scratching.

Stencilling is the method whereby an artist grinds up pigment into a fine powder and mixes it with water. The artist then sprays the mixture from the mouth over the object being stencilled, which is held against the rock. When the object is

Plate 3.1 Composite stencils, resembling emu tracks but made by stencilling of the tips of boomerangs, Carnarvon National Park, Queensland. (G. Walsh)

removed, a negative silhouette outlined by splattered paint remains on the rock face.

Hand stencils are most common. The hand is usually placed with the palm flat against the rock, giving the negative impression a relatively sharp outline. If the back of the hand is held against the wall, the outline is much more diffuse. Sometimes a stencilled hand will appear to be lacking some fingers or finger joints, but careful examination has shown that often these apparent mutilations are trick stencils, produced by bending back the fingers. Other trick stencils have been made, such as large emu tracks made by stencilling the tips of three boomerangs (plate 3.1).

Feet as well as hands are stencilled and occasionally one finds a stencil of a pair of baby's feet, where the baby has been held up against the wall. Very rarely, a whole person is stencilled, as in the Tombs site in the Mount Moffat section of Carnarvon National Park, Queensland. Stencils of items in everyday use such as boomerangs, axes or dilly bags (collecting bags) are quite common, and can be valuable in the information they provide about prehistoric material culture in a region. For example, boomerangs have not been part of the equipment of

Aborigines of the Kakadu region in the Northern Territory in historic times, but stencils of boomerangs in rockshelters there show that this was not always the case.

Much less common than stencils are prints, positive impressions of relatively soft, flat objects dipped into wet pigment and pressed against the rock surface. Again, hand prints are most numerous but prints of other objects occur, such as grasses in the early art of Arnhem Land. Stencil art reaches its height in Australia in the art of the Central Highlands of Queensland, as described in chapter 10. (The locations of the main rock art regions in Australia are shown in figure 3.1.)

Rock painting or freehand art is the technique whereby an artist mixes ground-up pigment with water and then paints the rock surface by hand. The paint can be applied by a wide range of methods, ranging from finger-painting to the use of a fine brush made from the chewed end of a twig.

While a painting is a mark made by adding wet pigment to a rock surface, a drawing is created by the application of dry pigment. Drawings are often made by use of a piece of charcoal, presumably from the campfire, and are especially common in sites in the Sydney region.

Figure 3.1 Principal rock art regions in Australia

Engravings are marks made by removing material from the surface of the rock. Pecking is a method of engraving involving making precise, deep nicks in the rock surface usually by indirect percussion, using a sharp pointed tool of stone or bone with a hammerstone. The design is pecked into the surface by use of the hammer and chisel technique. Pounding is similar, but involves direct percussion or bruising with a stone hammer, producing a diffuse mark on the art surface by direct percussion. Abrasion uses repeated friction to make a continuous linear groove, by rubbing the rock surface to and fro with a stone, bone or wooden tool. Finally, scratching also occurs, with shallow lines being made by light scratches with a stone tool.

Some sites contain pictures made by only one of these techniques, others have three or more, and sometimes painting and engraving are combined in the same figure. Generally, engravings stand the ravages of time much better than ochred art. Extremely weathered engravings can be seen on rock slabs or "pavements" in open sites exposed to the elements. Other engravings are protected by the ceiling of a rockshelter or cave. Some engravings are of great antiquity. In a few rockshelters pieces of the engraved walls or ceiling have fallen on the earth floor and become covered with later occupational debris such as the remains of campfires. In others the level of the shelter floor has risen due to the gradual accumulation of earth, charcoal, stone tools and food remains, gradually burying the lower part of the engraved back wall. Paintings do not usually survive burial under earth for thousands of years, but engravings last almost indefinitely in such situations.

A minimum age for rock art can be gained by obtaining radiocarbon dates for the charcoal or other organic material such as bone or shell associated with the buried engraving. It is thus possible to establish that the engraving must be older than the material which has accumulated around and above it. The remaining question is how much older. Evidence of this type comes from the rockshelter of Ingaladdi 1 in the Northern Territory, where John Mulvaney's excavation unearthed fragmented rocks bearing abraded grooves and bird tracks, below a 5,000-year-old layer and resting on a 7,000-year-old occupational floor.[1] The minimum age therefore for these engravings is 5,000 to 7,000 years. At Early Man site in north Queensland excavation showed that the engraved frieze on the rock wall extended below an occupational layer dated to 13,000 years, giving a minimum age for engravings of 13,000 years (see chapter 9).

There is strong circumstantial evidence from other caves that rock art is of even greater antiquity than this. At Koonalda Cave below the Nullarbor Plain charcoal from directly below wall markings gave a date of 20,000 years (see chapter 13). It is thought that the charcoal was derived from burning brush torches carried into the darkest recesses of the cave, where ceremonies were probably carried out. On soft surfaces these markings were made by fingers, on harder rock engraved with a stone, bone or wooden tool. The Koonalda wall markings are multiple finger lines or flutings and linear engravings (cf. plate 13.11). This style, which is reminiscent of the "macaroni" style of early European art, has now been found across 3,000 kilometres of southern Australia, from the Perth region in the west to the Snowy River in eastern Victoria.

A large and ancient body of archaic linear rock engravings have been identified in some 21 underground limestone caves in the Mount Gambier region of South

Australia by Robert Bednarik, founder of AURA, the Australian Rock Art Research Association. It seems probable that the tradition of finger markings of the digital flutings type is more, possibly, much more, than 20,000 years old, on the basis of the Koonalda evidence, the overgrowth in several sites of finger markings by reprecipitated carbonate and the major tectonic changes which have taken place in many caves since the markings were made.

Superimposed on the finger lines, but still likely to go back in excess of 15,000 years, are deeply carved circles and other motifs, termed by Bednarik the Karake style. Later still is a tradition of shallow incisions executed with single strokes, considered to be less than 10,000 years old.

Much more common than digital flutings are engravings of what has long been known as the Panaramitee style, also called archaic linear petroglyphs. Panaramitee in South Australia has been regarded as typical of this style, since it has an extensive series of engravings and was one of the first such sites recorded in detail. The motifs are dominated by tracks of birds and animals such as emus and kangaroos, and by circles, which take many different forms. The simple ring-like circle is very common, but infinite variations occur such as concentric circles (circles within circles), barred circles, circular spirals, fully-pecked disc-like circles, linked or overlapping circles, and hollowed-out eggcup -like pits.

One remarkable engraving at Panaramitee has been thought to portray the head of a crocodile, although this seems unlikely in view of the tremendous distance from crocodile country. It was removed in the 1960s for safe-keeping to the South Australian Museum on North Terrace in Adelaide, where it may be viewed (plate 3:2).

There are early engravings in several parts of the continent which resemble the Panaramitee style. They have a very narrow range of motifs. Macropod and bird tracks, circles and crescents predominate, and other linear motifs are common. While there is a marked degree of homogeneity in the motif range, the percentage which each motif forms of the art body varies dramatically from region to region.

It has always been considered that some engravings are of exceptional antiquity, on the grounds of the high degree of weathering and cracking, occasional portrayal of extinct animals such as the thylacine in the Pilbara, and the build-up of a thick layer of desert varnish. Desert varnish is a patina or surface sheen which builds up over the millennia on rock surfaces and the motifs engraved upon them (plate 3.3). It can be a thick black, shiny surface or a thin veneer invisible to the naked eye. It is found particularly in arid regions but it also occurs elsewhere.

Pioneering work on desert varnish has been done by Deirdre Dragovich of Sydney University.[2] Now the cation-ratio dating method has been developed. Analysis of a pinhead size sample of desert varnish from an engraved groove will give the date at which the desert varnish began to build up, that is, the minimum age of the engraving. However, a number of variables affect the growth of desert varnish, and it is still uncertain whether the cation-ratio method allows sufficiently for these unknowns.

A first set of dates on varnish from inside engravings has been produced by Ron Dorn in conjunction with Margaret Nobbs on one of the engravings sites (Karolta) she has recorded in the Olary region of South Australia.[3] The results are startling. If they are correct, engravings of circles, tracks of birds and macropods and

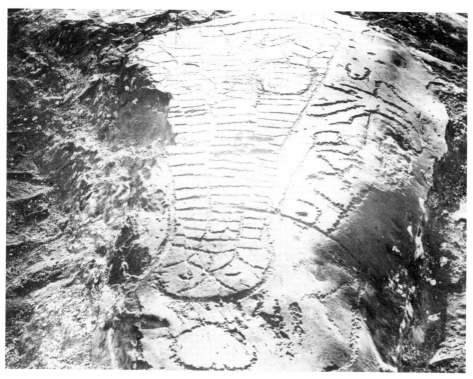

Plate 3.2 An engraving at Panaramitee resembling a crocodile head. It may now be seen in the South Australia Museum, Adelaide (R. Edwards)

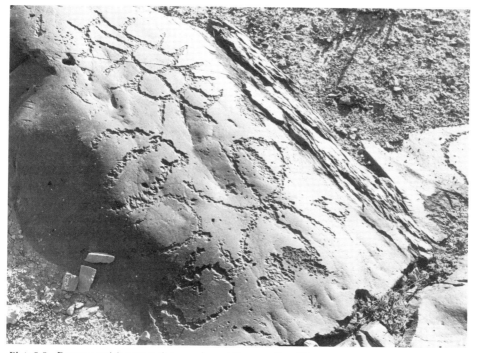

Plate 3.3 Desert varnish over rock engravings at Panaramitee, SA

abraded grooves were being executed 44,000 years ago in the Olary region, and similar motifs were being engraved right down the centuries until 1,000 years ago. Likewise at Sandy Creek rockshelter in north Queensland engravings were buried by charcoal dated to 32,000 years old.

Another extremely important new development is the discovery in south-west Tasmania of pigmented art considered to be more than 12,000 to 13,000 years old. This is the first time in Australia that pigmented art, as opposed to engravings, has been found in Pleistocene contexts. The sites are deep, dark limestone caves in an environment which is now rainforest, but which during the last glaciation would have been open alpine heathlands, well-suited to hunters (see chapter 20). No engravings have been found in the caves, but there are hand stencils and streaks and patches of red ochre. Analysis of the ochre from one cave in the Southern Forests has shown that blood was mixed with the ochre before it was smeared on the rock walls. The blood is likely to have been human blood, mixed with the ochre during rituals deep inside these dark caves.

This art is in complete darkness, something which is exceedingly rare among Australian sites. In prehistoric art hand stencils are a worldwife motif, exemplifying the common elements in human behaviour and cultural evolution on a global scale.

These cryptic signs on the rock are a symbolic statement about Aboriginal identity and religion, reaching out across the centuries. They show that pigmented art is likely to be as old in Australia as engraving. The fact that, until this find, nothing but engraved art had been found in Pleistocene sites does not mean that ice-age Aborigines did not practise painting or stencilling, but only that such pigmented art does not usually survive.

Certain patterns in the development of Australian rock art are beginning to emerge. Both pigmented and engraved art go back to the Pleistocene period, almost certainly more than 40,000 years ago. There seem to be two main phases in the development of Australian rock art. The major difference between the two is the development of figurative art, or in Bednarik's words "the advent of iconicity". Iconicity is defined as "the ability to abstract from a three-dimensional object to a two-dimensional depiction". Figurative or iconic motifs are ones which resemble things familiar to the observer, such as depictions of animals, birds, humans or artefacts. Non-figurative motifs on the other hand are linear or geometric, with circles, convergent lines and maze-like designs.

Non-figurative marks such as abraded grooves certainly exist alongside figurative ones in the younger phase, and other motifs such as hand stencils are likely to have existed throughout the sequence. Likewise it seems that tracks may have been engraved long before other truly figurative pictures such as silhouette or outline representations of humans, animals or birds.

Only further detailed research will clarify the question of the regional distribution and development of art styles. Nevertheless, there seems now to be fairly general agreement that there are at least two stages in the development of Australian rock art: an earlier, linear and geometric style and a later figurative style with innumerable regional variants. This sequence in broad terms seems to be continent-wide, although some regions appear to lack the earlier phase and some, like Tasmania, the later phase.

One of the major problems encountered in trying to ascertain the development of rock art is the lack of any technique for dating most art, particularly pigmented art. While there is strong circumstantial evidence that some rock paintings are at least 12,000 to 13,000 years old, there is as yet no method of obtaining absolute dates for when they were executed. Considerable research is being carried out in Kakadu National Park in the Northern Territory (see chapter 8), where some rock paintings in red ochre have become bonded to the rock and sunk deep into the wall, and others are covered with a transparent mineral skin of silica. It is hoped that methods of dating pigmented art will be developed, but meanwhile the earliest paintings in a simple figurative style in Arnhem Land are considered to be at least 10,000 years old.

It may be no coincidence that the two-stage development from geometric to figurative styles bears an uncanny resemblance to the two-stage development in stone tools from the early core tool and scraper tradition to the small tool tradition, as described in the previous chapter. Although the development of simple figurative art seems to have occurred earlier than that of the new, specialised small tools, which appeared around 5,000 years ago, both may reflect the trend to increasing regional diversity and complexity in Aboriginal society and culture. It seems that an initial period of relative homogeneity may have been followed by a flowering of local styles.

There is certainly great diversity among regional bodies of rock art in recent times. These vary widely in style, subject matter and technique. They range from the huge, colourful figures of the Laura area in Cape York Peninsula to the small but dynamic humans of western New South Wales paintings, from the circles and other small linear engravings of Tasmania to the life-size outlines of whales, fish and other fauna engraved in the Sydney sandstone.

Recently Rhys Jones has found in the Northern Territory "crayons" of haematite (fine-grained red ochre) 40,000 years old. They are in the basal layer of a three metre deep deposit at Malakunanja rockshelter, indicating that even Australia's earliest inhabitants practised some form of art.

The style of most Australian rock paintings is termed "simple figurative", characterised by simplified silhouettes in outline or infilled form of animal or human figures. Decoration is either absent or relatively simple, such as stripes or dots or the use of a second colour for the outline. Examples of the simple figurative style are the paintings of Victoria, New South Wales and Queensland and the rock engravings of the Sydney area.

The complex figurative style in contrast has a greater sophistication and stylisation, expressed by features such as a high degree of internal anatomy (the X-ray style), fine line work, grouping of figures into compositions and depiction of action. Paintings in this complex, polychrome style are the X-ray style in Arnhem Land and the Wandjina of the Kimberley, and the engravings of sites such as Woodstock in the Pilbara. The locations of the major regional styles are indicated on figure 3.1, and are described in the succeeding chapters.

CHAPTER FOUR

Western Australia: Perth and the South-West

Western Australia has a wealth of impressive geological sites, several of which are described below, and some of the most spectacular scenery in the continent. The diverse topography had a profound effect on Aboriginal culture, prompting the development of a rich mythology and rock art. The many caves and rockshelters of the Kimberley provided ideal locations for paintings of ancestral beings from the Dreamtime, whereas the granite and dolerite slabs of the Pilbara were a perfect medium for engraving similar subjects. The rock art of the painters and engravers of northern Western Australia is probably unsurpassed elsewhere in the continent, or even in the world.

Western Australia also boasts some occupation sites of great significance, including in the Perth area one of the earliest firmly dated Aboriginal campsites in Australia, on which the oft-quoted figure of 40,000-year-old occupation is based. Limestone caves in the south-west have provided similar evidence of early human occupation.

More than 13,000 Aboriginal sites have been recorded in Western Australia. The state sites authority is the Department of Aboriginal Sites of the Western Australian Museum, which administers the Aboriginal Heritage Act 1972–80 and keeps a site register. At June, 1989 this contained 13,006 sites: 2,483 in the Kimberley, 6,262 in the Pilbara, 1,684 in the Western Desert and goldfields, 1,457 in the south-west and 1,120 in the Perth metropolitan region. All these Aboriginal sites are protected by law, very few are open to the public, and in most cases, as noted below, permission to visit must be sought from both the Aboriginal custodians and the Department of Aboriginal Sites (see page 363).

A series of heritage trails are being developed in Western Australia. Preliminary information on some of those which include Aboriginal heritage is given here. Further information is available from the Western Australian Heritage Committee, Jardine House, 184 Saint George's Terrace, Perth (tel. (09) 322 4375). The Western Australian Tourism Commission is also a mine of useful information. (It is located at 16 St George's Terrace, Perth. (tel. (09) 325 3055) and has various regional offices.) Enquiries regarding national parks should be addressed to the Department of Conservation and Land Management (C.A.L.M.), P.O. Box 104, Como, W.A. 6152 (tel. (09) 367 0333).

Museums with quality displays on Aboriginal sites and culture in Western Australia include the Western Australian Museum in Francis Street, Perth, the Anthropology Department in the University of Western Australia, the Carnarvon Historical Society, and museums in Albany, Geraldton, Golden Mile, Kalamunda, New Norcia, the Welcome Centre in Port Hedland, Yalgoo and Yanchep.

Perth and the South

The south-west of Western Australia is a green oasis of karri and jarrah forests and limestone caves, where giant kangaroos once roamed and Aborigines collected fine-grained chert from land now long submerged beneath the rising post-glacial sea. Human occupation of this distinctive cultural and natural region goes back 33,000 years in Devils Lair Cave in the Margaret River area (see page 39). Much of the world's water was locked up in huge polar ice sheets, and, at the time of lowest sea level — around 18,000 years ago — the ocean was between 50 and 100 kilometres further out along the south-western coast of the continent than

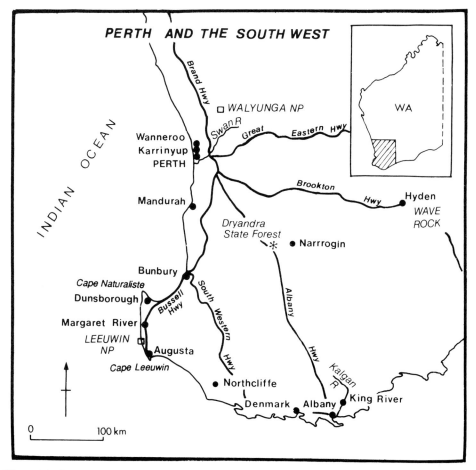

Figure 4.1   Perth and the south-west

today. As the ice sheets melted with the warming-up of the climate at the end of the ice age, the oceans rose.

Proof that Aborigines exploited this coastal strip before it was drowned by the rising sea was provided by some detective work by archaeologists and geologists trying to find the source of a distinctive type of stone used for artefacts before but not after about 4,500 years ago. The stone is a unique type of fine-grained rock known as Eocene chert, a fossiliferous (fossil-bearing) silicified limestone formed in the Eocene period between 54 and 38 million years ago. The source of the Eocene chert found on early campsites such as Walyunga and Dunsborough on the western coastal plain remained a mystery, for no outcrops or quarries for the material seemed to exist in the region (figure 4.1).[1] Then a geologist deduced that the source must lie west of the present coast. This was dramatically confirmed when offshore exploration bores drilling for oil brought up samples of identical chert.

This distinctive chert provides a useful marker of campsites used before the sea reached its present level about 6,000 years ago. Some was reused after the sources had become unavailable, but it is not found on sites younger than 4,500 years old. Its presence or absence thus distinguishes between older and younger sites on the west coast. Certain popular places, such as river crossings, valley junctions, or food gathering areas such as swamps or yam grounds, were used both in the earlier and later periods, and many of the earlier campsites may now be under the sea. Nonetheless, a major increase in population seems to have occurred, with ten times as many young sites without Eocene chert as old, pre-sea-level-rise sites.

The well-watered and forested south-west supported a large Aboriginal population known as the Nyungar people, because of the family of language dialects they speak. These people developed a rich material culture. They had kangaroo skin cloaks and bags, possum skin belts and feather necklaces, carried smouldering banksia cones under their cloaks for added warmth, and used unique kodja axes and taap saw knives (figure 4.2).

There is also a great deal in the south of Western Australia for anyone interested in palaeo-environment, ancient landforms and caves. One of the most

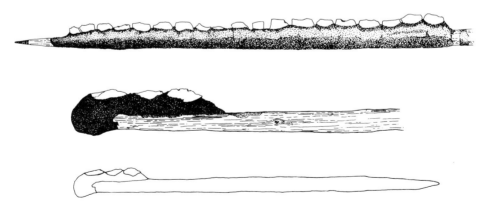

Figure 4.2 Hafted implements from south-western Australia. The barbs are small, sharp-edged quartz flakes set in plant resin. *Above:* a death spear. *Centre and below:* a taap knife, showing its head, with a total length of 44 centimetres. (After C. Dortch 1984, p.53)

spectacular landforms is Wave Rock (see page 43), where the lower slopes of an isolated granite outcrop or inselberg have been eroded into a massive wave-like cliff.

Outstanding cave formations are found in the Leeuwin-Naturaliste National Park on the coast south of Busselton and some 300 kilometres south of Perth. The ridge which runs from Cape Naturaliste to Cape Leeuwin is of granite and gneiss partly overlain by limestone, much of which has been eroded by acid groundwater into large caves. Many caves are open to the public, and can be reached from Caves Road, which runs parallel to the coast between it and the Bussel highway. Crystalline formations are seen in a wonderful variety of shapes at caves such as Yallingup, 40 metres below the ground. Some caves which lie over impermeable bedrock contain lakes and pools, in which the limestone formations are reflected. The remains of extinct animals are preserved in caves such as Jewel and Mammoth (see page 41). This is also the wine-growing region of the Margaret River, so a day of site-visiting can be rounded off with a glass of wine at one of the many vineyards.

Devils Lair

One of the most important archaeological sites in Australia is the limestone cave Devils Lair, twenty kilometres north of Cape Leeuwin and five kilometres inland from the coast. (The cave is not open to the public and can only be viewed by special arrangement with the Western Australian Museum.) In this dimly lit, earth-floored chamber of some 75 square metres archaeologist Charles Dortch[2] has found evidence of 33,000-year-old Aboriginal occupation. There is a rich 3 metre deep deposit of animal bones, revealing the diet of prehistoric people during the last ice age. Regular items on the menu seem to have been wallabies, possums, bandicoots, native rats and mice, snakes, frogs, lizards, bats and birds, emu eggs and freshwater shellfish.

The lowest layer containing artefacts is radiocarbon-dated to 33,000 years and has also produced several bones of extinct giant kangaroos such as *Protemnodon* and *Sthenurus*. Some of the bones are fractured, and archaeologist Jane Balme claims that there is good evidence that prehistoric hunters preyed on the megafauna.[3] Occupational debris, including cooking hearths, dated between about 28,000 and 6,000 years ago, shows that regular, if sporadic, use was made of the cave as a camping place. Most of the deposit was sealed under a 12,000-year-old layer of flowstone, and in recent times the large number of bones of the Tasmanian devil and its prey gave the cave its name of Devils Lair.

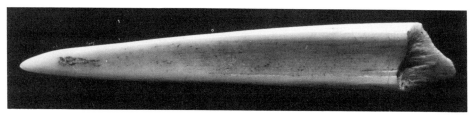

Plate 4.1 Bone point from a 22,000-year-old layer in Devils Lair. (Courtesy C. Dortch and WA Museum)

The limestone environment has preserved bone as well as stone tools, and Devils Lair has yielded what are at present Australia's oldest bone tools, 22,000-year-old bone points (see plate 4.1). Some of these were probably used for sewing skins together to make cloaks to ward off the glacial cold, for their size, shape and the use-polish on some of the tips suggest skin-working. One of the most exciting finds from Devils Lair was the discovery of three 12,000 to 15,000-year-old bone beads, now on display in the Western Australian Museum (figure 4.3). No parallels for these exist in contemporary Aboriginal culture, and they are the first indication in Australia that ice-age Australians wore ornaments.

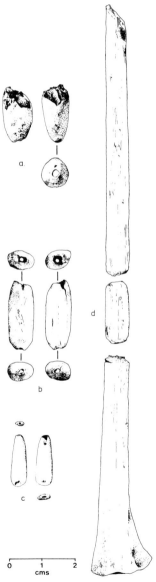

Figure 4.3   Three bone heads from Devils Lair (on the left) and a modern kangaroo fibula from which a short segment has been cut, showing the first stage of the manufacture of a bead. The beads are between 12,000 and 15,000 years old. (After C. Dortch 1984, p.66)

Jewel Cave

Jewel Cave, 8 kilometres north of Augusta and 37 kilometres from Margaret River, is open to the public and is noted for its beautiful limestone formations, including one of the longest straw stalactites known. It has also yielded remains of the Tasmanian tiger, *Thylacinus cynocephalus*, the Tasmanian devil, *Sarcophilus harrisii,* and an extinct koala, *Phascolarctos cinereus.*

Mammoth Cave

Mammoth Cave, 21 kilometres south of Margaret River and 33 kilometres from Augusta, is well known for its fossil remains and is open to the public. It contains a bone deposit more than 37,000 years old, with such extinct species as the Tasmanian wolf, *Thylacoleo carnifex,* the long-beaked echidna, *Zaglossus,* kangaroos like *Sthenurus,* and *Zygomaturus.* Remarkable evidence of what seems to be deliberate cutting, breaking and burning of the bones of these giant extinct megafauna has been found at Mammoth Cave.[4] The pattern of charring found on the bones is more consistent with deliberate cooking of carcasses than with accidental burning in bushfires. This is the best evidence yet in Australia that Aborigines hunted and ate these animals, possibly contributing to their eventual extinction.

Quininup Brook, Leeuwin-Naturaliste National Park

Aborigines regularly camped beside a series of small waterfalls and pools at Quininup Brook between 18,000 and 10,000 years ago.[5] The site is now near the beach, but at that time the sea would have been at a much greater distance. There are several areas of scattered debris from working stone, and also several clusters of stone that people must have carried there. Their purpose is unknown; they are not associated with camping debris or artefacts. (Remember that Aboriginal artefacts may not be collected). Access to the park is off Caves Road.

Northcliffe, D'Entrecasteaux National Park

At Northcliffe near Pemberton an excellent visitors' information centre has been developed by the Department of Conservation and Land Management. This orientates people to the parks and karri forests of the region, and highlights the traditional Aboriginal way of life. Aboriginal occupation of the D'Entrecasteaux region goes back at least 8,000 years. Aboriginal campsites and stone quarries are found in the Northcliffe area, and shell middens on the coast between Manjimup and Albany.

Denmark heritage trails

A variety of Aboriginal sites are known in the Denmark area, including rockshelters, stone arrangements, ochre deposits, stone quarries, fish traps and open-air campsites. The Wilson Inlet heritage trail (a 9 kilometre walking trail from Ocean Beach Road to Crusoe Beach in Denmark) introduces the visitor to

Aboriginal fish traps and features a display on traditional Aboriginal life on the south coast. This is in the (man-made) Minang shelter, 3.4 kilometres along an easy track from the historic Post Office.

The Mokare heritage trail, is a three kilometre walking trail commemorating Mokare, leader of the Minang tribe in the Albany region, which formed part of the larger Nyungar Aboriginal group of the south-west of Western Australia.[6] Mokare (pronounced Mo-ka-ri) acted as guide and interpreter to Dr Thomas Braidwood Wilson on his 1829 expedition into the Denmark district. A rich variety of plant and birdlife can be enjoyed on this trail, which meanders past paperbark trees along the banks of the Denmark River between the traffic and railway bridge. (Note that the east bank may be flooded in winter.)

Occupation goes back 19,000 years in the Albany region, where archaeologist Bill Ferguson has made a detailed study of Mokare's domain. The oldest evidence of habitation comes from the Kalgan Hall site, an open-air camp in the grounds of the Kalgan town hall, where a 2.5 metre excavation revealed occupational debris radiocarbon-dated to more than 18,850 years ago. This site is near the lowest ford on the Kalgan River, where many Aboriginal trackways came together.

Oyster Harbour fish traps, Albany

Well-preserved Aboriginal fish traps are increasingly rare in Australia, for they are extremely vulnerable to destruction by both natural and human agency. Few examples survive in Western Australia, so this relatively intact site is of high heritage significance, and is in the Register of the National Estate. It lies 10 kilometres north-east of Albany in a national trust reserve on the northern shore of Oyster Harbour, south of Nanarup Road. (Take Barameda Road off Morilla Road down to the foreshore reserve.)

The fish traps consist of eight semicircles of low stone walls lying along the

Plate 4.2   Oyster Harbour Aboriginal fish traps. (WA Museum)

shore for about a kilometre, with various associated smaller rings of stone (plate 4.2). The stones used to build the wedge-shaped walls are of a local dark, lateritic material and are irregular in size and shape but generally about 15 centimetres across. A natural reef forms the end of one trap, and another is bounded almost entirely by reef. Aborigines used the appreciable ebb and flow of the tides to catch the fish. Fish which swam into the enclosures on a high tide were then stranded when the tide went out, and were caught by hand or spearing.

Wave Rock

Wave Rock is in arid country four kilometres from Hyden, and is a major tourist attraction of the region (plate 4.3). The wave-like appearance of the rock has been created by the elements eroding the surface little by little over the millennia, forming an undercut. The distinctive vertical bands of colour are due to rain washing natural chemical deposits down the sloping face of the rock, which is 2,700 million-year-old granite. The granite cliff is 50 metres high and is part of an isolated outcrop known as an inselberg or "island mountain".

Bates Cave art site

North of Wave Rock and 18 kilometres north-east of Hyden are "the humps", massive residuals of granite rising spectacularly above the gently rolling landscape. A large flat rock known as Kings Rock contains a gnamma hole or rock well, and there are rock paintings in a cave below a large, free-standing boulder on

Plate 4.3   Wave Rock. (WA Tourist Commission)

the east side of the humps. The cave is 12 metres long and 5 metres wide, and has more than 50 hand stencils in red ochre and white pipe-clay on the walls and ceiling. There is also one linear design in the entrance cavern.

There is a story associated with Bates Cave concerning a young Aboriginal woman who fell in love with a warrior of a forbidden tribe. Her punishment for disobeying the society's laws was to give birth to a cross-eyed son. Her son, Mulka, was declared an outcast and took refuge in this cave. His crossed eyes made it impossible for him to hunt for his food, and he was forced to eat young children. He grew to be a giant on this diet, and his hand stencil can be seen high on the walls and ceilings of the cave. The tribal elders finally decided to rid the area of Mulka and chased him all the way to Dumbleyung. There he was killed and his body was tossed onto an ant heap without proper burial.

There is no evidence of cannibalism in this region and the gory details were probably to warn people to obey society's laws on marriage and to take heed of territorial boundaries. Similar cautionary tales are common all over the world.

Dryandra ochre trail

West of Bates Cave in the Dryandra State Forest, a walking trail goes past a pit where the Nyungar Aboriginal people used to quarry ochre. The ochre pigment was used for body and artefact decoration as well as for rock art.

The Dryandra area is one of the most scenic in the wheatbelt, and its magnificent woodlands of wandoo, powderbark, brown mallet and bushland thickets shelter numerous native mammals and birds, providing food in abundance for the Nyungar. Hardwood from eucalypts was used for spears, boomerangs and digging sticks, and corkwood from the Christmas tree *(Nuytsia floribunda)* for shields.

The 5 kilometre long ochre trail commences in wandoo woodland off Tomingley Road near the Dryandra arboretum, and leads through upland powderbark and kwongan (heath) vegetation past the Aboriginal ochre quarry. Access to the main Dryandra forest area is off the York Williams Road to the west and the Narrogin Wandering Road to the east. It lies 160 kilometres south-east of Perth and 20 kilometres north-west of Narrogin. Signposts to Dryandra are on the Albany Highway at North Bannister, on the Great Southern Highway at Yornaning and Cuballing, and at Narrogin.

Perth region

Yaberoo Budjara heritage trail, Wanneroo

This 28 kilometre-long walking trail on the western side of Wanneroo Road takes in a number of Aboriginal mythological sites in the Wanneroo area, 50 kilometres north of Perth. It links Lake Joondalup, Neerabup and Yanchep National Parks, highlighting features of Aboriginal, natural and historic significance. The route follows a traditional Aboriginal track linking the coastal plains and inland lakes. Most of the trail is set on the track that the serpent, Waugul, is said to have carved out of the earth in the Dreamtime. Further information and leaflets are available from the Western Australian Heritage Committee.

Wanneroo scarred tree

This is one of the very few scarred trees known in the metropolitan area. As such, it is significant to Aboriginal people in the region. Two large scars — one facing east and the other west — are visible on an old but living jarrah tree. These scars were caused by Aboriginal people removing large sheets of bark, possibly for making bark shelters, shields, dishes or carrying baskets. Both scars probably date from the early days of European settlement, for metal axe marks are visible but there is substantial regrowth of bark around the scars, indicating a considerable passage of time since the sheets of bark were prised off the tree.

The tree lies on the southern verge of Church Street off Wanneroo Road, adjacent to number 85 Frederick Road, in Wanneroo. It features on the Lake Joondalup heritage trail, which commences at Hawkins Park on Boas Avenue. (Trail brochures are available from the city of Wanneroo.)

Star Swamp heritage trail

Other scarred trees lie on the Star Swamp heritage trail in the same north metropolitan region, in the Karrinyup area. This is a 1.4 kilometre long walking trail which is also suitable for wheelchair users. The trail commences at Groat Street, and the Aboriginal camp and scarred trees lie near the northern end close to the Mary Street entrance.

Orchestra Shell Cave, Wanneroo

This limestone cave opens onto the top of a 15 metre-high ridge rising steeply from the eastern margin of Lake Nerrabup, east of the Wanneroo Highway about 10 kilometres north of Wanneroo and 35 kilometres north of Perth. There are interpretive signs on site, and it may be visited by special arrangement with the Department of Aboriginal Sites. Visitors should take torches and be very careful not to disturb the earth floor or to touch the soft rock walls.

An Aboriginal site of great archaeological significance, the cave contains both rock art and a prehistoric occupational deposit, and has been studied in detail by archaeologist Sylvia Hallam of the University of Western Australia.[7] The entrance is some 7 metres wide and almost 2 metres high, and leads down a steep slope into a half-dome shaped cave measuring about 18 metres by 12 metres. The cave, named for its shape, is reasonably spacious and light right to the back, and would have provided a warm, dry haven from winter rains and a cool refuge in summer. Radiocarbon dates on charcoal in the earth floor deposit showed that Aboriginal people used this cave at least 6,500 years ago, and analysis of animal bones in the deposit suggests that it was also from time to time a carnivore's den, the most likely candidate to have left telltale chew marks on the bones being the Tasmanian devil.

The most exciting feature of Orchestra Shell Cave is the markings on its walls. The relatively smooth surface of the whole eastern side of the ceiling is covered with faint markings, some of them overlain with a calcitic encrustation, suggesting considerable age. The markings are too narrow and sharp in cross-section to have been made by fingers, but must have been made with some sort of sharp engraving tool. There are at least four different "designs" — a set of grooves splaying out from a single stem, sets of wide-spaced straight parallel grooves, short very deep individual cuts, and curving crisscrossing sets of usually fivefold narrow-spaced parallel grooves.

These markings are reminiscent of those in other Australian caves such as Koonalda on the Nullarbor Plain. There is no doubt that they were made by human hand, probably many thousands of years ago when the limestone was rather softer than it is now. It is clear that engraving implements were used. These were probably both single- and multi-pronged, and it has been suggested that the parallel marks derive from the use of a set of animal's claws with five digits, such as those of the Tasmanian devil.

Orchestra Shell Cave is one of only two similar early engraving sites so far discovered in West Australia. It is thus of great archaeological significance in tracing the development of prehistoric art in this part of the continent.

Upper Swan River site

One of the oldest firmly dated human occupation sites yet found in Australia is an open-air campsite on the bank of the Upper Swan River, north of Perth. It lies on an ancient floodplain some 20 metres above the present floodplain bordering the Swan River between Perth and Walyunga, on the north side of the river and east side of the road within sight of the Upper Swan bridge. The site is now in the Register of the National Estate, and the deposits containing artefacts have been stabilised and protected from further erosion. Visits can be made by arrangement with the Department of Aboriginal Sites.

Like many archaeological sites, this ancient campsite was found by chance, in this case by an alert archaeologist, Bob Pearce, who noticed men digging in a clay pit belonging to a brick factory.[8] He stopped his car to have a look, and found stone tools of quartz *in situ* at a depth of 70 to 90 centimetres. Radiocarbon dating of charcoal associated with artefacts revealed that the site belongs to between 40,000 and 38,000 years ago. About 900 deeply patinated stone artefacts were recovered, and are now in the Western Australian Museum in Perth. The local Aboriginal community have taken a strong interest in the find, and are actively involved in management of the site.

It is hoped that the Aboriginal community will allow some signs to be erected to explain and interpret the site to visitors, for like many archaeological sites of major scientific importance it is not visually impressive in itself and the artefacts are housed elsewhere for safety purposes. Nevertheless, beneath the grassy banks lies evidence that Aborigines were already camping and hunting in the south-west of the continent 40,000 years ago. Indeed, this is the site on which is based the oft-quoted figure of a minimum of 40,000 years for Aboriginal occupation of Australia.

Walyunga heritage trail

A short walking trail beside the Swan River in Walyunga National Park, 40 kilometres via the Great Northern Highway north-east of Perth, reveals Aboriginal myths, traditional lore and uses of the river, landscape and local flora and fauna. It is an 850 metres easy walk along the bank of the Swan River, linking Walyunga Pool and Boongarup Pool, and incorporating a visit to an important Aboriginal campsite.[9] This was frequented from over 10,000 years ago till historic times by Aboriginal groups who brought a great variety of stone materials with them from many distant regions. The Nyungar Aboriginal people believe that the rainbow serpent, Waugul, travelled along the river and left behind stone such as chert and quartz for making tools. Over one million stone artefacts have been found on the site, some of them made of Eocene chert from sources now under the sea. (This site is protected by law like all Aboriginal sites in Australia, and not a single artefact may be removed.)

Coondebung's Kalleepgurr heritage trail

The Nyungar community designed this 6.5 kilometre long trail, which takes in Aboriginal sites, natural flora and fauna and an attractive waterfall. Visitors are introduced by an Aboriginal guide to the concept of the Dreamtime, and creator beings such as Waugul, the rainbow serpent, and Tjitti Tjitti, the willy wagtail. This trail is in the Brigadoon area adjoining Walyunga National Park, but can only be explored by groups accompanied by an Aboriginal guide from the Nyungar community. Arrangements for tours can be made by telephoning the community on (09) 342 6230.

CHAPTER FIVE

Western Australia: The Murchison and Cue Regions

The story of Western Australia goes back further than that of anywhere else in the continent. Here can be seen the beginning of life on earth. Australia's oldest dated mineral is 4.1 billion-year-old zircon from Mount Narryer; one of the most weathered landscapes in the continent is found in the granite of the Pilbara, dating between 3.1 and 2.6 billion years; and one of the earliest forms of life on this planet has not only been found fossilised, but is still living in Western Australia today. This is the stromatolite, a growing structure formed from particles of mud or silt allied with tiny micro-organisms.[1] In the Pilbara fossilised stromatolites

Plate 5.1   Stromatolites at Hamelin Pool, Shark Bay. (K. McNamara)

have been found (at a site inappropriately named North Pole Well) in rocks dating 3,450 and 3,550 million years old, providing the oldest firmly established evidence for life on this planet.

Near Kalgoorlie there is evidence that between 2,800 and 2,700 million years ago, stromatolites grew on the margins of volcanic hot springs. Volcanic eruptions would have showered the stromatolites with hot ash and other debris, killing but also helping to fossilise them. The stromatolite boulders can now be seen weathering out of the softer volcanic ash surrounding them in rocks at Kanowna, just east of Kalgoorlie. Similar stromatolites still grow today in volcanic springs in Yellowstone National Park in North America.

Impressive large domed stromatolites also exist at Thuragoody Bore east of Wiluna in the Western Desert; these fossils are a mere 1,700 million years old. Their living descendants still exist on the west coast of Western Australia, at Shark Bay and in coastal lakes, particularly in saline Lake Thetis near Cervantes, in hypersaline lakes on Rottnest Island, in the freshwater Lake Richmond at Rockingham, and in the northern end of brackish Lake Clifton between Mandurah and Bunbury about 100 kilometres south of Perth. All stromatolites seem to develop in environments rich in calcium carbonate, either limestone or lime-rich sands. These living stromatolite platforms can be visited, but must on no account be disturbed.

The west coast

Shark Bay

The finest living examples in the world of one of the earliest life forms on this planet, stromatolites, are in Hamelin Pool, an intertidal and shallow water shelf of Shark Bay in the Carnarvon region of the west coast (figure 5.1). The pool is at the southern end of the easternmost inlet of Shark Bay, bordered by low sand dunes. Stromatolite means "mattress stone", and hundreds of black clumps resembling soft rock jut from sand or mud or in deeper water grow in columns up to three metres tall. They vary in shape from large clubs to columns, cylinders and complex branching shapes (plate 5.1).

These are living colonies of primitive, single-celled plants bound by secretions of lime. The stromatolite mats visible today are alive, and have been building up over thousands of years at the rate of about half a millimetre annually. They are survivors of one of the world's earliest life forms, found fossilised in rocks up to 3.5 billion years old.

The microscopic plants which grow in mats are called cyanophytes, and represent the earliest form of life on earth, and the first to put oxygen into the air. They commonly grow in mats like algae, and here at Hamelin Pool are left in peace to build, since the backwater is landlocked on three sides and the outlet is partially blocked by the Faure Sill, a shallow bank of sand and sea grass. The dehydrating effect of sun and wind sometimes makes the water twice as salty as normal sea water.

Stromatolites differ from normal fossils such as shells or bones, which are actual parts of animals, because they are formed by the activity of micro-

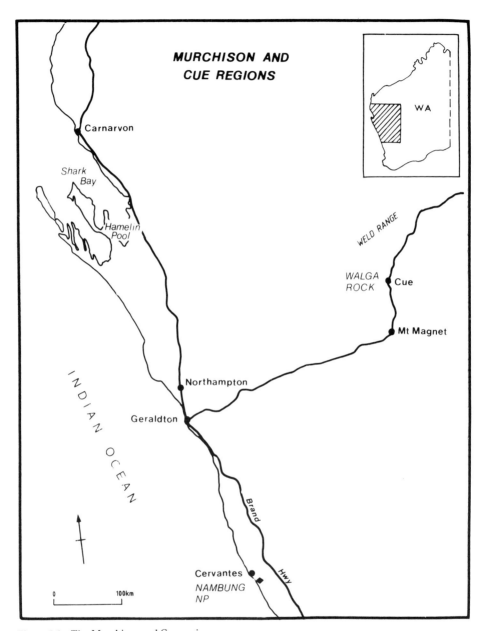

Figure 5.1   The Murchison and Cue regions

organisms, which trap, bind and precipitate sediment. The constructing micro-organisms are mainly microscopic bacteria-like organisms, the cyanobacteria, which trap fine particles of sediment from the water and bind them together with a film of mucus which they secrete. Stromatolites develop as countless layers of sediment are trapped by the microbial mat. One simple growth pattern occurs when some of the buried filaments become active in daytime and push upward through the layer of sediment towards the light, to form the next organic layer or lamina.

Stromatolites have been around since Day One of the world's evolutionary story, and some of the finest living examples of this ancient life form can be seen today on the north-western coast of Western Australia. This area is consequently under consideration for nomination to the World Heritage List for its scientific significance. Shark Bay has another attraction; it is a refuge for dugong and for a community of friendly bottlenose dolphins, which love to come and play in the shallows of the Monkey Mia area. The area is reached from the Shark Bay turn-off at Overlander Roadhouse on the North West Coastal Highway, 700 kilometres north of Perth.

Willi Gulli paintings, Northampton district

Four small rockshelters containing Aboriginal paintings and stencils lie two kilometres north-east of the coast near Northampton, and are open to the public. They are reached from the Horrocks Beach Road. On the north-west side of Bowes River Valley a gravel road turns off south-west towards the sea 17.6 kilometres west of Northampton. On the north side of the gravel road the rockshelters are situated in a scarp of Cretaceous marine sandstone about 5 metres in height, between 15 and 75 metres from the road over its first half kilometre. The easternmost site is the major site. Other roads lie to the north-west and north-east of the sites, and there is a quarry for road material immediately above them.

The rockshelters contain both rock art and occupational debris, and seem to have been used as camping places for several hundred years or longer. The paintings were first recorded in 1914 by W.C. Campbell, and the name Willi Gulli appears on old maps of the district and is said to mean "place of the curlew".

These sites contain the largest numerical concentration of motifs known in the south-west of Western Australia. The paintings are in red, white, black and yellow. The white figures stand out vividly whereas those in red ochre are hard to discern and presumably much older. Subjects include human figures, lizards, emu feet, shield-like designs, a seven-stroke symbol and some spectacular white

Plate 5.2 Hand stencils and a painting of a snake at Willi Gulli

snakes up to two metres long (plate 5.2). There are also chains of small white dots painted in one metre-long vertical lines or coils, and symbols resembling fringed pubic aprons. Stencils in white pigment derived from pipe-clay of hands and boomerangs are numerous; both right and left hands have been stencilled and some of them are very large, clearly belonging to adult men. The wide variety of motifs and good preservation of at least the paintings and stencils in white makes these sites well worth a visit.

The Pinnacles, Nambung National Park, Geraldton district

Nambung National Park contains the dramatic Pinnacles Desert, where spikes and knobs of limestone, some taller than a house, others smaller than a pencil, stud the sands (plate 5.3). These bizarre monoliths began to form when rainwater percolated through high, mobile dunes of lime sand, which had been blown inland. Lime was leached from their upper layers, cementing the lower sand into a soft limestone.[2] Stabilising plants deposited an acidic layer of soil and humus over the dunes, accelerating the leaching process. A hard layer of calcrete formed under the soil horizon, and this is now visible as a capping on many pinnacles. Over the centuries the subsurface limestone eroded as plant roots crept down cracks in the calcrete topping and water seeped down the channels. The pinnacles are the remnants of that eroded limestone layer, exposed as the prevailing wind blew away the surrounding quartz sand (figure 5.2). Over much of the Pinnacles Desert there is what looks like a forest of petrified twigs, but in reality they are fossilised plant roots or rhizoliths, up to 20 centimetres in height.

The age of the pinnacles is uncertain, but it seems likely that they were formed between about 80,000 and 15,000 years ago, in environmental conditions associated with a drop in sea level. The process of formation was entirely subterranean, but there is evidence that they were exposed on at least one

Plate 5.3   The Pinnacles, Nambung National Park. (WA Tourist Commission)

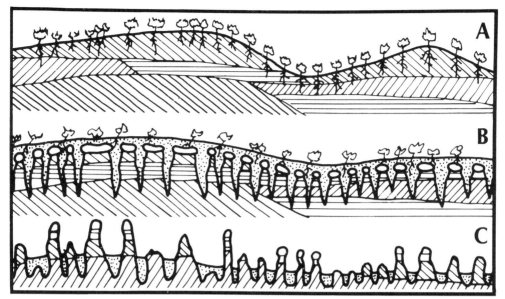

Figure 5.2 Schematic cross-sections of the development of the Pinnacles, Nambung National Park. A: The dune being stabilised by vegetation. Tap roots penetrate deep into the developing limestone, which hardens around the roots. Groups of parallel lines represent dune bedding. B: A hard layer of calcrete has developed. In this and the underlying limestone, solution pipes have formed. The insoluble residue from the dissolution of the limestone accumulates in the pipes. C: After prolonged sub-surface weathering, only a few residual stumps of limestone are left, swathed in quartz sand. When the wind has blown this sand away, the residual limestone stumps jut into the air as pinnacles, a few capped by the remnants of the old calcrete layer. After K. McNamara, *Australian Natural History,* vol. 22 (10) 1988

occasion more than 6,000 years ago. Archaeologists have found artefacts made of fossiliferous Eocene chert cemented to the base of some pinnacles. This raw material was derived from offshore quarries which were submerged by the post-glacial rise in sea level more than 6,000 years ago. It is thought that the pinnacles were later again covered by sand dunes, and may have only been re-exposed within the last century.

The Pinnacles lie about 260 kilometres north of Perth, and are reached from the Brand Highway, turning west approximately 30 kilometres north of Cataby Roadhouse; Cervantes is 50 kilometres from the Brand Highway and The Pinnacles are 17 kilometres south-east of Cervantes. (There are also regular coach tours from Perth.)

Cue area

Walga Rock, Cue district

The impressive granite monolith of Walga or Walganna Rock rises 50 metres above the grasslands and mulga scrub of the surrounding plains in the Murchison goldfields region (plates 5.4 and 5.5). The site is open to the public and is signposted. It lies 37 kilometres west of Cue and 30 kilometres west of Austin Downs homestead. A well-defined subsidiary track leads south-west from the

Plate 5.4   Walga Rock

creek crossing and windmill, which are within clear view of the rock on the road
west from the homestead. The track ends at the south-west end of the rock,
where there is a camping ground near the rockhole and the northern end of the
painted rockshelter, which faces west.

The name Walga means ochre or painting in the Warragi language, and this is
one of the most extensive painted sites in Australia. The rockshelter is shallow
but about 60 metres long, and its back wall is covered with paintings throughout
its length. Some are so high above the earth floor that scaffolding must have been
used to paint them. There are so many superimpositions that no single motif
stands independent of the others, except the famous ship at the shelter's northern
end.

The ship has at least two masts, possibly a funnel, ratlines, rigging and square
portholes in the hull. Beneath the ship are four rows of wavy lines which some
observers have interpreted as a series of symbols of a script resembling Arabic,
but it now seems more likely that they represent water.

This ship painting some 325 kilometres from the sea is a riddle, and there has
been much speculation and a little research as to its origin. Two old desert
Aborigines were recorded as saying in 1926 that a long time before a girl in the
tribe who had blonde hair and blue eyes had made the painting. As she had done
this in a place restricted only to initiated men and was forbidden by her sex to
make paintings, she had been killed. No evidence has been found to corroborate
this story. Other theories maintain that the painter was a survivor or descendant
of a survivor of a ship wrecked off the coast, such as the *Zuytdorp*, although the
ship motif does not represent a Dutch colonial vessel. Or perhaps it was the work
of an Afghan, in view of the resemblance of the "waves" to Arabic writing, or an
Asian stationhand working on Austin Downs station in the 1920s? The white paint
used in this motif has been analysed and is the same and comes from the same
source as the white pipe-clay used in other white paintings at the site, which may

Plate 5.5 Painting of a ship at Walga Rock

indicate an Aboriginal painter recording his first impression of a ship and the ocean.

The other paintings in the rockshelter are clearly affiliated in style with the art of the desert. The colours used are red, white and some yellow, the red ochre being transported from the Wilgie Mia ochre mine, 65 kilometres to the northeast (see below). There is a large number and range of motifs, dominated by non-figurative designs such as single and multiple (usually three or four) parallel meandering or wavy lines, arcs and U-shaped outlines, singly or back to back.

Although there are circles, dots and spirals, the true concentric circles characteristic of desert art do not seem to be present. The few figurative motifs include paintings of large lizards, an anthropomorph and bird and animal tracks, and stencils of hands and artefacts. Some paintings carefully emphasise the natural contours and bulges of the rock surface.

A small excavation was done in the floor of the rockshelter in 1978 by a joint Australian-French expedition led by Charles Dortch of the Western Australian Museum and the late Professor Francois Bordes.[3] The deposit is about one metre deep, and shows that Aboriginal people had been camping there intermittently for several thousand years.

Walga Rock is an elongated oval shape about 1.5 kilometres long by half a kilometre wide and is oriented north-east to south-west. A climb to the summit is well worthwhile, both for the panoramic view and to see a modern Aboriginal painting site in a small rockshelter in a jumble of boulders just below the summit. The motifs are an unusual mixture of traditional subjects like snakes painted in a traditional way with European-style paintings such as landscape and trees. Although Walga Rock still has significance to Aboriginal custodians, ceremonies are no longer held there and they have agreed that it may be visited by the general public.

Wilgie Mia Ochre Mine, Cue district

The most extensive and well-preserved Aboriginal ochre mine in Australia is Wilgie Mia, on the southern side of the Weld Range 70 kilometres north-west of Cue. The public should contact the Department of Aboriginal Sites for advice on possible visits, and obtain a permit from the Western Australian Aboriginal Lands Trust for entry to the reserve.

This mine is remarkable for its massive chambers, the use of scaffolding, the outstanding quality of the ochre, vast trading network, associated mythology, ethnographic information and the antiquity of the site. On the northern side of a hill, Nganakurakura, Aboriginal miners excavated an immense open cut, between 15 metres and 30 metres wide and 20 metres deep. (European miners dug a large tunnel into this pit from the southern side, and this now makes the most convenient approach.) The pit slopes steeply down into a dimly lit cavern where various small galleries branch off, formed as the Aboriginal miners followed the seams of red and yellow ochre.

The quarrying was on a much larger scale than elsewhere in Australia, and an estimated 15,000 cubic metres of material has been mined from the deposit. Scaffolds of poles bound together with kangaroo sinew and placed on piles of rocks were used to follow up some of the veins of ochre out of reach from the chamber floor. This is stratified in places up to a depth of 6 metres, and excavation of a pocket recess in the north-east wall of the main chamber revealed short digging sticks (20 to 50 centimetres long by about 3 centimetres wide) and hammerstones made from river cobbles or large flakes two or three times the size of a fist. Half a tonne of artefacts were found by archaeologist Ian Crawford in one small excavation, perhaps because there was apparently a traditional taboo on taking any tools out of the mine.

Radiocarbon dates on wood from the base of the excavation show that ochre has

Plate 5.6   Wilgie Mia ochre mine. (Courtesy WA Museum)

been mined at Wilgie Mia for more than a thousand years. The ochre was quarried by men hammering fire-hardened wooden digging sticks as wedges into the seams of rich ochre to break up walls of hard haematite. Light was provided by fires kept burning on the floor of the chamber, as a thick layer of white ash bears witness. The excavated material was then carried up the northern slope where the lumps were broken up to extract the ochre. This was then pulverised, dampened within water, and worked into balls for trading purposes.

Because of its deep red colour, high-covering power (opacity) and fine powdery texture, Wilgie Mia ochre was highly prized, and was regarded by Aborigines 300 kilometres away as the best of the various known ochre sources in the interior. It was used across a wide expanse of Western Australia and is said to have been traded as far afield as Queensland. Some of its importance stemmed from the belief that the deposit was created by the death agony of an ancestral being, a giant kangaroo, who was speared by the evil spirit, Mondong. The dying kangaroo leapt to Wilgie Mia hill, where the red ochre is his blood, the yellow his liver and the green his gall. One last leap took him to another hill, which marks his grave. This hill lies three kilometres to the south-west and is known as Little Wilgie. An open pit about 50 metres by 18 by 5 metres was excavated there to extract the red and yellow ochre. This site was more important mythologically than the much more extensive workings at Wilgie Mia, and was apparently mined first, which would imply an antiquity of more than a thousand years.

The ochre mine was regarded with great fear, except by elders who were its custodians. Those leaving the site traditionally walked out backwards and swept away their footprints, so that Mondong could not follow and kill them. Photographs from the early 1900s show these rituals being enacted (plate 5.6).

CHAPTER SIX

Western Australia: The Pilbara

The art of the ancient engravers reached its height in Australia, and possibly the world, in the Pilbara region of Western Australia. In contrast to the Kimberley, there are almost no caves or rockshelters in the Pilbara and consequently very few paintings, but instead an exuberant style of rock engraving flourished in prehistoric times, surpassing all others in Australia in both quality and quantity. This body of rock art is elsewhere unparalleled in sheer numbers and density of sites and individual figures, artistic sophistication, stylistic complexity, technical achievement and antiquity of cultural tradition. The total number of engraved figures is in the order of hundreds of thousands, possibly even more than a million.

The visual impact of the Pilbara engravings is without equal. Large areas of outcropping rock, particularly granites, granophyres and dolerites, have a black or very dark brown surface or patina due to concentration of iron oxide in the surface layer. (It is no coincidence that this is also Australia's iron ore province.) When this patina was removed by the engraver's pounding or abrasion, the light, freshly exposed subcutaneous rock contrasted strongly with the dark surrounding surface. This striking colour contrast forms the image in many Pilbara engravings. Other engravings show no colour contrast and are visible only because of the deep pounding made into the rock, because repatination has occurred over a period of thousands of years.

The rock which forms much of the Pilbara is 2,600 to 3,100 million years old, making it one of the oldest, most weathered landscapes in Australia.[1] Symmetrical conical granite outcrops rise like islands from the sandy spinifex-clad plains. Many of these outcrops bear engravings. The prehistoric artists showed a preference for the darkest granite, which produced the clearest and most striking visual images, often visible for a considerable distance. Seed-grinding patches — oval patches of rock worn smooth from women's grinding of grass seeds into flour — are frequently close to or even on top of engravings, and stone tools are often found in the same areas. Production of rock engravings here therefore seems to have been a part of everyday life, and at least some sites were not secret-sacred. Likewise on the coast shell middens are sometimes associated with groups of engravings.

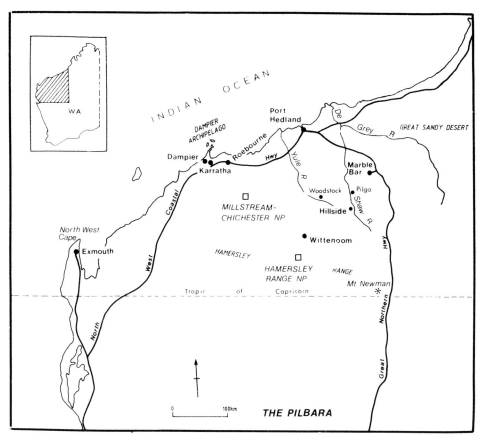

Figure 6.1 Map of Pilbara

The Pilbara region of north-west Australia is roughly bounded by the De Grey River and the Great Sandy Desert on the east and the Tropic of Capricorn on the south (figure 6.1). The scenery is arid but impressive, with rugged ranges and some of the deepest, most dramatic gorges in the continent. Aborigines have been living in this landscape for at least 26,000 years. Traces of human occupation of this order of antiquity have been found in two rockshelters in the Mount Newman area,[2] and in one on North-West Cape.[3] This is the Mandu Mandu rockshelter in Cape Range National Park, where archaeologist Kate Morse has found the first Australian evidence for the exploitation of marine shellfish during the Pleistocene.

Rock types which have been engraved are varied ranging from the limestone ridges of Port Hedland, dolerite boulders of offshore islands and the Black Ranges, granite conical hills of the Upper Yule and Shaw Rivers, to the metamorphosed sediments of the Hamersley Range.

There are at least two distinct phases of engraving, each with its own technique and repertoire of motifs. In the first phase abrasion was used, linear motifs and outlines of figures being abraded into the rock to depths of as much as a centimetre. The resulting grooves have a smooth polished appearance and texture, and have weathered back to the colour of the surrounding rock. This

Plate 6.1   Gallery Hill, Woodstock (WA Museum)

process of repatination takes many thousands of years, probably a minimum of ten thousand. Subjects of these early engravings are kangaroo and bird tracks, circles, spirals and arcs, the outlines of large creatures such as kangaroos and emus, and some rare outline human figures.

The second phase of engraving is characterised by shallow figures pecked out of the rock by direct hammering or indirect percussion using stone hammer and chisel. These pecked, lighter coloured engravings have a much wider range of subjects. As well as numerous animal and bird tracks and non-figurative designs, there are many reptiles, animals, birds, artefacts such as spears, shields and boomerangs, and above all human figures.

Subjects of the art are extremely varied. On the coast marine creatures are common; and inland, as well as the ubiquitous tracks of birds and animals, circles, arcs, spirals, spears, boomerangs and non-figurative motifs, there are naturalistic engravings of animals, often life size, and a wealth of human figures, engaged in dramatic compositions including fighting, running, dancing, hunting and love-making. Some humans are realistic, others are anthropomorphous, involving supernatural features such as pincer-like hands and feet with only two digits, two-toed tracks, protruding muzzles resembling kangaroos or dogs, antennae-like projections waving from their heads, and greatly enlarged genitals. They are usually portrayed with legs pointing in random directions, as if floating rather than standing on the ground. These novel anthropomorphs were originally termed Kurangara, since they were believed to be related to the Aboriginal cult of that

Plate 6.2 Woodstock figures at Gallery Hill, characterised by protruding "muzzles", head "antennae", thin flexible limbs, forked heads and feet and enlarged genitals.

name. But this now seems unlikely, and the Aborigines have no knowledge of them, so they have been renamed Woodstock figures, after the site where they are most prolific (plates 6.1 and 6.2).

These Woodstock anthropomorphs usually show strong colour contrast, indicating that they are among the younger engravings. The youngest art is an exuberant celebration of life, particularly of fertility and sex, but it also has a haunting spiritual quality. Other Pilbara engravings are deeply engraved and weathered back to the colour of the parent rock, surviving evidence of an age-old, rich cultural heritage. Although engravings are no longer being created, they are part of a living culture and Aboriginal people are sensitive to visitation. Certain sites are restricted and interested persons should contact the Department of Aboriginal Sites or local Aboriginal organisations.

Hamersley Range National Park

Some Aboriginal rock art is found within this huge national park, which is 270 kilometres south of Port Hedland and is reached from the North West Coastal Highway on the Wittenoom road, which crosses the park. The Hamersley Range rises above the plain in flat-bedded layers of Precambrian sediments which were on the seabed, 2,000 million years ago. This massive block of weathered rock is one of the world's oldest land surfaces. The northern scarp of the arid plateau of spiky hummock grass and stunted mulga trees is broken by twenty major gorges, with walls up to 100 metres high shading cool, tree-lined creek beds and large permanent pools.

In the gorges the horizontal beds of shale and conglomerate rock are darkened by deep bands of red iron ore and seams of blue asbestos in the cliff walls. A memorable viewing point is where four tremendous canyons meet, at the junction of Red Gorge with the equally deep but narrow canyons of Joffre, Weano and Hancock Gorges. From a lookout on the narrow spine between Weano and Hancock Gorges there are awe-inspiring views vertically down several hundred metres into the intersecting clefts.

These oases in the desert country were regularly used by Aborigines as camping places, and traces of their passing can be seen in some rock painting and engraving sites. Adequately protected rock surfaces are few and small in the banded iron formations of the Hamersley Ranges, which form angular slabs of rock that tend to break off from the walls and ceilings of rockshelters, presenting only small and discontinuous surfaces to the rock painters. Most paintings therefore are small in size, in the order of 10 to 20 centimetres high.

The best known site is in beautiful Dales Gorge in the north-east of the park about 60 kilometres south-east of Wittenoom, noted for its large circular pool and the Fortescue Falls. (Information about the rock art sites is available from the ranger.) Some paintings and engravings downstream from the waterfall include very faded traces of about 80 elongated human figures in yellow ochre (figure 6.2), 2 snakes, 7 vertically striped oval shapes, possibly representing weapons or sacred objects, and about 170 yellow and 82 red short vertical "tally strokes". Some 167 individual motifs have been engraved on the south side of the gorge for about a kilometre downstream, but most are extremely indistinct, although some human figures are discernible.

The most outstanding painting site lies just to the west of the mouth of Kalamina Gorge. Here clear, long, stick human-like figures in white pigment are

Figure 6.2 Deteriorating paintings in yellow ochre in Dales Gorge, Hamersley Range National Park. (After B. Wright 1968, fig. 850. The scale is 30 cm.)

superimposed on faint boomerangs. This site is about 1.5 kilometres from the road.

Paintings are also found in the upper Eastern Gorge, which runs into Wittenoom Gorge about nine kilometres south of Wittenoom. The paintings are all in orange ochre, lumps of which can be picked up in the creek bed. Beyond the waterfall about two-thirds of the way up the gorge the yellow outline of a kangaroo nearly 2 metres high is painted on a large flat surface in a protected position. The main gallery is almost at the head of the gorge. Here 164 marks have been painted on angular slabs more or less protected from the weather. The marks include dingoes, lizards, boomerangs and anthropomorphous figures, with long bodies, short limbs and long radiating hair or head-dresses. Most unusual are some six birds or bird men, with winged arms. Similar figures painted in white but with a more tapering, bird-like body are found at another Pilbara site, but birds in the engravings are quite different, whether in profile or front view owl-like figures.

There are few engravings in the Hamersley Range, probably because the banded iron formations do not usually display the same type of patina as the Pilbara granites and dolerites, so the contrast between a fresh engraving and the original patinated surface, although visible, has little visual impact.

The locality with the most paintings in the Hamersley Range is the gorge area in the Wittenoom and Mount Bruce districts. Near the mouth of Wittenoom Gorge on the north side of the range there are paintings in a cave about 1.5 kilometres east of the town, on the eastern side of a creek running down from a prominent hill. The small paintings have been made on the ceiling and on the underside of low laminated ledges at the back. Boomerangs predominate, about fifty-seven being painted in white, orange, black, black with white outline, black with red outline, red with white outline, and white with black outline. There are also twenty-three human figures, four dingoes, five white circles, two white hands, two white kangaroo prints and one red emu track. Among the paintings and on the vertical edges of rock are several rows of short vertical strokes or "tally marks", about 10 centimetres long and in a wide variety of colours.

A most unusual feature of this site is the wide variety of colours used. White and black have been mixed to produce grey figures, and some of the human figures are grey outlined in red. Such a combination of materials to make another colour was very rare in Aboriginal rock art.

Millstream-Chichester Range National Park

This park, 80 kilometres south of Roebourne, is noted for its scenery and Aboriginal sites. There are many mythological sites, such as those associated with the deep pools of the Fortescue River in the Millstream area. The Chichester Range encompasses a tableland dissected by the headwaters of the Harding, George and Sherlock Rivers, and includes many groups of Aboriginal rock engravings.

Woodstock engraving sites

One of the finest and most prolific rock art site complexes is the Western

Plate 6.3   Rock engraving in the Pilbara, W.A. (H. McNickle)

Australian Museum Reserve of Abydos-Woodstock on the Upper Yule River, centred on the old Woodstock homestead some 170 kilometres south of Port Hedland just to the east of the Great Northern Highway from Wittenoom to Port Hedland. Here outcrops of suitable dark granite coincide with abundant supplies of water. More than 200 granite outcrops, usually weathered into conical heaps of red-brown boulders, have been engraved with thousands of figures by Aborigines over many millennia (plates 6.1, 6.2 and 6.3). A preliminary survey by Bruce Wright, of the Western Australian Museum, in the 1960s identified more than 3,000 individual engravings.[4] Visits to the reserve can only be made with the permission of the Department of Aboriginal Sites of the Western Australian Museum.

The major concentrations are Gallery Hill, where several hundred engravings are found on the north-facing slope, and Maynard Granites (formerly Egina Granites), a conical hill surrounded by a sloping granite pavement or apron. Here there are engravings on both the hill and the pavement, including some long snakes and a faint but exquisite figure of a running pregnant woman on the pavement (figure 6.3). There are also rock wells and seed-grinding patches, and the only painting site found in the reserve, a small rockshelter beneath a granite boulder with very faint red images.

The human figures make the most impact on the visitor. Some of them are naturalistic, but many are the part-human, part-supernatural or anthropomorphous figures now widely known as Woodstock figures after this, the type site. They generally have a long thin body, a head with a protruding muzzle and antennae-like projections, thin bending arms and legs without knee or elbow joints, exaggerated genitals and forked hands and feet. Sometimes they appear as individuals leaping or dancing, but often they feature in dramatic compositions of fighting, hunting or copulation.

This corpus of rock art has been described as worthy of the World Heritage List, and as "the Lascaux of Australia". There is a compelling spirit of place about the Woodstock art. In the early morning the engravings glow red as the first light reaches them; in the evening shadows cast by slanting rays of the setting sun throw more and more shallow engravings into relief, and the rocks seem to come alive with figures.

Spear Hill rock engravings sites

A series of about thirty-five engraving galleries, located on boulder piles, rock outcrops and flat pavements are found in Black Range east of Woodstock and east of the Upper Shaw River in the vicinity of Spear Hill, 66 kilometres south-west of Marble Bar on the Marble Bar to Hillside station road. Permission to visit these sites must be sought from the Department of Aboriginal Sites, the Aboriginal custodians and the landowner. Spear Hill, just to the north of the road, is a

Figure 6.3 Woodstock engravings. A running pregnant woman on a rock slab at Maynard Hill. (Courtesy J. Clegg)

striking dome-like structure of pink granite, 2 kilometres by 1.5 kilometres in extent and about 70 metres high. All over the hill are large rounded boulders and attractive, unusually large trees of Minnirichi wattle, reaching a height of 10 metres. These gave the hill its name, since the wood is extremely hard and was used for making spear tips, according to local Njamal Aboriginal people.[5] The summit of Spear Hill was also used for initiation ceremonies at one time, but the ceremonial ground has now been moved to another site. Two small rockshelters near the summit have outlines of boomerangs, hand stencils and faint traces of paintings, which are very rare in the Pilbara.

One of the puzzles about Spear Hill is that it is by far the largest and most conspicuous outcrop in the area, but bears only five individual engravings, whereas several thousand are found at other less prominent sites in the vicinity. Howard McNickle, who has made a particular study of the Spear Hill rock art complex, believes this is because Spear Hill is of a coarse granite, a far less suitable engraving medium than the finer and darker-patinated granite which occurs as a line of much smaller but prolifically engraved outcrops to the north. This line of low hills runs in a west-east direction for 17 kilometres from the west bank of the Shaw River in the west to the east side of Black Range to the east of the highway.

The sites in these low hills number about 35 and vary from small rockpiles a metre or so in height to symmetrical conical hills of considerable height or complex outcrops with several summits. (A site was here defined by a continuous extent of granite unbroken by vegetation.) Pilga homestead lies close to the Four Mile Creek right among several of the most outstanding sites. There are also many seed-grinding patches on the pavements or aprons at the base of conical hills, appearing as bright areas on the granite where the surface has been ground perfectly smooth.

The engravings are mainly figurative, and cover a wide stylistic and chronological range. There are elaborate panels of engravings featuring anthropomorphous figures, flying creatures, speared animals, hunting scenes, bird, animal and human tracks, and numerous geometric and abstract designs (cover plate). Some of the figures are lifesize or larger; one horizontal anthropomorphous figure on the side of a boulder is 2 metres long, but the largest figures are found on pavements, where they reach 4 metres or even 5 metres. The same chronological sequence from tracks, animal and bird figures and geometric designs to a wholly figurative style focusing on stylised human figures is apparent at the Spear Hill sites as at Woodstock.

There are many fine, naturalistic engravings of large animals such as emus and kangaroos, and more than half of these animals appear to be part of hunting scenes, being transfixed by spears or hit by boomerangs. Often several weapons are associated with a single animal. Kangaroos with joeys in the pouch also feature. One extremely rare motif is a flock of what appear to be five flying birds above a panel of human figures. Another is a design apparently depicting a string of yams, on a high location in the most westerly site overlooking the Shaw River.

Jaburara heritage trail, Karratha

A three-and-a-half kilometre-long trail overlooking Karratha township highlights the cultural heritage and natural history of the district, and guides the visitor round excellent representative examples of some of the main types of Aboriginal sites in the Pilbara. It traces the history and culture of the Jaburara, the traditional inhabitants of this area, and wends past a number of Aboriginal sites. These include stone quarries, shell middens and camping places, rocks where women used to grind seeds into flour, and numerous rock engravings.

Engravings are found on the ridge top south of the Dampier Salt Shakers Lookout, some of them identified by a sign. Further examples are on the approach to Rotary Lookout. One large engraving is on a flat rock on the left of the trail about 10 metres before the lookout, and an exceptionally clear figure of a kangaroo has been carved on the side of the large rock near the approach to the lookout. (The best time to photograph this is morning or midday.)

The trail is steep and rugged in parts and two to three hours are needed to appreciate it fully at a leisurely pace. It commences at the information bay and carpark on Karratha Road below the water tanks, and finishes at Karratha Community Library. Water should be carried and precautions taken against sunburn or heat stress. Leaflets and further information are obtainable from the Dampier Lions Club, CALM or the WA Heritage Committee.

Burrup Peninsula

North of Karratha and north-east of Dampier the Burrup Peninsula juts out into the sea towards the many islands of the Dampier archipelago. The peninsula's Aboriginal name is Murujuga, meaning "hip bone sticking out". Burrup Peninsula is renowned for its wealth of rock engravings, and includes such famous panels as the Dampier climbing men (plate 6.4). (A cast of this may be seen in the Western Australian Museum in Perth.)

More than 10,000 engravings occur on jumbled boulders in massive scree slopes. Over 500 sites have been recorded and vary widely in size, form, technique and subject matter.[6] The number of engravings at any one of these sites ranges from 1 to 1,177, but 96 per cent of sites have fewer than 10 engravings. Some engravings can be seen in a large fenced compound established by Woodside Offshore Petroleum Pty Ltd after some 1,793 engraved boulders were moved out of the way of their North West Shelf Gas Project. Many other engravings are still visible *in situ* on vast slopes of tumbled granophyre boulders. One of the most prolific sites is a valley on the right about one kilometre from the end of the road from Dampier to Hearson's Cove. Here the concentration of rock art is so dense that almost every boulder is decorated, and fresher images have been pecked over earlier, less obvious ones. Similar concentrations are found in many rock-pile areas around King Bay and in a valley east of Withnells Bay.

There is a wide range of subject matter in the engravings, but almost 60 per cent are geometric or non-representational forms such as circles. Human figures predominate among the figurative or representational art, but there are also numerous animals, birds, fish and other marine fauna. Many of these can be identified to genus level, for instance stingrays, groper, bream, flounder, unicorn fish, whales, dolphins and turtles. Among the birds are waders in silhouette with long necks and curved beaks, some shown with fish in their beaks. Terrestrial animals include euros, wallabies, lizards, snakes, and dog-like animals with

Plate 6.4 Dampier Climbing Men site, Burrup Peninsula. The scene may represent young men climbing a tree during an initiation ceremony. (WA Museum)

striped backs, which seem undoubted depictions of the Tasmanian tiger or thylacine. Since these have apparently been extinct in mainland Australia for some 3,000 years, this sets a minimum age for these engravings.

Unusual subjects in this rock art are eagles depicted in frontal position with wings outstretched, rows of human figures holding hands, "climbing men", double-headed animals, part-human part-bird figures, and humanoid faces with owl-like eyes, some with miniature human bodies. These faces are usually deeply pecked and heavily patinated. Faces have also been found resembling archaic faces found in the Cleland Hills in Central Australia and along the Canning stockroute in the Durba Hills south of Lake Disappointment.[7]

Other types of Aboriginal sites on Burrup Peninsula are shell middens and campsites, stone quarries, grinding grooves and seed-grinding patches, hunting hides, a few rockshelters with occupational deposits, and some 130 stone arrangements, such as single standing stones, walls and pits. Standing stones are natural column-shaped stones which have been stood in a vertical or near-vertical position by wedging them in gaps between boulders. A dramatic group of some ninety-six standing stones near a rock well on a knoll stand out against the skyline near the southern shore of one of the bays, and another group of at least 300 lies on the southern end of the peninsula. Such stone arrangements are often associated with totemic centres, where ceremonies are carried out to perpetuate or increase food plants or animals or to bring rain at the end of the dry season.

CHAPTER SEVEN

Western Australia: The Kimberley

The Kimberley is one of the least known, most rugged parts of Australia, which encompasses an area of about 422,000 square kilometres. It is a region of ranges and gorges, some 800 kilometres by 650 kilometres, in the extreme north of Western Australia, bounded on the west and north by the sea, on the east by the Ord River, and on the south by the desert (figure 7.1). Precipitous cliffs bound the coast, 12 metre tides make boating dangerous, and deeply cut gorges dissect the plateaux and ranges of the hinterland.

A particularly notable landform is the Napier Range, which runs some 250 kilometres from north-west to south-east in the west Kimberley and is about 3 kilometres to 5 kilometres wide. This is part of a giant reef of Devonian limestone, probably 1,000 kilometres long, which formed about 360 million years ago under the sea. At that time a vast tropical sea reached around the Kimberley and extended into Central Australia. Now stranded on land, the Napier Range is the finest example of a fossilised barrier reef to be found anywhere in the world. Its sheer walls and crenallated ridges rise between 50 metres and 100 metres above the surrounding plain, and marine fossils in its weathered walls can be viewed in three national parks, Tunnel Creek, Geikie and Windjana Gorges (see pages 73–74). Layers of fossils and strata of the ancient limestone reef are exposed in cross-section, opening a window onto the fascinating marine life of the Devonian period before the evolution of reptiles and mammals.

Human occupation of the Kimberley region goes back at least 18,000 years, the age of the earliest campsite debris from Miriwun rockshelter in the Ord River valley. (This excavation by Charles Dortch of the Western Australian Museum was a rescue dig, and the site is now under the waters of Lake Argyle.) The excavation revealed a two-stage cultural sequence, from flakes in the lower layers to an industry characterised by finely made stone spear points over the last 5,000 years. The Kimberley region is well known for symmetrical spear points with serrated edges fashioned by pressure-flaking; initially produced in stone, they were later made from bottle-glass and telephone insulators.

The artistic skill of Kimberley Aborigines is seen both in these pressure-flaked bifacially worked points, and in carved baobab nuts and pearl shell pendants intricately carved with geometric designs. Examples of these items can be seen in

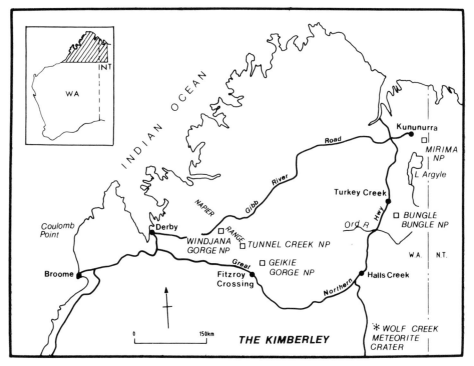

Figure 7.1   The Kimberley

museums in Perth, Darwin and elsewhere. The most renowned aspect of
Aboriginal culture in the Kimberley, however, is undoubtedly rock art. The
Kimberley has some incredibly large, colourful and varied rock paintings, which
are among the most spectacular examples of the art of non-literate people
anywhere in the world (plate 7.1).[1]

The many rockshelters of the Kimberley provide excellent camping places,
especially in the wet season, and wherever the rock surface is suitable have often
been decorated with paintings. In the east Kimberley snakes tend to be dominant
both in rock art and mythology, whereas in the west the famous Wandjina figures
predominate.

Wandjina (pronounced Wand-gin-a) are ancestral beings envisaged as having
human form, but often three times life size. They are spirits of the clouds, the
makers of land and sea and human beings. They control the ultimate sources of
life, and bring the life-giving rains of the wet season. At each place where a
Wandjina came to the end of his time on earth, he was transformed into a
painting, and his spirit is embodied in his portrait. The Wandjina paintings are
therefore of great significance to local Aborigines, who believe them to be the
work of the Wandjina themselves. The paintings still provide the focus for the
telling of the Wandjina stories and performing of associated songs and rituals.
The stories tell of the arrival of the Wandjina, who came out of the sea or sky into
the land, hunted, travelled, fought each other, built fish traps and caves, and
eventually painted themselves onto the rock walls.

Wandjina have characteristics of both humans and clouds. The paintings are usually huge and colourful, being painted in red, yellow or black pigment (mixed with water and occasionally resin), often on a background of a brilliant white, produced from the mineral huntite. They represent the places where ancestral beings responsible for thunder, lightning and the monsoon rains came to rest.

The figures are extremely stylised, being portrayed with head halo, eyes and nose but no mouth. Kimberley Aborigines have explained that they have no mouths because they contain the rain as well as the thunder and lightning; if they had mouths, they would release unceasing rain upon the land. Sometimes the whole figure is shown with decorated body, but often only the head and shoulders, face or even just the eyes surrounded by a halo is shown.

The elaborate head-dress which all Wandjina wear represents both hair and clouds, and the rays which emanate from the head-dress are both feathers which Wandjina wore as decoration and the lightning they control. The predominance of white in the paintings is associated with the towering white cumulo-nimbus clouds which herald the advent of the monsoon. These are believed to be Wandjina, who control fertility of humans and animals and regeneration of all life, through their power over storms, cyclones and the spirit world.

In some sites large snakes or crocodiles are painted in the same colourful style, and are said by local Aborigines also to be Wandjina spirits. In the east Kimberley the rock python replaces Wandjina in human form as the dominant subject, and

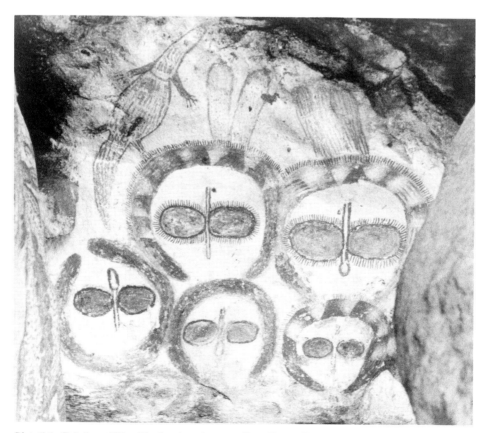

Plate 7.1 Painting of Wandjina heads and a crocodile at Derre, Kimberley. (WA Museum)

there are some outstanding paintings of the ancestral python travelling with its babies. Other sites contain finely painted figures in what is known as the Bradshaw style. These paintings in red ochre are often only 25 centimetres to 30 centimetres high, but they are remarkable for their animated scenes of dancing, hunting and fighting. The humans wear elaborate head-dresses, armbands and tassels, painted in great detail. They are often covered by later Wandjina paintings, and are presumed to be much older; Aborigines say that they were done by the old people in the places where they camped. Unfortunately currently none of these sites is open to the public, but enquiries may be addressed to Aboriginal traditional owners and/or the Department of Aboriginal Sites. Some sites may be made accessible by special arrangement.

An Aborigine in Derby, Sam Lovell, founded Kimberley Safari Tours in 1981. It takes small groups of visitors on tours into the very heart of the Kimberley, including some of the outstanding rock art sites of the Gibb River area, such as those by the large waterhole in Manning Gorge. Sam Lovell's unrivalled knowledge about the land, where he grew up and worked as a stockman, give these tours a special quality for the visitor, and recently earned him the Sir David Brand medal in recognition of his contribution to Kimberley tourism. (Contact him through Western Australian Tourism Commission.)

A heritage trail is being developed from Derby. Leaving Derby Tourist Centre, the Pigeon heritage trail involves a drive or cycle trail around four sites in the town of Derby and a drive out to Windjana Gorge and Tunnel Creek National Parks. This trail has a strong Aborigial emphasis, relating to the resistance leader, Jundumurra (Pigeon), and the beliefs of his people the Bunuba.

Much of the Kimberley is remote and many areas can be dangerous if caution is not exercised. It is essential to carry spare fuel, water and food. During the wet season — mid-December to March — many roads tend to be impassable. Before travelling, enquiries should be made from appropriate bodies, such as the local police station on the Main Roads Department in Derby (telephone (091) 91 1133).

Lurrujarri heritage trail, Broome

A heritage trail leads along the coast from north of Broome, following an Aboriginal song cycle and interpreting the significance of the coast, its flora and fauna, and its traditional use by Aboriginal people. The trail starts at Minarringy (Coulomb Point within a CALM nature reserve) about 80 kilometres north of Broome. Access from the Northern Highway is via Beagle Bay Road and Minarringy Road (Quandong Road) at the turnoff for Willies Creek.

The Lurrujarri trail follows the coast southwards from Minarringy for 80 kilometres to finish at Minyirr (Gantheaume Point) near Broome. It is divided into six sections with seven camping or starting points which are all accessible to vehicles and provided with heritage trail information signs. Following the path of dreamtime ancestors, the trail should be followed from north to south, but any section may be selected for a single day's walk. The trail passes old Aboriginal camping grounds, mythological sites and a wide variety of seasonal bush and sea foods.

(Further details can be obtained from the Western Australian Heritage Committee in Perth, C.A.L.M. or from tourist offices.)

The Lurrujarri heritage trail follows part of a Dreaming track, an Aboriginal song cycle which originated from ancestral beings who created all the landscape features we see today. Such song cycles are used to pass on from one generation to the next a detailed description of the land and how it has been shaped by ancestral beings of the Dreamtime. The songs encode the law and are still sung ceremonially today by tribal Aborigines. This song line also sets the pattern of an age-old route of trade and exchange which originated in the Kimberley and extended as far as Uluru (Ayers Rock) in Central Australia.

Windjana Gorge National Park

Aboriginal paintings in the renowned Wandjina style can be seen in this narrow canyon, cut through the fossil limestone Napier Range by the Lennard River, 150 kilometres north-east of Derby and 19 kilometres off the Gibb River road. The river flows only in the "Wet", but some deep pools shaded by the 90 metre high multi-coloured cliffs remain throughout the "Dry". The gorge is about 4 kilometres long, and the limestone has weathered into caves and rockshelters which have been decorated with paintings, including ancestral Wandjina figures. Walking is the only way to see this gorge, and there is a 3.5 kilometre-long walking trail, which winds along the gorge from the camping area. It may be possible to visit Aboriginal rock art sites by special arrangement with park rangers.

At the entrance to Windjana Gorge a large vertical rock represents the rock python which is a major ancestral being in the belief system of the Kimberley. In the middle of the gorge another massive rock stands in a pool of water in which baby spirits are said to be found. The spirits of children are believed to live in water, particularly freshwater pools, and to come from Wandjinas, the guardians of spirit children.

Tunnel Creek National Park

A huge natural tunnel has been eroded by Tunnel Creek right through the limestone of the Napier Range (plate 7.2). This remarkable geological phenomenon is 750 metres long, 3 metres to 12 metres high and 15 metres wide, but is pitch black throughout much of its length. Visitors can take a walk through the icy waters of Tunnel Creek to get a close-up view of the fossil reef, but powerful torches are needed and this is not a place for the claustrophobic. The tunnel is often populated by thousands of fruit bats (also known as flying foxes), which inhabit the open collapsed section in the middle of the tunnel. Tunnel Creek used to be known as Cave of Bats, and it is a memorable experience to witness at dusk the beating of thousands upon thousands of wings as the fruit bats go out to feed. Stalactites descend from the roof in many places, and some Aboriginal paintings decorate the walls.

Tunnel Creek is of significance to local Aborigines, and is renowned as the favourite hideout of the Aboriginal leader, Pigeon or Jandamarra, who was shot dead by a police tracker in 1897 after a three-year manhunt through the King Leopold Ranges. The Pigeon heritage trail commences in Derby and enables the visitor to follow in the footsteps of this remarkable Aboriginal resistance leader.

Plate 7.2   Tunnel Creek. (A.A. Burbidge)

The park is open to the public and lies 180 kilometres east of Derby. It is reached from the turnoff on the Gibb River road to Fitzroy Crossing, 125 kilometres east of Derby.

Geikie Gorge National Park

Geikie Gorge (pronounced Geeky with a hard "g" as in "go") is the longest, best known and perhaps most beautiful gorge in the Kimberley. Located 280 kilometres east of Derby and 21 kilometres north-east of Fitzroy Crossing, it is 8 kilometres long and was formed where the Fitzroy River cut through the limestone barrier of the Napier Range. It was named after the British geologist, Sir Archibald Geikie. The range is a fossilised limestone reef some 360 million years old, and the cliffs are studded with fossilised sea shells. As well as marine fossils in the Devonian limestone, other relics of this period are sea creatures like sawfish and one species of shark, the Bull shark, 350 kilometres inland from any ocean — biological curiosities which over the millennia have adapted from a salt to freshwater environment.

In the summer wet season when the Fitzroy River is flowing, the gorge can turn into a raging torrent, as evidenced by the limestone walls bleached to heights of more than 16 metres. At the height of the dry season it is filled with an extensive waterhole, acting like an oasis in this part of the south-west Kimberley. The abundant bird, animal and plant food made Geikie Gorge an attractive area for Aborigines, and several sites, including mythological and burial sites, are found in the vicinity. There are crocodiles, but they are the freshwater species. River trips are available in the dry season, and there is a rewarding walk along the west bank to the western wall of the gorge.

Wolf Creek meteorite crater

The second largest meteorite crater on the earth's surface, Wolf Creek Crater, is a geological site of worldwide significance.[2] The site, in arid country 133 kilometres by road south of Halls Creek, was discovered by Europeans only in 1947 during an aerial reconnaissance of the Great Sandy Desert basin. Formed when a huge iron meteorite crashed into the earth's surface, perhaps sometime during the last million years, the crater is an almost perfect circle varying between 870 metres and 950 metres across and 61 metres deep, although in-blowing sand has now raised the level of its interior by some 10 metres. The rim is formed of piles of broken quartzite rocks and is 27 metres wide at its maximum thickness, with an extremely steep inner slope (plate 7.3).

The crater rises up to 35 metres above the surrounding plain, and is best seen from the southern flank, where the massive piles of jumbled red-brown quartzite blocks are particularly striking. From the top of the rim the almost perfect symmetry of the crater can be seen. The inner slope of the crater wall is 30 to 40 degrees, and that of the outer wall 10 to 15 degrees. The crater floor is basically flat, composed of sand around a central area of light gypsum with a number of sinkholes. A surprising number of quite large trees grow inside it.

Aborigines of the local Djaru group call the crater Kandimalal, and tell how it was created by two giant rainbow snakes which moved across the country. Sinuously slithering over the arid landscape, they formed the nearby Stuart Creek and Wolf Creek. One then plunged into the earth. The huge, circular crater is the hole where he emerged. The site lies in a small national park on the southern fringes of the Kimberley region and on the northern edge of the Great Sandy Desert, and may be reached from a turnoff on the Great Northern Highway to Balgo and Carranya, 16 kilometres south-west of Halls Creek. Camping is available just to the east of this road and 5 kilometres north of Carranya Station.

Plate 7.3   Wolf Creek meteorite crater. (A.S. George)

The Bungle Bungle (Purnululu) National Park

This region enshrines some of Australia's most spectacular landforms, but it is so remote that the park was only declared in 1987. The bizarre bell-shaped towers for which it is renowned are best viewed from the air, the north-east part of the massif being particularly impressive. Scenic flights are available both from Kununurra and Halls Creek (figure 7.2). Road access is off the Great Northern Highway, 250 kilometres south of Kununurra, 55 kilometres south of Turkey Creek and 109 kilometres north of Halls Creek, on the Spring Creek track. From the west this strictly four-wheel-drive track leads into the massif along boulder-strewn creek beds and steep jump-ups, the 55 kilometres taking about five hours. It is unsuitable for caravans or trailers and is often impassable in the wet season. It is closed in January, February and March and possibly longer, depending on the seasons. (Check with CALM rangers in Kununurra.)

The track brings one to "Three Ways", and excellent views of the spectacular region which Aboriginal traditional owners call Purnululu. The massif itself is called Kawara and every feature of its 400 square kilometres has an Aboriginal name. Rock paintings are found in some of the shelters, caves and gorges, favourite motifs being ancestral beings from the Dreamtime, crocodiles, fish and

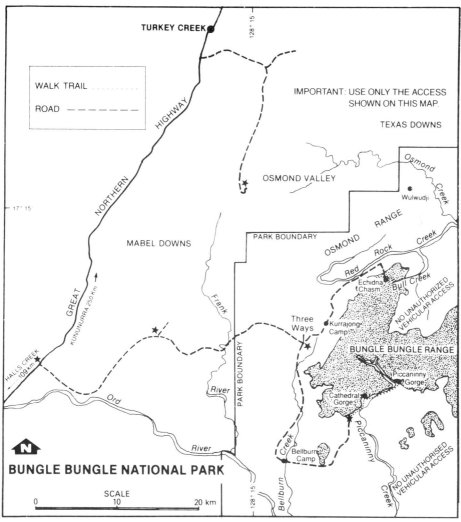

Figure 7.2 Bungle Bungle (Purnululu) National Park. (Courtesy Department of Conservation and Land Management, Perth, Western Australia)

stencils of children's hands. (Few, if any, of these paintings are available for public viewing).

The most impressive rock formations are on the southern flank, where wind and weather have sculpted the soft, brittle sandstone into beehive-shaped domes (plate 7.4). These are reached by a 29 kilometre-long track which leads round the south-western corner of the massif to end close to the rock walls. From there visitors proceed on foot to see massive gorges and cliffs over 200 metres high, such as Cathedral Gorge, one hour's easy round trip from the Piccaninny Creek carpark. A 9 kilometre walk from the carpark leads to a huge slash through the massif known as Piccaninny Gorge. This is the point where Piccaninny Creek emerges from the massif. Eight to ten hours should be allowed for the round trip

Plate 7.4   Bungle Bungle National Park. (C. Totterdell)

on this 18 kilometre walk. West of Piccaninny Creek another dramatic gorge leads 500 metres between sheer walls clad with tiny ferns to the cool green depths of a permanent pool.

The conical domes of the Bungle Bungle were formed from soft Devonian sandstone laid down in horizontal beds some 350 million years ago, and the bands of alternating dark and light sediments reflect changes in the moisture content and texture of the layers. The striking horizontal orange and black bands have developed along bedding planes and are formed by alternating protective skins of silica (orange or lighter colour) and lichen *(Microthelia arterrina)*, which makes up the darker bands. Beneath the encasing coloured skins the rock is white and friable. So intense has been the weathering that these strange tiger-striped domes now soar vertically up out of the plain to as high as 300 metres. This vast array of sandstone towers ranks as the finest example of ruiniform or sandstone tower topography in Australia and one of the most outstanding examples of its type in the world. The sandstone is extremely fragile, and visitors are warned not to touch or climb on the towers.

Mirima (Hidden Valley) National Park

Hidden Valley lies only 3 kilometres east of Kununurra, and is readily accessible by ordinary car. The road leads from Kununurra between steep escarpment walls to the broad river flat of Lily Creek with its permanent pools. Gradual erosion of the quartz sandstone by Lily Creek and its tributaries has created an intricate maze of twisting valleys, amphitheatres and rocky hills. The rock is about 300 million years old and the horizontal strata or layers in which it was laid down can be seen clearly.

Mirima is the name given to this area by the Miriuwung people, whose ancestors left a rich legacy of rock paintings, engravings and artefacts. Above Lily Pool there are axe grinding grooves, and a signposted walk leads to them. A number of Aboriginal paintings in rockshelters also exist in the network of interlocking valleys and stony hills, and one is signposted and open to the public.

CHAPTER EIGHT

The Top End of the Northern Territory

The Top End of the Northern Territory is of great significance in the prehistory of Australia as one of the three possible main entry points to the continent from the Asian region. During most of the last 100,000 years a land bridge linked the Top End to Papua New Guinea, when sea level was as much as 150 metres lower during the last ice age. This means that the easiest route by which ice-age immigrants would have reached the Australian continent would probably have been via Papua New Guinea into the region now known as Arnhem Land (figure 8.1). It has therefore always seemed likely that early occupation sites might be found there.

Archaeological work in the area commenced in the 1920s, and the first Pleistocene sites were discovered in Arnhem Land in the 1960s. A strong impetus to research was given by the Alligator Rivers environmental fact finding study of 1972–73, in conjunction with the development of uranium mines within the region and the establishment of the Kakadu National Park in western Arnhem Land. Kakadu or Kakadju is the name of the language spoken by Aboriginal people of the coastal lowlands. Aboriginal ownership of the land known as Kakadu National Park was recognised under the Aboriginal Land Rights (Northern Territory) Act of 1976. Then in November 1978 the traditional owners leased 6,144 square kilometres of their land to the Australian National Parks and Wildlife Service as stage 1 of the Kakadu National Park, to be managed as a park for all Australians. Stage 2 (6,926 square kilometres) was proclaimed in February 1984, and 70 per cent of this is Aboriginal land. Stage 3 of the park (presently under land claim) encompasses another 6,700 square kilometres to the south, stretching almost to the Katherine River (figure 8.2, plates 8.1 and 8.2).

Considerable research into the prehistory of the Top End has been done over the last three decades, largely by archaeologists from the Australian National University such as John Mulvaney, Jack Golson and Carmel Schrire (then White) in the 1960s, Harry Allen and Johan Kamminga in the 1970s, and a group led by Rhys Jones, Betty Meehan and Jim Allen in the 1980s.[1] Current archaeological fieldwork is being carried out by Hilary Sullivan and Ivan Haskovec in Kakadu, and by myself, Bruno David, Ian McNiven, Valerie Attenbrow and Bryce Barker, supported by Earthwatch in the Katherine region.

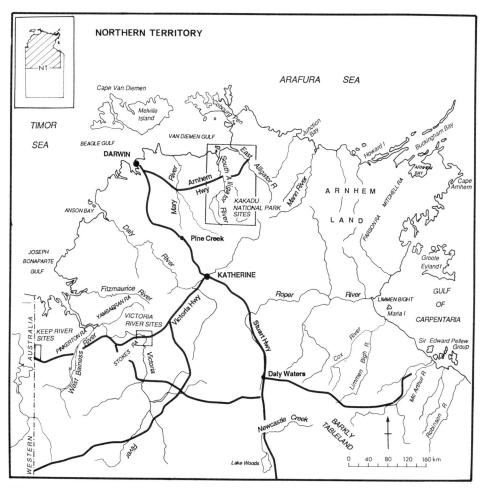

Figure 8.1   The Top End of the Northern Territory

Some of the earliest evidence of human presence so far discovered in the Top End comes from a rockshelter in Deaf Adder Gorge in the south of Kakadu National Park. It is in an area called Nauwalabila by Aborigines and the site is now known as Nauwalabila 1. (It has also been called the Lindner site after local explorer, Dave Lindner.) The rockshelter was formed by a huge boulder which at some time fell off the edge of the nearby escarpment. The sloping slab of sandstone shelters a flat soft black sandy floor, on which lay stone tools such as spear points. The archaeological potential of the site was recognised by Rhys Jones and Betty Meehan when they were taken there by Dave Lindner in 1972, and excavations were carried out there by Johan Kamminga in 1973 and by Rhys Jones in 1981 and 1989. Two old Aboriginal men, who remembered camping in the shelter with their families as small boys and thus depositing the topmost layer of habitation debris, took part in the latter excavation and helped to uncover the basal layers. The past way of life that the excavation revealed appears to have continued in an unbroken tradition.

Stone tools were found down to a depth of almost 3 metres below present

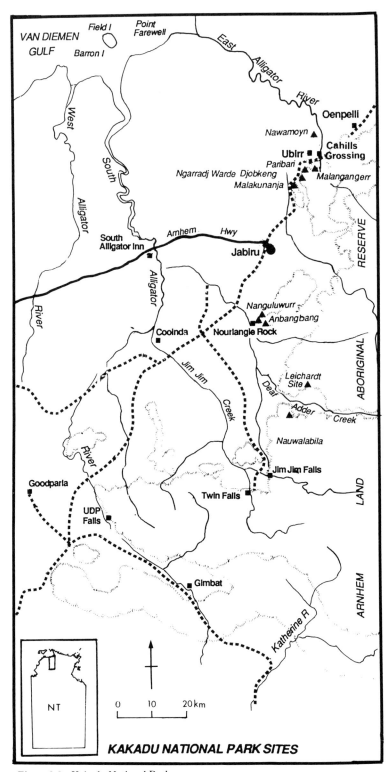

Figure 8.2   Kakadu National Park

ground level, and a radiocarbon date of about 20,000 years was obtained on charcoal at a depth of 1.7 metres to 1.9 metres. The top 2.4 metres of deposit was fine sand which built up steadily over a period of at least 25 to 30 millennia. Below the sand was a layer of weathered sandstone rubble some 40 centimetres thick resting on large rocks and red sand. Stone tools lay within the basal rubble, heavy weathered quartzite flakes, which, when snapped, revealed a thick chemically weathered skin on their outer surface.

The Nauwalabila site is of particular significance for several reasons. It reveals continuous occupation throughout the height of the last glaciation, when there appears to have been a break in occupation of some other sites in the Kakadu region. The stone artefacts in the basal rubble are probably more than 40,000 years old, which makes Nauwalabila one of the oldest human occupation sites yet discovered in Australia. The site also contains vital evidence of change in the landscape. When hunters first inhabited the rockshelter, the surface of the ground was 3 metres below its present level. Since that time the ground level both within the shelter and of the extensive sandsheet plain outside has risen 3 metres. Why, straight after human arrival in the valley was there this sudden build-up of sand, with the rate of sediment accumulation increasing a thousandfold? The answer seems to lie in Aboriginal impact on the environment. When Aboriginal people reached the Top End more than 40,000 years ago, they used fire extensively both for cooking and as an aid in hunting and gathering, as their modern descendants still do. In the Kakadu environment this caused massive slope instability and erosion, leading to the build-up of sediment on valley floors such as Deaf Adder Gorge. Dramatic change came to Kakadu during the last ice age not because of climatic change but because of the one new factor in the equation, humans with their firesticks.

The most important discovery so far in Arnhem Land is the recent find by Rhys Jones and Michael Smith of stone tools dating to 50,000 years in the rockshelter of Malakunanja 2. The dates, obtained by the thermo-luminescence method, form a consistent sequence, making these Australia's oldest firmly dated traces of

Plate 8.1   Typical outliers, Kakadu National Park

Plate 8.2   The wetlands of Kakadu, Ja Ja billabong

human presence. Even more remarkably, "crayons" of high grade ochre or haematite were in the same layer, indicating that some form of art was being practised by Australia's first inhabitants. Below the basal layer were three metres of sterile sand, suggesting that this rockshelter may well have been one of the earliest homes of Australia's first migrants.

The prehistoric story of the Top End can be divided into four principal phases: pre-estuarine, estuarine, freshwater and contact. These phases are reflected in the material from archaeological deposits, sediments and pollen sequences, and are mirrored in the subjects of the rock paintings.

The early phase has been called pre-estuarine because Kakadu lay about 350 kilometres inland during the last ice age. Sea level at its lowest was then about 150 metres lower than at present and the current coastline was a flat plain which extended northwards to link Australia to Papua New Guinea. Kakadu was then far from the sea or estuaries, but the availability of abundant fresh water, food resources and rockshelters must have made it an attractive habitat for settlement.

In the earth floors of rockshelters a series of occupation deposits containing stone tools and charcoal from ancient campfires have been found. The handful of excavated sites have produced some remarkable discoveries. The earth floor in one of these rockshelters, Malangangerr, in open woodland just west of Cahill's Crossing on the East Alligator River, was excavated by Schrire and radiocarbon-dated to 23,000 years old (plate 8.3). Recent re-excavation by Rhys Jones and Michael Smith has revealed occupation down to a depth of 2 metres, with the lowest sands giving thermoluminescent dates of about 50,000 years ago. This shelter is a deep overhang in a residual outlier

Plate 8.3   Malangangerr rockshelter, which contains evidence of 50,000-year-old occupation

of the Arnhem Land Plateau. There are a few paintings on the shelter's back wall and shells, the remains of ancient meals, are visible in the earth floor and in the upper levels of the deposit.

The stone tools in these lower sands were characterised by flaked core tools, steep-edged scrapers, utilised flakes and, most remarkably, by small ground-edge axes with grooves on their sides. These stone axeheads have their cutting edges ground to a sharp chisel-like blade, with a groove round them to facilitate hafting to a handle (figure 8.3). (They are usually known as axes but hatchets is the more correct term for small light hafted axes which are used with one hand.) When they were first discovered it was thought that there must be some mistake, for such sophisticated ground-edge tools had never been found in contexts older than 4,000 years ago before in Australia. However, careful investigation and further radiocarbon dates confirmed Schrire's initial findings. The technique of grinding stone tools and producing a bevelled working edge belongs to the post-glacial Neolithic period in Europe, but in Japan, Papua New Guinea and tropical Australia this technique of hammer-dressing and grinding axe blades dates back more than 20,000 years. These Arnhem Land ground-edge axes are therefore amongst the world's earliest evidence for the technology of polishing and edge-grinding tools.

Another shelter, Nawamoyn, just a little north of Malangangerr, produced a

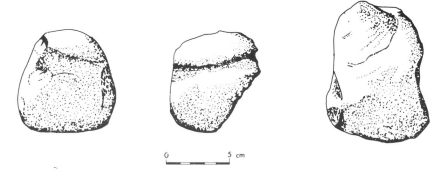

Figure 8.3   Ground-edge axes from Kakadu National Park, with grooves for hafting, more than 20,000 years old. (After C. White 1967 and 1971)

very similar sequence of sediments and artefacts, with a date for the base of occupation of about 21,500 years, and again ground-edge axes were in the lowest layer. These have also now been found in a few other Arnhem Land sites, including Nauwalabila 1, where flakes of dolerite showing ground faces with striations from use-wear on them were found throughout the top 1.4 metres of the deposit, the lowest example of these flakes off ground-edge axes coming from the 14,000-year-old level. Below this were pieces of volcanic rock which, because of its hardness, is the characteristic material used to make ground-edge artefacts, but these had been so heavily chemically weathered that their original form was not readily discernible. At a depth equivalent to an age of about 25,000 to 30,000 years, in Rhys Jones' words, "were several extremely weathered lenticular objects of volcanic rock, which were of exactly the same shape as Schrire's Pleistocene hatchet heads, though again, the weathering on our examples was so great that a definite ascription to this tool type cannot be made, though we strongly suspect this".[2]

Throughout the same 25,000- to 30,000-year-old layer at Nauwalabila 1 were slabs of sandstone showing evidence of grinding and hard, heavy pieces of haematite with grinding facets on their surfaces, indicating that they had been used as a source of pigment. Ochre in a wide variety of colours occurs in the lower levels of all these ice-age sites, and there is some evidence that the ochre was ground up and pulverised. Small circular hollows, similar to those that are visible nowadays on flat shelves of rock in innumerable Top End rockshelters, are clearly as old as the covering sands (that is, more than 18,000 years) at Malangangerr and Nawamoyn. At another shelter, Malakunanja 2, to the south near Ja Ja billabong, 18,000-year-old charcoal is associated with a grinding hollow and two flattish mortars, one bearing clear traces of ochre.

A study of the art of more than a thousand rock galleries in the Top End has been carried out over many years by George Chaloupka of the Northern Territory Museum in Darwin.[3] He believes on several grounds that the Arnhem Land rock art has considerable antiquity. The occurrence of ochre and ochre "crayons" with ground facets produced by use in pre-18,000-year-old layers in several sites, and the paint palette of an ice-age artist at Malakunanja 2, is clear evidence of the use of paint, and thus the attainment of aesthetic perception, by ice age people in Australia.

Plate 8.4 Thylacine high above the main gallery, Ubirr, Kakadu National Park. The white streak across its body is waterwash.

Extinct animals are portrayed in the early rock art.[4] There are more than a dozen representations of striped animals bearing a striking resemblance to the thylacine or Tasmanian tiger, and unmistakable, detailed representations of the Tasmanian devil. It is likely that both these animals became extinct in northern Australia more than 3,000 years ago. Other extinct animals which have been tentatively identified in Arnhem Land rock paintings are the long-beaked echidna (*Zaglossus*) and the marsupial tapir (*Palorchestes*). Both are thought to have been extinct in Australia for at least 18,000 years, but *Zaglossus* still exists in Papua New Guinea. A representation of the Tasmanian tiger can be seen on the overhang above the main gallery at Ubirr (plate 8.4).

The paintings assigned by Chaloupka to his early phase on the grounds of style and subject matter are all in red ochre, which has bonded the rock and stained the design deeply into the wall. Some art panels are covered with a surface coating of a transparent mineral skin, implying deposition under environmental or climatic conditions very different from the present. The most likely times are the dry, semi-desert conditions which are thought to have pertained in the Top End at the height of the last glacial period about 18,000 years ago, or possibly the tropical humid but inland and relatively cool climate which preceded it, 25,000 and more years ago, which again has no counterpart today.

This early pre-estuarine art is dominated by depictions of land animals, in contrast with the predominance in the later style of saltwater crocodiles and estuarine fish such as barramundi. It is therefore thought that the early-style paintings predate the post-glacial rise in sea level and development of estuarine conditions which were complete by about 6,000 years ago.[5]

Full of scenes of expressive movement, this early art has been named by Chaloupka the "dynamic style". There are exquisite human figures and animated compositions from everyday life, such as dances, kangaroo and emu hunts, battle and mortuary scenes (figure 8.4). As many as sixty figures appear in one painting, apparently conceived and executed by a single artist. Most figures wear long head-dresses decorated with feathers and tassels, and some have necklaces and armlets. Later there followed a style in which human beings were simplified to a stick-like form.

This is the earliest known narrative art in the world. Today's Aborigines have no direct knowledge of these paintings, but describe them as the work of Mimi spirit people from the Dreamtime, who were the first to paint and who taught this skill to the Aborigines. According to local tradition, the paint used was a mixture of red ochre and blood.

If Chaloupka's chronological sequence is correct, as seems very likely, some of the "dynamic figure style" paintings may be as old as the Upper Palaeolithic art of western Europe. Arnhem Land would thus hold one of the longest developmental sequences of art in human history.

Figure 8.4 Dynamic style female figure with spears and dilly bag, Kakadu National Park. (After E. Brandl 1973)

Plate 8.5   Fish in X-ray style at Nanguluwurr, Kakadu National Park. (R. Edwards)

The rising of the sea at the end of the ice age had a profound effect on both prehistoric economy and culture. The sea, or at least estuarine conditions, reached as far inland as the foot of Kakadu cliffs. Animals of the pre-estuarine savannahs such as antilopine wallaroos and emus were forced to move further inland and they eventually disappeared from the rock paintings. The thylacine became locally extinct, but for the first time the dingo began to appear as a motif.

The "estuarine" rock art was so naturalistic that it is possible to identify the particular species portrayed, such as barramundi, mullet and the lesser salmon catfish. A wide range of colourful pigments was used — white, yellow, red, orange, brown and black. Styles varied both regionally and chronologically, but the most prevalent was the X-ray style, in which the artists painted the internal organs and bone structure of a subject within its external form. Many X-ray figures are visible in the rockshelters at Ubirr. X-ray art is not unique to Australia, but it reaches its highest development here in the art of Arnhem Land (plate 8.5).

Figures were often painted as a full silhouette in white pigment, and then the internal schematised anatomical features were drawn and decorated with other colours. Unfortunately the pipe-clay usually used for white pigment is often unstable, and waterwash and weathering have damaged or destroyed many of these paintings.

The post-glacial rise in sea level may have led to the birth of the tradition of the rainbow snake. Generally associated with stories concerning floods and rain, which could reflect the rising sea, this ancestral creative being is estimated to have swallowed up several hundred metres of land each decade or even each year. The change from pre-estuarine to estuarine conditions and its appearance seem to belong to between 6,000 and 7,000 years ago, which would make the rainbow snake tradition the longest continuous religious belief documented in the world.

The lightning man, Namarrkon, is similarly depicted for the first time in the estuarine period. Namarrkon is responsible for the thunder, lightning and violent electrical storms of the wet season. When he becomes angry, he releases the lightning by striking the clouds or ground with the stone axes attached to his head, elbows and knees. A characteristic representation of Namarrkon can be seen in the main gallery of paintings at Burrungkuy or Nourlangie Rock (see figure 8.6).

There are also changes in the types of artefacts portrayed in the rock art. In the pre-estuarine period the dynamic-style figures do not have spear-throwers nor do their spears have stone tips or multiple prongs. Instead they seem to use barbed single-piece wooden spears thrown by hand, ground-edge axes and boomerangs. These artefact types have all been found in archaeological deposits 10,000 years old or more. Stencils of boomerangs also appear in the rock art, but interestingly, boomerangs were no longer in use as weapons in Arnhem Land in historic times except as musical instruments imported from the desert to the south.

In paintings of the estuarine period the boomerang has disappeared but new tool types occur, such as spear-throwers, multi-pronged spears and spears with hafted stone tips. Stone spear points make their first appearance in the occupational deposits of Kakadu between 6,200 and 5,700 years ago, on the evidence of the Nauwalabila 1 excavation. Hafted stone adzes or chisels were introduced later, about 3,500 years ago.

The estuarine environment is reflected by shell middens in many rockshelters, such as Ngarradj-Warde-Djobkeng (excavated by Harry Allen in 1977), in an outlier south-west of Cahill's Crossing in Kakadu National Park (see plate 8.1). What Allen showed was that there was a shift from shell species typical of mangroves and mudflats in use between about 4,000 and 1,500 years ago to freshwater species, especially freshwater *Velesunio* mussels, in the uppermost layer of the site.

It seems that after the arrival of the sea and its fringing mangroves about 6,000 years ago, the river banks gradually silted up and levees formed. Eventually the inflow of saltwater became blocked by the levees, so that the areas behind them formed swamps. Given the torrential downpours of the wet season in this monsoonal region, the areas behind the levees were rapidly transformed from sterile saline plains and tidal flats to freshwater swamps immensely rich in food for hunter-gatherers. The waters became thronged with magpie geese, ducks, pelicans and myriad other birds. Food plants multiplied; there were wild rice, waterlilies and large lotus lilies with their edible tubers, and most important of all, the spike rush, which is very similar to the Chinese water-chestnut.

This dramatic environmental change in Arnhem Land took place between 1,500 and 1,000 years ago, and the creation of these freshwater swamps led to a great increase in the intensity of occupation of the entire plains and wetland area (see plate 8.2). The rich wetlands supported a large Aboriginal population, reflected in the remains of goose-hunting camps on their edges, open campsites stretching for as much as a kilometre and littered with literally thousands of stone tools.

The way of life of the goose-hunters is also portrayed in paintings of the last millennium. Men are depicted carrying bundles of "goose spears" (short, light reed shafts with sharp hardwood tips), and women are shown poling rafts across the swamps to collect goose eggs and waterlily tubers. Representations of long-necked turtles, file snakes, magpie geese and waterlilies now abound, together with barramundi, catfish and other subjects of the estuarine period. In spite of the formation of the freshwater swamps the major rivers remained brackish and home to the huge saltwater crocodiles, which have penetrated far inland. These "salties" are man-eaters (and woman-eaters) and may be encountered in almost any water in the Top End except Katherine Gorge, where only the smaller, shy and comparatively harmless freshwater crocodile is found.

A vivid picture of this freshwater period has come from the excavation by Rhys Jones of the massive cave of Anbangbang in the cliff called Burrungkuy by Aborigines and Nourlangie Rock by white people (see below). This site was amazingly rich in organic food remains and artefacts made from wood, bone and shell, and the high density of occupational material in the upper levels is matched by only a few other sites on the continent.

This freshwater environment was basically that seen by the first white man to cross Arnhem Land, explorer Ludwig Leichhardt, who in 1845 reached the edge of the Kakadu escarpment between Jim Jim and Twin Falls. He was near the end of his journey to Port Essington, and was down to his last bullock, when he descended to the wetlands and met large groups of Aboriginal people, who welcomed and fed his party. They were thriving in their land of plenty, and even today Aborigines describe these wetlands as "our supermarket".

Aboriginal contact with foreigners goes back at least to the seventeenth century, when Indonesian fishermen sailed their parahus each year from Macassar to northern Australia in search of the delicacy, trepang — also called sea-slug or beche-de-mer. Paintings of parahus and stencils of steel Macassan axes and knives are found on the walls of rockshelters, and items such as dugout canoes, didgeridoos and smoking pipes were adopted into Aboriginal culture, but otherwise foreign visitors seem to have had little impact until the coming of the Europeans.

The last known traditional paintings done by local Aboriginal custodians were of a goanna and an agile wallaby in 1972. Now there seem to be no more traditional rock painters to carry on the art, but similar motifs and techniques are still used in bark painting, which is now the dominant art of the Top End. Both rock art and archaeological sites occur widely across the Top End, but only those sites which are in national parks or reserves and which may be visited by the general public without special permits are described below.

Further information on Kakadu is available from the Australian National Parks and Wildlife Service, PO Box 71, Jabiru, NT 0886 (tel. (089) 79 2101; there is also an excellent visitors centre near Jabiru. Information on other sites which are open to the public should be sought from the Northern Territory Government Tourist Bureau, PO Box 1155, Darwin, NT 0800 (tel. (089) 81 6611). The bodies with a statutory role in site protection are the Aboriginal Areas Protection Authority, the Conservation Commission and the Museum (see page 362). A visit to the museum in Darwin in Conacher Street on Bullocky Point is highly recommended; not only for the exhibits and bookshop but to enjoy lunch or dinner at the Beagle restaurant overlooking the bay.

Kakadu National Park

Ubirr, Kakadu National Park

Ubirr is a residual sandstone outlier of the Arnhem Land Plateau, situated west of the East Alligator River, about one kilometre north of Cahill's Crossing, at the northern end of Kakadu National Park. Rising abruptly out of extensive alluvial plains and low laterite covered ridges, Ubirr (previously known as Obiri Rock) is composed of several large rock outcrops, affording extensive views of the wetlands. Weathering and erosion of the sandstone has given rise to many caves and overhangs, together with ripple marks, cross-bedding and some pebble beds.

Its proximity to the rich food resources of the river, swamps, woodlands and nearby rainforest thickets made Ubirr a focus of prehistoric occupation. Over 120 rock painting sites are located in the numerous rockshelters. There is a wide range in styles of painting, and Ubirr contains many outstanding examples of Aboriginal rock art, in particular the decorative X-ray style, which here reaches possibly its highest development. Several sites contain elaborate X-ray paintings of fish, kangaroos and other animals.

There is a one kilometre-long walking track to view the main Ubirr galleries, and it is best to head west first, making a clockwise loop. The first site is at ground level, on the south-east side of a major rock residual, and is dominated by a 240 centimetre-long yellow arch with red outline, a painting of the rainbow snake.

From here, follow the track north-eastwards around the foot of the outlier to the main gallery, which is situated under a deep overhang on the south-western side of a high, isolated monolith. The shelter is lofty, with a smooth curving back wall about 15 metres long and 2 metres high, a perfect "canvas" for prehistoric artists. A frieze of polychrome X-ray paintings decorates this wall. Fish, painted in many colours are the dominant motif, and are superb examples of the X-ray style. Most of the fish are barramundi; other subjects are turtles, kangaroos, goannas and human figures. Small figures of men executed in white pipe-clay or red ochre clearly depict Europeans; one smokes a pipe, wears clothes and has his hands in his pockets, others are in the characteristic white man's stance of hands on hips.

On the outside, left-hand end of the huge overhang above the main gallery is a clear portrayal of a Tasmanian tiger or thylacine (see plage 8.4). Its rear has been damaged by waterwash, but the stripes on its back are still clearly visible. This painting is thought to be at least 3,000 years old. In the opposite direction to the south-east of the main gallery the track continues to a small site bearing several paintings, in particular a magnificent figure of a hunter, Mabuyu, with barbed spears, spear-thrower, goose-wing fan and a large dilly bag suspended from his neck.

Opposite the main gallery is a track leading to the hilltop art sites and lookout. One of Australia's finest galleries of Aboriginal art is in an open rockshelter high on this outcrop. A frieze of running figures is painted in white on the flat, smooth back wall, and was first recorded by C.P. Mountford in 1949. The composition is outstanding in Aboriginal art for its animation and fluidity of movement. It depicts a series of men in motion, each figure differing from the others in outline, decorations and in the arrangement of weapons (plate 8.6).

> . . . From left to right, the first man is running; he has ornaments on his elbows, a bag hanging from his shoulder, a goose-wing fan, a spear in one hand, and a small spear-thrower in the other. The second figure is about to launch a barbed spear. He is carrying a goose-wing fan and two long-bladed spears. The third man has arm ornaments and a long string bag hanging from his shoulder. He is carrying a short-barbed spear at the level of his body. The fourth figure is in a running position, with a single-barbed spear and spear-thrower in one hand and three multi-barbed spears in the other. He has a head-dress, and a carrying-bag hanging from his shoulder. The fifth figure is also running. In one hand he is carrying a small spear and a spear-thrower while in the other he has a goose-wing fan and three multi-barbed spears. He also has arm ornaments and a long carrying-bag. The sixth man is standing with the sole of one foot resting against his knee. He carries a spear and spear-thrower in one hand. An arm ornament hangs from his elbow and a goose-wing fan from the forearm. The seventh and last man is in a running position. He also has a spear and spear-thrower in one hand, barbed spears in the other, and a long carrying-bag hanging from his shoulder.
> In the extreme right of the gallery is a freshwater tortoise, in X-ray art. In the centre of the frieze are two long-bodied triangular-faced Namarakain women who have been painted over the running men. Between their fingers the Namarakain women are holding the loop of string by means of which they travel from place to place during the hours of darkness".[6]

This well-preserved frieze is an excellent example of the animated figurative art found at many sites in the Alligator Rivers region, and probably derives from the last millennium, the period of goose-hunting in the extensive freshwater swamps. On boulders on the floor of the shelter grinding hollows are noticeable (plate 8.7); often such hollows bear red staining, and contemporary Aborigines generally believe that they were formed in the process of grinding up purple plums and other bush fruits, but another use may have been to pulverise lumps of iron oxide to make red pigment.

A scramble up to the lookout on top of this outlier is rewarded by a panoramic

Plate 8.6   Frieze of hunters, Ubirr, Kakadu National Park

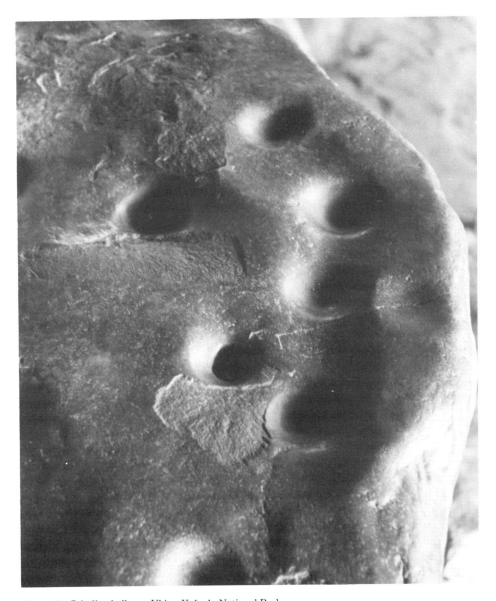

Plate 8.7 Grinding hollows, Ubirr, Kakadu National Park

view out over the floodplains. In the other direction, east of the Mountford gallery, is a site with a rock floor. Many colourful fish and other subjects are painted on its low roof.

Birndu (Ngarradj-Warde-Djobkeng), Kakadu National Park

Ngarradj-Warde-Djobkeng is the name of a spectacular group of rock residuals on the western end of a large outlier north-east of Ja Ja billabong and some five kilometres south-west of Cahill's Crossing (see plate 8.1). The name means literally "the cockatoo splits the rock", for local Aboriginal people believe that in the Dreamtime the escarpment at this point was split by the sulphur-crested cockatoo.

Four main art sites are located in close proximity to each other, together with a 10,000-year-old occupation site. This is a long open shelter in the cliff at the base of the outlier facing west, with a large area of earth floor. Excavation by Allen of part of the 2.5 metre deep deposit revealed occupation extending back 10,000 years, with a rich array of food remains including fish, shellfish, crabs, geese, tortoise and the bones of large and small marsupials. At Ngarradj there was an important shift from the lower and middle midden levels, with mangrove-estuarine species of the tidal flats such as cockles and whelks, to the topmost levels where these species were replaced by freshwater *Velesunio* mussels. This indicates change from an estuarine to freshwater environment, which occurred at this site about a thousand years ago.

Artefacts were found throughout the deposit, including edge-ground axe fragments, rectangular scrapers, stone and bone points, utilised flakes and one or two shell artefacts. Three-quarters of the stone artefacts were points, which were probably hafted onto the end of spears, since 80 per cent of them were snapped off at the tip with transverse fractures probably caused by impact.

The back wall of this rockshelter is covered with an abundance of colourful paintings, including a battle scene involving more than ten warriors with upraised spear-throwers. A little way from this site a gallery with many hundreds of paintings extends along a rock ledge which runs the whole length of the cliff-face about ten metres above ground level. Access is by means of a narrow rock shelf. Here is found a remarkable small painting known as the "mosquito man". It resembles a mosquito, but is more likely to be a Nadubi spirit. These dangerous, evil spirits had feather-shaped, magical barbed spines protruding from their limbs, and would shoot them into people travelling alone.

Two of the main art sites lie on the summit of another large rocky residual, which is honeycombed with shelters and caves. These would have enabled Aboriginal people to take shelter from rain and wind from any direction. Motifs are in the X-ray and the dynamic styles. On top of the adjacent outlier which rises above these shelters is a deep rockshelter extending for about 100 metres across the hill, and a fine view is obtained from its top. The art of Ngarradj-Warde-Djobkeng is outstanding in its variety of colours and subjects, which include sorcery paintings, spirit figures, a giant serpent, hunters, fish and kangaroos.

Nanguluwurr

To the east of the Jabiru-Pine Creek road on the northern side of the Nourlangie Rock massif lies the rockshelter of Nanguluwurr, an extensive and significant painting and occupational site, previously known as Nangaloar. A bush road leads to the site but this has been converted to a walking track by the park managers, who are anxious to protect such art galleries from dust raised by vehicles. However, Nanguluwurr is well worth the walk. The shelter extends for some 70 metres along the base of a high sandstone cliff, above a scree slope. In one corner there is a small spring, which provides a welcome trickle of cool water. In the centre of the site there are rocks with grinding hollows and an earth floor containing an occupational deposit. A small excavation by Kamminga and Allen revealed 750-year-old occupation, but it is likely that slabs of roof-fall cover older occupational deposits. Some of the paintings in the shelter are in the dynamic pre-estuarine style, and paintings are found in areas such as the ceiling of an eight metre high overhang. These paintings are now completely out of reach, even with the aid of a bush-timber ladder, suggesting that rock ledges on which the artists stood have since collapsed.

Most of the rock art styles of Kakadu are represented here. Underneath a high overhang small figures in the dynamic style run across the wall, wearing large head-dresses and carrying spears and boomerangs. Hand stencils surround them, some with the three middle fingers held tightly together. Below are painted outlines of hands and forearms, and nearby an outline painting of Namandi, a malignant spirit, with dilly bags hanging from his arms.

One of the most striking figures in the gallery is a ship painted in white ochre. It is fully rigged and trails a dinghy; remarkable detail is shown, including the anchor and anchor chain. There is also a finely painted series of fish in the X-ray style, and a short-necked turtle. These were painted around 1964 by "Old Nym" Djimogor, a Wardjag man who was a friend of Najombolmi, the painter at Nourlangie Rock.

Burrungkuy (Nourlangie Rock)

Burrungkuy is a prominent sandstone outlier rising to 265 metres at the south-west end of the Nourlangie Rock-Mount Brockman massif.[7] With its many rockshelters and good supply of food and water, it was highly suitable for prehistoric occupation. The best known art site in Kakadu is probably the main Anbangbang gallery (plate 8.8), located at the base of the massif, about 400 metres gentle walk along the track from the carpark east of the large billabong (figure 8.5).

On the way to this main gallery there are two other large rockshelters to the

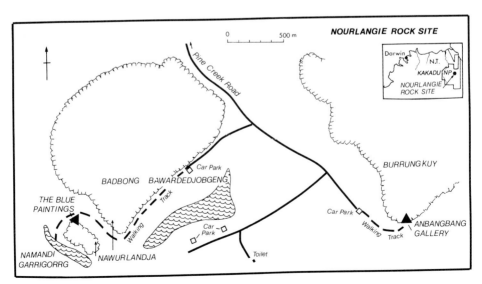

Figure 8.5   Nourlangie Rock. (After H. Sullivan, Australian National Parks and Wildlife Service)

Plate 8.8 Anbanbang gallery, painted in 1964 by Najombolmi, Nourlangie Rock, Kakadu National Park

Figure 8.6 Anbangbang gallery, Nourlangie Rock. 1. Namandjolk: the dangerous spirit. 2. Namarrkon: the lightning man. The lightning is depicted in the lines joining the head and feet. The objects attached to the head, elbows and knees of the figure are garramalg (stone axes), used to produce thunder and lightning when struck against clouds or the ground. 3. Barrkinj: wife of Namarrkon. 4. guluibirr: saratoga. 5. Family groups of men and their wives. Two of the women are depicted with milk in their breasts. The people travelled through the area on their way to a ceremony. (After Australian National Parks and Wildlife Service)

Plate 8.9 Anbangbang shelter, with a record of 6,000-year-old occupation, Nourlangie Rock, Kakadu National Park

north (left) of the main walking track. Steps lead off uphill to a lookout, occupation site and art site. The Anbangbang occupation site is situated about 20 metres above the plain and is the largest shelter in the region, formed by a massive quartzite rock which has fallen from the cliff high above and come to rest on two other huge rocks on the scree slope (plate 8.9).[8]

Generations of Aboriginal people have camped here in the wet season, for the site gives excellent protection from the rains. The shelter is reasonably well-lit and is some 40 metres long by 20 metres wide, with adequate headroom over most of the floor area. Part of the occupation deposit was excavated by Jones, and yielded the richest collection of organic materials ever obtained from an excavation in Australia.

In the upper levels were innumerable remains of past meals such as fish, freshwater turtle, fragments of fur, eggshell from crocodile and goanna eggs, freshwater mussel shells, and bones of flying foxes, lizards, wallaroos and other macropods. Altogether more than seventy species of animals were hunted and brought back to this cave. Plant foods such as tubers and tree fruits were equally important, and there was intensive exploitation of the rhizomes of waterlilies. As well there were thousands of artefacts made from bone, shell, bamboo, wood and string as well as stone, including firesticks, bamboo and reed spear shafts, lengths of fibre and hair twine and pieces of woven bags.

The remains suggest that the cave was used over the last 6,000 years primarily during the wet season as a base camp for a group of men and women, who carried out a wide variety of domestic tasks there. Paintings adorn the sloping back wall of the shelter, and there are grinding hollows on several large flat boulders across its floor. Other paintings are found on the uphill side of this shelter and on other rocks in the vicinity.

The main art site at Burrungkuy is about 400 metres north-east of the occupation cave, and can be reached without climbing any steps. It is a large fairly open rockshelter. Until the 1960s this shelter was used by Aborigines for camping. A small excavation in its earth floor revealed occupation going back 2,500 years. In 1964 the great rock-painter, Najombolmi, known to Europeans as Barramundi Charlie, camped in the shelter for the last time and executed perhaps his finest painting. He had seen the depopulation of his land and the disintegration of much of Aboriginal society, so he decided to "put the people back into the shelter".

He painted two family groups of men with their wives, some of whom are shown with milk in their breasts, ready to people the land again. Then he built a platform and painted mythic beings high on the wall, Namarrkon the lightning man, his wife Barrkinj and Namandjolk, a dangerous spirit (figure 8.6). The lightning man is responsible for thunder, lightning and storms, and has stone axes growing from his head, arms and knees with which he strikes the clouds to release the lightning. (The band encircling his body represents the lightning.) To the left of the main frieze is the single male figure, Nabulwinjbulwin, a dangerous spirit who kills women by striking them with a yam and then eating them. To the right is a narrow passageway which contains a number of other painted figures including Namarrkon.

There is another large gallery only some 50 metres away, screened by tall trees. Well-preserved spirit figures lie just below the ceiling, and the wall of conglomerate rock also bears hand stencils and paintings of kangaroos and guns.

Nawurlandja (the blue paintings), Little Nourlangie Rock

The blue paintings site is a small overhang on the northern side of a low sandstone outcrop just south of Nawurlandja or Little Nourlangie Rock. A walking track leads to it and a few other small paintings sites from a carpark on the northern side of the Nawurlandja billabong (see figure 8.5). The low overhang shelters a silt earth floor, where a small test excavation by Rhys Jones in 1981 revealed stone tools and occupation to a depth of 68 centimetres. Charcoal from this layer was radiocarbon-dated to 8,000 years old, but 20 centimetres below this resting directly on the basal clay was a piece of hard haematite with striations from use as a pigment. Jones therefore believes that "there is evidence at this site of some sparse occupation in terminal Pleistocene times" (that is, about 10,000 years ago).

Paintings adorn the back wall of this shelter (figure 8.7). Like those at the main Anbangbang gallery, they were executed in 1964 by Najombolmi or Barramundi Charlie. An innovation here is the use of a new exotic pigment, blue paint made from Reckitts Blue washing powder, but in all other respects the paintings are in the traditional X-ray style. They depict women and a man, various species of fish, a goanna, waterlily bulbs, and most interestingly, a pig-nosed or Fly River turtle. This turtle was thought to occur only in the southern rivers of New Guinea. This painting was the first evidence for European scientists that this species occurred in Australia, and it was only in 1973, after this painting had been identified as representing the pig-nosed turtle, that the first live specimens of this species were collected in local rivers. Access to this site is only with permission from ANPWS.

Katherine region

Katherine Gorge National Park

This spectacular gorge bisects an ancient sandstone plateau, 32 kilometres north-east of Katherine. The Katherine River has carved into the ranges along rectangular fault lines, incising a deep gorge with dramatic vertical walls (plate

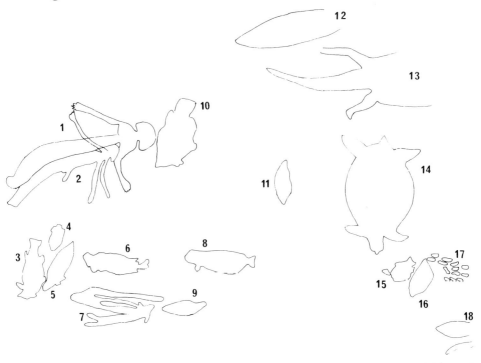

Figure 8.7 Nawurlandja (the blue paintings), Nourlangie Rock. 1. dalug: woman. 2. bininj: man. 3. madjabarr: mullet. 4. bodjal: primitive archer fish (rare). 5. bindjarang: eel-tailed catfish. 6. madjabarr: mullet. 7. dalug: woman (with contorted limbs). 8. ammagawari: large catfish. 9. malalalg: immature barramundi. 10. nageidmi: black bream. 11. bindjarang: eel-tailed catfish. 12. galalba: ox-eye herring. 13. galawan: goanna. 14. warradjan: pig-nosed turtle. 15. njalgan: archer fish. 16. bindjarang: eel-tailed catfish. 17. angoidjbang: waterlily bulbs. 18. dolpo: small unidentified fish. (After Australian National Parks and Wildlife Service)

Plate 8.10 Katherine Gorge National Park

8.10). Very few places in the principal gorge afford space to walk along the river banks, so it is necessary to visit by boat. (Boat trips or canoe rentals are readily available from the foot of the gorge.) Between the gorges there are shallow pools and rapids, and many rockshelters and alcoves in the cliff faces, some of which bear Aboriginal rock paintings.

Between the first and second gorges there are some paintings at the foot of the cliff. These are on the left-hand side facing up the gorge, opposite the canoe-mooring beach and the lower end of the canoe-portage walkway. The paintings are above a huge boulder where the foot of the cliff rises to a high point, and are reached in about ten minutes easy walk across rock slabs from where tourist ferries moor or canoes are beached. Subjects include over-lifesize human figures and the timid freshwater crocodile, which haunts the tranquil deep pools of the gorge.

Other painting sites lie further up the numerous gorges, and can be visited by hiring a canoe for a few days of exploring, camping on small, golden beaches and safe swimming in warm, clear water.

Kintore Caves reserve

Located 15 kilometres north-west of Katherine, Kintore Caves are of considerable scientific and archaeological significance, but are normally closed to the public. Permission to visit should be sought from the Conservation Commission's Katherine office. The horizontal limestone cave system is complex and extensive, with a main chamber and several subsidiary openings. Part of the floor of the main cave was excavated in 1963 by John Mulvaney, who found a deep stratified deposit, with a stone tool sequence showing a transition from large hand-held tools in the early layers to small specialised stone spear points and other hafted artefacts in the upper levels. Rock art is present in both the main cavern and some of the subsidiary openings. Both engravings and paintings occur, including abraded grooves and a painting of a snake. In style and subject matter the art has links with that of the Wadaman to the south-west.

Cutta Cutta Cave Nature Park

Engravings are also found in the Cutta Cutta caves near Katherine, which are open to the public. The park lies west of the Stuart Highway 27 kilometres south of Katherine. A self-guiding walk leads past weirdly weathered towers of limestone, 500 million years old, to a collapsed doline known as Cutta Cutta to the Jawoyn Aborigines. Underground tours of this cave are available. It contains many different formations, some Aboriginal engravings, the rare golden horseshoe bat and relics of an ancient marine fauna, the blind shrimp, which is almost colourless and has no eyes.

Gregory National Park

This region of sandstone plateaux and gorges lies south of the Victoria Highway around the Victoria River Crossing, 195 kilometres west of Katherine and 320 kilometres east of Kununurra. The region is being developed as the Gregory National Park, centred on what was previously the property of Bullita. Of particular note are Victoria River Gorge in the north (figure 8.8) and Jasper Gorge in the south-west. Between them lies the Stokes Range massif, rising to 250 metres to 300 metres above the surrounding plains and dissected by many sheer cliffs and gorges over 100 metres deep, most of which contain permanent water. In the summer monsoon waterfalls cascade down from the cliffs.

This scenic area contains numerous Aboriginal sites, including Dreaming places, stone arrangements, paintings, engravings, occupation sites, old earth ovens, ochre and stone quarries and stone hawk traps.[9] There is a rich concentration of sites in the area round the Victoria River Crossing and in Jasper Gorge, with more than 30 art sites.

Some of the largest paintings in Australia are found here. Particularly impressive are huge snakes, anthropomorphs, crocodiles, stingrays and swordfish. Other subjects are human beings, mammals, birds, and bush foods. Figures are often over a metre long, and are usually executed in silhouette view in red or yellow. Some figures are outlined in a continuous or dotted line in a contrasting colour and occasionally there is additional internal decoration. An unusual feature of this distinctive art style is the combination of the techniques of painting and engraving on a single figure.[10]

In the Victoria River region there are paintings of the lightning brothers, who

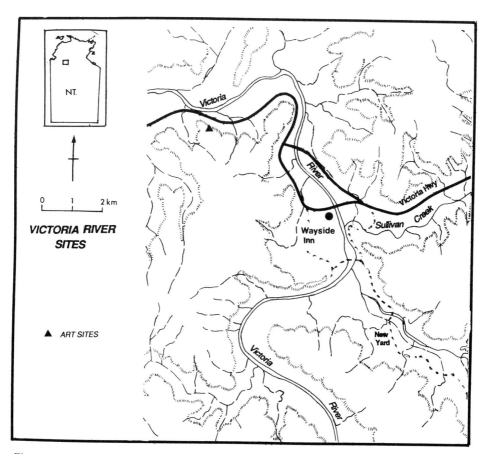

Figure 8.8 Victoria River Crossing area, Gregory National Park

are major figures in the mythology of the Wardaman people of the area west of Katherine.[11] The story relates how Yagjagbula, the older brother, had his beautiful wife stolen by his tall, handsome younger brother, Jabaringi. The two brothers fought with boomerangs until Jabaringi's head-dress was knocked off, the women stopped the fight and the lightning brothers painted themselves onto the rock wall. Traditionally each year at the end of the dry season in about October rain-making ceremonies were held at the lightning brothers sites. One of the rituals which was used to bring the rain was to take a sharp stone and rub or abrade grooves into the rock, "to cut Old Man Rock" and make him bleed.

One painting site in the vicinity of Victoria River Crossing is being made accessible for public viewing by the Conservation Commission with the agreement of Aboriginal traditional owners. This is the Wiyuwuti site, some seven kilometres west of the roadhouse, at the base of a long cliff on the southern side of the road. A climb up through spinifex grass leads to a massive, whiteish indentation in the cliffline (figure 8.8 and plate 8.11). Paintings are found along more than 100 metres of this rockface. Most are large, with stripes or other internal decoration. There is a big red kangaroo, a giant stingray, white hand stencils and an unusual white striped anthropomorph shown in profile.

Plate 8.11   The site of Wiyuwuti, Gregory National Park, Victoria River region

Particularly notable is a huge, striped anthropomorph painted horizontally across the wall (plate 8.12).

Other art sites may be viewed by special arrangement, on foot or perhaps via a boat trip from the roadhouse upriver through the spectacular Victoria Gorge.

Plate 8.12   A striped anthropomorph at Wiyuwuti. (The scale is marked in 5 cm.)

Plate 8.13   Ancestral beings at Garnbu-wuya, a hawk Dreaming in Wardaman country west of Katherine

Plate 8.14   Ancestral beings at Garnawala, Wardaman country west of Katherine

Enquiries regarding which sites are open to the public for viewing should be made
to the Conservation Commission.

Most of the rock art of this region is on private cattle properties, inaccessible to
the public, but some sites may possibly be visited on a tour from Innesvale
homestead (tel. (089) 750 720) or on Billy Harney's Jankangyina Aboriginal tours
(bookings via Northern Territory Tourist Bureau, tel. (089) 72 2650). Billy Harney

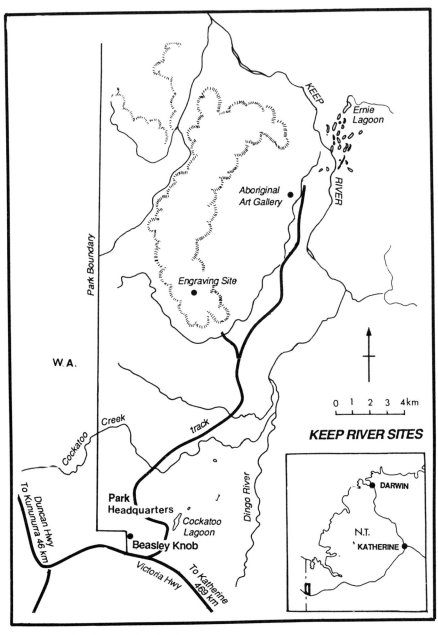

Figure 8.9   Keep River National Park

Plate 8.15   The site of Nganalang, Keep River National Park

is the son of the late Bill Harney, author and first ranger at Uluru, and he speaks both English and his mother's language, Wardaman. He conducts tourists to Aboriginal sites in the vicinity of Yingalarri waterhole (plates 8.13 and 8.14).

Keep River National Park

This park lies north of the Victoria Highway 460 kilometres west of Katherine and only 3 kilometres east of the Northern Territory-Western Australia border. It lies within the Victoria River district of the Northern Territory, but is much closer to Kununurra than to Katherine. The Keep River National Park is in a remote area and is little developed, but is noted for its striking sandstone landforms, fauna and Aboriginal rock paintings. A series of paintings, engravings and occupational sites is found in rockshelters and water-worn caverns in outcrops in open forest near the edge of the flood plains and in the Keep River gorge (plate 8.15). The sites were used in the wet season by the Miriwun people. One of these sites is currently open to the public, and is reached by a ten minute walking track north from the car park (figure 8.9).

The rockshelter lies in a relatively isolated outcrop and is 18 metres long but the back wall is split into two by an archway through the outcrop. The site is called Nganalang (pronounced Nunalum), after the white cockatoo lady, who poked her nose-bone through the rock, making the hole. The art is prolific, with a wide variety of motifs including hand stencils, snakes and two large anthropomorphous figures placed on the high, flat ceiling. On the lower wall beneath the paintings are numerous abraded grooves, most of which are long, fine lines, but some are combined to form bird tracks or other geometric designs.

Three other art sites are located at the edge of the main outcrop only two kilometres north of the park camping ground. Their paintings are rather weathered, but one of the rockshelters has on its earth floor a large boulder almost completely covered with deep circular engraved pits.

A number of other art sites have been found within the park, including paintings, stencils, engravings and even figures moulded out of beeswax. Stencils are common; as well as stencils of hands and occasionally feet, there are stencils of boomerangs, stone tools and other objects. The Keep River paintings are distinctive in style, with large figures in vivid colours. Particularly striking are large snake-like figures. One is painted in red with a white and yellow outline and is 24 metres long and over 1 metre wide for most of its length. This is by far the largest figure recorded in the region, and possibly in the whole of Australia. Another meandering, 5 metre long snake-like figure has a conspicuous animal-like head and ears. This body of art forms an important link between the art of the Kimberley to the west and the Victoria River district to the east.

CHAPTER NINE

Queensland: The North

Some extraordinary fossil finds in Queensland give a vivid picture of this part of the continent as far back as the time of the dinosaurs. Ninety-five million years ago, in what is now arid north-western Queensland, dinosaurs left at least 1,200 of their footprints stampeding through a patch of mud on the edge of a lake. The large dinosaur which caused the panic was a carnosaur, a carnivore standing about 2.6 metres high at the hips. Its footprints can be seen at Lark Quarry Environmental Park near Winton (see page 111). Many other finds from the age of the dinosaurs are on display in the Queensland Museum in Brisbane, together with 20 million-year-old unique fossil fauna from the newly discovered Riversleigh site described below. (For locations see figure 9.1.)

Human occupation in Queensland began at least 37,000 years ago. More than 5,200 Aboriginal sites have been recorded in the state, and entered in the computerised database of the Cultural Heritage branch of the state government (see page 362). Those wishing to visit Aboriginal sites in Queensland should contact this branch, which will put them in touch with the ranger in each region, for directions to sites. Regional archaeologists are stationed in Cairns, Townsville, Rockhampton and Brisbane, and can be contacted through the Division of Conservation of the Department of Environment and Heritage.

Recorded Aboriginal sites include, in order of frequency: artefact scatters, paintings, shell middens, stone arrangements, scarred trees, engravings, burials, quarries, axe grinding grooves, wells, earthen arrangements or circles, hearths and ground ovens, fish traps, stone circles, carved trees, dwellings, pathways, weirs and other rare site types. This order of frequency is based on the recording of the more obvious archaeological features such as rock art sites and by the concentration of archaeological surveys in the south-east of the state near the modern centres of population. Thus in more remote areas much of Queensland's rich Aboriginal heritage no doubt still remains to be discovered.

The prehistoric story of the north-east of Australia, which is now the state of Queensland, is described in two parts: the tropical north and the semi-tropical to temperate south-east. (The other regions are omitted because they contain virtually no sites which are open to visitors.) Within these broad geographical divisions sites are described in the order which best enables the story to be told, so

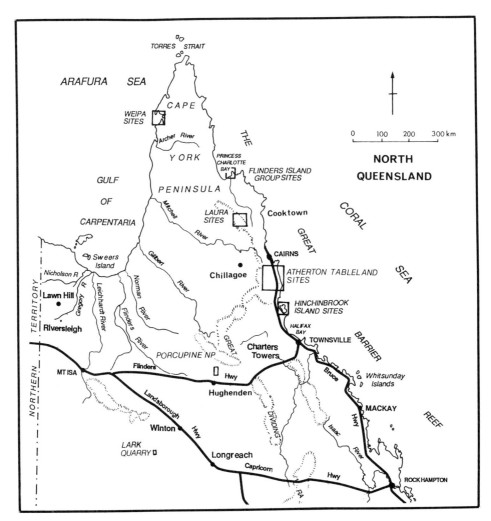

Figure 9.1   North Queensland

the arrangement may be chronological, thematic or regional. (In north Queensland it is chronological and regional, in the south-east thematic and regional.)

The Pleistocene antiquity (more than 10,000 years old) of human arrival in Queensland is supported by several archaeological sites. In far north-west Queensland traces of occupation well in excess of 17,000 years old have been found in a cave in the Lawn Hill National Park, for heavily patinated stone tools were found well below the shell which gave this radiocarbon date.[1] The site is remarkably rich, with a density of 50,000 stone artefacts and half a million pieces of animal bone per cubic metre of deposit.

The prehistoric environment was reconstructed through careful analysis of the sediments, bones, shells and stone tools. The high degree of weathering of the deposit, heavy mineral staining on the bones and patination on the artefacts suggest that human occupation commenced at least 30,000 years ago and possibly much earlier. At that time it was considerably wetter than at present, but from about 22,000 to 15,000 years ago it was very dry, peaking around 18,000 years ago. The Gulf of Carpentaria coastal plains became semi-arid, but the Lawn Hill gorge with its permanent waterholes has remained an important focus of Aboriginal occupation till the present day.

Other Pleistocene sites have been discovered at Sandy Creek shelter 1 (32,000 years) near Laura in Cape York Peninsula and at Fern Cave near Chillagoe (25,000 years). Recently Bruno David found 37,000-year-old occupation in Nurrabullgin Cave on spectacular Mount Mulligan near Chillagoe. (Tours available only from Kuku Djungan Aboriginal Corporation (19 Fenwick Street, Mareeba 4880, tel. (070) 92 3797).

Most of the Aboriginal sites visitors can now see date from a much more recent time. They give a picture of traditional Aboriginal society in the immediate prehistoric period, its way of life, customs, technology, economy and above all its rock art. Queensland has a rich legacy of Aboriginal art, with a particularly notable concentration in the Laura region on Cape York Peninsula.

North-west Queensland

Lark Quarry Environmental Park, central western Queensland

Dinosaur footprints are the main feature of this environmental park south-east of Mount Isa and about 120 kilometres south-west of Winton on the west side of the road to Jundah and Stonehenge (figure 9.2).[2] (The journey from Winton takes about two hours over a dirt road which becomes dangerous or impassable in wet weather; the site is best visited in the dry season between April and September, when drinking water should be carried.) Here evidence of a dinosaur stampede has been miraculously preserved in stone. What seems to have happened is that 95 million years ago some small animals, the size of emu chicks, were gathered near a lake when a big carnosaur took a swing to the left across an open mud patch. The small animals were trapped, and they huddled together for protection.

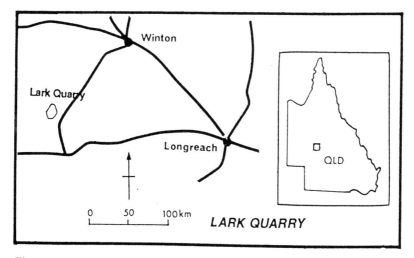

Figure 9.2   Location of Lark Quarry

Then the carnosaur turned right, his eyes possibly on a victim. The small ones seized their chance and stampeded back over the mud.

Three types of dinosaurs are represented, and more than 1,200 of their footprints are preserved in the rock which formed from the mud patch. The mud was dry enough to retain the tracks, yet sufficiently moist to prevent cracking and the footprints remained. Water carried sand and silt into the tracks and layers were built up and compressed to form the rock seen today. In a further 35 million years dinosaurs became extinct, and the face of the land changed. A low range of hills formed where once a lake had been, but over the millennia erosion cut into the hills and the fossilised footprints were again visible. After an observant local property manager noticed them in the 1960s, excavation of up to one metre of soft sandstone overburden by Queensland Museum staff and volunteers revealed graphic evidence of life in the age of the dinosaurs over a triangular area of 209 square metres, which is now roofed and has been opened to the public by the Queensland National Parks and Wildlife Service and the Winton Shire Council.

Figure 9.3 Dinosaurs: Coelurosaur on the left and Carnosaur on the right, with their tracks. (After National Parks and Wildlife Service, Queensland)

The large animal that caused the panic was a carnosaur, a carnivorous dinosaur standing about 2.6 metres high at the hips with a walking speed of 8 kilometres per hour (figure 9.3). Its maximum recorded footprint is 64 centimetres and its mean stride 1.7 metres. The small animals, with footprints about 10 centimetres long, were the ornithopod, a herbivorous small dinosaur standing about 12 centimetres to 60 centimetres at the hip (about bantam to half-grown emu size) with a running speed of 10 kilometres to 30 kilometres per hour, and the coelurosaur, about the same size as an emu chick, 15 centimetres to 25 centimetres at the hip, able to run at 10 kilometres to 15 kilometres per hour and an omnivorous dinosaur, eating eggs, insects and plants. The calculations of scientists have shown that about 240 individuals stampeded in a group.

This is the world's largest known group of footprints of running dinosaurs, and a huge cast of the main slab may be seen adorning the wall in the foyer of the Queensland Museum in Brisbane.

Riversleigh

Moving on to 20 million years ago in the Early Miocene epoch, there are the Riversleigh fossil finds, which are in the process of re-writing the books on the evolution of Australian mammals (figure 9.4).[3] Riversleigh lies north of Mount Isa in the far north-west of Queensland; it is private property but organised tours are available through the North West Queensland Tourism and Development Board, Mount Isa. Riversleigh fossils can be seen at the impressive new Riversleigh

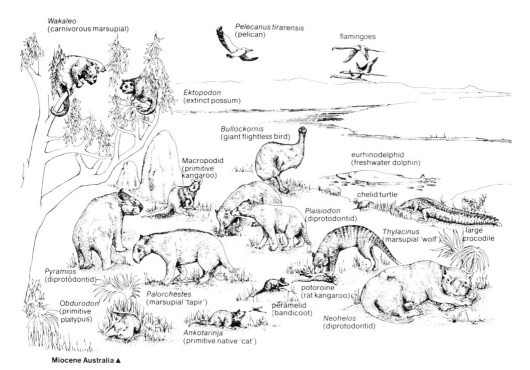

Figure 9.4 Miocene fauna. (Peter Murray, *Australian Prehistoric Animals,* Methuen, 1984: frontispiece)

Museum in Mount Isa, the Queensland Museum in Brisbane and at the Australian Museum in Sydney. In addition, a public display has been created by the Australian Geographic Society at the most accessible and oldest Riversleigh fossil deposit, "D" site, on the road from Mt Isa to Lawn Hill.

The Riversleigh project, led by Michael Archer, Suzanne Hand and Henk Godthelp of the University of New South Wales, has unearthed some of the richest and most significant terrestrial vertebrate fossil deposits in the world, in terms of understanding the history of marsupials, bats, egg-laying monotremes and other unique Australian animals. From what Archer and his colleagues have already learned, it is clear that 20 million years ago the Riversleigh region was totally different from the vast areas of semi-arid savannah woodlands that cover it today.

The ancient vegetation was dense rainforest teeming with life. In the trees were innumerable leaf-eating possums including ancestors and cousins of today's ringtail possums, miniscule feathertail possums, large cuscuses and brushtail possums, other less familiar omnivores and even a tiny ancestor of today's koala. This lush mantle of tall trees shaded cave-riddled limestone cliffs inhabited by millions of bats, overlooking a forest floor dotted with shallow freshwater pools. Small lakes held lungfish, an ancestral platypus *(Obdurodon),* a variety of crocodiles including a six to seven metre species (that may also have been terrestrial), and enormous turtles. Ferns, mosses and flowering plants provided a soft green carpet, over which foraged a wide range of herbivorous marsupials including strange "ordinary" herbivorous kangaroos, omnivorous and even carnivorous kangaroos and sheep- to cow-sized but wombat-shaped browsers (a species of *Neohelos*).

A wide range of smaller marsupials, including dasyurids and bandicoots, also haunted the forest floor. A python (initially named *Montypythonoides!*) seven metres long, slithered along the branches, and carnivorous predators such as a panther-sized marsupial "lion" (genus *Wakaleo)* and a small but wolf-like Tasmanian "tiger" stalked their prey. Giant flightless birds twice the size of emus, tiny geckos, dragons and an army of strange frogs were also part of the cast of actors on this ancient Tertiary stage.

One of the most bizarre creatures added to the prehistoric menagerie is a unique mammal temporarily dubbed "Thingodonta" and now formally described as *Yalkaparidon.* Its teeth are like those of no other mammal known anywhere in the world; the combination of long rodent-like lower incisors, the number of cheek-tecth and the strikingly specialised molar teeth which could only cut rather than grind food make this a completely new mammal, the first new order of mammals discovered in Australia since the 1800s. *Yalkaparidon* would have had fur and been about the size of a rabbit, but its teeth were like tiny scissors; all it could do was cut and snip, but what did it eat?

There is a gap in the Riversleigh story after the Middle Miocene, but about 3 to 5 million years ago in the Pliocene a new scene unfolds. An ancient cave deposit along the Gregory River now known as Rackham's Roost has provided a window into this period of Riversleigh's history. Here thousands of carnivorous ghost bats dropped pieces of their prey onto the cave floor. During the millions of years that the teeth and bones of these prey, together with those of some of the predators, accumulated in the refuse on the floor of this ancient cave, they became fossilised.

Finally, the ravages of time removed the surrounding cave walls, but left the last vestiges of them visible at the edges of the deposit.

The next significantly different act in the revelation of Riversleigh's history is a Pleistocene terrace deposit along the Gregory River, perhaps 50,000 years old. By this time humans were probably on the stage and were possibly hunting the rhinoceros-sized *Diprotodon* found here. It was a ponderous, slow-witted creature of wombat-like build. Although its skull was half a metre long, its brain was barely as large as a tennis ball. It would probably have been relatively easy prey for hunters.

Much further research needs to be done; it is estimated that only five per cent of the fossil-rich deposits have been discovered as yet. The accumulation at Riversleigh of this treasure trove of the past, bone-rich layer upon bone-rich layer, represents the pages of a remarkable prehistory book, written in stone over the last fifteen million years. (For further information and tours or participation in Riversleigh expeditions, contact the Riversleigh Society, PO Box 281, Gordon, NSW 2072, or Lloyd Campbell, Campbell Coaches, Mount Isa, Qld 4825.)

Lawn Hill National Park

North of Mount Isa and 140 kilometres north of Camooweal lies Lawn Hill National Park, where Lawn Hill Creek has cut spectacular gorges in its course from the dissected north-eastern part of the Barkly Tableland through the Constance Range to the plains of the Gulf of Carpentaria. Sheer red cliffs falling as much as 70 metres to clear, emerald-green permanent pools in a series of gorges, together with lush remnant rainforest species such as cabbage tree palms, cycads, pandanus, vines and creepers, give this region an extraordinarily beautiful, oasis-like quality.

There are numerous Aboriginal campsites, mussel shell middens and art sites. The paintings were mainly done freehand in red ochre, principal subjects being snakes, bird tracks, boomerangs and humanoid figures. Engravings also exist, some of them covered in red ochre. This suggests that the engraved motifs were of special significance, and were repainted as part of ritual ceremonies at the site. A readily accessible, signposted site is Wild Dog Dreaming. Another, Rainbow Dreaming, requires a canoe (hireable) to cross Middle Gorge. Both sites are not far from the National Parks and Wildlife Service centre and an excellent campground (bookings required in the dry season).

Fish traps in the Gulf of Carpentaria

At various places along the southern shoreline of the Gulf of Carpentaria and the adjacent islands, fish traps have been constructed by Aborigines from local rock. Located on mudflats, rock shelves and beaches, they all occur below high water mark, either as single features, in groups or as a series of complexes (plate 9.1). Their total lengths range from approximately 20 metres up to a kilometre. The rock walls are usually between 50 centimetres and 90 centimetres high and act as barriers to trap fish, dugong and turtle as the tide recedes. Prey are chased into the shallows or speared with a multi-pronged fishing spear. Some of these fish traps are still in use.

Plate 9.1 Aerial photograph of fish traps in the Gulf of Carpentaria at Gaabula (Bayley Point), North Queensland. (G. Connah and A. Jones, University of New England)

More than 40 identifiable fish traps survive on the shoreline of the southern Gulf of Carpentaria between Bayley Point and the mouth of Moonlight Creek some 30 kilometres north-north-east of Burketown. Another 300 fish traps are situated on the Wellesley Islands in the gulf, with particular concentrations on Bentinck, Mornington, Sweers, Allen and Forsyth Islands. Shell middens are sometimes associated with the fish traps. The only traps which can easily be visited are those on Sweers Island, which are within walking distance of the tourist resort. Most of the other traps may be viewed only after consultation with the relevant Aboriginal council, and are only accessible by four-wheel-drive and/or boat.

Kalkadoon Cultural Centres, Mount Isa

A centre displaying traditional arts, crafts and lore of the Kalkadoon people has been developed in the lower floor of a large, disused tank and reservoir in the grounds of the Frank Aston Museum at the top of Rotary Hill in Mount Isa. Features are artefacts and weapons, a replica of a cave with rock paintings, and a simulated traditional camp with hut. Another Kalkadoon cultural centre well worth a visit is next door to the tourist office.

Sun Rock paintings and Browns Creek engravings, Mount Isa

Visits to some rock art sites in the Mount Isa region can be arranged by contacting one of the Kalkadoon centres in Mount Isa, or the Cultural Heritage branch in Brisbane. Currently, two sites are open to the public. At Sun Rock paintings have been executed in red ochre.[4] The paintings are on a quartzite rock face adjacent to water and have probably occasionally been washed by floods, but nevertheless may be quite ancient. Often where red fine-grained red ochre has been used, a "bonding" tends to develop between the pigment and the rock. At this site the tiny grains of ochre have penetrated into minute cracks in the rock, which means that the paintings should continue to survive for many more centuries.

The figures appear to depict humans, possibly clan elders since some of them wear large head-dresses, of the type used in traditional dances and ceremonies in this region. The paintings are so old that local Aboriginal people no longer know their exact meaning, but the large snake which figures prominently in the painted design indicates that this may have been a fertility or totem centre for the snake. It has also been suggested that the smaller (and perhaps younger) human figures represent youths, and that the site may have been an initiation centre for the snake totem.

Many rock engravings survive in the hard and durable micaceous quartzite of the Mount Isa area. Major waterholes were a focus of traditional Aboriginal life in this arid region, and at Browns Creek there are engravings which are weathered and cracked with age and appear to be many thousands of years old. The pictures include large wheel-like motifs, spirals, animal tracks, curvilinear shapes and numerous pits or depressions found singly or in rows across the rock face. The wheel-like design is common at engraving sites in north-west Queensland. Its meaning and that of the other motifs is no longer known, but they were probably used as symbols to teach traditional law to the younger members of the clan.

Cape York Peninsula

Quinkan country

Some 350 kilometres north of Cairns, at the base of Cape York Peninsula centred on the small township of Laura, is a sandstone plateau about 10,000 square kilometres in area, extending from Cooktown on the coast to the Hann River in the west. River valleys have dissected this plateau into a series of impressive ridges capped with steep cliffs. On the slopes below are huge blocks of rock that have sheared off the cliffs over the millennia. In both these boulders and the cliffs are innumerable wind-worn caves and rockshelters that provided ideal living places for Aborigines and ideal walls for their art.

Evidence from archaeological excavation on the floor of one of these rockshelters named "Early Man"[5] has shown that not only has the region been inhabited for at least 13,500 years, but that the art is also of this antiquity. It may indeed be much older. In the Early Man shelter heavily weathered and patinated engravings cover the back wall in a diagonal frieze and clearly continue below the present ground surface (plate 9.2). Excavation revealed the presence of engravings on the rock wall below an occupation level containing charcoal dated to 13,000 years, which must therefore be older than this.

Plate 9.2   Early Man site, Laura area

The engraved designs have been influenced by natural contours of the rock surface, for example natural hollows have been emphasised by outlining or filled with engravings. The most common motifs are gridded designs, three-pronged marks resembling bird tracks, circular forms and extensive mazes. Rather similar engraved designs occur at two shelters in the Koolburra area I excavated in 1981 and 1982, which dated back to 8,500 and 7,500 years.[6] Excavation of Sandy Creek shelter in 1989 by Michael Morwood has revealed much older occupation, going back 32,000 years. This was associated with a buried panel of pecked rock engravings, mainly small circular pits on a sloping rock slab. At the same depth of 3 metres the site's discoverer, Percy Trezise, in an exploratory excavation in the 1960s unearthed a remarkable axe made from pink quartzite. Not only did it have notches on the sides to lash it to a handle, but also its working edge was ground rather than flaked. This find therefore extends the minimum time-depth of edge-grinding technology in Australia back to 32,000 years, and makes this the earliest known edge-ground axe in the Asian region. (Ground-edge artefacts have been found in Japan dated to between 30,000 and 27,000 years, and in the New Guinea highlands at 26,000 years.) Unfortunately all these sites are in remote areas only accessible by four-wheel-drive on private property, and there is no public access to them. However, some of the glories of Cape York rock art can be seen at three site complexes which are open to the public near Laura (figure 9.5), and others may be viewed with special permission from the Ang-Gnarra Aboriginal Corporation of Laura.

Twelve kilometres south of Laura there are two signposted rock art complexes, close to the west side of the road. These are Split Rock, where there is a carpark and walking track up to the sites, and Guguyalangi, which is linked to Split Rock and the road by a signposted trail (figures 9.6 and 9.7 and plate 9.3). You can walk either way, or just visit Split Rock galleries. If you start at the northern, Guguyalangi end, the walking track leads up to the first level of the tableland, where there is a view

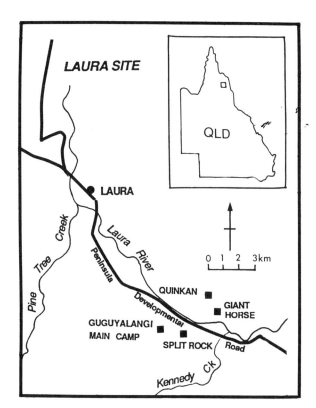

Figure 9.5 Laura area

Figure 9.6 Location
of Guguyalangi and
Split Rock galleries, Laura

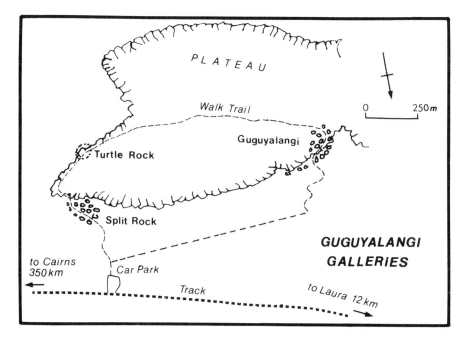

north over a vast expanse of country, with Cape York Peninsula stretching into the
far distance. This would be the highest point between Laura and the Cape. The

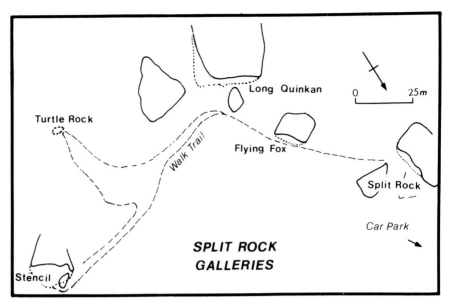

Figure 9.7   Split Rock galleries, Laura

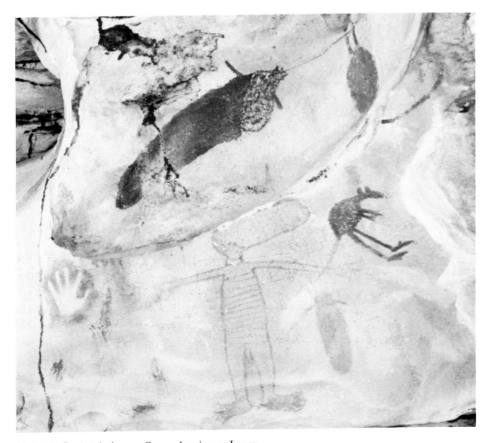

Plate 9.3   Rock paintings at Guguyalangi, near Laura

track winds through the broken edge of the escarpment until it reaches the first of the art sites, where the subjects are mainly hand stencils done with local red ochre.

Other art sites are found in sheltered overhangs and small caves further on as the track passes between massive sandstone blocks. Motifs include tall spirit beings with helmet-shaped heads, the Quinkans, after which part of this region has been named the Quinkan Reserve. The sinister Quinkans with their angular figures, pendulous ear lobes and staring eyes are evil spirits who live in rock crevices and lure the unwary to destruction in their dark hiding places. Other

Plate 9.4 Imjim spirit figure at Split Rock, shown with typical elongated ears, with stone axes on his elbows and a knobbed appendage on which he hops across the countryside

subjects relate to hunting and food, such as yams, nonda fruit, dilly bags and birds. There are 12 art sites at Guguyalangi, and art forms include stencils, paintings and some pecked engravings.

A small climb leads onto the top of the tableland from where the track runs south towards the other side of the escarpment. Here you can see the main road stretching away to the south. The massive outcrop that has become known as Turtle Rock is also visible with its distinct resemblance to a turtle's head. The track winds its way around the edge of the rock face and down steps to the Split Rock galleries. The first gallery near the steps contains some stencils, pecked engravings and a few paintings, mainly human figures. Heading west towards the large boulders which form the main Split Rock galleries, the track comes to another gallery adorned with tall Quinkan spirits painted in thin red lines, small humans and kangaroos. Next is the flying fox gallery, with various animals and flying foxes, shown hanging upside down from the trees as they do each night. The last gallery is Split Rock itself, containing many paintings, including an excellent figure of an echidna, shown in plan view as is normal in Cape York art. There is also an Imjim spirit figure with typical large ears, stone axes on his elbows and a knobbed appendage. Aboriginal informants told Percy Trezise in the 1960s that Imjim spirits lived on frogs, bounced around like kangaroos at night on their appendage, and could bounce half a mile in one hop (plate 9.4).

Plate 9.5 Horse's head and Quinkan spirit, Giant Horse site

Other galleries are Mushroom Rock and Giant Horse, which lie on the eastern side of the road between Split Rock and Laura. The Ang-Gnarra Aboriginal Corporation in Laura must be contacted to visit these sites. Giant Horse is an hour's uphill walk but well worth the climb. (A track goes to within five minutes' walk of the site, but the gates are usually kept locked.) In the main shelter one artist dramatically recorded his impression of a horse, a strange-shaped animal four or five times bigger than any living animal he had seen before. The horse is around six metres long and not only dominates a large rock wall, but dwarfs all the other paintings of traditional animals, men and spirits (plate 9.5).

Another dramatically large painting here shows a bucking horse and the rider, with reins and rifle still in hand, sprawled on the ground in front of it. Was this a narrative painting of an actual event, or was it sorcery, a last desperate attempt to use sorcery to rid the land of the white invaders? Other colourful figures crowd the surface, stingrays, bush turkeys and the ubiquitous skinny Quinkan spirits. In a subsidiary site round the corner there is a portrayal of what appears to be a pack rape.

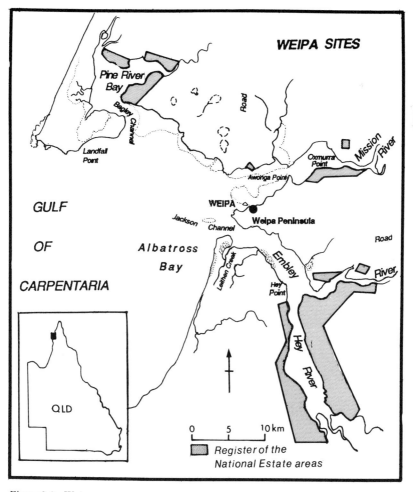

Figure 9.8 Weipa area

This body of rock art in the Laura area includes over a thousand sites and tens of thousands of figures. The paintings are larger and more colourful than most other Aboriginal rock art, with a wide variety of styles, techniques and subject matter. The art has been recorded largely through the initiative of Percy Trezise, bush pilot, explorer, painter and writer[7], and the Trezise family were mainly responsible for getting the area protected as the Quinkan Reserve, and are now involved in running a safari camp and guide service to the rock art of the region from their property of Jowalbinna near Laura. (Contact Trezise Bush Guide Service, PO Box 106, Freshwater, Cairns 4870, tel. (070) 55 1865.)

Weipa shell mounds

Huge shell mounds up to 13 metres high can be seen near the modern bauxite-mining town of Weipa on the western coast of Cape York Peninsula. The need to conserve the shell mounds is recognised by the mining company, Comalco, and the Napranum Aboriginal Community Council, who have both supported community action to establish the Uningan Bicentennial Nature and Recreation Reserve. This lies east of Awonga Point (Uwang) and Weipa North on the southern bank of the Mission River, and contains several mounds.

There are about 500 mounds along the banks of the shallow estuaries of four rivers, the Embley, Hey, Pine and Mission (figure 9.8)[8]. Most of these are within the Comalco mining lease. The shells are largely of one species, the cockle *(Anadara granosa)*, and it has been estimated that the mounds contain a total of 200,000 tonnes of shell, or about nine thousand million cockles.

Archaeological excavation has shown that the mounds are of human, not natural origin. Layers of charcoal, the presence of bone and stone tools and the predominance of one shell species are all features of a man-made midden (plate 9.6). Artefacts include barbs of fishing spears, made of bone or stingray, and

Plate 9.6 Shell midden at Weipa

wallaby incisor teeth split to form a toothed scraper, probably used to sharpen spear tips. One feature of the middens which archaeologists found puzzling at first was that more than half the cockle shells were not broken, but appeared to be intact and unopened. Local Aborigines have solved this riddle by demonstrating that heat is usually used to open the cockles and the flesh is removed without breaking the shell, which then closes again. The usual cooking method is to place the live shells in a heap on the ground and make a small fire of leaves and twigs on top of them; this creates sufficient heat to open the valves.

Most of the shell mounds are only one to two metres high, but some reach nine metres and the largest is thirteen metres high. Their shapes vary greatly; some resemble inverted cones with steep sides and others form ridges or heaps. Some mounds lie at the edge of mangrove swamps but others, including the largest ones, lie within 200 metres of high tide mark. The reason for developing high mounds in this low-lying and often waterlogged area would seem to be the need for a dry camp, free from insect pests, with a sea breeze and near the cockle beds. Excavation has shown that the mounds began to accumulate about 1,200 years ago. This fits with archaeological evidence from other parts of Australia for a period of increased activity, population expansion or "intensification" over recent millennia.

Flinders Group National Park

Some of the most spectacular island rock art galleries on Australia's east coast lie in the Flinders Islands, on the east coast of Cape York Peninsula, north of Bathurst Head between Princess Charlotte Bay and Cape Melville. The island group consists of five main continental islands and a number of islets (figure 9.9). There is no access to the islands from the adjacent mainland, but Owen Channel between Stanley and Flinders Island provides a safe anchorage for boats.

The Flinders Islands contain the most extensive and varied concentration of rock painting known to occur on any Queensland island. Subjects in this unique regional rock art body vary from sorcery figures to post-contact ships, and paintings are generally colourful and reasonably well-preserved. A distinctive feature of the art is the decoration of dotted lines found on many of the figures. Marine creatures dominate the motif range, as might be expected. Turtles, stingrays, fish and dugong are most common, and there are also jellyfish, birds, dingoes, emus, flying fish, crabs, painted bird and macropod tracks, moths and butterflies, boats and ships and a number of non-figurative motifs (figure 9.10).

One of the motifs unique to the art of this Princess Charlotte Bay region is the broad T-shape identified by local Walmbaria Aborigines as motjala which means moth or butterfly. Such figures are found both in the island and adjacent mainland sites, and Grahame Walsh recorded more than 800 in 60 sites in a recent survey.[9]

Major rock painting sites are located on Stanley and Clack Islands and on Bathurst Head on the mainland. On the north-east coast of rocky Stanley Island to the north of Owen Channel are three painted shelters, known as Endaen, Mildred and Ship shelters. The Endaen shelter is in a low cliff line only separated from the shore by a large sand ridge. It contains several representations of ships together with turtles, starfish, stingrays, moths/butterflies, dingoes, jellyfish and an emu. Another extensive array of ships is painted in Ship shelter, 200 metres to the east

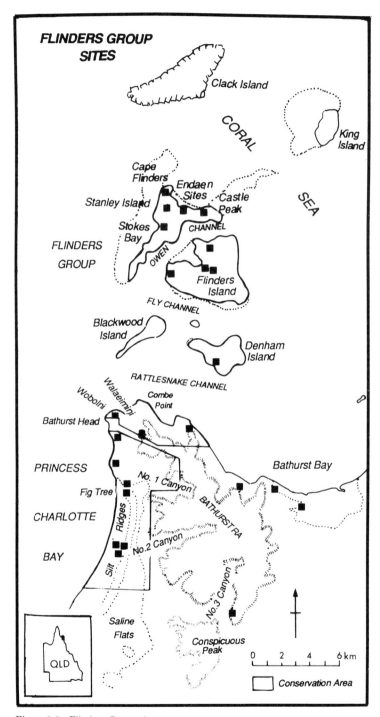

Figure 9.9 Flinders Group sites

of Endaen. Both of these sites are open to the public and provided with boardwalks and interpretive signs, and are reached by a signposted walking track. In Mildred Cave on the northern face of Castles Peak at the north-eastern

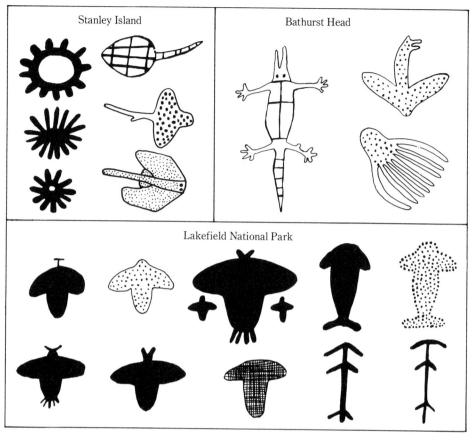

Figure 9.10 Flinders Group art motifs. The moths are usually between 20 and 30 centimetres long. (After G.L. Walsh 1984)

tip of Stanley Island, is a remarkably detailed painting in red with white outline of a lugger, the *Mildred*, towing a small dinghy.

Clack Island, a very small rocky island on the edge of a large reef to the north of the main Flinders Group, also contains extensive art sites. Difficulties of access in stormy weather mean that these are seldom visited, but they contain similar marine motifs such as dugong and crabs in the same polychrome decorative style as those on Stanley, together with many sorcery figures. Clack Island's Aboriginal name is Ngurromo, and it seems to have been a place of particular significance, especially for sorcery art.

On Bathurst Heads on the east side of Princess Charlotte Bay several rockshelters contain art. The large Walaeimini shelter above the bay just west of the tip of Bathurst Heads has paintings of starfish, frogs, humans, butterflies and moths, together with a few hand stencils. Another unnamed shelter, its mouth hidden with vegetation, contains exceptionally fresh-looking, vivid paintings, including a superb depiction of a sailing boat in full rigging.

While clearly some of the art is quite recent, belonging to the nineteenth or early twentieth century, archaeological work in the area by John Beaton has demonstrated that middens in Princess Charlotte Bay go back some 3,000 years, and that occupation on Stanley Island is 2,500 years old. Some of these middens are shell mounds several metres in height and are comparable with the shell mounds of Weipa on the west side of Cape York Peninsula.

Cairns-Townsville region

The Atherton Tablelands

The Atherton Tablelands, west of Cairns, may have been penetrated by hunter-gatherers as long ago as 45,000 years. This claim is based on a long pollen sequence in a core taken from Lynchs Crater, a flat-floored marshy depression which was originally a volcanic explosion vent, about 15 kilometres from Broomfield Swamp. About 60,000 years ago the vegetation resembled the vine forests of southern Queensland, with hoop pine the dominant species. Then about 45,000 years ago there was a massive increase in charcoal at the same time that the vegetation changed from rainforest to fire-adapted *Eucalyptus*. The only reasonable explanation for this change according to pollen analyst, Peter Kershaw, is the arrival of people with their firesticks.[10]

The volcanic origins of the Atherton Tablelands are clearly visible in the many craters which dot the region, particularly north of Malanda (figure 9.11). Many of these craters were produced by volcanic explosions, probably as the result of ascending lava reacting with groundwater. Several of these explosion craters or maars contain lakes inside their rims. Three such crater lakes which are national parks are Hypipamee Crater, between Atherton and Ravenshoe, Lake Eacham, 700 metres across, just off the Gillies Highway between Yungaburra and Gordonvale, and Lake Barrine, 1 kilometre in diameter, 5 kilometres to the east of Lake Eacham. The crater lakes are more than 60 metres deep, surrounded by rainforest and haunted by platypus, tortoises, brush turkeys, cassowary and innumerable smaller birds.

One of the most remarkable features of these craters is the existence of detailed and site-specific Aboriginal myths about volcanic eruptions in the area, even although the last eruption occurred more than 10,000 years ago. The Ngadyandyi, a tribe of the Atherton Tableland speaking a dialect of the Dyirbal language, have a myth which explains the origin of the three volcanic crater lakes, Yidyam meaning "large expanse of water" (Lake Eacham), Barany (Lake Barrine) and Ngimun (Lake Euramoo). It is recounted that two newly-initiated men broke a taboo and angered the rainbow serpent. As a result "the camping-place began to change, the earth under the camp roaring like thunder. The wind started to blow down, as if a cyclone were coming. The camping-place began to twist and crack. While this was happening there was in the sky a red cloud, of a hue never seen before. The people tried to run from side to side but were swallowed by a crack which opened in the ground".[11]

This is a plausible account of a volcanic eruption, and the Aboriginal storyteller also remarked that when this happened the country round the lakes was not rainforest as it is today but open scrub. Pollen analysis at Lynchs Crater shows that the present rainforest on the Atherton Tablelands is only about 7,500 years old; before that it was open scrub. The three volcanic lakes were formed a little

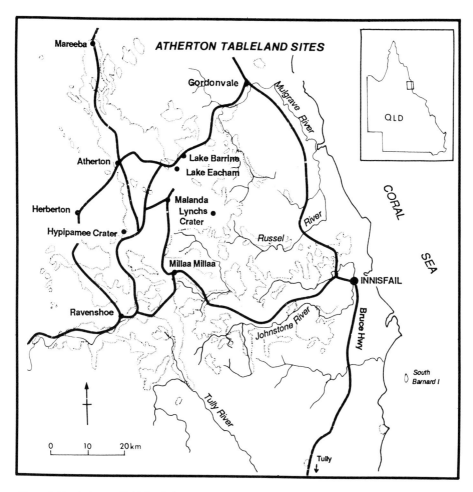

Figure 9.11   Atherton Tableland sites

over 10,000 years ago. This means that the oral tradition about volcanic eruptions and the spread of rainforest have been handed down from generation to generation for some ten millennia.

Chillagoe

Some 200 kilometres west of Cairns are the Chillagoe bluffs or towers of fossiliferous limestone, some exceeding 60 metres in height. These are some of the best developed examples of tower karst in Australia. The rock is a grey Upper Silurian to Lower Devonian limestone formed between about 434 and 416 million years ago, when Chillagoe was under shallow water in an environment similar to today's Great Barrier Reef.

In the Chillagoe-Mungana Caves National Park guided tours are available to several caves such as Royal Arch and Donna Cave containing spectacular limestone formations. Some rockshelters with rock art such as Balancing Rock are also open to the public. Others are on private property with no public access. Walkunder Arch Cave in the Chillagoe limestone is such a site. Bone is usually well-preserved in limestone caves, and this site has produced a long sequence of animal bone and stone artefacts, going back more than 18,000 years. The site is being excavated by John and Mireille Campbell of James Cook University.

Even older sites have recently been discovered in the Chillagoe region by Bruno David of the University of Queensland. These are Fern Cave, a large rockshelter containing both rock art and 25,000-year-old human occupational debris, and Nurrabullgin Cave, at 37,000 years currently the oldest site in Queensland.[12] (Tours available: see page 111.)

Hinchinbrook Island

Located just off Cardwell on the North Queensland coast 160 kilometres north of Townsville, Hinchinbrook is a loftly Great Barrier Reef island with diverse mangroves, heaths, *Eucalyptus* forests and pockets of tropical rainforest, separated from the mainland by a drowned river valley. It is the world's largest

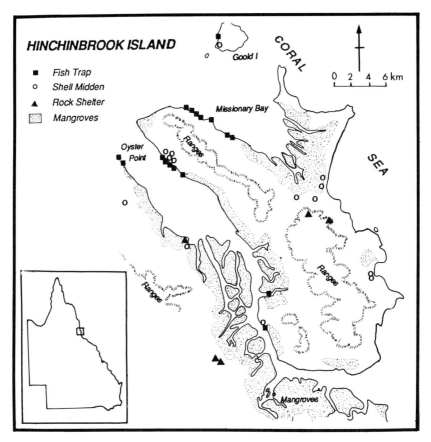

Figure 9.12   Hinchinbrook Island sites

island national park. Prehistoric Aboriginal occupation depended very heavily on the resources of the sea, and the main types of site are shell middens and fish traps (figure 9.12).

The fish traps are concentrated at Scraggy Point and Missionary Bay, on the northern and western sides of the island.[13] The combined total area of the tidal fish traps at Scraggy Point is about 2.16 square kilometres. The low walls are cemented together with the rock oyster, and fish and crustaceans such as the mangrove crab or "muddie" abound in the area. There are raceways, loops, poles, funnels, breakwaters and "arrowheads", all part of an elaborate automatic seafood retrieval system. The fish trapped as the tide fell would have been able to feed substantial groups of people for extended periods of time.

Judging both from early European accounts and from the number and size of the middens, it seems likely that there were fairly permanent villages of timber and bark near the fish traps on Hinchinbrook and the neighbouring Goold Island.

Hook Island, Whitsunday Passage Islands

This national park of 5,180 hectares is reached by yacht or launch from Shute Harbour. At Nara Inlet on the southern side of Hook Island about 30 metres above water level is an Aboriginal rock art site (figure 9.13). This is a long, deep rockshelter with a small pillar dividing it near the centre, and three panels of freehand paintings[14]. It is open to the public and interpretive signs and a boardwalk have been erected on the site. The paintings are predominantly geometric motifs, and include grid motifs, zigzags, circles, "arrows", "stars", crosses and "theta"

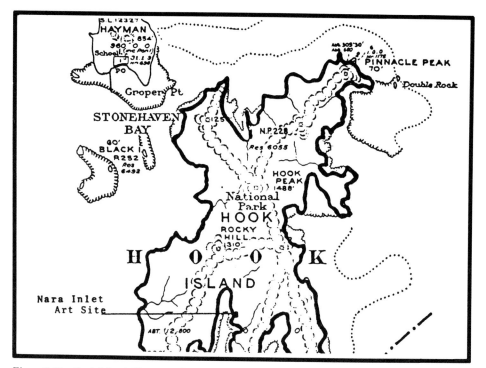

Figure 9.13   Hook Island. (Courtesy Queensland Forestry Department)

signs. The largest motif is 50 centimetres high. Unusual composite stencils in white pigment also occur, and the art is far more similar to that of the Central Highlands of Queensland than to paintings on nearby Dunk Island and the Flinders Group further north, where there is a figurative style featuring turtles, fish, birds and other animals.

Another rockshelter at Nara Inlet on Hook Island has been excavated recently by Bryce Barker of the University of Queensland, who obtained a date on the base of human occupational debris of 8,000 years. This is the earliest date obtained so far for human occupation of the Barrier Reef islands.

The Horn, South Molle Island, Whitsunday Passage Islands

An Aboriginal quarry site is located on top of a steep ridge near the Horn, the second highest peak on South Molle Island (figure 9.14). The quarry extends north along the ridge for about 60 metres and downslope for over 100 metres. The site is 1.5 kilometres east of South Molle Island Resort, and is intersected by a walking track some 30 metres from the ridge top on the eastern side. The quarry consists of four circular depressions about 80 centimetres deep. The rock is a hard, black volcanic basalt, ideal for making ground-edge axes. Evidence of Aboriginal exploitation of this superb stone is visible in the form of hammerstones and axe blanks (partially flaked large pieces).

Historical records tell how Aboriginal people who lived in the Whitsundays area at the time of first European contact frequently went to South Molle for stone, and then to other islands. Visitors are reminded that Aboriginal sites and artefacts are protected by law, and must not be disturbed.

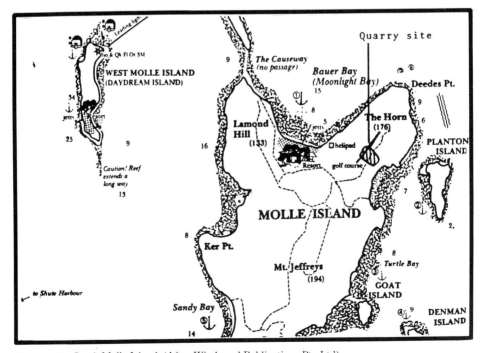

Figure 9.14   South Molle Island. (After Windward Publications Pty Ltd)

CHAPTER TEN

Queensland: The South-East

Archaeological discoveries have shown that for more than 20,000 years Aboriginal people have been living in a wide series of environments in what is now Queensland. They were in caves up in the Gulf country and the rugged ranges of Cape York Peninsula, in Kenniff Cave on the top of the Great Dividing Range at 770 metres above present sea level and camping out near the sea coast in the ancient Brisbane River valley in Moreton Bay (figure 10.1).

The most recent of these discoveries was the chance find of an ancient "transit camp", used intermittently by Aborigines for over 21,000 years, on the west coast of North Stradbroke Island.[1] Robert Neal of Queensland University and Errol Stock of Griffith University found shells, animal bones, flaked stone artefacts and charcoal in a 2.5 metre deep stratified archaeological deposit, at the foot of a large sand dune at Wallen Wallen Creek about 400 metres inland from the present coastline.

Twenty thousand years ago when sea level was some 140 metres lower, what is now Stradbroke Island was part of the mainland and the coast was between 12 and 20 kilometres to the east. The Wallen Wallen Creek site was then a temporary camping place on the main access route between the coast and the Brisbane River valley and mountains to the west. As the sea gradually began to rise some 17,000 years ago until it stabilised at its present level about 6,000 years ago, this high coastal dunefield was transformed into an offshore island. Other, perhaps even older, prehistoric sites may now lie deep beneath the waters of Moreton Bay.

This campsite affords a glimpse of the profound changes in coastal landscape and Aboriginal lifestyles occasioned by the rising of the seas. In recent times Aboriginal diet there included shellfish, fish and a few dugong. The far greater quantities of artefacts in the upper layers of the site and other evidence suggest a significant increase in human occupation of the offshore islands of Moreton Bay during the past few thousand years; this evidence accords with that from numerous shell middens on other sand islands such as Fraser and Moreton.

Pleistocene open campsites such as Wallen Wallen Creek are extremely rare in Australia and tend to be chance finds uncovered by erosion or developmental activities. The site is on a sand-mining lease, but is being protected by the

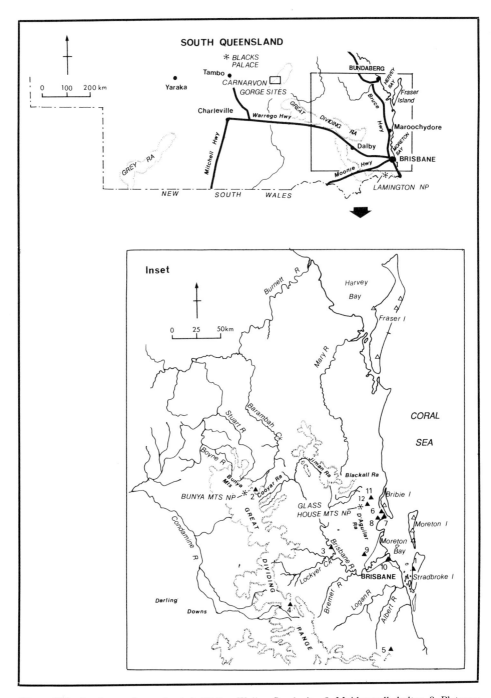

Figure 10.1 South-east Queensland. 1. Wallen Wallen Creek site. 2. Maidenwell shelter. 3. Platypus shelter. 4. Gatton shelter. 5. Bushrangers Cave. 6. Toorbul Point fish trap. 7. Sandstone Point midden. 8. Toorbul Point bora ground. 9. Samford bora ground. 10. Nudgee bora ground. 11. Landsborough grinding grooves. 12. Beerburrum bora ring

company, Consolidated Rutile Limited. There is nothing to see at this site since remains are all sub-surface and there is no public access except with special permission from the company, but examples of this type of site can readily be seen in the striking middens along the exposed coastlines of Moreton, Stradbroke and Fraser Islands (see below). On North Stradbroke Island more than 100 Aboriginal heritage sites have been recorded, with middens recorded at Polka Point in Dunwich, at Point Lookout in the north-east, and elsewhere.

South-east Queensland is a generally well-watered region with rich and varied food resources for hunter-gatherers. It is transitional between a tropical and temperate environment, with great variability in topography, flora and fauna. Like other regions in eastern Australia, it seems to have been sparsely populated during the Pleistocene, with only sporadic use of optimal sites and areas.

Then came a major environmental change, with the melting of polar ice caps causing a global rise in sea level and flooding of former river valleys such as that of the lower Brisbane River. Moreton Bay came into being, and when sea level stabilised about 6,000 years ago, extensive mangrove, mudflat and estuarine areas developed, which were fabulously rich in food. Coastal resources had been exploited before but never on this scale, for conditions during earlier times of fluctuating sea levels did not produce the biological abundance of the last 6,000 years.

The increase in resources led to population increase and social changes, such as the development of far-flung trade and marriage networks.[2] Many rockshelters were occupied for the first time between 6,000 and 5,000 years ago, such as Bushrangers Cave (see below), Platypus shelter on the upper reaches of the Brisbane River, Gatton shelter on the east of the Dividing Range and Maidenwell shelter on the eastern slopes of the Bunya Mountains. Huge gatherings of hundreds of Aboriginal people came together for the runs of sea mullet in Moreton Bay in winter, or the summer crops of bunya nuts in the Bunya Mountains.[3]

The largest remaining stands of bunya pines can be seen in the Bunya Mountains National Park, 240 kilometres north-west of Brisbane, off the Warrego Highway at Jondaryan or Dalby. The nuts are almond-shaped and about the size of a small hen's egg, and grow in large cones in the tree's distinctively rounded crown. The trees fruit every year but every three years there is a particularly abundant crop. Each tree had its individual owner, who was the only person allowed to climb it to harvest the nuts. He would use vines to help him climb the tree; traditionally toeholds were not allowed, although some are visible on bunya pines today, testimony perhaps to the period when traditional law had broken down. The nuts were eaten raw or roasted, tasting rather like roast chestnuts.

These bunya feasts could bring together 600 to 700 people from groups normally living up to 450 kilometres apart, from as far north as the Bundaberg region and as far south as the Tweed River. Marriages were arranged, and items such as possum skin rugs, hunting nets, dilly bags, shells, necklaces and weapons were exchanged. Their complex religious life is evidenced by the large number of ceremonial grounds which used to exist in the region; regrettably few have survived, but some examples are described below.

There is a marked increase in both the number of sites and in the intensity of site use since 4,000 years ago, as well as in the spread of new tool types, the development of labour-intensive food processing such as the large-scale processing of cycad nuts, and widespread changes in art systems. The last few thousand years were a period of change and development in Aboriginal society, well demonstrated in south-east Queensland through the work of John Beaton, Jay Hall, Peter Lauer, Ian Lilley, Ian McNiven, Mike Morwood, Robert Neal, Mike Rowland, Grahame Walsh, Ian Walters and other archaeologists.

In Moreton Bay there was a significant increase in site numbers and in the intensity of exploitation of marine foods such as shellfish within the last thousand years, evidenced at sites such as Sandstone Point (see pages 138-39).

The coast

Great Sandy National Park, Fraser Island

Fraser Island is the world's largest sand island, 120 kilometres long and up to 22 kilometres wide. There are only four small outcrops of volcanic rock on the island, three at Orchid Point in the north-east and one on the west coast. All the rest of the island is sand, together with tall rainforest where valleys between dune ridges have become filled with humus-rich soil. There are also many perched, freshwater lakes, formed when vegetable matter and minerals have combined to cement the beds of depressions among the high inland dunes well above sea level.

Aborigines exploited the rich marine resources of the island, and many of their middens can be seen along the east coast. (These may be viewed, but must not be disturbed in any way.) Peter Lauer of the Anthropology Museum, University of Queensland, (a museum worth a visit), has made a particular study of Aboriginal lifeways and prehistory on Fraser Island.[4] He has shown that Aborigines have been fishing and collecting shellfish on Fraser Island for more than a thousand years, and importing stone material for their tools from the mainland.

Fraser Island is 70 kilometres north-east of Maryborough, and can be reached by vehicular ferry from Urangan and River Heads. Four-wheel-drive vehicles are essential, and even for them, tracks are often impassable. The best time for a visit is between May and October.

Landsborough grinding grooves

West of the Bruce Highway about thirty-five kilometres south of Nambour and one kilometre south-west of Landsborough is a well-preserved group of grinding grooves. There are about 50 concave depressions worn into 3 separate sections of exposed sandstone along the bed of Little Rocky Creek, where Gympie Street crosses it on a wooden bridge. The grooves lie within 40 metres to the west and 80 metres east of the bridge. The site is signposted and partially fenced. Please do not walk or drive over the grooves, or light fires in the vicinity.

The grooves are generally about 30 centimetres to 35 centimetres long and 10 across. These dimensions are typical of grooves produced by manufacturing or re-sharpening the blades of stone axes. Suitable pieces of hard rock were selected from a quarry and shaped into an ''axe blank'' by flaking off any projections. The axe blank was then gradually ground to a sharp edge and polished by abrading it on sandstone, using water as a lubricant. Constant use of sandstone surfaces for this purpose produces oblong or dish-shaped grinding grooves. When axe blades became dull and blunt through use, they were re-sharpened, resulting in long, narrow, deep grooves.

This is the largest set of grinding grooves in the Brisbane region, with much of its original environmental setting undisturbed. The site also has historical significance, as the old Cobb and Company coaches once crossed the creek here, and marks left by steel-rimmed coach wheels can still be seen on some of the sandstone east of the bridge.

Glass House Mountains National Park

Behind the Sunshine Coast south-west of Maroochydore the spectacular Glass House Mountains rise abruptly from the coastal plains. The tallest hills mark the sites of volcanic eruptions about 25 million years ago. (Access is from the Bruce Highway between Glass House Mountains township and Beerburrum.) There are four small national parks around four of the major eroded volcanic plugs. The shape and position of these is explained by Aboriginal oral traditions, which recount how:

> Tibrogargan stands looking out to sea as he did in the ancient past with his children around him. Once he saw the seas disturbed and swelling. He collected the younger children and led them away to the mountains. He sent Coonowrin to help his mother, Beerwah, who was heavy with child. But Coonowrin ran to safety without her. So angry was Tibrogargan that he chased Coonowrin and when he caught him smashed him so hard on the head with his club that he dislocated his neck. So Coonowrin stands today with his crooked neck and Beerwah still awaits the birth of her child.[5]

This explains the two peaks whose faces are always turned away from each other, Tibrogargan and Coonowrin, and Coonowrin's crooked neck as he stands in shame, unable to face his father, since he deserted his pregnant mother, Beerwah, during the rising of the seas.

Beerburrum bora ring

This well-preserved bora ring lies north of Beerburrum and 2.7 kilometres south-east of Glass House Mountains township. It is signposted east from the Bruce Highway, and lies on a ridge with excellent views out towards the Glass House Mountains. The bora ring has a 5 metre wide embankment, enclosing a circular area about 22 metres in diameter. On the north side a slight depression in the ring suggests the possible existence of a path which once led off to another ring. Such rings were used by Aborigines mainly for male initiation ceremonies.

Moreton Island National Park

Moreton Island lies 50 kilometres north-east of Brisbane, and can be reached by vehicle ferries from Bulimba, Manly, Cleveland and Scarborough, and by passenger ferry from Redcliffe or Hamilton. (The island's roads are suitable only for four-wheel-drive vehicles, and there is just one resort, Tangalooma.) The island of almost 19,000 hectares is made almost entirely of sand. It is some 34 kilometres long and 11 kilometres wide at its widest point, with a surf beach running virtually unbroken along its eastern side. Wind-blown dunes surround high, forested dune ridges and perched lakes along the central spine of the island. These culminate in 285 metre high Mount Tempest, the highest stabilised coastal dune in the world.

Middens are concentrated on the north-east, north-west and south-west coasts.[6] Several archaeological excavations have been carried out, notably by Jay Hall of the University of Queensland, which have shown the strong reliance of the islanders on the resources of the sea: fish, shellfish and turtle. Dugong were also exploited, but may be fairly recent immigrants into Moreton Bay, attracted by the development there of seagrass beds which they require as fodder. Dugong were reported in their thousands by early European settlers but their bones are absent from middens on the island older than a few hundred years. The oldest site on the island found so far is about 1,500 years old, but it is likely that Moreton Island was inhabited well before this.

Toorbul Point fish trap

This is a well-preserved example of a stone-built fish trap, rare on the east coast. It was still in use in the 1950s.[7] The wall of local rock extends out from the shore over an area of about 75 metres by 35 metres in the form of a circle. At high tide the circle of stones is covered, but as the tide drops the fish which have come onto the mudflats to feed are caught as the water runs out through the stones.

The fish trap is easily accessible and is on the beach about one kilometre south of the Bribie Island bridge (on the mainland side) between Toorbul Point and Sandstone Point. Toorbul Point bora ground is five kilometres inland, and other bora rings have been recorded on nearby Bribie Island.

The pattern of prehistoric occupation would seem to have been that people gathered on the peninsula to visit relatives or hold ceremonies, had a base camp at Sandstone Point and collected fish from this fish trap only a short distance away. Fishing was the most efficient way of feeding large numbers of people gathered on the foreshores of Moreton Bay. Fish traps are now quite rare in the southern half of the continent, and there are only a few on the whole of the east coast.

One of the most remarkable fishing methods to be used by Aborigines in Moreton Bay was to train dolphins to herd schools of fish towards shore where they could be more easily speared or caught in nets. This is well documented in a number of historical accounts. It seems that

> So well did the Aborigines and porpoises understand each other that the blacks laid claims to individuals in the same way they do with dogs, and it was death by the law to kill or injure any of these. They have a very keen sense of hearing, and it was by this means that the natives were enabled to call them from a distance of a quarter of a mile or so when their services were required to drive a school of fish into the shallow water, where they could be taken with the tow-rows [scoop nets] or hand nets.[8]

Sandstone Point midden

This lies some three kilometres to the south-west of the Toorbul Point trap and the Bribie Island bridge, between the rocky outcrop of Sandstone Point and the extreme south-east corner of Godwin Beach. Its position below a wave-cut coastal cliff affords an unrestricted view of northern Moreton Bay, and it is easily accessible from Godwin Beach township to the south-west. The huge midden complex covers some 25,000 square metres and has been in use for more than 2,000 years.

The Sandstone Point midden was clearly a focal point for large ceremonial gatherings. It is the richest coastal midden site yet found in Moreton Bay, and is remarkable for the great quantity of fish bones it contains, possibly 90,000 specimens per cubic metre. This scientifically significant archaeological site has the potential to yield further invaluable evidence about the prehistory of Moreton Bay, and may be visited but not disturbed in any way.

Toorbul Point bora ground

In south-east Queensland the past ceremonial activities of Aborigines have left a material expression in earth-rimmed bora grounds and arrangements of stones. The Toorbul Point bora ground is in excellent condition and is probably the most well-defined and best preserved of its type in Queensland (figure 10.2). It is one of the very few remaining examples of a ceremonial ground where both rings and the connecting pathway are preserved. The rings were used for corroborees and ceremonies, particularly initiations, and for formal fights. The site is a public reserve, easily accessible and sign-posted and lies 13 kilometres east of Caboolture in the Brisbane area.

Bribie Island

There are both numerous middens and a bora ground on the island, and an excellent display on local Aboriginal culture in the Abbey Museum on the old Toorbul Point Road, Caboolture.

Brisbane area

Samford bora ground

The Samford bora rings are a well preserved, intact example of this type of Aboriginal ceremonial site, with a large and a small earth-banked circle connected by a pathway. They are in Samford about 30 minutes drive north-west of Brisbane, on a small reserve held in trust by the University of Queensland.

Nudgee bora ground

The Nudgee bora ring seems to be the only surviving bora ring within the city of Brisbane. It is preserved in a recreation reserve at the intersection of Nudgee Road and Child's Road in Nudgee, next to a waterhole and not far from the shore of Moreton Bay. The site consists of an oval mound approximately 50 centimetres high with diameters of 21 and 17 metres. Two large depressions exist in the mound, one of which may represent a gap for the pathway which previously led to

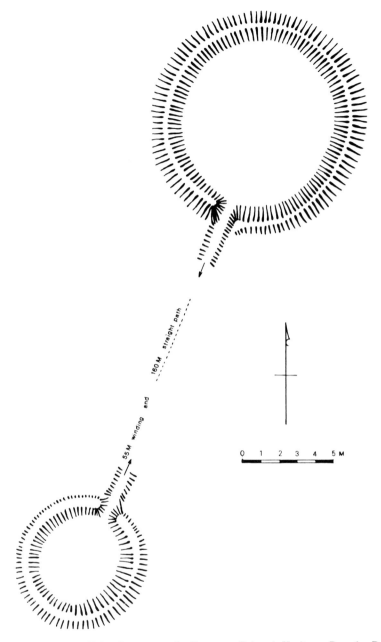

Figure 10.2 Toorbul Point bora ground. (Courtesy Cultural Heritage Branch, Department of Environment and Heritage, Brisbane)

a second ring. Historical records suggest that the pathway was originally about 300 metres long and led to a second ring on the western side on "Mr Kunde's farm", possibly in the vicinity of what is now Red Hill Road. This bora ground was apparently last used for ceremonial purposes about 1860. The site has been fenced and abuts onto playing fields to the north and ti tree swamp on the other sides.

Gold Coast area

Lamington National Park

This park, 100 kilometres south of Brisbane, is reached from Beenleigh via Canungra, or from Nerang via Beechmont. It contains many Aboriginal sites such as scarred trees and old campsites. Near Binna Burra is the Cooking Cave, where the remains of cooking fires and animal bones are visible. This is well-known and accessible to visitors, but please do not disturb any of the occupational material in the floor of this or other sites.

A spectacular large cave is Bushrangers Cave in the south-east of the park at over 700 metres above sea level just below Mount Hobwee, some 50 kilometres west of Southport on the Gold Coast and 1.5 kilometres north-west of the Queensland/New South Wales border gate. (Grid reference Tweed Heads 1:250,000 map 6301494; walk up on the Queensland side of the border, between two fences.) The cave forms a shallow arc behind a seasonal waterfall on the headwaters of the Nerang River, facing north-east over lush vine forest to the Numinbah Valley. It is a huge shelter, 60 metres long and up to 8.5 metres wide, beneath a soaring rhyolite cliff, with a spring at the south-eastern end supplying a year-round drinking supply (plate 10.1).

Plate 10.1   Bushrangers Cave. (J. Hall)

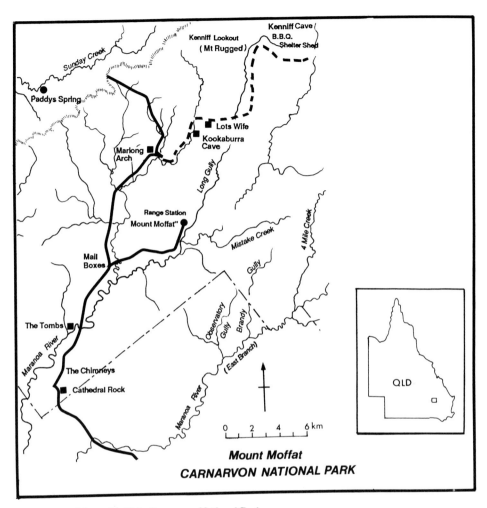

Figure 10.3   Mount Moffatt, Carnarvon National Park

This excellent camping place provided a hideout and stable for bushrangers operating in the Tweed Valley in the mid-nineteenth century. For 6,000 years prior to that it was home to Aborigines, who are thought to have used it as a short-term camp for groups travelling around or across the Lamington Plateau.[9] The remains of numerous prehistoric cooking hearths were found in the excavation by Jay Hall, together with burnt animal bone and a few artefacts can be traced by of stone. It is hoped that the source of these artefacts can be traced by mineralogical matching of the raw material of artefacts with prehistoric stone quarries.

The Central Highlands

Kenniff Cave and the Carnarvon Ranges

The Carnarvon National Park contains some of the most important archaeological sites and finest rock art in Australia; in particular the art of stencilling on rock reaches here its height of artistic expression. The park lies about 765 kilometres north-west of Brisbane and 470 kilometres west of Rockhampton. It can be approached by road either from Injune to the south or Rolleston in the north. There is an airport at Roma and an airstrip about four kilometres east of the park visitors' centre, camping area and lodge at the foot of Carnarvon Gorge.

The oldest site in the Carnarvon Ranges, Kenniff Cave, is not in Carnarvon Gorge but in an extension to the national park to the north-west on what used to be Mount Moffatt property. This is reached by driving some 200 kilometres northwards from Mitchell on the southern side of the range. (There are no facilities or fuel at Mount Moffatt, the tracks are rough and four-wheel-drive is desirable.) Kenniff Cave is about 22 kilometres north-north-east of Mount Moffatt homestead, past Junction Hill at the head of the southern branch of Meteor Creek, at an altitude of about 770 metres above sea level (figure 10.3 and plate 10.2). A track leads to the site which is protected against vandalism by a grille (keys available from the ranger).

Excavations in the 1960s by John Mulvaney[10] through three metres of occupational debris in the earth floor of Kenniff Cave showed that this site had been inhabited by Aborigines 19,000 years ago. Kenniff was the first archaeological site in Australia to be firmly dated to the glacial period, so its discovery caused much excitement. It is also still the "type site" for Australian stone tool industries; here Mulvaney found an unusually wide range of stone tools and set up a cultural sequence which has stood the test of time remarkably well. The lower industry, lasting from 19,000 to 5,000 years ago, consisted of large,

Plate 10.2   Kenniff Cave, containing evidence of 19,000-year-old occupation. (D.J. Mulvaney)

heavy hand-held stone tools such as choppers and dome-shaped scrapers, whereas the more recent industry saw the appearance of new specialised small tools and the technique of hafting.

Kenniff Cave also contains colourful rock art. Red, white, yellow and black pigments were employed and the motifs are mostly stencils of hands, feet and boomerangs. The colour was blown from the mouth around the object held against the rock wall. Some unusual stencils in the cave are a hafted axe, a pair of baby's feet, a shield and some weapons unknown in historic times. There are also a few freehand paintings of criss-cross and linear designs and a human figure. (The cave is fairly dark inside and flash is needed for photographs.) The cave averages about three metres of headroom, and is reputed to have been the hideout of the Kenniff brothers, the notorious bushrangers and cattle-duffers of the region. It is said that they even occasionally kept their horses inside the cave, to hide them from pursuing police. Not far away in Lethbridge Pocket, which you pass through to get to the cave, is the large flat rock where they cremated the bodies of their last victims.

Also on the Mount Moffatt section of the Carnarvon National Park is the Tombs, south-west of Mount Moffatt homestead. Human occupation of this large rockshelter, likewise excavated by Mulvaney, apparently began about 9,500 years ago, and it demonstrated the same change in stone tools as Kenniff Cave. The art is also similar; there are some 180 hand stencils, a few foot and boomerang stencils, and a remarkable red stencil of a whole human body with arms outstretched, as if guarding the site. This is Australia's largest known stencil. Other rare stencils are of a spear-thrower, kangaroo paws, and ovals which are likely to be Che-ka-ra shell pendants,[11] possibly of *Melo* or *Nautilus* shells. These are thought to have been traded down from the north Queensland coast, a distance of some 1,300 kilometres. There are also freehand paintings of bird tracks, rectangles and criss-cross patterns, the significance of which is unknown.

In this rugged Carnarvon Range outcrops of sandstone, about 150 million years old, are capped by harder basalt and have been worn by wind and water erosion into curious pillars and towers. A superb sandstone formation known as the Arch lies some six kilometres north-west of Mt Moffatt homestead, and contains numerous red handprints and linear engravings. Further up Marlong Creek from the Arch, on top of a steep bank, is Kookaburra Cave, as it is known locally from the apparent depiction of a kookaburra. (This is more likely to be a decayed hand print.) This cave contains stencils, deeply incised linear engravings and superb naturalistic human and macropod tracks.

The Carnarvon Gorge

The greatest concentration of Aboriginal sites in the Carnarvons lies in Carnarvon Gorge itself, and most of these are readily accessible to the visitor by the network of walking tracks (figure 10.4). The gorge is a spectacular twisting chasm, 32 kilometres long, with vertical white sandstone walls which soar up to 183 metres above the bed of Carnarvon Creek. There platypuses play in deep pools but sometimes the spring-fed creek disappears underground, only to surface again. Its banks are lined with the cabbage-tree palm, *Livistona nitida,* tree ferns, *Cyathea cooperi,* the cycad, *Macrozamia moorei,* and a myriad mosses and ferns,

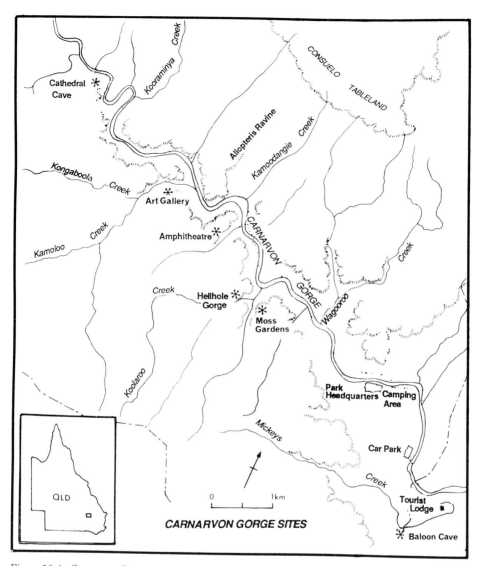

Labels within figure: Cathedral Cave, Kooraminya Creek, CONSUELO TABLELAND, Angiopteris Ravine, Kamoodangie Creek, Kongaboola Creek, Art Gallery, CARNARVON GORGE, Kamoloo Creek, Amphitheatre, Creek, Hellhole Gorge, Moss Gardens, Wagooroo, Creek, Koolaroo, Park Headquarters, Camping Area, Mickeys, Car Park, Creek, QLD, Tourist Lodge, CARNARVON GORGE SITES, 0 1km, Baloon Cave

Figure 10.4 Carnarvon Gorge

including the extremely rare *Angiopteris* fern with fronds over four metres long. Tributary gorges radiate from the main one, and the rock walls are honeycombed with caves and rockshelters.

There are some 50 Aboriginal sites in Carnarvon Gorge. Most of them are art sites, some of which were also used as camping shelters or burial sites. Some 5,500 "pictures" have been recorded in these sites, two-thirds of them in the two largest sites, the Art Gallery and Cathedral Cave (figure 10.5).[12] The main sites worth visiting for visitors with limited time are Baloon Cave (Baloon is an Aboriginal word for stone axe), the Art Gallery and Cathedral Cave (plates 10.3 and 10.4). All these are accessible, signposted and open to visitors. Baloon Cave is reached by a short easy walk through cabbage-tree palms from near Carnarvon

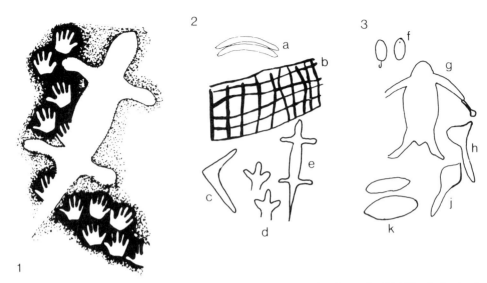

Figure 10.5 Rock art in Carnarvon National Park. 1. Goanna and hand stencils. 2.(a) Matched pair of hunting boomerangs (Art Gallery). 2.(b) "Net" patterns (Art Gallery and Cathedral Cave). 2.(c) V-shaped killer boomerang (Art Gallery and Cathedral Cave). 2.(d) Composite stencil of tracks, made from boomerang tips (Art Gallery). 2.(e) Freehand white goanna (Art Gallery). 3.(f) Che-ka-ra shell pendants (Art Gallery and Cathedral Cave). 3.(g) Freehand outlined humanoid figure (Cathedral Cave). 3.(h) Unusual Lil-lil type club (Cathedral Cave). 3.(j) Broad spade type club (Cathedral Cave). 3.(k) Shields or coolamons (Art Gallery and Cathedral Cave). (After National Parks and Wildlife Service, Queensland)

Plate 10.3 Cathedral Cave, Carnarvon National Park

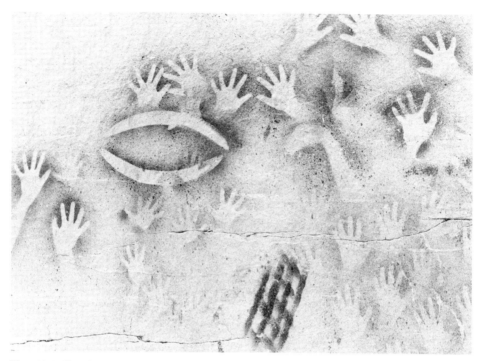

Plate 10.4 Stencils in Carnarvon National Park

Lodge, and is accessible to the disabled. Best viewing time is early morning, when the orange and red pigments stand out brilliantly against the white rock. The cave contains some striking stencils of large stone axes and over sixty hand stencils, including one with apparent mutilations, although it has been found that these distorted hands can usually be produced by bending back the fingers and only in rare cases are joints of the fingers really missing.

The major sites are the Art Gallery and Cathedral Cave. These are open to the public, well signposted and contain boardwalks and interpretive signs. The walk to and from the Art Gallery requires about half a day, and if Cathedral Cave is also visited, which is well worthwhile, a full day (and picnic lunch) should be allowed. Also worth a visit is the Amphitheatre on the south side and *Angiopteris* Ravine on the north side of the creek on the bend to the north before the Art Gallery. The Art Gallery is adorned with some of the finest stencil art in Australia.

The white sandstone walls of this 62 metre long rockshelter are covered with a vast network of colourful designs (which are best photographed in the middle of the day). It contains at least 1,343 engravings and 646 paintings and stencils. Among the engravings animal tracks and vulvas dominate. Numerous stencils of boomerangs range from the large V-shaped killer ones to a small leaf-shaped hunting type. Shields and coolamons (carrying dishes) have been stencilled, and stone tomahawks. There are also trick stencils: the impression of giant birds feet has been given, it seems by stencilling the tips of three boomerangs together.

The most striking of the art motifs are extensive "net" patterns, which are actually all composite stencils, made by multiple stencilling of a pair of spread fingers. Blowing pigment between the fingers produced a V-shaped positive line, and designs were formed by lines of overlapping stencils. Grahame Walsh, the expert on this stencil art, believes that this composite stencilling technique was used because it allowed a far sharper outline and more vivid colour than freehand painting on such coarse-grained and porous rock. There are also white "goannas", and when the light is suitable, a most unusual faint painted "face" with round eyes is visible below the large white "net". Engravings are concentrated in the centre of the wall, and feature animal and human tracks, zigzag lines, groups of abraded oval depressions (possibly symbolising nests of emus' eggs), and the human vulva, which is frequently portrayed and may have a ceremonial purpose.

The walls of Cathedral Cave are likewise covered with engravings, stencils and paintings. Red and purple are the predominant colours and hands the most common stencilled motif. There are also many stencils of weapons, including a broad-headed spade type of weapon (probably a type of flat club), and some Lil-lil throwing clubs, with the unusual feature that the "hump" is on the reverse side of the boomerang-type handle. In Queensland such clubs are known only from their stencilled images. Some thirty stencils occur of Che-ka-ra shell pendants, on some of which the string has also been stencilled. Among the freehand paintings, red and white "net" patterns predominate, whereas among the engravings animal tracks are most common. There are also a number of engraved "nests of emu eggs", one of which contains 21 "eggs". Panels of engraved tracks extend 90 centimetres below present ground level, and human occupation of Cathedral Cave goes back 3,500 years. One of the economic staple foods used from that time was the nut of the cycad, *Macrozamia moorei,* which is extremely toxic unless leached. Processing is a lengthy and complicated exercise, but the large nuts, when detoxified, were used as a staple carbohydrate food by Aborigines here and in various other parts of Australia.

Blacks Palace Reserve, Tambo region

Blacks Palace (also known as Marsden Cave) is the largest complex of art sites known from the Central Queensland Highlands. The art is spectacular, and includes engravings, stencils and colourful polychrome paintings[13] (plate 10:5). Eight art sites are in close proximity in a sandstone gorge, a group of axe-grinding grooves lies at its head, and another 34 art sites lie within a 10 kilometre radius. Blacks Palace was declared a Scientific and Recreational Reserve (R39) as long ago as 1933, and has been known and visited by Europeans since last century. Over the years there has been a good deal of vandalism, and Blacks Palace has the dubious distinction of being Queensland's most vandalised site. Originally there may have been as many as 200 bark burial cylinders in rock crevices at this site, but all have now disappeared. Nevertheless, most of the art is well-preserved and at last the site is being properly protected and presented to the public by the Queensland heritage authorities by means of a National Estate grant from the Australian Heritage Commission.

Access is via a track on Marston Station, which is approximately halfway between Tambo and Alpha. The site lies at the headwaters of the Barcoo River, at Australian Map Grid DP3520 on the 1:250,000 Tambo map; further information

Plate 10.5   Blacks Palace: Australia's largest stencil site, Central Queensland highlands. (G. Walsh)

regarding access may be obtained from the Cultural Heritage Branch of the state government in Brisbane.

The gorge is about 500 metres long and 200 metres wide at the open end. The brilliant white sandstone cliffs rise to a maximum height of 25 metres and eight rockshelters at their base along a 153-metre-long stretch bear rock art. This includes stencils, freehand paintings, abraded grooves and some pecked engravings. The main colours used were red, purple, brown, yellow and white. Substantial deposits of ochreous sandstone in all these colours occur about three kilometres east of the gorge, and it is very likely that these deposits served as the pigment source for the artists of Blacks Palace.

The rich array of art of Blacks Palace has been studied by Michael Morwood of the University of New England. He recorded 9,471 individual marks. Abraded grooves predominate, which were probably rubbed by Aboriginal visitors to the sites as a form of "signature". There are also engravings of tracks and vulvas (some filled in with red or yellow ochre), and various geometric motifs. Stencils are the second most common art form here, and include complex panels telling a story. Hand stencils are most numerous, but there is an unusually wide range of other stencilled items, such as human feet, boomerangs, steel axes, bird and macropod feet, spears, clubs, shields and dilly bags. There is also a faint yellow stencil of what appears to be a Snider carbine rifle.

The number and range of paintings is unusually high. Most of the 348 paintings are net, grid and zigzag designs, but there are also painted bird tracks, discs, ladder-like motifs, two lizards and a 9.8 metre long snake. There is an enormous amount of over-painting and superimposition of art techniques and motifs in the region. Freehand paintings in white pigment of net motifs with oval perimeters seem to be most recent, and pecked engravings precede the other art.

Blacks Palace's diversity of colours, techniques and motifs is only approached by two other sites in the region — the Art Gallery and Cathedral Cave described above. It is Australia's largest stencil art site, and probably the largest anywhere in the world.

CHAPTER ELEVEN

Central Australia

About 60 per cent of the Australian landmass in its centre and west falls within the arid zone. Rainfall in the region is sporadic and low averaging between 120 mm and 350 mm per annum, and much of the area is desert. For a long time it has been thought that penetration of the arid centre of the continent might have been beyond the capabilities of prehistoric hunter-gatherers until some time in the last few thousand years. The greatest barrier to the colonisation of Australia might not have been the crossing of the seas or the occupation of the tropical north but the extension into the dry heart. Aborigines were inhabiting the whole of the desert regions at the time of first European contact, including arid country which caused the death of several European "explorers", but how far back in time did this pattern go?

The first indications of a considerable antiquity for the occupation of Central Australia came in the early 1970s from the excavation of Puntutjarpa rockshelter in Western Australia by Richard Gould,[1] who found 10,000-year-old occupation in this harsh region of the western desert. Nevertheless until recently researchers such as Sandra Bowdler[2] believed that colonisation of Australia was coastal, ice-age occupation being confined to the coasts, major river valleys or lakes such as Lake Mungo in western New South Wales (see chapter 16) which, although within the semi-arid zone, is fed by waters from areas of higher rainfall and lies up a river valley only about 400 kilometres inland.

Evidence of 20,000-year-old underground flint-mining at Koonalda Cave[3] on the arid Nullarbor Plain in South Australia was likewise explained by relative proximity to the coast. Nor did the discovery of 21,000-year-old and 26,000-year-old occupation deposits in two rockshelters[4] in the Hamersley Ranges in the Pilbara region of Western Australia upset the coastal colonisation theory, because although they would then have been around 500 kilometres inland from the lower ice-age sea level, they were connected to the coast by rivers. Rivers such as the Fortescue, now usually dry, would then have held water because of reduced evaporation in the cooler glacial climate. The local environment would have been less arid and ice-age migrants could have gradually moved into the interior along such rivers.

A dent was put into this theory by the discovery of a cooking hearth containing

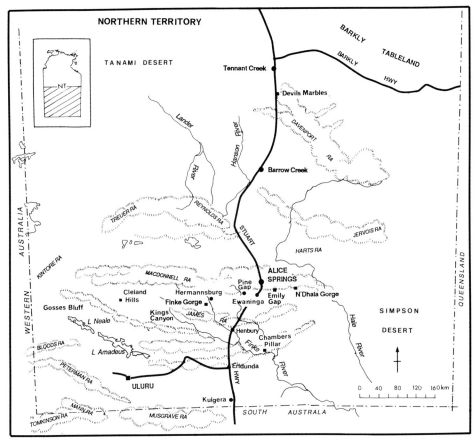

Figure 11.1   Central Australia

freshwater mussel shells dated to almost 14,000 years in the dunefields of the Strzlecki Desert,[5] but it was not until 1987 that the first proof came that the arid heart of Australia was inhabited in the ice age. This was the discovery by Michael Smith of the Northern Territory Museum of 22,000-year-old human occupation in the Puritjarra rockshelter, almost in the centre of the continent (figure 11.1).[6]

Puritjarra is a large rockshelter in the Cleland Hills, near the eastern boundary of the Western Desert, about 320 kilometres west of Alice Springs in the Northern Territory. (The site is not open to the public. The area is within the Haasts Bluff Aboriginal Reserve, and to enter Aboriginal land a permit must be obtained through the Central Land Council in Alice Springs. It may be possible on occasion to visit the area by special arrangement, but application should be made at least a month in advance to allow time for traditional owners to be consulted.)

This region of Central Australia is environmentally diverse, with spinifex grasslands and mulga woodland broken up by the complex topography of the central ranges. Rainfall averages less than 350 mm a year, but the ranges have some good natural water storage ranging from permanent springs and waterholes to deep rock "reservoirs" and soakages in creek beds. All of the rivers in the region, such as the Finke, are intermittent, but they usually contain some waterholes and soakages in their beds.

Puritjarra is a huge rockshelter, 45 metres across the entrance and about 20 metres high, in a cliff formed of a hard red sandstone, which has fractured both vertically and horizontally, resembling towering red brick walls (plate 11.1). An extensive array of rock art in stencil, engraved and freehand techniques is present. The stencils are dominated by adult hands, but also include unusual examples of artefact stencils, and there seems to be a change of pigment preference to white in the later phases of stencilling. The freehand art is mainly monochrome, with a few examples of bichrome, and includes "story panels" based on animal tracks. Engravings are relatively few, and feature motifs such as pecked circles and deeply abraded lines.

The shelter is situated close to the only permanent water in a region of 8,000 square kilometres, and provides about 400 square metres of level, shaded earth floor. It was used by Aboriginal people for camping until the 1930s, when the area became depopulated as the people moved onto missions and government ration depots in the western MacDonnell Ranges.

A small test excavation by Michael Smith late in 1986 revealed three stratigraphic layers. The uppermost is a loose, gritty light-brown sand containing intact cooking hearths, charcoal, flaked stone tools, grindstones, ochre and emu egg-shell. This layer spans the last 6,000 years, but also gives evidence of a major

Plate 11.1 Puritjarra rockshelter. The tiny figure sitting in the centre gives some idea of the vastness of the shelter. (G. Walsh)

increase in occupation of the region during the last 1,000 years. Layer 2 is compact, fine red clayey sand. The lowest artefacts found so far in the site come from this layer at a depth of 66 to 77 centimetres below present ground surface, and are associated with charcoal which gave a radiocarbon date of 22,000 years. Below this is the rubble of layer 3. A second season of excavation in 1988, funded through the National Estate Grants Program, uncovered two definite artefacts — a bifacially flaked core and a modified flake — and other dubious stone tools in this hard, compact layer. The minimum age for these artefacts is 38,000 years, and this is a conservative estimate on the preliminary thermoluminescence dating for this layer (M. Smith pers. comm.).

One fascinating find was a piece of red ochre associated with the 22,000-year-old charcoal. This suggests that art was being practised in the desert heart as elsewhere in Australia just as early as in other parts of the world such as the caves of France and Spain. By 13,000 years ago ochre was concentrated against the back wall of the shelter, a clear suggestion of rock art.

Between 22,000 and 13,000 years ago, the shelter was used only occasionally, and no more than a few artefacts were deposited each millennium. The climate was probably responsible for this low use, for between 25,000 and 16,000 years ago it was increasingly dry and windy, with widespread drying of lakes, extensive dune-building and an expansion of the arid zone. From about 7,000 years ago this site was used more intensively, with the most intensive use occurring during the last 2,000 years.

The main significance of Puritjarra is that, in one stroke, it more than doubles the known antiquity of human occupation of the arid heart of the continent. At last researchers know that even extreme aridity did not deter Aboriginal people from penetrating the harshest deserts of Australia more, possibly much more, than 20,000 years ago. Occupation of this antiquity has now been found in all the main environmental zones of the continent.

The Cleland Hills are also significant for their rock art, particularly the famous engraved "smiling human faces".[7] Not everyone believes them to be faces, but some certainly seem to have stylised eyes, nose and mouth in a heart-shaped face (figure 11.2 and plate 11.2). The "eyes" resemble concentric circles with a central

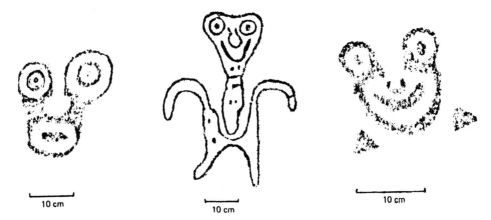

Figure 11.2 Human figures (?) at Cleland Hills. *Left:* asymmetric, "sad" face. *Right:* "happy" face with a curious body. (Drawings based on photographs by R. Edwards 1968)

Plate 11.2 A heart shaped face at Cleland Hills, damaged by rock fracturing and erosion. (G. Walsh)

pit, but the "nose" and "mouth" give a strong visual impression of a human face. They are all pecked and weathered and are quite small (about 30 centimetres high by 10 to 20 centimetres wide). One has a body with two legs and strange wing-like arms, another has two triangular pecked depressions on either side of the "chin" and two long vertical lines extending down from these, possibly delineating the sides of a body (plate 11.3). A further "face" motif in the same alcove has an extension from the "neck" area tapering to form a shape like an incomplete angular boomerang.

There is a great range of motifs present besides the 16 faces which are on record. Subjects include the ubiquitous tracks and circles, but also a pair of strange anthropomorphous figures seen in side view and an owl-like motif. Another curious figure is a solitary engraving on an exposed rock section of a dog-like creature. There was minimal patination on this motif, so it could be one of the area's more recent engravings. If it was intended to portray a dingo, its fresher appearance would fit with the estimated entry of the dingo into Australia about 4,000 years ago.

Parallels for these archaic faces have been found in equally weathered engravings in the Pilbara region of Western Australia, and it is thought that they have great antiquity. The Cleland Hills examples are clustered around Thomas "reservoir", a small gorge about 18 kilometres from Puritjarra containing a seasonal water source, which must have been a focal point for Aborigines living in this extremely dry environment.

Plate 11.3   A smiling face figure with "body" at Cleland Hills. (G. Walsh)

Both habitation and art continue in Central Australia from the earliest sites up to the present day. Within this long period perhaps the most important innovation was the introduction of distinctive seed-grinding technology, apparently some 4,000 years ago. Seed foods were among the most widely available, predictable and dependable foods available in this arid country.[8] In recent times edible seeds were harvested from a large number of trees, shrubs and grasses. More than 70 of the 140 known plant food species in Central Australia were exploited for seeds. In particular the seeds of five are considered to be staple foods: mulga, woollybutt grass, native millet, and the exceptionally nutritious pigweed with close to 20 per cent protein and 16 per cent oil content.

The hard mulga seeds were gathered, roasted in hot soil, then cracked and ground into flour on a millstone. Similarly grass seeds were gathered, winnowed and husked, and ground into a paste with water. Wet milling of seeds was done on large, flat-surfaced sandstone millstones with one or more long shallow grooves worn into the surface. The millstones usually weigh between 4 and 30 kilograms and measure from 40 to 60 centimetres long by 30 to 40 centimetres wide by 2 to 15 centimetres thick; the grooves are usually about 30 centimetres long by 10 centimetres wide by 1 to 2 centimetres deep. Millstones bear distinctive use-wear; the ground surfaces are smooth and finely abraded, and are often covered with a reflective polish, which is a silica polish or "sickle gloss" produced by seed-grinding. With the millstone a top-stone or muller was used; these are thin hand-held seed-grinding artefacts with an oval, rectangular or triangular shape and one flat or convex surface which often also exhibits use-polish. They are much smaller than the millstones, averaging 100 to 250 grams in weight, 8 to 10 centimetres in length and 1 to 3 centimetres thick.

Millstones have been found in archaeological deposits in arid Australia such as Puntutjarpa and Intirtekwerle (James Range East) rockshelter,[9] which lies near Deep Well some 100 kilometres south-east of Alice Springs. The original excavation at the latter suggested 10,000-year-old occupation, but further investigation by Smith revealed that major habitation at the site did not commence till around 850 years ago, with very sparse occupation extending back 5,000, not 10,000, years. The stratigraphy suggested that a massive build-up in the level of the sand plain has taken place over the last 5,000 years, the ultimate origin of the sediment being the Simpson Desert dunefield. This means that many sites in Central Australia are likely to be deeply buried by sand if they are older than 5,000 years.

At present the only two sites with long cultural sequences spanning the last 10,000 years in the Red Centre are Puritjarra and Puntutjarpa. At Puntutjarpa the lowest of the specialised seed-grinding stones comes from a layer estimated to be about 3,500 years old, at Puritjarra they are confined to the last 2,000 years and at James Range East to the last 700 years, where they make up 10 per cent of the stone artefacts. These specialised seed-grinders therefore appear to have developed in Central Australia not more than about 4,000 years ago, although other types of grinding apparatus are known from Pleistocene contexts elsewhere. Other widespread changes in the toolkit follow this development in Central Australia. For example, at Puritjarra around 3,000 years ago distinctive new artefacts appear such as backed blades.

The same pattern has been found in a number of other prehistoric sites, both rockshelters and open campsites, across Central Australia; in each case an ephemeral use of the site is followed by much more intensive occupation, represented by a high density of millstones and chipped stone artefacts and a dark-grey layer with burnt animal bone. This major upsurge in intensity of site use seems to have occurred only during the last 2,000 years.

What is the explanation of the development of a seed-gathering economy? The most likely answer would seem to be that it resulted from a need to produce more food in a time of stress, caused either by an increase in population or an unfavourable environmental change, or both. There is some evidence from the pollen record at Lake Frome and elsewhere[10] that a relatively wet phase from about 7,000 to 4,200 years was succeeded by a long dry period from 4,200 to 2,200 years ago. This environmental stress could have provided the catalyst for the development of seed-grinding.

It is also likely that population was increasing in the centre of Australia as in other parts of the continent, and nearing the carrying capacity of the land, so that the land could not support more people without the development of new food resources. The fact that specialised seed-grinders were produced only during the last 4,000 years suggests that the new technology was not just a reaction to environmental stress, which had happened before, but that the population density was also significantly higher than during earlier arid periods. In other words there were more mouths to feed at a time when water, and hence food, were increasingly scarce.

Seeds are high-cost resources in terms of labour and time. From five to eight hours of one person's time (usually a woman's) were required to collect and process one kilogram of flour from grass or acacia seeds. This meant that seeds tended to be exploited mainly when other better alternative plant foods such as fruits, roots and tubers were not available, although Aborigines appreciate diet variety and the sweetness of at least some of the seed foods. The use of seed foods was nonetheless a fundamental part of the recent Aboriginal pattern of land use throughout the arid core of Australia. It enabled population to be maintained at existing levels even in drought years and during the lean period of the annual cycle late in the dry season, when other bush foods were rapidly depleted. It also meant that large ceremonial gatherings could be held. Some seed foods such as that known as mungilpa grow on claypans in prolific quantity, sufficient to feed several hundred people for a few days or longer. People gathered for ceremonies when it was ripe.[11]

Aborigines in Central Australia have been called the lizard eaters, but they could equally well be called the seed-grinders. These desert people inhabited the most hostile environment in Australia and consequently were the most nomadic in the continent in the continual seasonal round of foraging for food and life-giving water. Nevertheless they found time to develop a remarkably rich and complex religious and artistic culture.[12] There are literally millions of artistic representations and other sites scattered through the Red Centre, and many of these sites are still maintained by their traditional owners. A small selection of prehistoric sites which are open to the public is described below.

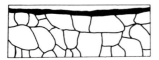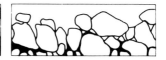

Figure 11.3 Granite weathering at the Devils Marbles. *Left:* a single mass of granite was divided by joints into rectangular blocks. *Centre:* more rapid erosion of the corners and joint lines gradually rounded off the blocks. *Right:* less resistant rock was eroded away, and harder boulders became separate and more rounded. Reproduced with permission from *Scenic Wonders of Australia*, Reader's Digest (Aust.) Pty Ltd, 1976, p. 289

Devils Marbles Conservation Reserve

On both sides of the Stuart Highway near Wauchope, 97 kilometres south of Tennant Creek, are the Devils Marbles, a group of huge, spheroidal granite boulders dominating the surrounding undulating arid plains. These dramatic egg-shaped rocks are an important Aboriginal Dreaming place, the rocks being eggs layed by the rainbow serpent in the Dreamtime. The Devils Marbles is a registered sacred site — that is, a site of traditional significance to contemporary Aboriginal people, registered by the Aboriginal Areas Protection Authority.

This rare geological formation results from spheroidal weathering. The original granite mass broke along joint planes into roughly rectangular blocks up to 7 metres high, which were then gradually rounded into almost spherical boulders by erosion and the flaking away of the surface layers (figure 11.3). This spheroidal weathering is caused by continual expansion of the rock by day and contraction at night, due to the extreme changes of temperature experienced in such arid environments. At the same time oxidation of some minerals in the granite weakens the rock, producing flaking of the surface layers. Brown and red iron compounds present in the granite produce wonderfully glowing colours in the light of the setting sun, and sunset is the best time to visit this particular site.

Kweyunpe: Pine Gap Conservation Reserve

Aboriginal paintings can be seen in this reserve in Pine Valley, only about 16 kilometres south-west of Alice Springs and west of the Stuart Highway on the southern flank of the MacDonnell Ranges. The reserve lies a kilometre east of the Joint Defence Space Research Facility at Pine Gap, and the last road to the right before reaching the latter is followed across a cattle grid to a parking and barbecue area. Several rockshelters containing paintings and debris from prehistoric occupation lie within the reserve, which is open to the public. The rockshelter at the western end of a low sandstone ridge closest to the fence and parking area has been partially excavated, together with another at the eastern end of the ridge, which contained occupation dating back 2,000 years.[13] The rock art is not very well-preserved, but the motifs are extensive, varied and characteristic of the rock art of Central Australia. There are both hand stencils and hand imprints in red and purple, together with several concentric circles, linked circles, bird tracks, bars, large U-shaped arcs, long vertical elliptical symbols and snakes. Some of the motifs are painted in two colours, and Aboriginal traditional owners of the Arrernte (pronounced Arunta) people have explained that the red ochre was applied first, left to dry for three days and then the white pipe-clay was applied. There are also a few weathered engravings — pecked tracks and circles — near an ephemeral rockhole in the bed of a small creek about halfway along the ridge. The Kweyunpe sites are of significance to the Arrernte people, and were first described by anthropologists Spencer and Gillen in 1899.

Emily and Jessie Gap Nature Park

These two rocky gaps contain a rare resource in this arid region — semi-permanent water. Emily Gap lies 8 kilometres east of Alice Springs and Jessie Gap a little further east. Both are dramatic gorges cut through the rocky quartzite spine of the east MacDonnell Ranges. Both are registered sacred sites and contain some rock paintings.

The Udnirr Ingita site at Emily Gap is significant to present-day Arrernte Aborigines as a caterpillar Dreaming, with other sites in the MacDonnell Ranges, which have a remarkably caterpillar-like form. On the eastern side of the gap shallow alcoves in the rock walls are decorated with impressive, tall caterpillar Dreaming figures, painted in vertical red and yellow stripes. The lines represent the decorative designs painted on men participating in ceremonies at the site. The paintings mark the place where Intwailuka, ancestral hero of the Arrernte, cooked and ate caterpillars on his Dreamtime journey. Aboriginal custodians believe that these paintings were not painted by human agency but were laid down in the Dreaming, and have been there "since the beginning". This is why custodians are particularly sensitive about them and they are classed as tywerenge (pronounced churinga) or sacred objects. The paintings may be viewed but no photographs of them may be published. Sometimes it is just a simple short walk to this site, but when the gap's sandy floor is full of water, there is no access to the paintings. Similar paintings exist on the eastern side of Jessie Gap but they are not so well-preserved.

N'Dhala Gorge Nature Park

Near the historic Ross River homestead, 89 kilometres east of Alice Springs, is N'Dhala Gorge (pronounced En-dala), which is a major focus of engravings, studied in 1980–81 by Sarah Forbes of the Australian National University.[14] The track from Ross River homestead leads southwards through strongly dissected sandstone country to a carpark at the south-eastern, downstream end of the main gorge (figure 11.4). In steeply dipping sandstone ranges rising to 700 metres above sea level, the gorge has been incised by a creek which then flows across several kilometres of low-lying sandplain to meet a west-east tributary of the Ross River.

The main gorge runs from south-east to north-west and is about a kilometre long; a walking track leads up to it, initially across alluvial flood plains through which the usually dry stream channel winds, and in the upper reaches between escarpment faces above talus slopes strewn with giant boulders. An 800 metre long side gorge runs northwards from the main gorge on its northern side approximately 300 metres from its downstream end. (For the visitor this side gorge is easy to miss; it enters the main gorge on the right about a quarter of a kilometre from the carpark, where the creek bed is close to the rock wall.) This side gorge is 20 metres wide at the maximum and averages only 10 metres, whereas the width of the floor of the main gorge ranges from 20 to 80 metres.

A water supply persists in N'Dhala Gorge after the surrounding country has dried out. This made it a natural focus for prehistoric occupation. There are several rockholes and the water in the more sheltered rockholes remains long after the stream beds have stopped running after rain. There is one semi-permanent rockhole in the side gorge, some 200 metres from its southern end, which usually contains water; it is a narrow crevice in the rocks approximately 1.5

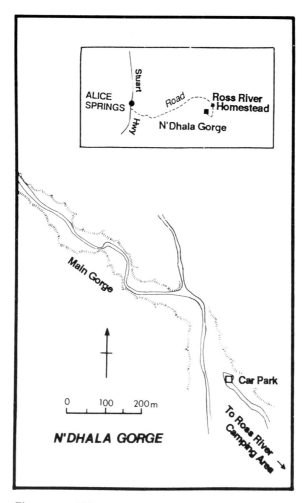

Figure 11.4 N'Dhala Gorge

metres deep, and holds a small amount of water long after all other rockholes in both gorges are dry.

The sheltered microclimate of the gorge makes it a favourable environment for an abundance of trees and shrubs, in contrast to the arid surrounding lowlands and ranges. The most common trees and shrubs are the cypress pine, native fig, ghost gum, bloodwood, whitewood, corkwood, ironwood, native fuschia and various species of *Grevillea* and *Acacia*.

Almost 6,000 engravings (5,982) have been found in N'Dhala Gorge, dispersed in 819 discrete areas of artistic activity or "sites", which may be individual engraved boulders or discrete clusters of engravings on the same rock surface such as a continuous cliff face. In addition there are two painting sites (in the side gorge), a hunting hide and a number of traces of habitation, including grinding stones. There are 438 engraved sites in the main gorge and 240 in the side gorge. The number of engravings at each site ranges from one to 268, but 76 per cent have less than 10 and 20 per cent contain only one motif.

Engravings are found in a wide variety of localities, from cliff faces to the tops and sides of large boulders, small rocks or horizontal rock slabs. The prehistoric artists showed a preference for engraving on horizontal surfaces; in 35 per cent of cases a horizontal surface has been selected rather than a sloping or vertical one. This is not explicable in terms of environmental factors but must be a cultural preference.

Almost all (97 per cent) of the engravings are pecked, a series of deep pecks in the rock being placed next to each other to achieve a precise solid line. These were produced by the technique of indirect percussion, using a sharp, hard tool of wood or bone and a hammerstone rather like a hammer and chisel. A very few engravings are shallow, very fresh-looking marks with diffuse edges produced by simple direct pounding.

The pecked engravings are older than the pounded ones, and most of them are patinated to the same colour as the surrounding rock, whereas the younger, pounded ones stand out fresh and white. It has not yet been possible to establish their absolute age, but most are likely to have an antiquity of many millennia.

The most common engravings are pecked solid areas of no specific shape (18 per cent) or marks which are indistinct (5 per cent), probably because of their great age, but many others are distinguishable and 78 individual motif types have been identified. Among these tracks of macropods (15 per cent) and birds (12 per cent) are most common, followed by plain circular rings (6 per cent) and deeply engraved circular pits (5 per cent). There are also several examples of wavy irregular lines, curvilinear mazes, sets of U-shaped concentric lines, concentric circles, rayed figures from a stalk and anthropomorphous figures. Like most early engravings sites in Central Australia the majority of motifs (in this case 44 per cent) are non-figurative, comprising circles or other motifs which appear geometric or abstract to the outside viewer, but which would have had specific symbolic meanings to the original artists. Among figurative motifs tracks predominate markedly.

Some of the most unusual subjects are anthropomorphs, with huge head-dresses on top of small but unmistakably human bodies. These figures probably depict ancestral creator beings. A striking pair of these anthropomorphs is found on a large sloping rock slab at the top of the main gorge, where the walking track terminates (plate 11.4). Another pair is located near the foot of the main gorge in a dramatic position overlooking the junction of two creeks.

Another unusual motif which occurs fairly widely at N'Dhala Gorge is a rayed figure from a stalk. These motifs appear fern-like at first glance, but they may well have a ceremonial significance, since some have a forked appendage on the bottom possibly representing legs and a penis. A particularly fine panel of these figures is found on a large sloping boulder immediately to the left of the walking track in the lowest part of the main gorge, among the first engravings past the carpark.

The size of the engravings varies from 1 centimetre to 224 centimetres, with a mean size of 13.7 centimetres; half of them are less than 10 centimetres. The mean width of the engraved lines is 2 centimetres, with 47 per cent being 1 centimetre wide. Generally the artists did not increase the width of motifs with increased length, but there is one interesting exception to this. As the tracks of birds or macropods get longer, they also get fatter. In other words, when

Plate 11.4   Rock engravings at N'Dhala Gorge Nature Park

representing tracks the artists retained realistic proportions. It may be significant that the lines which make up the fern-like rayed figures with stalks do not increase in thickness on the taller figures, perhaps indicating that they are not part of the natural world but rather ceremonial or supernatural. Analysis of width/length relationships may therefore be a useful way of trying to distinguish between naturalistic and non-naturalistic motifs in prehistoric art.

The engravings were probably executed over many thousands of years, and although it has not so far been possible to find out their absolute age, the relative extent of erosion on various motif types has been established. (Microscopic examination of engraved surfaces revealed that the amount of deterioriation of the calcium-based cement matrix between the mineral grains in the sandstone varied considerably; in recent engravings the matrix was nearly level with the top of the surrounding grains whereas in older engravings on the same rock surface the matrix had eroded away leaving the grains sticking out like mini rock towers.)

This microscopic examination of the extent of erosion of various motif types established a rough relative sequence of the most commonly repeated forms at N'Dhala Gorge. What emerged was that concentric circles are the oldest motifs, radiating line figures are later and tracks and naturalistic figures such as goannas later still. Moreover it is highly unlikely that all the engravings were made in a short period.

A study of the subject matter of the fresher engravings in comparison with patinated ones revealed that macropod tracks are more numerous in the recent engravings than earlier, whereas for bird tracks the opposite is true. This suggests that here a dominance of macropod tracks characterises the more recent engravings. This may mean that the engravings of the side gorge are more recent than those of the main gorge, since the side gorge has almost twice as many macropod tracks but fewer bird tracks, more human figures, fewer pits and fewer concentric U-shapes.

N'Dhala Gorge contains one of the most extensive arrays of rock engravings in Central Australia in a magnificent setting. There is a wide variety of motifs including both the characteristic circles and tracks of early desert art and some unusual subjects such as anthropomorphs. The majority of the engravings are considered to be of high antiquity, probably more than 10,000 years old.

Ewaninga Rock Carvings Conservation Reserve

In arid red sandplain country 39 kilometres south of Alice Springs lies an extensive group of prehistoric Aboriginal rock engravings, located on a small cluster of sandstone outcrops rising to 7 metres. These overlook a claypan, which acts as a natural bowl, holding water even after light rain and attracting many birds and animals. Long ago rockshelters beside the claypan provided good camping places for Aboriginal people, but now their roofs have collapsed in a jumble of sandstone blocks.

The soft and easily fractured red sandstone was a superb medium for Aboriginal engravers. The motifs are deeply pecked and have weathered back to the same colour as the parent rock. When engravings are newly made they stand out white and fresh, and it generally takes many hundreds or even thousands of years for the colour to revert to that of the surrounding rock. Cracks across the

Plate 11.5   Ewaninga Rock Carvings Conservation Reserve

Plate 11.6 Chambers Pillar Historical Reserve. (D. Chinner, Conservation Commission)

engravings caused by natural weathering also indicate considerable antiquity. However, some are relatively recent, and their meaning is known to Arrernte Aboriginal custodians. The name Ewaninga is said to mean a place of rocks with small cave hollows.

A walking track leads visitors to the two main areas of prehistoric art, where a series of sandstone blocks are covered with a complex mass of engravings (plate 11.5). Some engravings are in such inaccessible positions that it is clear that the blocks have broken away from the main rock outcrops since the motifs were executed. Subjects are mainly non-figurative and include simple, barred and concentric circles, spirals, wavy and meandering lines and round, pecked-out hollows and pits. There are also what appear to represent animal and emu tracks, and the site is associated with emu Dreaming mythology.

Many of the engravings are very weathered, and are best seen in late afternoon or early morning, when shadow effects make the shallow peckings much easier to see. The Ewaninga engraved art is a good representative example of that of much of Central Australia. Its significance lies in the large number and wide variety of well-preserved engravings and their probable great antiquity.

Chambers Pillar Historical Reserve

This spectacular pillar of sandstone towers 50 metres above the surrounding open sand dune country, 160 kilometres south of Alice Springs on the edge of the Simpson Desert (plate 11.6). (Four-wheel-drive is required to negotiate the dunes around the pillar.)

Sandstone beds were laid down in the region 350 million years ago. Since that time the softer material has been eroded away by wind and rain so that all that now remains is this solitary column of pebbly sandstone.

Chambers Pillar was named in April 1860 by John McDouall Stuart, heading north on his first attempt to cross Australia, and it became a prominent landmark in European "exploration" of Central Australia, being visited by John Ross in 1870 and Ernest Giles in 1872. Long before, Aboriginal people had become familiar with the striking rock formations of this region, and explained their origins. In the Dreamtime, they said,

> the gecko ancestor Itirkawara [pronounced it-turk-kar-wara] left the Finke River and travelled north-eastward. As he travelled he grew into a huge and powerfully built man of superhuman strength and extreme violence of temper. On the way home to his birthplace he successfully challenged and killed, with his stone knife, a number of other unfortunate ancestors. Flushed with the ease of his successes he then disregarded the strict marriage code and took a wife from the wrong kin group. His enraged relatives promptly banished him and the girl. The two retreated into the desert, Itirkawara raging impotently in fury, the girl shrinking from him in deep shame. Among the dunes they became weary and turned into prominent rocky formations — Itirkawara into the Pillar, the girl, still turning her face away from him in shame, into the low hill to the north-east, about 500 metres away.[15]

This hill is known as Castle Hill.

There used to be very, very faint Aboriginal paintings in a small cave near the base of the pillar, but the cave was destroyed by an earth tremor several years ago. There are also historic graffiti of European explorers and early pastoralists.

Henbury Meteorite Conservation Park

This park 150 kilometres south of Alice Springs contains 13 craters formed 4,700 years ago when a meteorite shower came from the south-west and plunged to earth.[16] The metallic meteor, weighing thousands of tonnes, entered the earth's atmosphere at a speed of more than 40,000 kilometres per hour. The intense heat generated by the friction of the air against the meteorite would have made it incandescent until finally it disintegrated shortly before impact at Henbury. This is a site where one needs a good imagination, for all that remains now of this stupendous impact is a series of shallow craters.

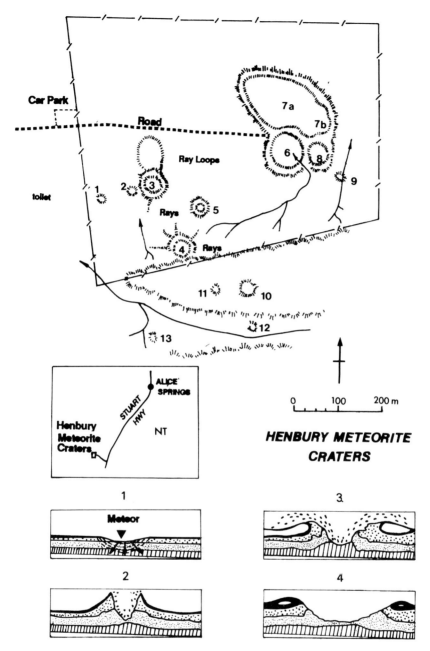

Figure 11.5 Henbury meteorite craters. *Impact Crater Formation.* 1. A shock wave spreads from the point of impact and compresses the rocks. 2. The rocks react against the compression and expand, thrusting material up and outwards. 3. Some rock layers fold back; others break, ejecting fragments, some of which form rays and ray loops on the ground. 4. The final crater 60 to 80 seconds after impact. (After Conservation Commission)

The Henbury "explosive" craters were excavated by meteorites which penetrated a short distance into the earth before breaking up with a massive release of energy (figure 11.5). As a result of the violent release of compressive forces, sheets of rock near ground surface were folded back to form the rims of craters and fragments of the meteorites were dispersed over a wide area. Several tonnes of these fragments have been recovered, many torn and twisted, resembling shrapnel. They are composed of iron (90 per cent) and nickel (8 per cent). The largest piece found weighed 100 kilograms, a chunk weighing 44 kilograms is on view in the museum in Alice Springs, and other pieces may be seen in the South Australian Museum in Adelaide and the Smithsonian Institute in Washington DC in the United States.

Three large craters are clustered together with ten smaller ones nearby. The largest crater is 183 metres wide and 15 metres deep with a rim 6 metres above ground surface, and the smallest is 6 metres wide and a metre deep with a rim only a few centimetres high. Some of the craters have associated ejecta rays and loops which are patterns of ejected material. These phenomena are also present on the Moon and other planets in the Earth's solar system, but are apparently unique on Earth. Henbury meteorite craters have therefore been of great importance in helping scientists to understand the formations visible on other planets. Prior to and during the manned Moon missions they were used for familiarisation purposes by the United States National Aeronautic and Space Administration personnel.

The 16 hectare park is open to the public and there are walking tracks and basic facilities (but no shade or water!). The craters lie 150 kilometres south-west of Alice Springs, in a rocky area at the base of a sandstone ridge on the northern side of the Bacon Range. The turnoff from the Stuart Highway is 136 kilometres south of Alice Springs, from where travellers head west for 8 kilometres on the road to Kings Canyon, and then north for 5 kilometres.

Gosses Bluff

Gosses Bluff is one of the best-documented and most significant comet impact structures in the world.[17] It lies some 160 kilometres west of Alice Springs and 50 kilometres west of Hermannsburg, and a good view of it is obtained from the Tylers Pass trigonometric station, 16 kilometres north of the bluff (plate 11.7). It is a registered sacred site, and a permit for a visit is required from the Aboriginal

Plate 11.7   Gosses Bluff comet impact crater. (Bureau of Mineral Resources)

Areas Protection Authority. Access is through Aboriginal land, so a second permit is needed from the Central Land Council.

This astro-geological feature is an erosional remnant of a huge crater produced by impact of a comet, an agglomeration of frozen carbon dioxide, ice and dust. The crater is about 4 kilometres in diameter, with a sub-circular ring of sandstone hills with steep outward-facing cliffs. The hills stand about 180 metres above the level of the surrounding plain and 250 metres above the internal "Missionary Plain". The area contains Aboriginal hunting hides, old campsite evidence and rockshelters with red hand stencils.

The ring of hills that can be seen today is all that now remains of the core of the original crater. An estimated 2,000 metres of erosion since the time of the impact about 130 million years ago has removed all trace of the original outer rim. The core was formed when deeply burned sediments were disrupted by the release of massive compressive forces built up as the comet struck the earth. The pressure release upturned sedimentary formations near the focus of impact; subsequent erosion has left only some of the more resistant sandstone formations forming upstanding relics of the crater core. Satellite images of the area indicate that the original crater was some 20 kilometres in diameter, for the bluff has a large "halo" which probably represents the extent of affected rock.

No material of extra-terrestrial origin has been found at Gosses Bluff, but there are in the area smaller structures known as shelter cones. These are cone-shaped fractures with distinctive "horsetail" marks on their surface which are produced by the type of extreme shock generated by the impact of a comet or meteorite. Study of the shatter cones has enabled scientists to determine that the object which struck the Earth at Gosses Bluff probably had an extremely high velocity (40 kilometres per second or 144,000 kilometres per hour) and low density (1.3 grams per cubic centimetre). This indicates that the object was a comet, and that on impact energy of the order of 22,000 megatonnes of TNT was released. In other words the comet which struck Central Australia about 130 million years ago released one million times more energy than the Hiroshima bomb.

Uluru (Ayers Rock–Mount Olga) National Park

Uluru National Park covers an area of 1,325 square kilometres of arid country, approximately 450 kilometres by road south-west of Alice Springs (some four hours drive on sealed road). It is on the World Heritage List as well as the Register of the National Estate and is an Aboriginal national park, in that it is a park that has been declared essentially on land owned by Aboriginal people. "Declaration of Aboriginal national parks adds a vital new dimension to the concept of Australian national parks, by presenting Aboriginal cultural aspects as a primary consideration in park management and by recognising the benefits to all of cooperative management."[18] At present the Commonwealth of Australia and the Northern Territory lead the world in the concept and development of national parks on traditionally owned land, with joint management between Aboriginal people and the federal government (represented by the Australian National Parks and Wildlife Service) in the case of Uluru and Kakadu, or in other cases such as the Cobourg Peninsula, the Conservation Commission of the Northern Territory.

Uluru is arguably the most distinctive symbol of the Australian landscape. (Uluru

Plate 11.8   Uluru. (D. Roff)

is pronounced oo-loo-roo, with the emphasis on the first syllable, as in other Pitjantjatjara words.) This stark red monolith rising out of the desert almost in the centre of Australia conveys a powerful image of the age-old nature of the continent and symbolises its inhospitable nature.

The park's two outstanding features are the huge monolith of Uluru (Ayers Rock) and the dramatic rock domes of Kata Tjuta (the Mount Olga group) (plates 11.8 and 11.9).[19] Kata Tjuta means many heads, and the smooth conglomerate residuals, unbroken by caves, give exactly that impression. Thirty-two kilometres away Uluru towers 340 metres above the red desert and sand ridges, with a circumference of 9.4 kilometres. Around its base are rockshelters and caves weathered into fantastic shapes, suggestive of many explanations.

Aboriginal owners of the rock, Pitjantjatjara and Yankunytjatjara people who refer to themselves by the collective name of Anangu, explain the formation of Uluru and Kata Tjuta in terms of Tjukurpa (pronounced djoo-koor-pah), the traditional law that guides daily life and explains existence and all features of the landscape.[20] Virtually every feature within the park is explained as the visible imprints of the activities of particular Tjurkurpa ancestral beings. Each of these sites is a tangible proof that the events of the Tjukurpa actually took place. Tjukurpa is a religious philosophy; when Anangu describe features within Uluru or Kata Tjuta, they refer to religious, not scientific, explanations.

Contemporary Western explanations are more prosaic, and go back not to the time of creation but only to the Proterozoic era about 1,200 million years ago.[21] Then this part of the earth's surface was a folded, rocky area which was being

Plate 11.9   Kata Tjuta (Mount Olga group). (D. Roff)

weathered and eroded. Slowly it was depressed and innumerable layers of sediments were deposited on top of the hard granite, gneiss, lava and quartzite still visible today as large rounded pebbles in the conglomerate rock of the Olga Gorge.

Later, about 600 million years ago, massive pressures began to fracture the southern end of the basin of Lake Amadeus, a large salt lake to the north of Uluru. The great pressure pushed the rocks of the Amadeus basin some 50 kilometres northwards, where rocks finally overrode the basin's edge. Severe folding resulted, and ranges of mountains arose composed of a vast mixture of rocks from earlier times. Rapid erosion of the ranges ensued, the granite and other materials collapsed into gullies, and were swept down creeks, rounded and deposited in thick layers in the sinking Amadeus basin. In some places the delta deposits were pebbly and boulder-strewn, in others sandy. The pebbly beds became the conglomerate of Kata Tjuta, and the sandy deposits became arkose, a type of sandstone rich in feldspar, of which Uluru is composed. It has been discovered that the conglomerate extends to a depth of 6 kilometres below present ground level. Subsequently, movement of the basin tilted the Kata Tjuta conglomerates about 30 degrees and the Uluru arkose 75 degrees, and erosion gradually reduced them to residuals. About 70 million years ago Uluru was an island in a huge lake; the many caves and "bays" around its base were carved out by weathering and erosion at this time. Erosion continues, and the fine red sands which surround the residuals are derived from the weathering of the ancient rocks.

The caves around the base of Uluru are adorned with hundreds of rock paintings (figure 11.6). These are found in two principal groups, on the southern side at Mutitjulu (pronounced moor-ti-djoo-loo) and on the north-western side directly north of "the climb". These can be seen on the Mutitjulu and Mala walks. This

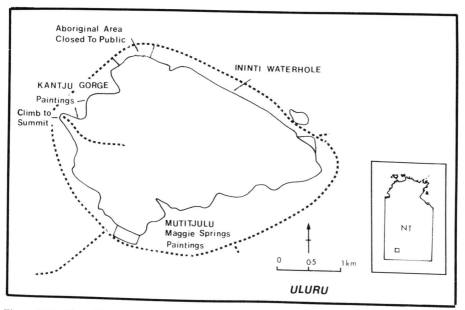

Figure 11.6   Uluru (Ayers Rock)

body of rock art, whilst generally poorly preserved, is a good representative sample of the art of the Western Desert.

Most of the paintings belong to the secular part of Aboriginal life and decorate the walls of rockshelters used as traditional camping places. Subjects include distinctive "tree" or "fern" type motifs, animals, reptiles and tracks (even a camel's track at the main Mutitjulu site!), together with many circles and other motifs whose meaning is now unknown. Rock painting was still being done in 1940, but since then there has been serious deterioration, mainly caused by visitor pressure and environmental degradation, particularly the loss of vegetation which used to protect the shelters from the disastrous effects of sand-blasting by the desert winds.

Engravings have fared better, but there is only a small number of engravings at Uluru, mainly near Ininti waterhole, whereas engravings are more common than paintings at Kata Tjuta, which lacks the caves and rockshelters of Uluru.

Most art sites are open to the public, and the Anangu and Australian National Parks and Wildlife Service have developed an excellent brochure: *An Insight into Uluru*, with an introduction and information on the Mutitjulu and Mala self-guiding walks. (It is VITAL to obtain this from ANPWS offices or the Visitors Centre in Yulara Village, as there is NO on-site information.)

The huge monoliths of Uluru and Kata Tjuta are not only remarkable geological phenomena, but also have important cultural, aesthetic, environmental and scientific values, as well as great symbolic significance for Aborigines and non-Aborigines alike.

Watarrka (Kings Canyon) National Park

This newly declared national park lies approximately 325 kilometres west of Alice Springs, and is reached via Wallara Ranch. Kings Canyon is a valley below soaring red walls and is one of the most spectacular gorges in Central Australia. A walking track leads from the carpark up the spur on the left-hand side of the valley onto the top of the cliff. Thence it wends its way between deep fissures and strange rock formations along the plateau top until it is possible to scramble down into the valley of the main creek. Deep permanent rock pools occupy the bottom of this steep-sided, shaded gully, which can be followed down for a few hundred metres until it ends halfway up the cliff face at the head of the canyon. Here there is a beautiful rock pool and a magnificent view out along the cliffs which form the sides of the canyon (plate 11.10).

Cycads *(Macrozamia macdonnellii)* are found in this gully and in other well-shaded and watered areas. The cycads are among about 60 rare or relict plant species, which have survived in this "oasis" from a period when dinosaurs walked a wetter, more fertile Australia, more than 50 million years ago. The flora and fauna of Kings Canyon are very rich; at least 572 different plant species have been recorded there, together with about 80 species of birds.

Some traces of past Aboriginal use of the canyon survive, and engravings occur at a rock pool within the canyon on its western side. There are many occupation sites, engravings, stencils and a considerable number of paintings in the Kings Canyon region, especially along the southern escarpment of the George Gill Range beside a series of permanent springs, such as Lila (Reedy Rockhole) and Wanmara (Bagot Spring). Occupation going back more than 2,600 years has been found at Wanmara.

Finke Gorge National Park (Palm Valley)

Four-wheel-drive is needed to reach this national park, as the last 16 kilometres into the park follows the sandy bed of the Finke River. The Finke River has the

Plate 11.10 Kings Canyon National Park

Plate 11.11 Rare palms in Finke Gorge National Park (Palm Valley). (D. Chinner Conservation Commission)

distinction of being claimed as the oldest river in the world, on the basis that its course has not changed in more than a million years. The park is 19 kilometres south of Hermannsburg and 138 kilometres west of Alice Springs, from where tours in four-wheel-drive buses are usually available.

The most notable features of the park are the 50 kilometre long twisting Finke Gorge and Palm Valley, where stand 3,000 or more relict palm trees which occur nowhere else in the world (plate 11.11). These unique cabbage palms *(Livistona mariae)* have survived in this area from a time when the climate in Central Australia was much wetter. Cycads, *Macrozamia macdonnellii,* are also present in the gorge. Except for these relics sheltering in damp gorges along the Finke River, palms are found only in the east, north and north-west of Australia, in such places as the gorges of the Bungle Bungle National Park in the Kimberley.

The lush green of these bushy palms, cycads, ferns and mosses growing by rock pools along Palm Creek is in strong contrast with the bare sandstone cliffs and barren ranges of the surrounding country. This lost valley holds great traditional significance for Aboriginal people, and a large sandstone residual, Initiation Rock, was once the site of initiation ceremonies for Arrernte youths. There are also rock engravings in the valley.

Rainbow Valley National Park

A new national park is currently being established south of Alice Springs, about 25 kilometres east of Orange Creek homestead. Striking, multi-coloured rock formations and a large claypan are the focus of an area which central Arrernte Aborigines call Wora or Urre and Europeans — Rainbow Valley. About 2 kilometres east of Wora is a rockhole and large engraving site with over 1000 individual engravings. The motifs are mainly arcs, circles and tracks, but there are several more complex designs, including one resembling a "Cleland Hills face". The rockhole and engravings lie a few hundred metres up a small gully, and near the mouth of the gully is a small rockshelter with about ten paintings of circles and tracks. Excavation of a stratified occupational deposit here has yielded a record of at least 3,600 years.

CHAPTER TWELVE

South Australia: The North

South Australia covers an area of more than a million square kilometres, but nine-tenths of this vast expanse averages less than 380 millimetres of rainfall per annum, and there is only one major permanent river, the Murray. The land was not always so arid, and a series of internationally famous fossil sites contain evidence of very different past environments. The story begins in the Flinders Ranges at least 1,000 million years ago with microscopic plant remains found in the Skillogalee Dolomite. At this time Australia formed part of a huge single continent called Gondwana, which included Antarctica, South Africa, India and South America. Shallow seas stretched inland as far as what was to become the Flinders Ranges, where traces of the first life on earth are still visible in the form of fossilised remains in sandstone and limestone.

The oldest, best preserved animal fossils in the world have been found in the Ediacara Reserve and elsewhere in the Flinders Ranges (figures 12.1 and 12.2). There, about 650 million years ago, in the Upper Precambrian age, soft-bodied marine animals made mainly of water, such as jellyfish, died in muddy patches on a beach and were covered in sand, becoming fossilised in sandstone.

Marine organisms are also found in limestone of the Early Cambrian age, about 500 million years old, in Wilkawillina Gorge, where fossils of *Archaeocyatha*, a sort of cross between a sponge and a coral, are preserved in fine detail with well-defined stratigraphy. These limestone deposits were part of a huge reef containing *Archaeocyatha*, a reef then stretching over tens of thousands of square kilometres from Kangaroo Island to the Alice Springs area.

Some of the dry lakes of the Lake Eyre region afford another glimpse into the past between twenty million and one million years ago. At that time there was a vast inland system of freshwater lakes and rivers. The Lake Palankarinna Reserve and other nearby salt lakes such as Lakes Kanunka, Pitikanta and Ngapakaldi, 70 kilometres east of Lake Eyre and 100 kilometres north of Marree, have yielded a rich menagerie of fossilised animals (plate 12.1). From the early Miocene about 20 million years ago come an amazing variety of vertebrate fossils: pelicans, flamingoes, ducks, lungfish, an ancestral koala and even crocodiles. A younger fauna occurs in the Pleistocene about one million years ago, an age which was generally warm and wet. Birds, fish, turtles and crocodiles still abounded

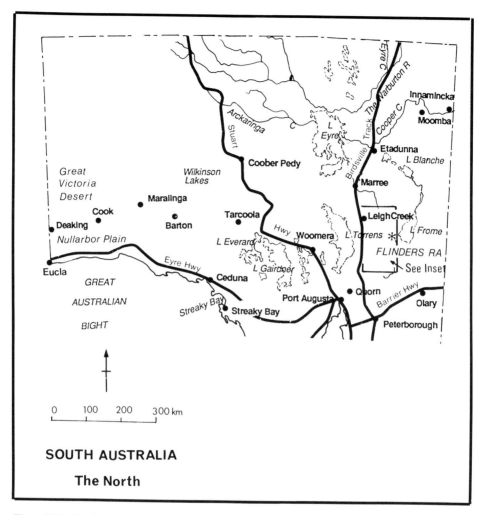

Figure 12.1 South Australia: the north

around lakes like Palankarinna, together with herbivorous marsupials feeding on the lush green vegetation of the plains. Sediments of the later Pleistocene in the same region have a rich complement of bones of fish, reptiles and marsupials, including *Diprotodon australis* of wombat-like build but the size of a rhinoceros.

A particularly notable site for *Diprotodon* is Lake Callabonna Reserve, 180 kilometres north-east of Leigh Creek. Set in the arid desert area of the north-east of South Australia, Lake Callabonna is one of numerous dry salt lakes which teemed with crocodiles and birds a million years ago. Long after the lush green vegetation disappeared in the increasingly arid environment, the giant lumbering *Diprotodon* remained, together with the huge emu-like bird, *Genyornis Newtoni,* a giant wombat, *Phascolonus,* and various now extinct giant kangaroos such as *Protemnodon* and *Sthenurus.*

The quest for water may have been the *Diprotodon's* downfall, for many animals died about 70,000 years ago after becoming bogged and sinking deep into sticky clay in the ancient lake bed. The skeletons were gradually encrusted with

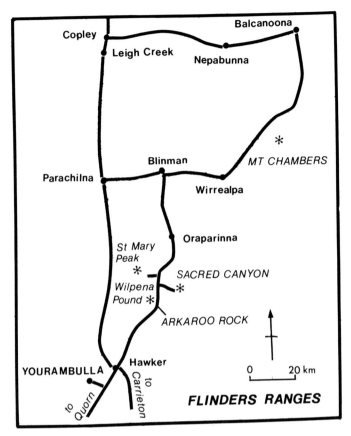

Figure 12.2   Flinders Ranges

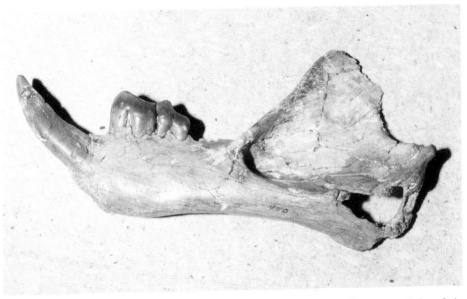

Plate 12.1   Lower jaw of a "Wakaleo", ancestor of the marsupial lion, 12 million years old, from Lake Ngapakaldi. (B. Macdonald and SA Museum)

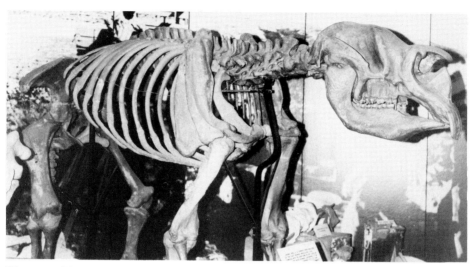

Plate 12.2   Diprotodon skeleton. (B. Macdonald and SA Museum)

gypsum-cemented clay which resulted in extraordinary preservation of feet, footprints, hides, hair and even stomach contents. Skeletons are now weathering out of the ancient lakebed, which is a veritable graveyard of Australia's largest marsupial.

Analysis of the stomach contents of a *Diprotodon* which died about 70,000 years ago has shown that it was living largely on saltbush, probably from necessity rather than by choice. A trackway of *Diprotodon* footprints has been preserved across part of Lake Callabonna, and a complete skeleton of one of these massive extinct marsupials can be seen in the South Australian Museum in Adelaide (plate 12.2).

The most visible legacy of prehistoric Aboriginal society is usually rock art, and South Australia has an exceptionally rich heritage of rock engravings and paintings. Engravings are found both in rockshelters and on open-air rock pavements, slabs and boulders in the northern part of the state, particularly in the Olary region[1] and the Flinders Ranges. The motifs are dominated by tracks of birds and animals such as kangaroos and by circles. Some of these ancient engravings appear to tell a story, such as one of the tracks of a large bird seemingly walking away from a nest full of eggs, but the meaning of most cannot be understood either by Aboriginal custodians or by archaeologists.

The Flinders Ranges are notable both for their engravings and paintings, and several Aboriginal rock art sites are open to the public. Archaeological evidence gathered by Ron Lampert of the Australian Museum, Philip Hughes of the Australian National University, Elizabeth Williams of the Australian Heritage Commission and others[2] at localities such as Hawker Lagoon has shown that Aboriginal people lived in this region at least 15,000 years ago. The age of the rock art is unknown at present, but at least some of the engravings are likely to be of a similarly great antiquity.

Descendants of the Adnyamathanha people still retell myths explaining the creation of these spectacular ranges, and these have been collected and published recently by linguist, Dorothy Tunbridge.[3] The ceremonial life of the

Adnyamathanha is no longer practised in its traditional form, but the Dreaming places where events took place during the creation period are still well remembered. Many such sites contain paintings and engravings, and some of Australia's largest ochre mines are also found in the Flinders Ranges.

Further information about sites open to the public may be obtained from the Aboriginal Heritage Branch and National Parks and Wildlife Service (see page 362). Some 3,700 Aboriginal sites are on record in South Australia.

Flinders Ranges

Ediacara Reserve

Traces of the first life on earth in the form of fossils of jellyfish and other soft-bodied marine animals dating from the late Precambrian era, about 650 million years ago, were found in this part of the Flinders Ranges by the geologist R.C. Spriggs in 1946. Marine jellyfish, sea pens and worms, soft corals, echinoderms and trilobites, an ancient crustacean resembling an enlarged pill bug, and other obscure animals unrelated to modern zoological groups were stranded in tidal flats bordering lagoons along an ancient coastline, some 650 million years ago, to be covered with sand and preserved as fossils in the sandstone. They are remarkably well-preserved as casts or moulds in the red, weathering rock, and constitute the oldest abundant and diverse marine fauna known to science.

The Ediacara Reserve of 21 square kilometres is in the Flinders Ranges about 15 kilometres east of Lake Torrens. It must be emphasised that all collecting is legally prohibited (with heavy penalties for contravention) except by permit from the South Australian Museum, which has a superb collection of the fossils on display in Adelaide.

Yourambulla art sites

The name Yourambulla is derived from the language of the Adnyamathanha or hill people of the Flinders Ranges, but the correct name for the Yourambulla Range is Yuralypila Vambata and for the caves Yuralypila Ithapi. Yuralypila are the twin rocky peaks immediately to the east of the Yourambulla painting sites, on the southern extremity of the Yourambulla Range, visible from the Hawker Road. Tradition has it that two men of different moieties, or kinship divisions, camped where the peaks now are when on a journey from the south and northeast. The larger, southern peak is thought to be the Ararru man and the smaller one the Mathari man, the two Adnyamathanha moieties being called Ararru and Mathari.

The story is told how there was a wicked old woman who lived in the valley at Yuralypila (meaning two men, and lying between the twin peaks and Mount Elm on the Yappala Range to the west), where there was then a large lagoon (which still fills occasionally), and an Aboriginal camp. She used to invite her relatives to her camp, where she killed them because she liked eating liver. She killed them in their sleep, removed their liver and threw the bodies into the large waterhole. The stone formations of the cliffs on the eastern side of Mount Elm (visible from Jervis

Plate 12.3   Yourambulla Caves main site. Flinders Ranges. (G. Walsh)

lookout) are said to be the spears and boomerangs standing up where all visitors placed them when entering camp.

When the two young men arrived at the camp they became suspicious about all the empty wurlies (bough shelters), and then found the remains of their murdered relations almost filling the waterhole. That night when it was dark the men went out and got two logs about the same size as themselves, put wallaby skin rugs over them, and lay in wait. They saw the old woman creep up and start dealing heavy blows with her throwing stick to the apparently sleeping forms. Then the man who belonged to the same line as the woman killed her, and threw her into the waterhole also. They then took off along the range, Warru Warldunha, to the north-east.[4]

Several caves and rockshelters around Yourambulla contain paintings, and three have been opened to visitors (plate 12.3). These are located about 10 kilometres south-west of Hawker off the main Hawker-Quorn road, and lie at the southern end of Yourambulla Range, with extensive views over the surrounding country. A 15-minute walk up the left-hand track leads to the main shelter, and two other shelters with grilles lie to the east at roughly the same height. The motifs have largely been painted with black pigment rather than the much more common red ochre. They are non-figurative linear designs such as rows of short parallel lines and concentric arcs, although some emu or other bird tracks occur. There are also barred circles in red ochre, and some unusual U-shaped designs. The main panel may well have been the work of a single artist, applying black pigment carefully with his fingertip. The black and red figures have a strong visual impact against the light-coloured siltstone rock, but their meaning is unknown. Surface campsites with flakes from stone-tool manufacturing are also found in the area, and probably were associated with ceremonies once carried out at Yourambulla. One of the major campsites is that at Hawker Lagoon, mentioned above.

Arkaroo Rock, Wilpena Pound

Wilpena Pound, Ikara, is said to have been created by the Akurra, two giant serpents whose bodies now form the walls of the pound. The head of the male Akurra forms Ngarri Mudlanha, St Mary's Peak, on the east side, and the female is Wilkalanha, Beatrice Hill, on the west.[5] The pound is probably South Australia's best known landform, representing an outstanding example of a perched synclinal basin bounded by relatively sheer walls (figure 12.3).

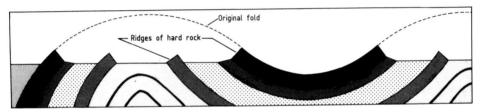

Figure 12.3 The basin of Wilpena Pound is ringed by sandstone ridges, which are the remains of large hills formed by earth movements squeezing sedimentary rocks into folds. Erosion has worn away the softer layers, leaving only ridges of hard rock. (Reproduced with permission from *Scenic Wonders of Australia*, Readers Digest (Aust.) Pty Ltd 1976, p. 210)

At the south-eastern corner of the pound is the large rockshelter known as Arkaroo Rock, which contains both Aboriginal paintings (protected by a grille and boardwalk) and occupational debris. This may be reached by a 1.5 kilometre long signposted walking trail of moderate grade from a carpark off the Blinman-Hawker Road, 15 kilometres from Wilpena. (Allow one to two hours for the visit.) The rockshelter is on the downslope side of a quartzite monolith, which has detached from the outer cliff face of Wilpena Pound and has come to rest in a small gully near the base of the Pound wall. Excavation of the shelter floor by Neale Draper has revealed two zones of occupation, the lower going back 6,000 years. The paintings feature reptile and human-like figures, bird tracks, snake-like lines, barred circles and "leaves" in red, yellow, white and black pigment. Some motifs were drawn with dry lumps of ochre, charcoal or manganese. Others were painted with wet pigment, which was mixed with water or animal fat and applied with the finger or a brush made from bark, hair or chewed twig ends.

Sacred Canyon

A narrow rocky gorge, reached from a turn-off one kilometre north of the road into Wilpena Pound, has become known as Sacred Canyon, for more than 100 Aboriginal engravings line its siltstone walls, near small seasonal pools of water. Engravings are scattered on both sides of the lower gorge but the majority lie where the canyon broadens out into the lower amphitheatre. This main gallery is roughly circular, its walls rising vertically on the upstream side. More than 150 engravings lie on these walls, bisected by the cleft through which the creek flows. Higher up the gorge is the upper amphitheatre, which has both engravings and a small cave with faint paintings in red ochre. (The best time to see and photograph the engravings is before midday, for they tend to stand out well in the morning light but shadows from the cliffs can make them sometimes difficult to see in the afternoon.)

The engraved motifs are mainly circles and other linear designs, such as concentric arcs and inverted U-shapes, together with a few bird and kangaroo tracks. The circles are remarkable for their large size, ranging from 8 to 48 centimetres in diameter. Superimpositions of one engraving on another suggest that they were executed on a number of occasions over a lengthy time period.

Mount Chambers Gorge

Mount Chambers lies about 80 kilometres north-east of Blinman; the turnoff to the east of the Wirrealpa-Balcanoona road at the junction with the road to Mulga View is signposted. Mount Chambers is known to the Adnyamathanha as Wadna Yaldha Vambata (boomerang crack hill), and is the focus of at least four myths.[6] It features in a story explaining the presence of brown coal deposits at Leigh Creek, the creation of Wilpena Pound, and the travels of two first-stage initiates or Valnaapa, who, after killing an emu, discarded parts of it at various places as it went bad, where it appears today as deposits of green copper oxide.

Another story tells how the Mount Chambers Gorge was created by the blue wren, Yuduyudulya, who hurled a returning boomerang at the eastern end of the mountain, making a big gap. The boomerang went right through the mountain and spun round towards the west, but on the way back it hit the top of the western end, and came to rest there, where it can still be seen, sitting like a knob on top of Wadna Yaldha Vambata. Expanses of white quartz are feathers used by Yuduyudulya.

Mount Chambers Gorge has sheer rock walls rising for more than 150 metres on either side, and is a favourite habitat for the euro, commonly called the hill kangaroo, which has left numerous tracks or pads up the less steep part of the gorge. Spectacularly large engravings occur before the entrance to Mount Chambers Gorge in a small subsidiary gorge entering the main Mount Chambers Creek from the north (figure 12.4). Follow the track into Mount Chambers Creek and continue along the track to a fork. The right-hand fork 9 kilometres from the main road leads to Mount Chambers Gorge, but take the left-hand fork to the end of the track, where two small creeks enter Mount Chambers Creek. Follow the right-hand creek upstream for approximately 300 metres to a small cliff. Engravings are on the cliff face on the left-hand side of the creek.

Motifs include circles, animal and bird tracks and linear patterns. About 150 metres to the north-east is the major engraving site, with over 150 engravings pecked on the cliffs on both sides of the creek (plate 12.4). Subjects include single

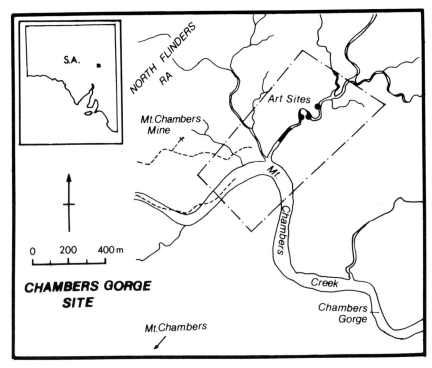

Figure 12.4   Chambers Gorge

Plate 12.4   Engravings in Mount Chambers Gorge. (B. Ross)

and concentric circles, animal and bird tracks, lizards, barred and tailed circles, a row of circles linked by a bar, and many other linear designs. Elderly Adnyamathanha informants have interpreted the engravings as associated with initiation ceremonies and food preparation. Animal tracks within circles were said to represent that species being cooked in a ground oven. Circles, lines and human footprints were associated with ceremonial rings and the smoking ovens used in initiations. Most engravings are large, and this is one of the most striking panels of engravings in Australia. Further engravings lie between 70 and 110 metres further up the creek, where it bends to the east, the engravings being predominantly on the cliff face on the left-hand side. (The best time to view and photograph the engravings is before midday. Please do not touch (or touch up!) the engravings, as this would accelerate deterioriation and any interference with Aboriginal sites is forbidden by law.)

Red Gorge, Copley

Many impressive engravings lie in Red Gorge on Deception Creek, about 20 kilometres east of Copley. It is a popular local picnic spot on North Moolooloo Station. (Telephone Copley 6 for permission.) Access is south from Copley-Depot Springs Road via Manners Well turnoff to Gorge Well and a rough track to Red Gorge, visible to the north-east. Numerous well-preserved engravings extend from the creek to the top of the 80-metre-high cliffs. Subjects include circles, tracks, humans, animals and birds[7]. Very rare motifs are dingo tracks, turtles and humans, some with boomerangs, clubs or spears.

Lyndhurst ochre cliffs

An Aboriginal ochre quarry is located 5 kilometres north of Lyndhurst. The cliffs of red ochre extend about 6 kilometres north-south and in places 2 kilometres from west to east, their western boundary being the old abandoned narrow-gauge railway line. Approximately 5 to 30 metres high, the ochre cliffs are naturally sculptured into impressive formations. This ochre was used by Aborigines, along with that from other ochre quarries in the Flinders Ranges, in an extensive trading network.

Bookartoo Historic Reserve, Flinders Ranges National Park

This renowned Aboriginal ochre quarry lies about 25 kilometres south-east of Parachilna within the Flinders Ranges National Park in the Heysen Ranges north of Wilpena Pound, but it can only be reached by bushwalking. Permission to visit is required from Aboriginal custodians (via the Aboriginal Heritage Branch of the Department of Environment and Planning).

   The area is stained red from ochre and extensively mined; two tunnel openings and five pits are still visible. Originally access was via a narrow tunnel entrance to a large chamber, but this cave has now completely collapsed, leaving only an opening measuring 75 by 70 metres and 2 metres deep, and a number of smaller pits, less than a metre wide, dug vertically or at an angle into the hillside. The ochre is a deep red-brown to red-purple in colour, is soft and contains 70 per cent iron oxide and some mica, which gives it an unique sheen. It was therefore highly prized for decorative purposes such as body painting and continued to be exploited by Aborigines until 1939.

The Bookartoo mine is still of significance to Aborigines of the Flinders Ranges, and is a major mythological site. The ochre was said to be the blood of a dog, Manindi, and complex rituals were carried out before ochre collection. This Parachilna ochre, as it was known, had special qualities such as its sheen, brilliant colour and fine texture, and was unrivalled by any of the other ochre mines of the Flinders Ranges. It was held as sacred and was sought after by Aborigines from as far afield as Cloncurry in Queensland, 1,500 kilometres away as the crow flies.

The North-East

Some Aboriginal sites in the north-east are open to the public. These include large Aboriginal stone quarry sites around Innamincka. Innamincka Historic Reserve contains a cairn marking explorer Robert O'Hara Burke's memorial, where his body was found by the search party after the ill-fated Burke and Wills expedition. Also within the reserve are many hundreds of rock engravings around Callamurra waterhole on Cooper Creek (plate 12.5). On the opposite side of Cooper Creek from Callamurra there are stone arrangements at Coongie Lakes, and an extensive series of middens.

Nullarbor Plain

The Nullarbor Plain and its surrounds constitute the largest arid karst landscape anywhere in the world. Nullarbor means "no trees", and this desolate, arid plain is largely treeless, although stunted black oaks are found on the fringes. Elsewhere low shrubs such as bluebush and saltbush are prevalent. Underneath the vast plain there are extensive cave systems, some with subterranean rivers. Although the caves generally lack "decoration" some are extremely long, with cathedral-sized chambers and large lakes. These caves provide water and living places for animals, but also sometimes acted as a trap for the unwary. Several caves contain mummified and fossilised remains of animals which fell into sinkholes and blowholes. Limestone, because of its high alkaline content, preserves bone and other organic material extremely well. The region is therefore likely to contain some of the oldest, best preserved and richest Aboriginal sites in Australia.

By 34,000 years ago Aborigines were living in Allen's Cave below the Nullarbor Plain, and mining chert, camping and creating art in deep dark caverns such as Koonalda Cave (see pages 188-91). In Koonalda Cave at the base of the wall containing criss-crossing patterns of finger markings and engravings, charcoal from charred sticks assumed to be from brush torches used to light this totally dark part of the cave has given an age of 20,000 years. This is strong circumstantial evidence for the ice-age antiquity of Aboriginal rock art.

About 40 Aboriginal sites associated with caves or dolines (conical depressions in limestone which may be many metres in diameter) have been found on the Nullarbor. Hand stencils occur in twenty, stone artefacts or other evidence of

Plate 12.5 Engravings at Callamurra waterhole, Innamincka Historic Reserve. (M. Nobbs)

occupation in nine, stone arrangements in nine and flint-mining in two. One cave has a stone arrangement with a substantial growth of stalagmite on top of the cairns, evidence of their considerable antiquity. Other sites occur on the surface of the plain, such as open campsites, stone quarries and at least three stone arrangements.

An exciting new discovery on the Nullarbor Plain has been the finding by Scott Cane of the Australian National University of prehistoric human and animal footprints preserved in the floor of an old salt lake west of Ceduna. The prints are set in lithified mud (mud which has become stone) and have been radiocarbon-dated to 5,500 years ago. They probably formed as people and animals walked around the lake to obtain food and water, while the lake bed was still soft. Very dry environmental conditions must have followed, so that the prints were not obliterated before they became fossilised. The human footprints appear to be those of an older woman with a broad short foot of about size 6½ and a young man, with a clear arch and a size 9 foot. This is only the second site in Australia where human fossil footprints have been found.

A complete carcass of a thylacine (Tasmanian tiger) was found on the floor of a cave now named Thylacine Hole on the Western Australian side of the Nullarbor. Radiocarbon dating has shown that it died 4,600 years ago. It had been mummified by the extremely dry air, its fur, tongue and left eyeball still intact. This incredibly well-preserved thylacine is now on display in the Western Australian Museum in Perth. The youngest thylacine skeleton to have been found in mainland Australia came from another Nullarbor Cave, Murra-el-elevyn, and is about 3,300 years old.

The Mirning occupied the southern fringes of the Nullarbor Plain from Twilight Cove to the vicinity of Eucla. They exploited the timbered country extending some 20 to 30 kilometres inland, but rarely went far out onto the treeless plain. A snake called Ganba or Jeedara was said to inhabit the caves, and he could pass through underground passages to the sea.[8] He was believed to have pushed up the sea cliffs in the Dreamtime so that he could swim along beneath them. The strange noises which sometimes come from the blowholes, called moonyungara, along the foot of the cliffs were thought to be the sound of Ganba breathing.

Murrawijinie Caves painting sites

Within the Nullarbor National Park, 300 kilometres west of Ceduna, there are a few Aboriginal hand stencil sites. Murrawijinie Cave number 1 is a shallow sinkhole 8.5 kilometres north of Nullarbor station homestead, containing hand stencils (in three groups of four, five and two) on the wall and a boulder on its northern side. The hand stencils in red ochre are faint due to natural weathering, and two stencils have been severely eroded by water since they are on a boulder and open to the weather. Seven hundred metres to the east is another sinkhole, Murrawijinie Cave number 3, which has 59 hand stencils on its eastern side, close to the cave entrance, approached by walking down a talus slope. Two vertical rock panels contain 18 to 20, and others occur on the roof, some in smooth circular cavities. The hands are stencilled in a bright-red ochre, and many are well defined, showing individual characteristics such as fine pointed or spatulate fingers.

These art sites are important in view of the rarity of Aboriginal art on the Nullarbor and for their evidence of Aboriginal presence in this inhospitable region.

Koonalda Cave

Aboriginal people made use of the caves of the Nullarbor as long as 34,000 years ago at Allen's Cave near Eucla and probably from about 24,000 to 15,000 at Koonalda Cave. (Koonalda Cave is at present closed to the public, and can be visited only by special permission of the Aboriginal Heritage Branch of the Department of Environment and Planning.) This crater-like sinkhole had two big attractions in prehistoric Australia; it held permanent water and nodules of some of the finest raw material for stone tool making available in Australia (figure 12.5 and plates 12.6 and 12.7). This shiny material is usually called flint, but is actually chert and chalcedony. Quarrying was carried out underground, sometimes without a glimmer of natural light, and the nodules were carried up to the surface of the plain to be fashioned into tools. In the first dimly lit cavern about 100 metres inside the entrance and 76 metres below the surrounding plain, ancient campfires, pieces of chert and other occupational debris were found by Alexander Gallus. Later, Richard Wright[9] of Sydney University excavated a pit 6 metres deep. Charcoal from the lowest layer gave a date of 24,000 years.

One of the most remarkable discoveries in Koonalda Cave was the presence of

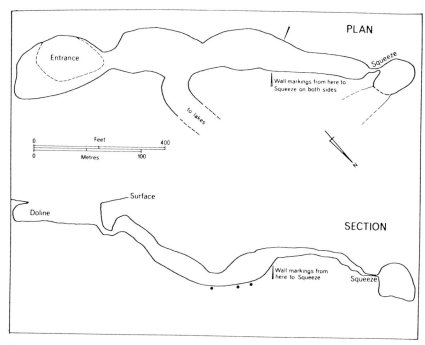

Figure 12.5   Koonalda Cave. (After R.V.S. Wright 1971)

Plate 12.6   Koonalda Cave excavation. (R. Edwards)

Plate 12.7   Wall markings in Koonalda Cave. (R. Edwards)

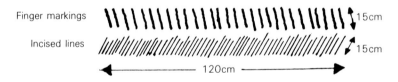

Figure 12.6   Herringbone design in Koonalda Cave. (After R. Edwards and L. Maynard in Wright, ed. 1971)

Pleistocene engravings in complete darkness in deep inner passages, some 300 metres inside the entrance. These vary from finger markings where the rock surface is soft to lines incised with a stone or stick in the harder surfaces. The lines resemble the so-called macaroni style of European cave art. Some appear to be random criss-crossing lines, but definite patterns occur, such as grids, lattices and concentric circles. One interesting design is a herringbone consisting of 74 short diagonal lines incised in a row below 37 similar finger markings (figure 12.6). The fact that 37 is exactly half of 74 can hardly be coincidence, and suggests that these marks had some purpose and significance.

What that significance was to their makers will remain unknown, but this "art" of Koonalda is of great heritage significance. There is strong circumstantial evidence that it is of ice-age antiquity, for a large panel of engravings was found

15 metres below an ancient rockfall, and charcoal from just beneath the surface of the floor immediately below other markings was dated to 20,000 years. The charcoal is thought to have come from burning brush torches carried by early inhabitants to light their way along the dark passages; it seems likely that visits to these deep, dark inner recesses of the cave were made for ceremonial or ritual purposes.

These engravings were the first evidence in Australia that Aboriginal people carried out artistic activity in totally dark caves, and they demonstrate the considerable antiquity of Aboriginal art, which is comparable with that of the cave art of France and Spain. Koonalda Cave is also significant for its evidence that Aborigines had learnt to live in caves and exploit flint and other resources of this arid region in the ice age, some 24,000 years ago. Visits to Koonalda continued throughout the last glacial maximum between 18,000 and 15,000 years ago, when the sea reached its lowest level, the sea coast was about 160 kilometres further south, and the environment on the Nullarbor was as arid as it is today.

Hand Print Cave

Several other art sites have been found on the southern part of the Nullarbor Plain, one of them, Hand Print Cave, being only 15 kilometres west of Koonalda station and 2 kilometres south of the old Eyre highway. It is a small sinkhole where the circular entrance has collapsed on one side, providing a gentle talus slope to walk down into the silt-floored chamber. Several hand stencils can be discerned on the walls of this twilight zone of the cave. When illuminated, these impressions of hands stand out astonishingly clear and bright in a rusty red ochre. One panel contains six adult hand stencils and one made by a child or adolescent.

CHAPTER THIRTEEN

South Australia: The South

Neither the Mount Lofty Ranges nor Gulf Saint Vincent existed 600 million years ago, but only a massive tidal flat and shallow sea in the Adelaide area, into which poured silt, sand and mud (figure 13.1). The sediments continued to accumulate, but 100 million years later tremendous pressures within the earth buckled and folded the deep basin of sediments. A huge mountain range was thrust up, but it was then gradually eroded by wind and water. No plants existed to slow the process of erosion, which continued to flatten the Adelaide area again until 270 million years ago, when the Permian ice age began.

Dramatic evidence of this glaciation 270 million years ago can be seen just south of Adelaide in the spectacular Hallett Cove Conservation Park (see below), where rocks polished and scratched by the passing of Permian glaciers are clearly visible. After the glacial period the land slowly eroded for 265 million years, removing most of the glacial debris, until the Pliocene epoch. Then earth movements and faults began to uplift the Mount Lofty Ranges to submerge the lowlands into a shallow sea. Part of Hallett Cove became a sea floor on which dead shellfish and sand came to rest. The shellfish were fossilised in shelly sandstone, the faulting and uplifting of the mountains waned and they began to erode, gradually depositing a thick layer of clay onto the plains. Soils developed, and lush vegetation.

Elsewhere in South Australia the bones of extinct animals have washed into underground caves such as Victoria Cave near Naracoorte (see pages 207–10). Human hunters may have had a hand in the extinction of the megafauna; researchers do not know exactly when hunters arrived on the stage, but it was in excess of 40,000 years ago.

Eyre Peninsula

Coffin Bay, Lincoln district

A number of Aboriginal fish traps are located on Horse Peninsula in the Coffin Bay area, approximately 6 kilometres north-west of Coffin Bay township and 50

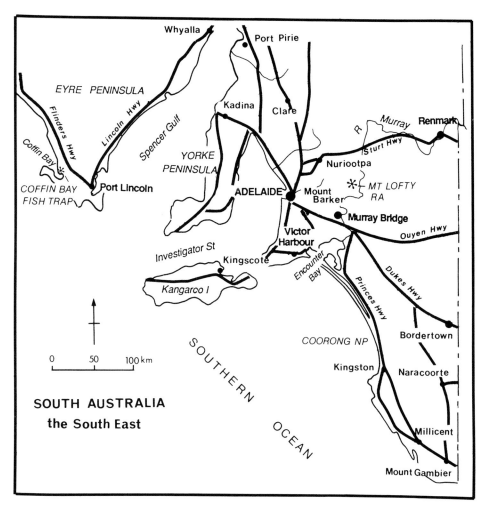

Figure 13.1 South Australia: the coast

kilometres west of Port Lincoln in the Coffin Bay National Park. (Access to the park is from the Flinders Highway 32 kilometres west of Port Lincoln.) One fish trap lies on an inlet beach in a sheltered bay on the south-eastern end of Horse Peninsula, another is 400 metres due west of it, and a third about a kilometre to the north on a tidal channel (figure 13.2). All can be reached by boat from either Mount Dutton or Coffin Bay township, and are clearly visible except at high tide.

Fish traps are rare Aboriginal sites, and the first and second sites are excellent examples of semi-circular traps designed to catch fish on a falling tide. They both consist of a curved wall of irregular limestone blocks on a gently sloping beach abutting onto a rock ledge which creates a natural back wall to the trap. There is a gap in the centre of the wall, which would have been blocked with stones, a net or bushes when in use to trap the fish after they had been swept or herded into the enclosure at high tide.

The third trap was built in a samphire swamp across a tidal channel; it can be reached by following the tidal channel inland for 200 metres and then taking the

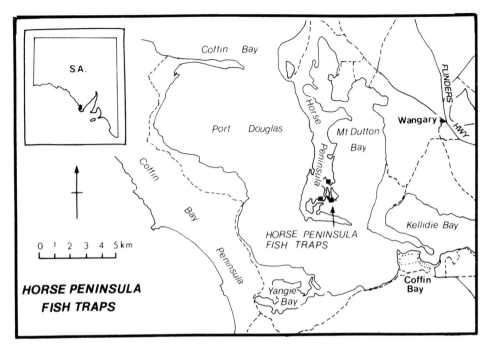

Figure 13.2   Location of Coffin Bay fish traps

fork heading north for 100 metres, whereupon the fish trap is clearly visible across the channel. It is a well-preserved, wavy wall, 16 metres long, with two small but definite gaps which would have been fitted with traps for the fish caught upstream of the wall at high tide.

Adelaide region

The city of Adelaide is now well provided with displays of Aboriginal art and artefacts. In 1989 the Aboriginal Cultural Institute, Tandanya, opened at 253 Grenfell Street, Adelaide 5000 (tel. (08) 223 2467). Tandanya provides a splendid venue for the fostering and development of Aboriginal art, culture and activities in the form of visual arts, a museum and performing arts. The South Australian Museum on North Terrace is also well worth a visit, particularly for its excellent displays on prehistory, prehistoric fauna and fossils.

Hallett Cove Conservation Park

Situated on Gulf Saint Vincent, 20 kilometres south of Adelaide, Hallett Cove is internationally famous for its evidence of the 270 million-year-old Permian glaciation, especially its superb glacial pavements. The site is best approached from the carpark and kiosk on Heron Way at the southern end of the park, which is reached from Adelaide by train or via the Main South Road, west on Majors Road, south onto Lonsdale Road, right at Cove Road, along Dutchmans Drive and right into Heron Way.

By following the trails to the stations marked from A to H you can read the story of the cove from 600 million years ago to the present day. The trail starts on the beach below the dark-purple, folded rocks of Black Cliff, made of siltstone compressed with sandstone. A climb up the cliff brings visitors to station B and dramatic evidence of the Permian glaciation, 270 million years ago. Glaciers of ice containing boulders and rock fragments left long parallel scratches in the underlying rock. This is one of the very few places in the world where you can see such ancient markings so well preserved (plates 13.1 and 13.2).

Boulders that have been carried along by the glacier are called glacial erratics, and two of them of quartzite can be seen at station C, which is reached by a track on top of glacial debris, originally soft clay and sand laid down in a basin of "meltwater" behind the retreating glacier. On the northern side of Waterfall Creek glacial debris lies on the upturned layers of the oldest, dark-purple folded rocks. Where they meet is a break in time or "unconformity", for a long period of erosion has removed intermediate layers.

There is a classic example of rock stress in the oldest rocks at station E. The rock is quartzite, a hard compacted sandstone formed from layers of sand in the ancient sea. During the folding process, tension cracks developed which were later filled with white quartz. A little further along the cliff top are crescent-shaped gouges in the hard quartzite rock below station F. As the ice moved over the bedrock, short cracks were opened at right angles to the line of movement. Like arrows, they point in the direction the glacier moved.

The white shelly sandstone of station G is 265 million years younger than the quartzite of station F. The shellfish fossils and gritty sand suggest that this rock

Plate 13.1 The "amphitheatre" with sediments spanning the last two million years, Hallett Cove

Plate 13.2   Parallel scratches are evidence of Permian glaciation, 270 million years ago, Hallett Cove

was formed on a sea bed a mere 5 million years ago in the Pliocene epoch, when earth movements submerged this area. Finally, the youngest rocks are found at station H in the "amphitheatre", spanning the last 2 million years or Pleistocene period (see plate 13.1). On top of the clay soils is a distinct white layer of hard limestone known as calcrete, which is an old soil layer now exposed to weathering.

The most recent change in the story of Hallett Cove was the gradual rise in sea level. At times of Pleistocene low sea level, the sea was as much as 150 metres below its present level and Gulf Saint Vincent was dry land. Now in the last 12,000 years the ocean has invaded Gulf Saint Vincent, carved out cliffs and shore platforms and formed the beaches and sand dunes. An Aboriginal campsite on a hillside facing north-east above Waterfall Creek may originate from the period when the sea was much further away, for the heavily weathered artefacts (now in the South Australian Museum in Adelaide) were the heavy Kartan type likely to be more than 15,000 years old. Some 400 core tools were found, the largest weighing 5.5 kilograms.

One of the riddles of this campsite is that the crude Kartan pebble choppers, horsehoof cores and hammerstones are all made of poor quality siltstone available close to the camp, whereas at the foot of the nearby cliff lie banks of fine-grained hard quartzite cobbles highly prized as raw material by stone tool-makers. The only convincing explanation is that when the sea level was low the quartzite cobbles were covered by scree and a talus slope of debris fallen from the cliffs and thus hidden from view, but this was subsequently washed away by the ocean pounding at the foot of the cliffs.

Figure 13.3 Kanmantoo rock paintings (not to scale). (R. Gunn)

Mount Lofty Ranges

Several small Aboriginal painting sites in the Mount Lofty Ranges east of Adelaide are reasonably accessible, and demonstrate a distinctive lively and colourful style of rock art. Permission to visit these sites should be sought from the Aboriginal Heritage Unit, Department of Environment and Planning, Adelaide, and occasional visits are also arranged by the Workers Educational Association.[1]

Kanmantoo painting site, Mount Barker district

Kanmantoo, or Native Valley as it is also known, is an excellent example of the Aboriginal painting style of the Mount Lofty Ranges (figure 13.3). The rockshelter of biotite schist faces west-south-west in a small cliffline about 2 kilometres north of Kanmantoo. About 80 marks have been painted or drawn on the walls and ceiling of the shelter, in red, white, yellow and black pigment. Subjects include figures resembling humans, lizards and an emu transfixed by a spear, a sun-like motif in yellow and white, anthropomorphs (part-human with head-dresses) and many linear designs. One human figure holds a boomerang, another is depicted in an unusual profile sitting position holding a weapon or shield, and one or two are shown with arms up and knees bent, apparently dancing. This art is both animated and colourful, and has a greater variety of subjects than other nearby sites.

Harrisons Creek, Mount Pleasant district

About 7 kilometres south-east of Tungkillo, a granite rockshelter containing paintings lies on the southern side of Harrisons Creek (figure 13.4). The paintings

Figure 13.4   Harrisons Creek rock paintings (not to scale). (R. Gunn)

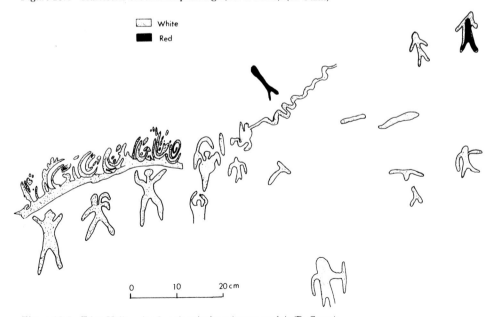

Figure 13.5   Eden Valley site 3 rock paintings (not to scale). (R. Gunn)

have been executed with brush or finger in red, black and white pigment. There are more than 20 paintings, and subjects include figures resembling snakes, lizards and humans, one holding a boomerang. One striking motif is a "fern" design in red and white. Overall, this site is a typical example of the rock painting style of the lower Mount Lofty Ranges.

Pyms shelter site, Mount Pleasant district

This is one of the most aesthetically pleasing and best preserved Aboriginal painting sites in the Mount Lofty region. The small shelter is formed from a large boulder of micaceous schist with an overhang facing north, and contains an occupational deposit as well as rock art.

Paintings in a bright-red ochre occupy the deepest part of the overhang. White lines outlining many of the paintings may be of European rather than Aboriginal origin. Subjects include figures resembling humans, the largest 26 centimetres long, macropod and emu tracks, dots, ovals and simple linear closed and open designs executed to take advantage of natural concave or convex formations in the rock.

Rockleigh, Mount Pleasant district

In the eastern Mount Lofty Ranges are several Aboriginal sites, rockshelters with paintings and occupational deposits, extensive campsites, cooking hearths and scarred trees.

Sugarloaf shelter, also known as South Rockleigh, is on the western side of a sandstone hill, facing north-west. More than 20 paintings in red ochre are on the rear wall, and there is a shallow occupational deposit in the floor. The motifs resemble emu tracks, humans or lizards; as well, a rake-like design and linear marks tend to follow projections and depressions in the rock face.

In the same area is North Rockleigh shelter facing south-west, with some ten figures visible, all painted in red ochre. Six seem to be human figures, one a human foot, and the rest are linear designs. A mesh grille and sign-posting have been completed at Rockleigh.

Eden Valley painting sites, Mount Pleasant district

Four small Aboriginal painting sites lie about 3 kilometres south-east of the settlement of Eden Valley (figure 13.5). Eden Valley painting site 1 is a small granite rockshelter facing north in a short, narrow, boulder-strewn gorge. The 35 paintings are well-preserved although covered with extensive graffiti. They are painted with brushes or fingers in red and white pigment, and are mainly of humans and linear designs, plus two white snake-like figures. Two additional techniques used here, stencil making and printing, are unknown at other Mount Lofty Ranges sites. An unusual feature is a simple curved linear design printed in white seven times in a row at this site.

The second painting site contains 41 well-preserved paintings and drawings in white, red and yellow pigment. Most figures are of human form or linear, but some unusual motifs also occur. One is a human figure in profile and another is a quadruped, possibly a horse. This was probably painted around 1860, and its fresh appearance in contrast with some other motifs suggests a time span of at least several centuries for the site.

The third and fourth art sites in the Eden Valley region are located just 20 metres apart in a rocky granite outcrop with a south-east aspect. Site 3 is distinguished by large numbers of stick-like human figures and lines and a very clear snake. Almost all the 47 motifs are drawn or painted in yellow or white. Site 4 has only nine white drawings, comprising a human figure, lines and simple linear designs and one bird, which resembles a wader or an emu.

Anthony Hill, Strathalbyn district

Aboriginal rock paintings are located on the walls and ceiling of a small sandstone rockshelter 4 kilometres north-west of Strathalbyn. It contains an occupation deposit and over 20 paintings in red ochre. A series of small, finely drawn human figures are portrayed, mainly in profile and exhibit unusually strong movement. The Anthony Hill site is the most southerly example of rock paintings in the east Mount Lofty Ranges, and the animated figures are atypical for the local region. There is also a canoe tree in the area.

Tjilbruke Dreaming trail

This trail runs along the coast from Adelaide southwards to Cape Jervis. Each Dreaming site is marked by a cairn, and a plaque tells the part of the story for each locality on the Dreaming track. The sites on this walking trail relate to the Dreaming hero, Tjilbruke, who travelled south from the Adelaide Plains to the shores of Gulf Saint Vincent, carrying his dead nephew whom he mourned. Where Tjilbruke rested, he wept, and fresh water springs were formed, even in the sea. (Further information is available from the South Australian Heritage Committee, c/o Department of Environment and Planning.)

Murray Valley

For thousands of years the Murray River has provided a focus for Aboriginal occupation, and its banks are rich with sites of all types. Of special note are the many scarred trees, river red gums bearing long scars where large sheets of bark were prised off to make canoes, shields, carrying dishes or other artefacts. Fish traps are also still evident at various sites along the Murray, especially in the south.

Overland Corner ochre mine, Barmera district

This Aboriginal ochre mine is a small reserve 1.5 kilometres east of Overland Corner Post Office on the Barmera Road and 100 metres south of the road opposite a cemetery. It lies in the uppermost slope of the breakaway between the plain and the deeply incised Murray River Valley. The red to mauve ochre occurs as a pocket within limestone, and chert is also present. A depression of approximately 36 square metres has been formed by extraction of limestone to obtain the ochre. The depth of the pit varies from half a metre to 1.5 metres, and a small cave about 2 metres long has been created, presumably where the quantity of ochre was greatest. The size of the workings indicates the importance of this ochre deposit for riverland Aborigines.

Swan Reach Aboriginal sites, Ridley district

Numerous traces of Aboriginal occupation are to be found 2 kilometres north-east of Swan Reach. Traditional lifeways are evidenced by campsites and trees which

Plate 13.3   Canoe tree at Blanchetown, Murray River. (R. Edwards)

bear long scars caused by the removal of bark to make canoes. One tree has traces of the toeholds cut by Aborigines when climbing the tree to hunt koalas or possums; such "possum trees" are now extremely rare. On the opposite bank are rock engravings in the limestone cliffs; only one other example of Aboriginal limestone engravings is known along the River Murray, at Devon Downs (see below).

Blanchetown canoe trees, Waikerie district

Canoe trees are trees with scars formed when Aborigines prised off sheets of bark to make canoes. Some of the best examples in Australia of such canoe trees are river red gums along the eastern bank of the Murray River opposite Blanchetown (plate 13.3). The trees lie in a historic reserve on the floodplain between the river and the lagoon, to the south of the road bridge and to the south or immediately north of Lock Gate number one.

Nineteen canoe trees survive here. The river red gums have particularly thick bark, and it was possible to remove large sheets of bark relatively easily during

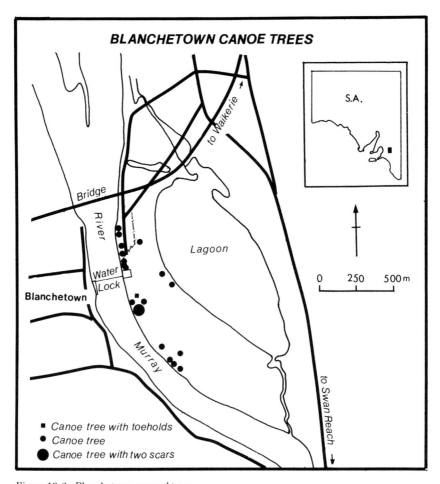

Figure 13.6   Blanchetown scarred trees

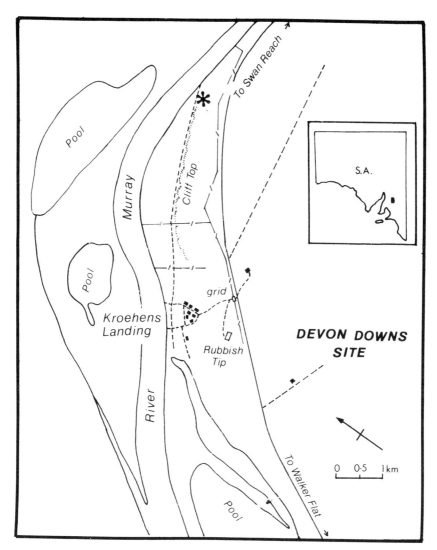

Figure 13.7   Devon Downs sites

the late spring or early summer growth period, when the sap flowed freely between the hardwood core of the tree and the bark.[2] One particularly fine example bearing two canoe-shaped scars stands close to the river's edge just south of the lock; another red gum with both a canoe scar and four toeholds still visible is just a little to the south in the same vicinity (figure 13.6).

Devon Downs rockshelters, Ridley district

On the eastern bank of the Murray River 8 kilometres north-east of Walker are some Aboriginal occupation sites of great archaeological significance. They lie at the northern extremity of a river flat where the river meets the limestone cliffline (figure 13.7). This is reached from the Walkers Flat-Swan Reach road, taking the track into Kroehen's Landing and then proceeding north-east for one and a half kilometres along the track and through two gates to the Ngautngaut Conservation Park. Opposite the end of the track is a small rockshelter containing some occupational debris, but the main site is the large shelter known as Devon Downs 1, which has engravings on its back wall and where a major archaeological excavation has been carried out.[3] Immediately to the north of it two further shelters also contain traces of occupation and engravings. Middens and open campsites occur in the vicinity, together with four scarred trees close to the river just north of the fence marking the western boundary of the park.

The main Devon Downs shelter was excavated in 1929 by Norman Tindale and Herbert Hale. This was the first archaeological excavation conducted in a systematic, scientific way in Australia, and was a remarkably advanced piece of fieldwork for its time. Although dug 20 years before the development of radiocarbon dating, excavated samples of freshwater mussels were later dated by this method, revealing that the deposit spans about 5,000 years. The 6 metre deep, well-stratified occupational debris was rich in animal bones, shell and bone tools, which survive well in the alkaline environment of a limestone rockshelter. The shelter seems to have been used occasionally throughout the last five millennia, particularly in wet weather, judging from extremely large quantities of ash in proportion to other types of debris, indicating the lighting of frequent campfires.

The earlier layers contained finely made, leaf-shaped stone Pirri points, generally thought to have been spear tips, but these apparently went out of use during the last 3,000 years. Another change which occurred about 3,000 years ago was in seasonal use; the presence of emu eggshell in the lower layers indicates winter or early spring occupation, whereas in the upper, post-3,000-year-old layers crayfish gastroliths indicate use in autumn. The shelter was used most intensively between 4,000 and 2,000 years ago.

The graves of four children were found within the shelter, in box-like structures made of stone slabs. Engravings were also found both on the roof of the shelter and in the deposit, where a slab engraved with linear designs and small circular pits in a 3,000-year-old layer provided the first evidence of the prehistoric antiquity of Australian rock art. (The artefacts from Devon Downs are in the South Australian Museum in Adelaide.) Engravings are very rare in the Murray River Valley, and one notable motif at Devon Downs is a large circle surrounded by rays, resembling the sun. Another excavated rockshelter with engravings of pits, bird tracks and linear markings is Fromms Landing near Walker Flat 18 kilometres downstream, but it is not open to the public. It produced a similar sequence of occupation to Devon Downs, and some notable finds such as the complete 3,000-year-old skeleton of a dingo and evidence of a flood 3,000 years ago, which was higher than that of any Murray River flood on record.

The Coorong and Mount Gambier district

The south-east corner of South Australia is known particularly for its caves, extinct volcanoes and magnificent coastline. This can be seen in a series of parks and reserves, where many traces of prehistoric Aboriginal life are visible, such as the shell middens of the Coorong and Canunda National Parks. Further to the east

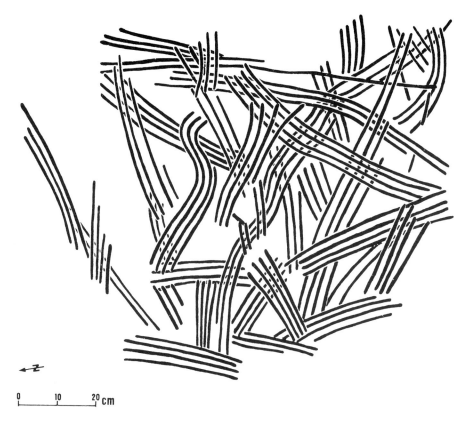

Figure 13.8 Rock art from Mount Gambier district. Finger flutings on the ceiling of Koongine Cave. (R.G. Bednarik, "Parietal Finger Markings in Europe and Australia", *Rock Art Research* vol. 3(1), 1986:48)

about 20 kilometres south of Mount Gambier there is a large midden near Port MacDonnell. It lies immediately south of the road leading west from Port MacDonnell to Cape Northumberland, and is open to the public.

Startling new evidence has come to light in the 1980s of an extremely ancient body of rock engravings in underground limestone caves in the Mount Gambier district of south-eastern South Australia. The discovery was made by Robert Bednarik, founder of the Australian Rock Art Research Association, and local resident and speleologist, Geoffrey Aslin.[4] Finger markings and engravings have now been found in more than 25 caves in the Mount Gambier region, and three succeeding styles have been identified.

The earliest and most common style is characterised by multiple finger lines or flutings on formerly soft surface deposits together with linear markings engraved with pieces of stone in harder surfaces on the walls of caves (figure 13.8). From the size of the finger lines it is possible to get some idea of the age of their makers, and one surprise was the high number made by juveniles. This style, which resembles the "macaroni" or "meander tradition" of early European cave art, has now been found over a distance of 3,000 kilometres along the entire south coast of Australia, from the Snowy River in eastern Victoria to Koonalda Cave on the Nullarbor Plain and the Perth region in the west.

Figure 13.9 The Karake style of rock art in Paroong Cave, Mount Gambier district. (G.D. Aslin, E.K. and R.G. Bednarik, "The Parietal Markings Project — A Progress Report", *Rock Art Research* vol. 2(1), 1985:73)

The finger lines tradition has not yet been securely dated, but is probably more, possibly much more, than 20,000 years old, on the evidence from Koonalda Cave, the overgrowth of finger grooves by a more recent deposit of reprecipitated carbonate in several sites and the major tectonic changes which have occurred in many caves since the markings were made.

Superimposed on finger lines in several Mount Gambier caves are deeply carved motifs, particularly circles. These may be incised, pounded or abraded, and the circles include concentric, dissected and other forms (figure 13.9). This style has now been termed by Bednarik the Karake style. (Karake is an Aboriginal word from the now extinct Buandik language of the Aborigines of the south-east of South Australia.) It is thought to be more than 10,000 years old, and like the preceding finger lines tradition, is entirely non-figurative. The latest style in the Mount Gambier caves is a tradition of shallow incisions executed with single strokes, which is believed to be less than 10,000 years old.

Several thousand of these engravings have now been found in the underground limestone caves of the Mount Gambier district, five of which also contain evidence of prehistoric mining of chert to make stone tools. This is already the largest known concentration of non-figurative cave art in the world, and no doubt many more discoveries are waiting to be made. These caves are generally on private property and the engravings lie in total darkness in inaccessible passages and chambers, so in order to protect this art from uncontrolled visitation and possible vandalism, site locations are being kept confidential.

The Mount Gambier district, as well as its heritage of archaic rock art, contains spectacular evidence of volcanic activity, which is readily viewed by every visitor. Part of the third largest volcanic plain in the world (23,300 square kilometres), the region's first eruption occurred about 2 million years ago. Mount Gambier and Mount Schank, 13 kilometres south of Mount Gambier, are volcanic cones, and plant remains from under the lava flows have been radiocarbon-dated to 5,000 years ago. The most recent volcanic eruptions in the area date from around 1,500 years ago. The crater of Mount Gambier contains four lakes filled with crystal clear sub-artesian water purified by filtering through the limestone bedrock. Particularly famous is Blue Lake, which has an average depth of 75 metres and is enclosed by steep sides up to 80 metres high. Curiously, the water level hardly fluctuates although the lake supplies the town with large quantities of water, and it changes its colour each year from grey to a brilliant turquoise blue in the summer months between November and March.

Another important site in the Mount Gambier district for Australian prehistory is Wyrie Swamp near Millicent, which contained the world's oldest known boomerangs. Excavation of part of this peat swamp by Roger Luebbers revealed the existence of a 10,000-year-old lakeside camp and both stone and wooden artefacts. It is extremely rare that wooden artefacts are preserved in Australian archaeological sites, so this was a great find. There were twenty-five in all, including digging sticks, a short simple spear, two barbed spears and nine boomerangs, which appear to be the returning type. The fact that specialised and sophisticated implements like returning boomerangs and barbed spears were in use 10,000 years ago came as a surprise to Australian archaeologists, who are eagerly awaiting full publication of this site by Dr Luebbers and display of the artefacts in the South Australian Museum in Adelaide. (Wyrie Swamp is on private property and is not open to the public.)

Naracoorte Caves Conservation Park

The limestone Cave Range in the south-east of South Australia is an area of classic karst topography, with flat to undulating landscape of marshland and hills containing many sinkholes, depressions and about 60 caves. Victoria, Alexandra and Blanche Caves are open to the public in the Naracoorte Caves Conservation Park, 14 kilometres south-east of Naracoorte on the Penola road. The caves are in rock known as Gambier limestone, which was laid down beneath the sea between 40 and 15 million years ago, and marine fossils embedded in the soft limestone walls can be seen in places, such as the entrance chamber of Alexandra Cave.

The caves began to form after the area rose above the sea. Water seeped down through cracks and gradually eroded the rock, making way for underground creeks which eventually formed large caverns. The water table subsequently lowered, leaving a system of dry caves with silt and clay floors. The Naracoorte Caves have excellent "decorations" (plate 13.4), formed as the limestone slowly dissolves with a mild acid of rainwater and carbon dioxide derived from the atmosphere and from rotting vegetation on the ground. When this solution of water and carbon dioxide percolates through the limestone ceilings of the caves, droplets form. For cave formations to grow, it is necessary for these droplets to hang there for eight to ten hours. During this time carbon dioxide and water

Plate 13.4 Formations in Alexandra Cave, Naracoorte. (B. Macdonald and SA Museum)

vapour are given off, and when the droplet falls to the floor a minute deposite of calcite is left behind (figure 13.10).

Cave "decorations" formed in this way on ceilings include stalactites (tapered and cone-shaped), straws (thin hollow tubes), shawls (thin sheets) and helictites, which grow in any direction and are thought to be caused by erratic capillary action. There are some particularly striking star-shaped helictites at Naracoorte. A similar process then takes place on the cave floor, forming flowstone and stalagmites which gradually grow upwards, sometimes meeting stalactites to form columns. Decorations of calcite are continuing to form beautiful, elaborate shapes in the wet or "live" Alexandra Cave, and wetas (cave crickets) cling to the ceilings and walls in the entrance chamber.

Impressive live decorations were found in Victoria Cave in 1894 and opened to

Water containing carbon dioxide penetrates the soil and enters joints in the limestone

The water acts as an acid, dissolving the limestone and forming a complex of cavities

Over thousands of years dripping water causes larger rocks to collapse, forming caves

Figure 13.10   The formation of limestone caves (Reproduced with permission from *Scenic Wonders of Australia*, Readers Digest (Aust.) Pty Ltd 1976, p.189)

the public in 1897, but it was not until the 1960s that the most scientifically significant chamber was discovered. The cave at a depth of about 20 metres below the ground has some 300 metres of passages and a series of chambers with ancient rockfalls cemented by flowstone, but in 1969 speleologists from the Cave Exploration Group of South Australia squeezed through a 25 centimetre high passage to emerge in a huge treasure chamber of ancient fossil fauna.

The bones are embedded to a depth of 3 metres in a soft silt deposit extending over an area of some 50 by 10 metres in the main 80 metre long fossil chamber, which is open for public viewing. The remains may have been washed into the cave by a creek or it may have been a carnivore's den. The most likely candidate is the rare marsupial cave "lion", *Thylacoleo carnifex*, which has been extinct for several thousand years.

Thylacoleo is generally believed to have been a flesh-eating animal, but its teeth differ from those of any living animal, either plant-eating or flesh-eating. Flesh-eating animals need sharp, pointed, interlocking teeth with which to hold their prey and tear off the flesh, but the marsupial "lion" had two upper tusk-teeth (incisors) which did not interlock with the lower incisors, but met them tip to tip. Its back teeth were not designed for chewing but were more like massive shears, for along each side of the jaw was a long razor-edged tooth which met a similar razor-edged tooth in the lower jaw. Although the non-interlocking front teeth of *Thylacoleo* would not have prevented the escape of a struggling victim, its forearms were remarkably long, with heavy paws. It may have killed its prey with one swipe from a heavy paw, for each toe had a claw and one claw was particularly large and sharp.

All the medium and large animals in the bone deposit are marsupials, many of them now extinct. Extinct creatures include the giant kangaroo, *Procoptodon rapha*, which was up to 3 metres tall, *Sthenurus,* a short-faced kangaroo which browsed on trees and shrubs, and *Zygomaturus*, a wombat-like lumbering creature about the size of a hippopotamus. They are certainly more than 10,000 years old and are generally estimated to be about 40,000.

Palaeontologists are still carefully unearthing the fragile remains of these ancient animals, peeling the layers away to build up a picture of the changes that occurred in the fauna of this region of Australia during the dramatic shifts in climate and environment during the last ice age in the late Pleistocene. A platform for viewing the dig and a museum housing excavated specimens have been set up inside the cave.

Victoria Fossil Cave, as it is known, is widely considered to be of world heritage significance in view of the diversity, antiquity, excellent preservation and wealth of content of its fossil bed. And two further fossil-rich chambers have now been discovered. This is the largest known accumulation of vertebrate fossils in a cave in Australia, and has been described by authorities as ranking in the first three of comparable deposits in the world.

Kangaroo Island

There are many ancient Aboriginal sites on Kangaroo Island, most of which date from before the area was cut off from the mainland by the rising sea about 10,000 years ago.[5] The island was called Karta, island of the dead, by mainland Aborigines. The first stone tools found on the island in the 1930s were therefore termed Kartan by their discoverer, Norman Tindale of the South Australian Museum. These large, heavy pebble choppers were discovered at Murray Lagoon, in what is now Murray Lagoon National Park. The paddock where they were found is near the ranger's house, a little hut and a palm tree, and is worth a visit both for the traces of the early Kartan industry still to be seen and for its wealth of waterbirds. (Visitors are reminded that collection of Aboriginal artefacts is illegal.)

Other Aboriginal sites can be seen in Flinders Chase National Park. An interpretive display is being developed by rangers at the park headquarters at Rocky River, and the site where Tindale found the bones of an extinct *Diprotodon* can be visited.

CHAPTER FOURTEEN

Victoria: The Grampians and the West

The great volcanic lava plain of eastern South Australia extends into western Victoria, covering a total area of some 23,000 square kilometres and containing nearly 400 extinct volcanic vents (94 of these are on the western plains of Victoria). Volcanic material has covered underlying marine deposits of limestone, but in places river erosion has exposed the sedimentary limestone.

Western Victoria contains some of Australia's youngest volcanoes. The volcanic eruptions began about 5 million years ago and have continued to as recently as 6,000 years ago. They produced cones of scoria, a rock formed from lava, at 165 to 200 metres above the surrounding plains. Molten lava poured out, covering the country in a blanket from a metre to 60 metres thick. Tongues of lava drained from beneath the main flow after a crust had formed on it, causing it to buckle and collapse. This led to the formation of the characteristic stony ridges separated by clay-lined troughs. Such ridge and trough formations can be seen around Mount Eccles and in the Stones Faunal Reserve near Macarthur (see below), Mount Napier near Hamilton and Mount Rouse near Penshurst. In other places such as Skipton, Byaduk and Pomborneit lava tunnels or caves have been formed where a stream of liquid lava flowed out from under the main lava flow after a crust had formed on it and the resulting cavity remained intact.

A lava cave at Mount Hamilton contains the bones of many animals, some of them now extinct in Victoria, which were trapped at the bottom of a 3 metre deep shaft, now the cave's entrance. Low gently sloping cones such as Mount Hamilton were produced by the accumulation of many basaltic lava flows.

Among Aboriginal sites, the special features of Western Victoria are the rock painting sites of the Grampians, and the extensive networks of fish traps constructed on inland waterways such as Lake Condah. These sophisticated eel harvesting and water control strategies seem unique to the Aboriginal engineers of the western district.

Mount Eccles National Park

Situated 335 kilometres west of Melbourne and 42 kilometres south of Hamilton, Mount Eccles National Park is reached from the Hamilton-Port Fairy road at

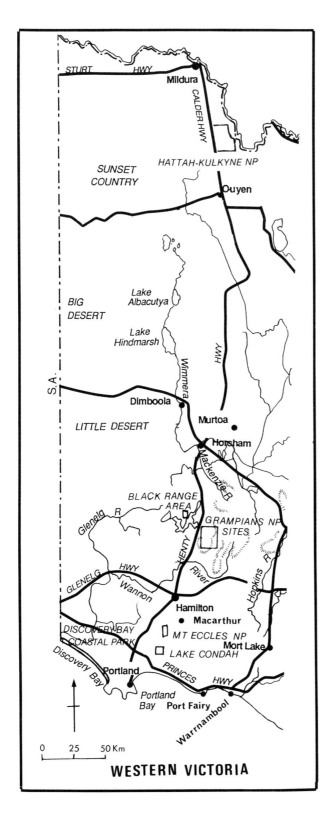

Figure 14.1   Western Victoria

Macarthur (figure 14.1). A great variety of volcanic forms can be easily seen in this 5,470 hectare park, and there is access for the disabled. Mount Eccles is a 196 metre high mound of scoria, a lightweight rock formed from lava, beside a steep-sided, deep-water lake, Lake Surprise. The lake is in a volcanic crater bounded by a low rim of lava fragments and rock debris. Lake Surprise is a volcanic sink, caused by the withdrawal of the lava column down the volcanic pipe, resulting in the collapse of the top of the crater. The blocked vents of the volcano, active some 27,000 years ago, now lie beneath the green waters of the lake, which is some 700 metres long and 180 metres wide. The water seems to come from underground springs; it falls each summer but returns in winter to a maximum depth of 13 metres.

Walking tracks lead through manna gum woodland around the lake, and at the northern end there is an ancient lava flow and a cave-like lava tunnel of basalt, where solidified drips of lava hang down from the ceiling. Above the south-eastern edge of the crater is Mount Eccles, a steep-sided, rounded cone of volcanic debris heaped up to 196 metres high from successive eruptions. Its slopes are formed of scoria, and are dangerously unstable to walk on.

Tower Hill Game Reserve

Another volcano is Tower Hill near Warrnambool, which last erupted some 23,000 years ago. It has a wide crater now filled with water like Mount Eccles. In the centre of the crater are numerous scoria cones formed by later eruptions, and a visitors' centre has been built on one of these. Clearly visible in the walls of the outer cone of Tower Hill are bands or layers of volcanic ash deposited by the series of eruptions (plates 14.1 and 14.2).

Plate 14.1   Lake view, Tower Hill volcano site near Warrnambool, with small cones formed at a later stage in the volcanic activity on the broad maar crater floor, now a lake. (Promotion Australia)

Plate 14.2 Tower Hill volcano site, showing layers of volcanic fragments in the tuff ring exposed in a former quarry. (Promotion Australia)

Mount Richmond National Park

Near the coast of Discovery Bay, 33 kilometres west of Portland, is Mount Richmond, a volcanic cone rising gently to 229 metres above the flat, forested plain. The solidified cone of volcanic ash, dust and pumice is largely covered by wind-blown sands from the shifting dunes of Discovery Bay. A walking track leads to the summit, where there is a lookout platform over the surrounding forests of manna gum and brown stringybark.

Discovery Bay Aboriginal middens

Discovery Bay Coastal Park between Portland and the South Australian border, 20 kilometres west of Nelson, contains extensive evidence of Aboriginal occupation. The stark, remote, windswept coastline within the park comprises a 50 kilometre long continuous open beach, huge rolling sand dunes parallel to the shore and a string of freshwater swamps and lakes. The largest swamp, Long Swamp, is an excellent waterbird habitat. It has been estimated by archaeologist Michael Godfrey[1] that more than 1,000 archaeological sites, most of them shell middens, lie within this coastal park, and this was clearly an important and productive habitat for Aboriginal hunting, gathering and fishing.

Most of the middens are less than 200 metres from the shore, although shell middens can be found up to 1.5 kilometres inland. Some middens have been excavated (plate 14.3). Radiocarbon dates from those composed of *Mytilus planulatus* (mussel) shells and located in the *terra rossa* soils which underlie the unconsolidated sand dunes show that these early prehistoric campsites are at least

Plate 14.3 Excavation of a shell midden in Discovery Bay National Park. (M. Godfrey)

8,500 years old. The younger middens are usually in a single layer on or near the surface of the dunes and are dominated by *Brachidontes rostratus* (beaked mussel), when adjacent to rock platforms, or by *Donax deltoides* (pipi) when by the open beach. Some are stratified and contain stone artefacts and burnt hearth stones.

The earliest site so far discovered is Bridgewater South Cave, a limestone cavern in an exposed escarpment overlooking the Bridgewater Lakes near Tarragal at the extreme eastern end of Discovery Bay. This cave was originally occupied before 11,000 years ago.[2] The early inhabitants only used the site sporadically and hunted the grey kangaroo, pademelon, potoroo, bandicoot, wombat, ring-tailed, brush-tailed and pygmy possums, and to a small extent seals, fish and shellfish such as pipi (at that time of low sea level the ocean was 25 kilometres away from the site). Later, part of the cave's ceiling collapsed, but the shelter was used more intensively during the last 500 years, when shellfish such as pipi and mussel were added to the diet.

A signposted, interpretive walking trail which features Aboriginal middens and food plants, has been set up in Discovery Bay Coastal Park.

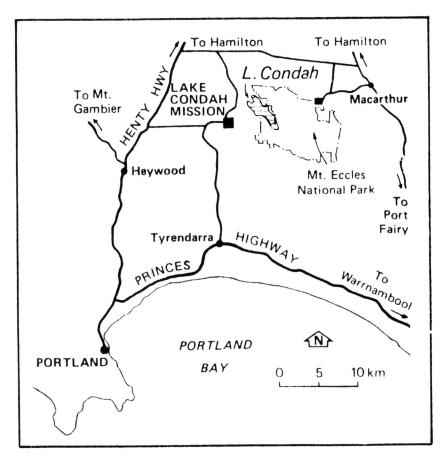

Figure 14.2   Location of Lake Condah. (Courtesy of the Kerrup-jmara people, Lake Condah)

Lake Condah fish traps

Forty kilometres north-east of Portland and fifteen from Heywood lies the Lake Condah area (figure 14.2), where Aboriginal people, the Kerrup-jmara, have established the Lake Condah Aboriginal Mission Tourist Development, to which Aboriginal and non-Aboriginal visitors are invited to learn more about the Aboriginal history and culture of the western region of Victoria.

Outstanding amongst the traces of local historic and prehistoric society is a huge system of Aboriginal stone fish traps and canals connected to Lake Condah (figure 14.3 and plate 14.4).[3] Before the land was drained for European agriculture, the annual rains of autumn and winter used to turn vast stretches of western Victoria into marshes each year. Land which is now dry paddocks was then extensive wetlands, at least from late autumn through to late spring, where Aborigines constructed an elaborate network of canals and traps.

The building materials for the stone walls were the blocks of black volcanic basalt from the Mount Eccles stony rise lava flows which litter the district, and

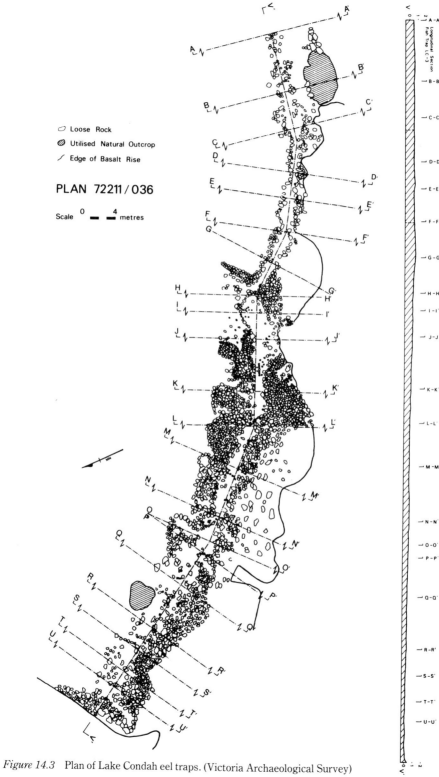

Figure 14.3   Plan of Lake Condah eel traps. (Victoria Archaeological Survey)

Plate 14.4   Lake Condah eel traps, after heavy rain. (Victoria Archaeological Survey)

the tools were digging sticks. Stone walls of up to a metre high and more than 50 metres long were built, and at Lake Condah canals were dug a metre deep and as much as 300 metres long. (Elsewhere in the western district an Aboriginal-made channel which links drainage basins across a watershed is over one kilometre long.) Fish swam into the narrow channels blocked with stone walls, and were caught in nets woven from reeds or traps inserted in the gaps in the stone walls.

Eels were probably the main species caught, and specially designed pots were used to catch the eels during their annual migrations, upstream in spring and downstream in autumn. These long, narrow, eel pots were made from plaited rushes or strips of bark with a willow hoop at the mouth (figure 14.4; examples can be seen in the Museum of Victoria in Melbourne). The fishermen used to wait behind the trap to grab the eels as they swam out from the narrow end of the pot, killed them by biting them on the back of the head, and threaded them on a stick to take them back to camp. The eel is a temperate freshwater species, *Anguilla australis occidentalis,* which grows to more than a metre long and the thickness of a man's arm.

This sophisticated piece of hydraulic engineering modifed the natural topography to construct a reliable system of catching fish and eels. It has been estimated that no more than 20 people were needed to operate the traps once they were built. The traps are located at different heights, and as the lake rose or fell, different traps came into operation one after the other, taking advantage of both rising and falling water. In June 1977 after a period of heavy rain Peter Coutts and other archaeologists from the Victoria Archaeological Survey were able to observe and record how the system operated. As the level of Lake Condah rose, the lower channels and traps were flooded. Water began to spill into rocky hollows and form pools. As each pool was filled, the water spilled out and raced along stone channels to fill the next series of pools, activating another series of traps.

This ingenious and efficient method of harvesting eels and fish allowed the Aborigines of the western district to follow a semi-sedentary way of life based on

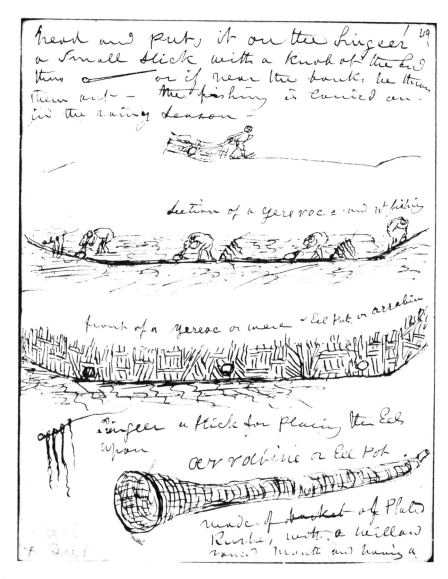

Figure 14.4 Eel traps in Western Victoria, sketched by G.A. Robinson in 1841. *Above:* the front of a yereoc or weir, with eel pot or arrabine set into the holes in the weir. *Left:* lingeer or stick for placing the eels on. *Below:* arrabine or eel pot made of plaited rushes. (After Robinson 1941, courtesy Mitchell Library)

a diet of fish, ducks, emus, plains turkeys, kangaroos and vegetable foods such as *Convolvulus,* tubers of the daisy yam and the starchy rhizomes of bracken ferns.

Stone houses with semi-circular bases and doorways all facing the same way are visible at Lake Condah, and the finding of stone tools in some of these indicates that their use goes back to prehistoric times. Their stone walls stood about a metre high and the roofs were of bark or rushes supported on a wooden frame (figure 14.5). The remains of a considerable number of houses have been identified, and many were found in one paddock, suggesting that Aborigines here were living in a large, reasonably permanent village. If most of the houses were occupied by one

Figure 14.5 Stone houses in Western Victoria. Several dozen stone structures have been found in a village by Lake Condah. (Artist's impression by D. White, the *Age*, 29.1.81)

family, the population of this prehistoric village would have been several hundred people.

Visits to the Kerrup-jmara people's Lake Condah Aboriginal Mission Tourist Development can be arranged through the ranger, Lake Condah Mission, PO Box 25, Heywood, Vic. 3304 (tel. (055) 78 4242), or Yarwang-i Cultural Learning Centre, Windermere Road, Lara, Vic. 3712 (tel. (052) 82 3429), or the Victorian

The Grampians (Gariwerd)

In contrast with northern Australia, only 130 Aboriginal rock art sites are known in Victoria, and over 100 of these are located in Gariwerd, Aboriginal name for the Grampians,[4] situated in western Victoria some 280 kilometres west of Melbourne between Stawell and Ararat on the east, Horsham in the north and Hamilton in the south (figure 14.6). (At Hamilton there is the Hamilton Aboriginal Keeping Place, which is open to the public.) They cover an area of about 2,500 square kilometres, and are composed of striking, rugged sandstone ridges, rising abruptly above the surrounding plains. The sandstone layers are tilted, rising steeply on the east and more gently on the west. The parallel, weathered ranges run north-south for about 100 kilometres, and the most impressive landforms are found in the Wonderland area near Halls Gap. In 1984 most of the ranges (167,000 hectares) were made into the Grampians National Park, Victoria's largest and most imposing national park. Access is off the Western Highway from Ararat, Stawell or Horsham, or off the Glenelg Highway from Dunkeld, and at Halls Gap (Budja Budja) there is both a

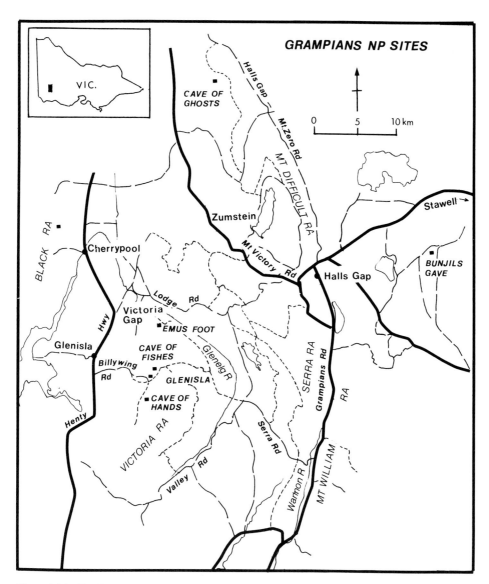

Figure 14.6 The Grampians

National Parks Interpretive Centre with displays on Aboriginal culture, and the Brambuk Aboriginal Living Culture Centre.

All of the rock art sites in the park are in rockshelters at the base of cliffs or beneath isolated boulders. Very few sites are at any distance from water, and minor and sparse occupation sites occur throughout the ranges, but more of the major habitation sites are on the periphery. It seems that easy access was a prime concern. The largest and most prolific art sites are usually located in accessible rockshelters on the less steep western slopes. These tend to contain traces of habitation in their earth floors, whereas art sites in very remote and rugged parts of the ranges generally contain less occupation debris and fewer painted motifs. Although it is clear that at least some art sites were used for sporadic camping, the quantity of stone tools found is low. This suggests that the function of art sites was either mainly ceremonial, or may simply indicate that the sites were only used as campsites for brief periods.

The Grampians rock art consists of paintings and a small number of drawings, prints and stencils; there are no engravings. This may be a function of the hardness of the local quartzose sandstone or granite, but since such rock has been engraved in other parts of Australia it seems more likely to be culturally determined. Most of the paintings are in red ochre, although white, black and yellow were also used.

The motifs are almost always small in size, with most less than 20 centimetres long. Most common subjects are "bars" or "tally marks", emu tracks, diminutive, simple human figures, and linear designs such as barred circles or grids. There are also lines, a very few kangaroo tracks, hand stencils, handprints and a few complex designs. Notable features of the Grampians rock art are the predominance of red ochre and the almost complete lack of bichrome paintings, the rarity of kangaroo figures and the small size and simplicity of the human figures and other motifs. Small, simple, red human figures and "tally marks" are dominant. These are probably the most widespread motifs both in space and time in Australia, so they give no clues to the age of the paintings or any links with other regions. This is the most southerly rock art on the Australian mainland, and contrasts markedly with the much richer and more spectacular art of New South Wales and South Australia, and with Tasmania, where no figurative paintings have yet been found but where more than a dozen sites have engravings or ancient hand stencils.

Aboriginal occupation of the Grampians goes back to at least 5,000 years, and ochre was found in the deposit in the main Glenisla rockshelter from at least 1,800 years. This suggests but does not prove that rock painting has been going on for more than 1,800 years, since ochre was also used to decorate artefacts and the body for ceremonial purposes.

There are three main groups of art sites with slightly different characteristics. The principal one, with the greatest preponderance of human figures, is focused on the catchment of Cultivation Creek in the Victoria Range. The northern group and those in the Black Range have fewer human figures and more geometric linear motifs and animal tracks. Twenty kilometres to the east of the Grampians lies the unique Bunjil's Cave, the only site to contain large figures (see figure 14.8) Sites which are in the Register of the National Estate and accessible to the public with protective grilles in place are described below in some detail as an aid to the visitor to appreciate the complexity of the sites. These are not visually spectacular but form a significant body of rock art, which repays unhurried examination. Many of the shelters are rather dark and it is necessary to accustom the eyes to the shade in order to see the faint motifs.

Cave of Ghosts, Mount Stapylton

In the very north of the Grampians north-west of Halls Gap ghostly human figures are painted on a shallow rock overhang. There are 16 figures painted in white pipe-clay and now faded by water-leaching. They average 20 centimetres in height.[5] The rockshelter is gridded and open to the public, and is a pleasant walk of about 4.5 kilometres from the Mount Zero picnic ground, via Pohlners Track.

Flat Rock shelter

In the same area another set of paintings lies on north-facing overhanging cliffs about 1.5 kilometres north-east of Mount Zero picnic ground. The main shelter is 25 metres long, with the art mainly on the ceilings.[6] The condition of the paintings is fair to good, with many very clear figures. Some 163 have been identified, all in red ochre with a mean size of 8 centimetres. Motifs comprise bars, emu tracks, handprints, kangaroo tracks, ovals, and various other indeterminate marks.

Black Range sites

The Black Range,[7] on the western side of the Grampians, contains at least seven art sites, three of which also have occupational debris in the earth shelter floor, including shell from emu eggs. Charcoal from ancient campfires in the middle of the occupational deposit in one of the shelters (number 2) has been radiocarbon-dated to some 3,300 years old, and it is estimated that the earliest habitation is at least 4,000 years. Excavation of a smaller art site to the north by Caroline Bird gave a basal date of 5,000 years.

The largest shelter (# 3) has 56 paintings and 2 hand stencils in red; motifs include emu tracks (19) and one kangaroo track, lines (14), 2 "stars", 2 "crosses", 2 complex and 3 simple designs and some 13 fragments. Another art site (# 2) is very close to the picnic ground and contains 81 figures spanning 13 motif types. Predominant are lines, simple designs, emu tracks and human figures, which dominate this site, but are absent in shelter 3. An unusual feature at this site is the extensive spiral design in the largest shelter.

The Black Range sites are west of the Henty Highway 13 kilometres south-west of Brimpaen, and due west of Cherrypool. The Black Range track is followed to a carpark and picnic area, 900 metres south-east of Rees Road. A 600 metre long walking track leads south uphill. Shelter 2 is reached after 200 metres; the track continues on down and across to the main northern cliff of Double Head Mountain in Black Range. After 400 metres visitors arrive at shelter 3. Both sites face north-east and both have grilles to protect the art.

Camp of the Emu's Foot

Located along Matthews Track 4 kilometres south-east of Victoria Gap and Glenisla Crossing in the western Grampians are four groups of paintings on the walls of sandstone rockshelters at the base of the steep, 30 metre high, northern rock face of the Victoria Range. The shelters face out north-eastwards over the broad Glenelg Valley. A signposted walking track leads to the largest shelter (B). Another site (A) with 13 poorly preserved paintings dominated by lines lies immediately to the west, and two other shelters with 17 and 23 motifs respectively lie a short distance along the cliff face to the east.

The main shelter contains a substantial archaeological deposit, including many fragments of burnt emu egg and freshwater mussel shell. There are 57 motifs painted in red ochre, including 16 human figures (some rare horizontal ones), 3 emu tracks, 3 lines, 7 simple linear designs such as a barred oval, and 1 left-hand stencil. The size of the motifs ranges from 4 to 111 centimetres, and the westernmost group of paintings is a major composition, which, were it not so faded, would have been the most striking graphic panel known in the Grampians. The placement, arrangement and uniformity in design and execution of the motifs suggest deliberate composition.

The name of the site is reported to derive from local mythology. One of the very few recorded myths dealing with the Grampians tells how the giant emu, Tchingal, created Victoria Gap by striking the ground with his foot while giving chase to the crow, War. He then rested in the vicinity for the night before continuing the chase.[8] Emus are now abundant on the flats around the ranges and even on the ridge tops. Emu egg-shell, often burnt, is quite commonly found in Aboriginal habitation sites, and was abundant in the excavated occupational deposits here and at Glenisla 1. Unexpectedly, emu tracks are not a dominant motif at this site.

The next shelter to the east (C) contains both occupation and red paintings in two groups of human figures, simple designs resembling human figures and fragments. All the paintings in this shelter are of the same colour, technique, size and form, and seem to have been executed at the same time. On a low cornice the rock has also been battered. This is common in many Grampians shelters (with or without art), and probably had a non-utilitarian function related to Aboriginal religion. Another 150 metres to the east is the smallest shelter (D) in this group, where again human figures are the dominant motif.

From detailed study of the art and superimpositions in these four rockshelters Robert Gunn discovered that hand stencils occur in only the first phase of art, that freehand paintings occur after hand-stencilling ceased, that drawings with dry pigment are the latest artistic technique (prior to European graffiti), and that the form of the human figure changes over time.

Cave of Fishes, Cultivation Creek

Located some 9 kilometres east of Glenisla homestead on the upper reaches of Cultivation Creek, this low sandstone rockshelter known as the Cave of Fishes or Brimgower Cave[9] is one of the few sites in the Grampians with a high number (22) of yellow paintings and a high number of red drawings (figure 14.7). It also has an unusual shape, with a main shelter at the north-east and a smaller one on the north-west corner, connected by a low curl of rock and a "tunnel". There is art, although fairly weathered, in both alcoves and the "tunnel".

The colours are red and yellow ochres, and the 269 motifs include 231 paintings in wet pigment and 38 drawings in dry pigment. Red "bar" motifs predominate (165), together with human figures (53), lines (15), simple designs (8), emu tracks (2), dots (1) and fragmentary motifs (22). There are also three anthropomorphs according to Gunn, one of which is 60 centimetres tall with long arms outstretched in the north-west alcove. Two other drawings in red on the ceiling of the main alcove are regarded by Gunn as anthropomorphs. The name Cave of Fishes derives from the mistaken identification of human figures as fish by the cave's first European "discoverers".

Figure 14.7 Paintings in Cave of Fishes, Grampians. (R.G. Gunn and Victoria Archaeological Survey)

The main site is protected by a grille, and sign-posted from the road. It lies about 2.5 kilometres north-east of Buandik picnic ground, and access is via a jeep track known as the Goat Track.

Glenisla shelter (Billimina)

The main Glenisla rockshelter is the most prolific single art site in Victoria, with more than 2,680 motifs.[10] It also contains a significant, excavated occupational deposit, estimated to go back at least 5,000 years. (There is considerable occupation debris below a radiocarbon date of 1,620 years on charcoal in the middle layers.) The shelter seems to have been inhabited intermittently, and the animal bone present indicates that its occupants were hunting wallabies, kangaroos, bandicoots, lizards, native cats and bush rats and collecting emu eggs. The stone tools recovered included grindstones, anvils, hammerstones, scrapers and backed blades, and seem to have been part of a maintenance toolkit, for mending wooden artefacts like spears or making new tools.

Glenisla 1 is the larger of two shelters situated about 300 metres west of Cultivation Creek and 20 minutes walk from the Buandik picnic area next to the Billywing pine plantation. A signposted walking track leads up to the site, which is an hour's drive from Halls Road along Glenelg River Road, Lodge Road and Red Rock Road.

The rock is a very hard, fine-grained quartzose sandstone, and the paintings are well-sheltered on the overhanging back wall, where they extend to a height of 2.7 metres over a length of 10.5 metres. Almost all are done in red ochre, either a fine-grained vermilion or a coarser purplish-red, but there are also a few yellow figures and one white figure. The whole wall is covered with more than 2,000 bars or tally marks, including three groups of about 300 each. This is the only site in Victoria with a whole wall covered in tally strokes; only small groups or rows occur at other Grampians sites. Most are vertical strokes about 10 centimetres long and 1 to 2 centimetres wide. They are thought to have been made with the finger, because they are generally wider at the top than the bottom and clearer in the middle, where the finger rubbed against the wall, than at the edges. A few of the bars have been repainted, and some have human figures superimposed over them.

The significance of the bars or tally marks is unknown, but the site has been known to Europeans since 1859 and there is some ethnographic information from the owner of Glenisla homestead in the second half of the nineteenth century, Samuel Carter, who wrote: "In very olden times before the arrival of whites, they congregated in large numbers at a rock in the Victoria Range near Glenisla — this rock is still marked with natives' pictures and signs, though rather disfigured by white people writing names over the stone. They counted times by moons and would draw strokes on the rock representing the number of moons that they had been there."[11] Carter's Aboriginal informants were not from the immediate area, but if he was correct, the vast number of strokes on the rock would imply considerable use of the site. Other explanations are also possible. They could be marks made to record the number of participants in ceremonies, lists of any kind, such as the number of days spent on a journey, a series of songs or sites, or the "line" of a ceremonial cycle, designs such as herring-bone on a shield, or simple symbolic decorations of the wall.

Other motifs are some 50 human figures, 10 emu tracks, 8 hands and 3 human feet, 2 or 3 birds, 2 probable boomerangs, 24 dots and a number of indeterminate marks. The human figures well illustrate the very simple and stylised human representations found in the Grampians, but contain several variants. The Glenisla art also has some previously unrecorded features, and this is one of only two known sites in the Grampians with paintings of birds, probably emus, although drawings of emus occur nearby.

About 200 metres downhill south-east of Glenisla 1 is a small painted shelter known as Glenisla 2,[12] in an isolated sandstone tor near the base of the hill slope some 50 metres from Cultivation Creek. The 18 motifs are mainly simple linear designs painted in a uniform orange-red wet pigment. Both these painted shelters lie in the immediate vicinity of the rock holes and pools of Cultivation Creek, but a third site[12] lies in a small shelter a 700 metre walk eastwards up the ridge crest, at the western end of a large outcropping ridge some 50 metres up the southern slopes of a short valley. The site faces north-east, and the faint paintings in red ochre are distinguished by an exceptionally high percentage of emu tracks among the 31 motifs. There are also four variations in the form of the emu track portrayed.

Cave of Hands, Deep Creek (Manja)

The Cave of Hands[14] faces north at the base of a spectacular sandstone cliff between Hut and Deep Creeks in the Victoria Range (Billawin), in the same region but south of the Glenisla rockshelters and 2 kilometres south of the Buandik picnic ground. It is 7 kilometres south-east of Glenisla homestead, and is reached by the 4 kilometre long, signposted Harrops walking track. Steel grilles have been erected to protect the rock art, which is relatively well-preserved, with many reasonably clear hand stencils.

The main site is a very large open shelter, and is the only rock art site in Victoria containing a high number of hand stencils. These are all in red ochre except for one in white pigment. There are 31 stencils of left hands, 19 of right, and 30 indeterminate. Other motifs present are bars (41), kangaroo tracks (10), emu tracks (9), bird tracks (3), human figures (39), and a number of other lines and designs. There are some 233 motifs in the main shelter and 34 in the smaller adjacent shelter to the right.

Bunjil's Cave

Bunjil's Cave lies in a scenic reserve 10 kilometres south-south-west of Stawell and 19 kilometres east of the Grampian National Park. There is a signposted access track to a picnic area 100 metres west of the shelter.[15] A scarred tree which may be associated with the art site lies 600 metres north-east of the shelter. The paintings are in a small, deep alcove on the southern face of a large granite tor, and are protected by a steel grille. There is no evidence that the shelter was ever used for camping, and it seems likely that this was a purely ceremonial site.

There are 13 paintings and drawings. The main motif is the large squatting human figure of Bunjil with arms akimbo and internal body decoration (figure 14.8). To his right are two dingo-like animals back to back. These three figures

Figure 14.8 Bichrome painting of Bunjil in Bunjil's Cave, Grampians. (R.G. Gunn and Victoria Archaeological Survey)

are unique in Victoria as they are all bichrome paintings in red and white. Analysis of the chemical composition of the pigments has shown that the original painting of Bunjil and the two dogs was certainly done by Aborigines with natural pigments, but that some over-painting with non-natural materials occurred later. The site has suffered considerable vandalism over the years, and the other motifs are now fragmentary.

Bunjil was the supreme, all-father creator figure in the Aboriginal religion of south-eastern Australia, according to information collected in the nineteenth century by anthropologists Brough Smyth and Alfred Howitt. A supernatural God-like being, he was reputed to have created the first people, produced many of the natural features of the landscape and led each tribal group to its present territory. He gave them their artefacts, together with the laws, customs and rituals with which to organise their society. His particular concerns were the initiation of novices into manhood and the making of medicine-men or "men of high degree". His name was known only to the initiated men, and he could only be approached by those men of high degree whom he had himself chosen. He had two wives and one or more sons, and at the end of his time on earth he ascended into the sky where he lives in "some place beyond the sky" and is represented by a star. After death the spirits of all mortals also go up to the sky and return to the spirit world.

Bunjil's Cave is arguably the most important rock art site in Victoria. Because the Aboriginal interpretation of the meaning of the art is available, it has undoubted Aboriginal religious significance, it contains the only known extant representation of Bunjil in Victoria, it is well-preserved and is unique in the state for its complex form, large size and use of more than one colour.

CHAPTER FIFTEEN

Victoria: The Centre and the East

Victoria has been distinguished by some of the major archaeological discoveries in Australia, particularly of human skeletal remains. The robust Cohuna skull, unearthed in 1925 by ploughing south of the Murray River, was only the second significant find of early man in the continent. Then in 1940 a 13,000-year-old skull was found in a quarry at Keilor (figure 15.1).[1] A quarry worker, James White, was standing on the quarry floor and swinging his pick into the silt when he felt it strike something hard. He dug out the object, washed it in the river, and found that he had put a hole into a fossil skull.

Extensive archaeological investigations of the Keilor area followed and are still continuing. The site is near the junction of Dry Creek and the Maribyrnong River, close to Melbourne airport, 2.5 kilometres north of Keilor and 16 kilometres north of Melbourne. The Victoria Archaeological Survey built a large, long shed over part of the site to protect the archaeological excavation which was going on inside during the 1970s and early 1980s, but unfortunately it has not proved possible to leave the site open to the public as originally planned.

As well as the skull found in what is now known as the Keilor terrace, some stone tools and a few bones of extinct giant animals have been found by Alexander Gallus and other workers in older deposits. Radiocarbon dates have been obtained on particles of charcoal and burnt earth, and the oldest evidence of human activity has been dated at 31,000 years. Earlier human occupation has been suggested for Keilor and, more recently, for a site near Warrnambool but these claims have not yet been substantiated.

Other major finds of prehistoric cemeteries in Victoria have been made at Kow Swamp, Coobul and Robinvale. Aboriginal people do not wish this human skeletal material to be on display nor are the sites open to the public, but the significance of the finds to the understanding of Australian prehistory is described in chapter

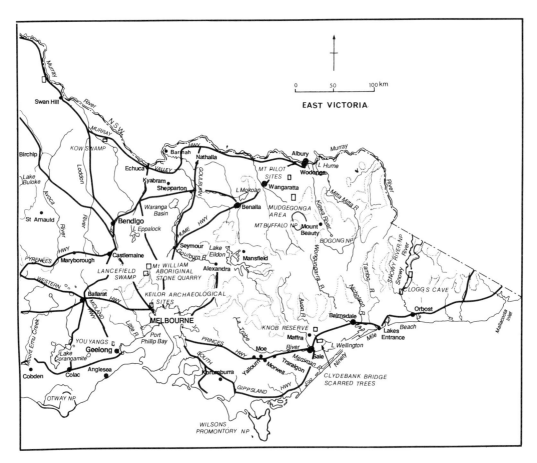

Figure 15.1   Central and eastern Victoria

2. Major displays on Aboriginal culture and an Aboriginal keeping place are in the Museum of Victoria in Melbourne.

Another important feature of prehistoric Victoria is its series of quarries of greenstone (altered volcanic rock of Cambrian age, predominantly amphibole hornfels). Greenstone is tough, fine-grained and shock-resistant and fractures readily and predictably, making it an ideal raw material for the manufacture of ground-edge axes. The piece of volcanic rock was first roughly flaked into the right shape and size, and then its cutting edge was ground to a sharp blade on a whetstone, usually of sandstone. Water was splashed onto it to aid the grinding process. The stone axehead was then hafted onto a handle of wood, usually by heating a strip of timber halfway along its length and doubling it over to form a loop, into which the blade was fitted. It was cemented in place with bindings and resin made from the sap of the grass-tree or, where available, the tough, sticky gum of spinifex.

Outcrops of greenstone occur throughout central Victoria, and stone from these quarries was mined by Aborigines and traded widely. Aborigines obtained greenstone from outcrops near Ararat, Maryborough, Glenthompson, Heathcote and the Howqua River, but the major quarry was at Mount William (see below).

Archaeologists such as Isabel McBryde[2] have succeeded in working out the distribution of axes from a number of these quarries. Once a quarry has been discovered, the distinguishing characteristics of the stone are identified by microscopic identification. Then thin sections — tiny slivers — of stone are sawn from ground-edge axes in museums and private collections, ground down to transparent thinness for examination under the microscope and compared with the "fingerprints" of the various quarries. In this way axes can be matched with quarries, and distribution maps drawn for the network of exchange from each quarry.

These distribution studies have shown that Aboriginal exchange of goods was complex. It was not determined merely by trade routes based on supply and demand or by the location of regional resources, but by social and political factors such as the affiliations of the local groups who owned the quarries. Investigation of anthropological and linguistic data has indicated that traditional trading networks tended to mirror social networks, of people who spoke mutually intelligible languages and intermarried. This is important evidence of the links between trade, language, belief system, social customs and group affiliations in at least this part of prehistoric Australia.

In this chapter, readers tour around central and eastern Victoria, beginning in the Lancefield-Geelong region, then heading east to Wilson's Promontory National Park, and finishing an anti-clockwise loop in the north along the Murray River and down to Carisbrook and Melbourne. In Victoria some 13,000 Aboriginal sites have been recorded, but few are visitable (refer Victoria Archaeological Survey [see page 363] or relevant Aboriginal traditional owners). Some Aboriginal sites around Melbourne are described in Gary Presland's excellent book, *Land of the Kulin.*

Mount William axe quarry, Lancefield

Sixty kilometres north-west of Melbourne and eight kilometres north-east of Lancefield to the east of the Lancefield–Pyalong road is the Mount William archaeological area. Mount William reaches 830 metres above sea level, and from its peak a ridge of Cambrian volcanic greenstone extends in a curve to the north-east (plate 15.1). Greenstone (amphibole hornfels) has the toughness, hardness and fine grain needed to make heavy-duty stone axes with ground edges. Signs of Aboriginal quarrying of this stone extend over an area of 60 hectares, now mainly masked by slope wash and growth of pasture grasses. A small portion of the site has been fenced with a two metre high chain mesh fence, and access is only possible with permission from the landowner and the Victoria Archaeological Survey.

Evidence of intensive Aboriginal exploitation of the outcrops and stone-working can be seen along a kilometre of ridge on the north-eastern slopes of Mount William.[3] Squat pillars of greenstone jut out on the skyline. Along the ridge's spine and at its south-western end large boulders have been quarried at their base, and downslope heaps of quarry waste and flaked stone have accumulated in piles up to 50 metres long. There are over 50 of these accumulations of broken stone. Buried stone was also mined, for more than 250 shallow circular or oval hollows, often several metres in diameter and a metre deep, had been dug out on the northern and eastern sides of the ridge by the Aboriginal miners in order to obtain

Plate 15.1 Mount William axe quarry, Lancefield. (Victoria Archaeological Survey)

stone from below ground surface. There are also 18 deeper, shaft-like pits cut down into the bedrock. Areas of sheared or jointed rock have been avoided.

Most of the mining pits have associated flaking floors, where the mined material was roughly shaped into a "blank" or "pre-form" for trading and later fashioning into a finished hatchet head with a ground working edge. Often in the centre of the flaking floor an undisturbed block of greenstone was left to serve as an anvil for this rough shaping process. Some 30 larger, distinct "flaking floors" are located separately downslope from the quarrying areas; these are circular mounds of flaked stone about 20 metres across.

The Aboriginal miners clearly had a sound knowledge of the nature of the outcrop, the varying quality of the material and the best technology to exploit it. Mount William was the centre of a vast trading network. More than half the axes were carried over 100 kilometres away from the quarry and 29 per cent travelled more than 300 kilometres.

The use of the quarry was recorded in the nineteenth century by anthropologist A.W. Howitt, whose informant, Barak, witnessed its final operations. It was "the stone tomahawk place" of the Wurundjeriballuk clan of the Woiwurrung tribe, who were part of the "nation" of the Kulin in central Victoria, an alliance of tribes with mutually intelligible languages and similar social organisation and laws. Axes were traded as valued goods and highly prized among the Kulin and their allies, but not to their traditional enemies, the Kurnai of Gippsland.

The last Aborigine responsible for working the outcrop was Billi-billeri, who died in 1846. He "lived at the quarry to take care of it and when he went away his nephew went to mind it". Tribes came from over 100 kilometres away to obtain this outstanding greenstone in exchange for other goods such as weapons, ornaments, belts or necklaces. Mount William axe stone was exchanged for reed spear-shafts from the Swan Hill area on the River Murray, 300 kilometres away, and for sandstone from St Kilda, Melbourne. The exchange rate is unknown, except for one instance of three axe blanks being traded for one possum skin rug. This shows the very high value placed on the stone, for it would take much longer to hunt, prepare and sew as many as 70 possum skins to make one rug than the hour or two of work needed to turn one axe blank into a finished tool.

This prehistoric axe quarry played a very important role in the social and economic lives of Aborigines who lived in central Victoria. It is a testimony to Aboriginal technical achievement, and illustrates the capacity of ancient Victorian Aborigines for organised effort and specialised industrial activity.

You Yangs Forest Park, Geelong

Aboriginal rock wells can be seen among the distinctive granite peaks of the You Yangs, which rise abruptly from the volcanic plains between Melbourne and Sydney. (The name You Yangs comes from the Aboriginal words Wurdi Youang or Ude Youang, meaning a big mountain in the middle of a plain.)

The park is 55 kilometres south-west of Melbourne and 22 kilometres north of Geelong. Access from the Geelong Freeway is signposted via Little River or Lara, or from Bacchus Marsh follow the Geelong Road and the side roads to Lara.

Reliable natural water is scarce in the You Yangs. Aborigines therefore improved the supply by creating rock wells in the granite, chipping away depressions or enlarging natural hollows. Some of these Aboriginal rock wells can be seen on top of Big Rock, 150 metres west of the Big Rock picnic ground north of the visitors' centre (plate 15.2).

Geelong Cultural Centre

There is an Aboriginal Cultural Centre at Geelong, called Yarwangi, where displays on regional Aboriginal culture may be seen.

Otway National Park

Many Aboriginal shell middens and other occupation sites lie along the 60 kilometres of spectacular coastline between Princeton and Apollo Bay, within Otway National Park, some 200 kilometres south-west of Melbourne. Otway peninsula is mountainous with forests of towering mountain ash and gullies of myrtle beech rainforest, mosses and ferns, but a narrow corridor of heathland borders the coast. On top of the cliffs at the tip of the peninsula Aborigines camped at Seal Point overlooking the eastern end of Crayfish Bay. This area lies about 2 kilometres east of Cape Otway lighthouse, 14 kilometres south of Apollo Bay and 15 kilometres south-east of Hordenvale.

Traces of shell midden can be seen for more than a kilometre along the cliff top, and at Seal Point the middens stretch back 100 metres from the cliff edge. There are some 16 separate sites within this area, one rockshelter containing shell midden and 15 open shell middens. One huge midden at the tip of Seal Point

Plate 15.2 Rock wells in the You Yangs Forest Park. (Department of Conservation, Forests and Lands, Victoria)

about 30 metres above sea level has been partially excavated by Harry Lourandos.[4] The site extends about 400 by 100 metres and 1.5 metres deep, and is eroding down the cliff face. At its eastern end there are ten circular depressions thought to be the bases of huts, as observed in use in the first half of the nineteenth century in western Victoria. The two easternmost hut depressions and some of the adjacent, stratified midden were excavated, and yielded traces of occupation going back 1,500 years.

The site probably served as a principal base camp and stone tool manufacturing centre in the Cape Otway region; it has been described by Lourandos as "the most complex and bountiful of all southwestern Victorian shell middens". It appears that the remote and mountainous Otway peninsula with its restricted habitable area was settled on a permanent basis only 1,500 years ago; vigorous searching by archaeologists failed to reveal any earlier occupation in the region. Once the camp was established, however, it was used intensively for much of the year, especially in spring and early summer during the sealing season. The inhabitants relied heavily on elephant seals, possums, fish (mainly Labrids), and shellfish from the nearby inter-tidal rock platforms. Microscopic examination of residues on the working edges of stone tools has shown that roasted rhizomes of bracken fern also played an important part in the diet. In the upper part of the midden there is a marked decline in the quantity of seal bones, and the elephant seal is largely replaced by the fur seal, but this was offset by increased consumption of fish and land animals such as possum.

Glen Aire rockshelters

Just outside Otway National Park on the west side of Aire River are traces of Aboriginal occupation in rockshelters formed in dune limestone at the base of a high calcarenite ridge. The sites have a superb view north across river flats to the Otway ranges, and are in a road reserve immediately south of the road from Glen Aire to Lake Craven, four kilometres south-west of Glen Aire and a hundred metres west of a large limestone quarry.

The two sites excavated by John Mulvaney in 1960[5] revealed 400-year-old stone and bone tools and bones of seals, seabirds and possums, as well as several species of shellfish. This is valuable evidence of the nature of recent Victorian Aboriginal culture in this region, and these are two of the few sites with good preservation of bone and other organic remains. Visitors are reminded that the collection of Aboriginal artefacts or other remains is prohibited by law.

Eastern Victoria

Wilsons Promontory Aboriginal middens

Within Wilsons Promontory National Park Aboriginal shell middens are numerous, and archaeological excavation[6] of some of these has produced important evidence about Aboriginal coastal lifeways and technology over the last 6,500 years.

The park lies 230 kilometres south-east of Melbourne, and is reached by turning south at Meeniyan or Foster from the South Gippsland Highway. There is a visitor centre and a display on Aboriginal culture at Tidal River, 32 kilometres inside the park entrance. The Aborigines knew this beautiful, rugged region as Wamoom, and gathered shellfish around its shores.

Most of the middens are on the west side of the promontory, between Shallow Inlet near the northern border of the park and the Darby River. There are concentrations at Oberon Bay and on the west side of Yanakie isthmus between Darby River and Cotters Lake, and at least some of this area is accessible by walking tracks. (Off the tracks the bush is thick and virtually impenetrable.) Along this coast of rock platforms and ocean beaches the middens lie in a series of superimposed dunes, the oldest dunes belonging to the glacial period when sea level was as much as 150 metres lower, Bass Strait did not exist and a tongue of dry land linked the promontory with Tasmania.

Plate 15.3   A scarred tree at Clydebank, Gippsland

The oldest human occupation on the promontory is 6,500 years old.
Archaeological evidence shows that about a thousand years ago Aborigines
changed their diet from rocky shore shellfish to sandy beach species. At the same
time their technology altered from a well-developed microlithic industry to the
use of less complex artefacts. The reasons for this dramatic change are not clear.

Knob Reserve, Stratford

Some of the very few axe grinding grooves found in Victoria lie on the top of a rocky sandstone knob, 25 metres above the River Avon. The area of sandstone is restricted and the grooves are few in number and small, but have considerable scarcity value in this region of south-eastern Australia. Nearby are several scarred trees, from which Aborigines removed sheets of bark to make canoes, shields or carrying dishes. This attractive, wooded reserve is only 2.5 kilometres south-east of Stratford.

Clydebank Bridge scarred trees, Stratford

Aboriginal scarred trees are becoming increasingly rare, and this group is particularly valuable because of the large number of generally well-preserved and varied scarred trees within a small area (plate 15.3). They lie on the north bank of the River Avon immediately east of the Bengworden Road where it crosses the river, 15 kilometres south-east of Stratford and the same distance north-east of Sale.

The site is on a narrow strip of land between the river and the swamps south and west of Ramahyuck Aboriginal Mission, which was occupied between 1863 and 1908. While some of the 18 scarred river red gums bear steel axe marks and date from the historic period, others are likely to be prehistoric, for this is a rich environment with much bird life on the wetlands and river, and has probably been used as a camping area by Aborigines for many centuries. The scarred trees include some very large canoe trees, many shield scars, and one tree with toeholds cut by Aborigines for koala or possum hunting.

Cloggs Cave, Buchan

Some of the oldest evidence of human occupation in Victoria has been found in Cloggs Cave near Buchan. Not only were there stone tools and charcoal from ancient campfires lit 17,700 years ago, but also, at the very base of the deposit, bones of extinct giant kangaroos, 23,000 years old. This is still the only known ice age site in south-eastern Australia in which bone and bone tools are preserved, so it is of great scientific significance. The cave lies four kilometres south-east of Buchan on the Orbost Road on the southern side of the Buchan River, and is visible from just west of the road bridge which crosses the river, as a tall dark cleft in a cliff near the top of a small hill (plates 15.4 and 15.5).

The site is on private property and is protected by a steel grille, but access for specialist groups may be arranged through the Victoria Archaeological Survey or the Victorian Speleological Association, with the agreement of the landowner. Other caves are open to the public in Buchan, where spectacular formations in the Devonian limestone can be seen.

I found the archaeological site in 1971 when driving along the Buchan-Orbost road to visit another site in the course of my study of Aboriginal prehistory in the Snowy Mountains region. I noticed the cave (formed by two intersecting geological faults) close to the crest of a hill, suggesting that the floor would be dry, unlike so many limestone caves which have a river running through them. I was

Plate 15.4 Cloggs Cave, Buchan

searching for a dry limestone cave which might have been inhabited in prehistoric times, in order to find remain of the meals of the hunter-gatherers and bone tools as well as stone tools. (Organic material is much better preserved in a limestone than in a sandstone or granite environment.)

Investigation revealed extensive smoke-blackening on the walls and ceiling, stone tools and fragments of mussel shell in the floor of the rockshelter, and a dimly-lit inner cave with a soft, dry earth floor: a perfect piece of prehistoric real estate!

Archaeological evidence from excavations at Cloggs Cave outlines its story with a reasonable degree of certainty.[7] Some 23,000 years ago, before Aborgines first camped in the cave, it was sometimes a lair of the Tasmanian tiger and devil, at other times the home of rock wallabies. Outside the cave the environment was similar to the present, with grassland and dry sclerophyll woodland bordering the river, but the climate was far colder and rather wetter than today's. Giant marsupials, such as the massive kangaroo, *Sthenurus orientalis*, still roamed the region, but became extinct later.

Then Aborigines began to use the cave about 17,700 years ago. At first they used simple flakes and pebble tools of local quartz, but gradually their toolkit expanded to include scrapers of finer-grained rock like chert and jasper. They paid only occasional visits to the cave, which was also a home for owls. The earth floor was fairly dry, but drips from the limestone roof gradually built up stalagmites, and from time to time small stalacites and the occasional large stone block fell from the ceiling.

As it became warmer at the end of the last glaciation between 13,000 and 9,000 years ago, use of the cave increased. In daytime the rockshelter was used, the north-facing ledges providing warm sitting places and a good vantage point out over the valley. At night fires were lit on the cave floor from *Eucalyptus* wood. The people gathered round, heating hearth stones and cooking food items gathered during the day such as possums, bandicoots, gliders, koalas, marsupial mice, rock and swamp wallabies and kangaroos. Men whittled with stone scrapers to make wooden spears and boomerangs, and rubbed hides with smooth river cobbles until they were pliable enough to be sewn together as cloaks. The possum or kangaroo skins were trimmed to size with sharp quartz flakes, holes were pierced with a bone awl, its tip ground and polished to needle-like sharpness, and sinews from the kangaroo's tail were chewed until supple enough to be used as thread.

The inner chamber of the cave was not used after 8,500 years ago, and the site seems to have been vacated until a thousand years ago, when hunter-gatherers camped in the rockshelter. They manufactured small backed blades there, probably to use as barbs on their spears, and ate mussels from the nearby river. This way of life came to an end when Europeans settled the Buchan Valley in the 1830s.

Plate 15.5 Cloggs Cave, Buchan, interior

Northern Victoria

Mount Pilot rock art sites, Beechworth

Rock art sites are rare in Victoria; there are very few outside the Grampians and those on Mount Pilot are isolated from other art sites in the north-east of the state. The exceptional paintings are unlike any others known in Victoria in both size and style of motifs,[8] and the Mount Pilot 1 site has both the largest single motif in Victoria and an apparent depiction of the Tasmanian tiger or thylacine, a painting probably more than 2,000 years old.

There are two art sites in granite rockshelters on the slopes of Mount Pilot (figures 15.2 and 15.3), 12 kilometres north of Beechworth, 11 kilometres south of Chiltern and 25 kilometres south-west of Albury-Wodonga. The more accessible site, Mount Pilot 1, lies only 150 metres south-east from the Mount Pilot Scenic Reserve carpark and picnic facilities reached from unsealed roads off the Beechworth-Chiltern road to the north of Mount Pilot. Situated on a steep hill slope 30 metres above the valley floor, the granite tor faces west at an elevation of some 300 metres above sea level; the summit and fire tower of Mount Pilot, about 500 metres to the south-east, rises to 510 metres.

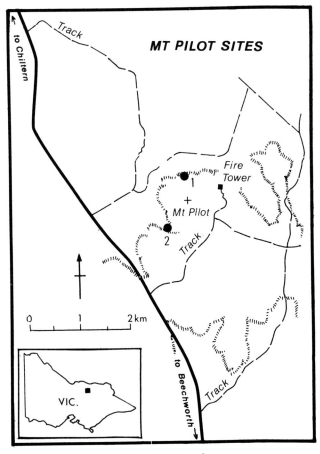

Figure 15.2   Location of Mount Pilot art sites

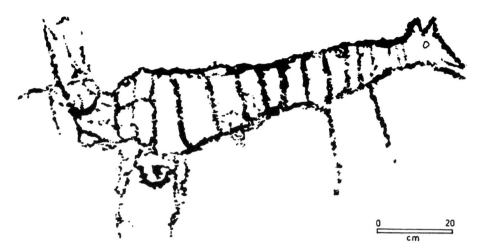

Figure 15.3 Thylacine in the Mount Pilot paintings. (Courtesy R. Gunn and Victoria Archaeological Survey)

There is a more obvious area of boulders and caves to the west, but the painted rockshelter occurs between two large granite tors on a steep slope. The shelter is roughly V-shaped in plan (eight metres wide by seven deep), with a steep rocky floor. The artwork is on the right-hand (southern) wall of the shelter, and is now fenced. There are only nine motifs and some of these are extremely faint. They were painted with a wet, red ochre, and there is some evidence of re-painting. Most of the pigment has fallen off the wall, and the motifs now exist only as a red stain which has impregnated the rock surface. This staining should last indefinitely, and implies substantial antiquity for the art.

The motifs include an outlined anthropomorph facing left in the top left of the panel, an outlined design possibly representing a snake with forked tongue facing right near the anthropomorph, and a long (246 centimetres) serpentine figure also possibly representing a snake facing to the right, which resembles a seam of biotite running across the top of the panel. The most outstanding figure is an outlined and infilled animal which has stripes across its back and most clearly resembles the Tasmanian tiger or thylacine (figure 15.3). A feldspar crystal within the granite has been incorporated into the design to represent the animal's eye. The thylacine is generally accepted (in spite of recent reported sightings!) to have been extinct on the Australian mainland for over 3,000 years, which would make this painting 3,000 years old, if its identification is correct. This would place it among the oldest rock paintings in Victoria. The site was probably of particularly significance to Aborigines, and associated with some form of special ritual.

A second small art site, Mount Pilot 2, lies 1.5 kilometres to the south-west, halfway up the western slopes of Barnes Gully above Bye Creek. The art alcove faces north-east in the centre of a group of large tors, to the right of a large tree. The major two motifs here are hollow-bodied human figures, a style unknown elsewhere in Victoria, although the more common bars, lines and emu tracks also occur.

In Beechworth there is an excellent regional museum, with a large collection of

Aboriginal artefacts. Of particular note are various types of wooden artefacts, carved with intricate designs with outstanding artistic skill.

Shepparton

There is an Aboriginal keeping place in the Shepparton International Village (PO Box 1386, Shepparton, tel. 058 21 8285), open every day. Another Aboriginal cultural centre is Dharnya in the Barmah State Forest near Echuca, where a rich collection of Aboriginal culture is displayed. The centre is actually built on an Aboriginal mound or "kitchen midden". Nearby, a walking trail has been established among the river red gums in the Barmah State Forest, where the visitor can view scarred canoe trees and other reminders of traditional Aboriginal life. Further information on the Dharnya centre is available from the Department of Conservation. Forests and Lands (see page 362).

Whroo Historic Reserve, Balaclava Hill, Rushworth

Within this reserve in north-central Victoria is the Whroo rock well, on a walking trail south-east of Balaclava Hill visitors centre, some 7 kilometres south of Rushworth, between Heathcote, Shepparton and Seymour. Whroo is said to be an Aboriginal word for lips or mouth, and the well is deep, with a capacity of about 110 litres or 24 gallons. It is 50 by 35 centimetres in diameter, and some 90 centimetres deep.

Hattah-Kulkyne National Park, Mildura

This park is located in the Murray Valley in the far north-west of Victoria. It is reached by turning off the Murray Valley Highway 4 kilometres east of Hattah, roughly 70 kilometres south of Mildura.

Aboriginal artefacts are on display at the visitors' centre, and there is much evidence to be seen of traditional Aboriginal life in the Murray Valley, such as middens, canoe and shield trees. One excellent example of a canoe tree stands by the shore of Lake Hattah on the nature drive near the visitors' centre.

Carisbrook stone alignment, Maryborough

The prime example in Victoria of an Aboriginal stone arrangement is that at Carisbrook, in the Maryborough region. Two curved parallel lines of small boulders (between 15 and 20 centimetres in diameter) form a boomerang shape, 27 metres long and about 2 metres wide. Nearby are cairns and two well-preserved circles of stones, with a diameter of between 2 and 3 metres. The site is on readily accessible farmland, but permission to visit and locational information should be sought from the local Aboriginal community or through Victoria Archaeological Survey.

Gellibrand Hill Park, Melbourne

A number of sites in Gellibrand Hill Park and the surrounding area tell us something of traditional Aboriginal lifeways in the Melbourne region. Surface campsites are typical of many of those found in the metropolitan region. In the park there are 8 scarred trees, where pieces of bark have been taken from river red gums to make canoes, shields, containers or shelters.

CHAPTER SIXTEEN

New South Wales: The West

Ancient sites in an ancient landscape characterise New South Wales, particularly the west of the state in the semi-arid region between Broken Hill and Balranald, which boasts most of the oldest Aboriginal sites in Australia (figure 16.1). The best known lie in the Willandra Lakes region, which contains Mungo National Park (see below), the only place in Australia which has been inscribed on the World Heritage List primarily for the significance of its Aboriginal sites.

In addition to its Pleistocene occupation sites, New South Wales boasts many rock art sites, and is particularly rich in engravings. The style of engravings varies greatly. In the west some are similar to those of South Australia and Central Australia and are mainly circle and track motifs, as in the classic Panaramitee style, but in other sites figures resembling humans and animals are prominent. Around Sydney outlines of large figures of spirit ancestors, humans, whales, fish, kangaroos and all manner of other creatures are engraved on the Hawkesbury sandstone. Rock painting is also marked by considerable regional variation both in subject matter and style, the most colourful and animated paintings being found in western New South Wales in the Cobar area.

More Aboriginal sites have been recorded in New South Wales than in any other state, probably because more archaeological work has been done there than elsewhere, because there are large centres of population and the state sites authority, the National Parks and Wildlife Service, has been particularly active. The number of sites on record is now more than 20,000. The vast majority of these are habitation sites, either occupational deposits in the floors of rockshelters or open campsites, ranging from a few stone artefacts scattered on the ground or small coastal shell middens to huge 30,000-year-old campsites beside ancient lake beds.

Other site types include burials, ceremonial stone arrangements and bora grounds, rock engravings, paintings, drawings and stencils, carved and scarred trees, fish traps, stone and ochre quarries and sacred sites of particular significance in Aboriginal religion. (In New South Wales historic Aboriginal sites such as mission stations are also recorded, but they are beyond the scope of this book.) One type of Aboriginal site which is almost confined to New South Wales is the carved tree. Carved trees have designs carved into the wood, whereas a tree

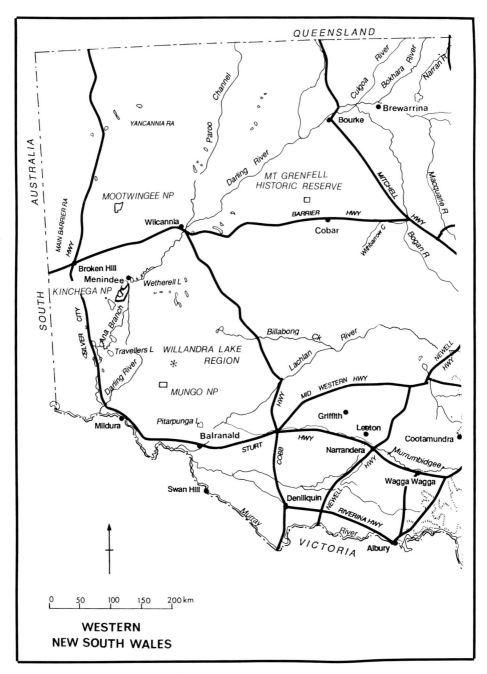

Figure 16.1   Western New South Wales

from which a sheet of bark has been removed to make a canoe, shield or other artefact is known as a scarred tree.

In spite of the very large number of Aboriginal sites on record in New South Wales, relatively few are promoted for public visitation, and most of these are described below. There is no public access to sites on private land but in some cases special entry can be arranged through the landowner and the National Parks and Wildlife Service. Further information is available from the National Parks and Wildlife Service (p. 362). The Australian Museum in College Street, Sydney is an excellent starting point to learn about the Aboriginal heritage of New South Wales. All Aboriginal sites and artefacts are protected by law, with heavy penalties for anyone who damages sites or removes any Aboriginal material.

In addition to its Aboriginal sites New South Wales has much to offer to those interested in understanding the landscape as it was before humans arrived on the scene. The east of the state boasts several groups of magnificent limestone caves, and the north contains the remnants of massive volcanoes. The west is distinguished by its ancient arid landscape, from which scientists have been able to learn much about past climates and environment.

Mungo National Park, Willandra Lakes region

Within the 600,000 hectare Willandra Lakes World Heritage region there is just one small national park, Mungo, 110 kilometres north-east of Mildura and 150

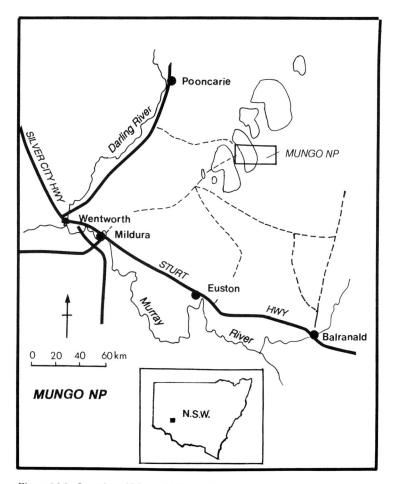

Figure 16.2 Location of Mungo National Park

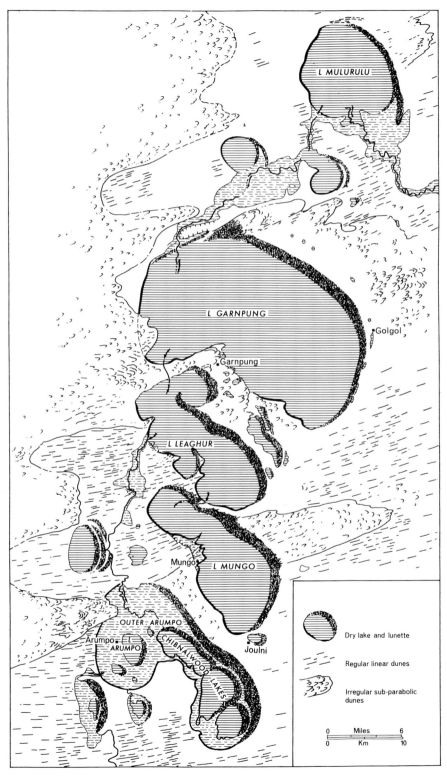

Figure 16.3   Willandra Lakes region: former freshwater lakes. (W. Mumford)

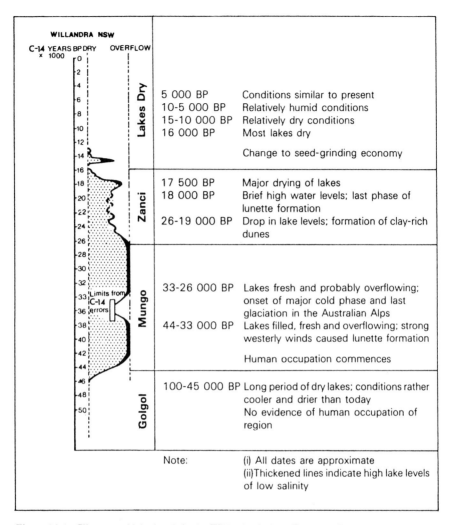

Figure 16.4   Climate and lake levels in the Willandra Lakes. (Based on Bowler *et al* 1976)

kilometres north-west of Balranald (figures 16.2 and 16.3). Car access from Mildura is through Boronga towards Wentworth, turning off at the Arumpo road, from Balranald and Ivanhoe from the Gol Gol road, and from Broken Hill through Menindee. The roads are unsealed and may be impassable after rain, and it is as well to telephone to Mungo, where there is a visitor centre (with excellent displays), in advance of arrival (enquiries 050 29 7292). The best time to visit is winter, and there is a ranger-guided drive tour during Easter and the winter school holidays.

Aborigines lived in the Willandra Lakes region for at least 40,000 years, when it was on the ancient channel of the Lachlan River. In this early period of occupation during the Pleistocene, conditions for hunter-gatherers were much more favourable than today. The climate was cooler and there was less evaporation which meant that lakes like Mungo were then full of fresh water (figure 16.4). But after 15,000 years ago the climate became much drier, the Lachlan River

Plate 16.1 Erosion of the ancient land surface in the Willandra Lakes World Heritage area. Differential erosion of old land surfaces produces residuals of hardened sand. These features are often consolidated by the roots of trees and shrubs. (J. Bowler)

changed to its present channel, and the lakes dried up, so don't bother bringing a boat, you are far too late!

Lake Mungo is about 25 kilometres long and on its eastern side is a high crescent dune of clay and sand, called the Walls of China by locals, possibly having been named by the Chinese labourers who built the Mungo woolshed in

Plate 16.2   Erosion on the Mungo lunette in the Willandra Lakes world heritage area. (J. Bowler)

1869. From the top of the Walls of China there is only flat mallee scrub to be seen stretching to the horizon, throwing into sharp relief the picture of what used to be a green oasis teeming with perch and the huge Murray cod, giant tree-browsing kangaroos, three-metre high emus and the massive *Zygomaturus*. These megafaunal creatures had become extinct in the Willandra region by the end of the last ice age around 14,000 years ago, probably from a combination of the drying up of surface water and hunting by Aborigines.

The story of Lake Mungo can be told, at least in outline, from 120,000 years ago, due mainly to the research work of geomorphologist Jim Bowler, who has made a number of outstanding discoveries in the area since the late 1960s.[1] The earliest sediments in the area, called the Gol Gol sediments, comprised a dune laid down about 120,000 years ago. About 45,000 years the lakes became full. From about 45,000 to 26,000 years ago, the lakes mainly remained full and sand from the lakeside beaches was thrown up on the lee, eastern shore to form a crescentic sand dune or lunette (plates 16.1 and 16.2). This dune consists of the Gol Gol, Mungo and Zanci units. The Mungo unit is the oldest sediment to contain stone artefacts or other remains of human presence; no such remains have been found in the underlying Gol Gol unit. From 26,000 to 16,000 years the lakes fluctuated, and by 15,000 years ago the Willandra Lakes were lakes no more.

While the lakes were brimming with freshwater fish and shellfish, Aborigines camped, fished and hunted on the soft sand dunes bordering their shores. They collected vegetable foods, mussels, frogs, yabbies (freshwater crayfish) and speared Murray cod weighing as much as 15 kilograms. They may also have used nets for fishing, for three-quarters of fish remains in the Pleistocene middens are of the golden perch, and all are of a similar size.

The diet also included land creatures, such as lizards and the brown-haired wallaby, together with emu eggs. This indicates that late autumn and winter were times when people camped at Lake Mungo, since emus lay their eggs from about April to November. Food was cooked on open campfires or in ground ovens (shallow depressions or pits containing a band of charcoal or ash and sometimes cooking stones or lumps of baked clay). Ground ovens were the traditional Aboriginal means of cooking large game and plant food, which clearly is an age-old technique; one cooking pit at Lake Mungo was dated to 30,000 years (plate 16.3).

Many stone tools, shell middens and campsites have been found around the shores, and the constant erosion of the sediments means that new material is constantly being uncovered. The earliest stone tools date to around 35,000 years ago and Mungo 1 is the site at which the old Australian core tool and scraper tradition was first identified. Core tools are large, heavy, hand-held chopping tools with a flaked cutting edge made on lumps of rocks (cores), used for heavy wood-working such as cutting down trees. A distinctive type of core is the "horsehoof", with a high domed shape like a horse's hoof, a flat base and steep overhanging edge (figure 16.5). Most horsehoofs were not core tools but cores produced in the manufacture of flake tools. Scrapers are usually smaller than core tools and made on either flakes or small cores, and those at Mungo often have steep edges, showing that they were frequently re-sharpened. They were probably used for scraping or cutting animal flesh, fur or sinew, or for chiselling, sawing, shaving or incising wood. The shape and the way in which they have been worn suggests that

Plate 16.3 Excavation of a Pleistocene hearth on the Lake Mungo lunette. (J. Bowler)

most of the stone tools were used to make wooden tools such as spears and digging sticks. Later tool types in this arid region include millstones for grinding grass seeds to make flour.

The most remarkable finds at Mungo have been the human remains. The world's oldest known cremation was found here by Bowler in 1969, and an even earlier burial shows that ritual was associated with the disposal of the dead 30,000 years ago. The 25,000-year-old cremation was that of a young woman. Her body was burnt and the bones collected, broken and buried in a small pit. This shows that complex rites could accompany death, including the death of a woman, and is a very similar ritual to that accorded to the dead in traditional Tasmanian Aboriginal society, which may have retained an extremely ancient custom which was originally more widespread. Remains of a campsite were found near the Mungo 1 cremation, with some 200 stone tools, campfires and the discarded remains of meals of animals, fish, shellfish and emu eggs.

The 30,000-year-old burial (Mungo 3) was an inhumation rather than a cremation, showing that there was a variety of burial practices during the Late Pleistocene as in present Aboriginal Australia. A tall man had been laid in a grave on his side with his hands clasped, and red ochre had been scattered over his body. Both he and the young woman were remarkably "gracile" and modern in physical type and very definitely belong to *Homo sapiens sapiens;* they do not differ markedly from the modern Aboriginal population, although having some archaic features and unusually small skulls and delicate bones.

Mungo is extremely significant in documenting the great antiquity of Aboriginal culture and society, and continuity both in physical type and in religious practices. It has also provided unique evidence on the adaptation of early Aborigines to a freshwater but semi-arid environment. Much further evidence is continuing to come to light, and remains of more than 100 hominids have now been found. While none of the burials and few of the other sites can be viewed by the general public, Mungo is like a landscape frozen in time. It has a surrealistic, sculptured beauty all its own.

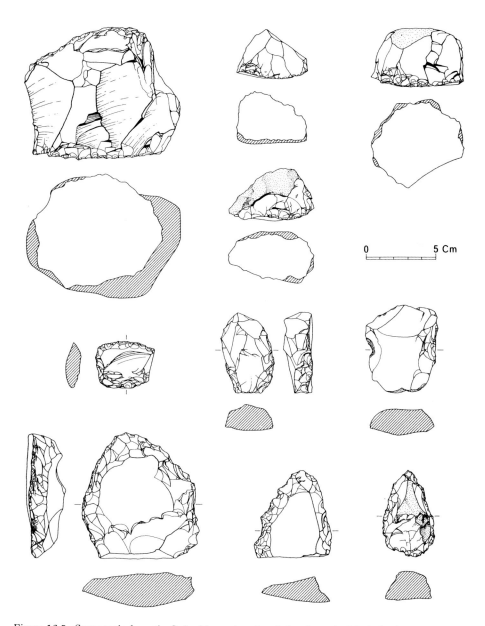

Figure 16.5 Stone tools from the Lake Mungo lunette, dating from the lake's freshwater phase. (J. Goodrum)

Mootwingee National Park, Broken Hill region

Mootwingee National Park covers a large part of the Bynguano Range, approximately 130 kilometres north-east of Broken Hill. The park lies east of Broken Hill to White Cliffs Road; the easiest access is north from Broken Hill along the Silver City Highway to the turnoff north of Yanco Glen to Mootwingee and White Cliffs. (The road is unsealed and is treacherous when wet.) Mootwingee National Park contains a rich array of more than 300 Aboriginal sites, and has long been particularly noted for its outstanding rock engravings and paintings.[2] The best known art lies within the Mootwingee historic site, which was closed to the public in the mid 1980s at the request of the local Aboriginal community, but extensive and formerly unpublicised galleries are now usually available to visitors. Some sites are only accessible by guided tours, but lucky visitors can have the memorable experience of being shown the sites by an Aboriginal guide, and so receive a unique insight into Aboriginal culture. Tours to the historic site are on Wednesday and Saturday, and generally every day during New South Wales school holidays. Rendezvous is in the camping area at 10 a.m. for the historic buildings and at 2 p.m. for Aboriginal paintings and engravings of Amphitheatre Gorge. Tours at other times may be prearranged, but in any case it is a good idea to check in advance with the Tourist Information Centre in Broken Hill (tel. 080 6077, corner of Blende and Bromide Streets) or with NSW National Parks and Wildlife Service District Office (tel. 080 88 0253, 6 Oxide Street, Broken Hill).

Aboriginal paintings and engravings can be seen on walking trails within the national park even if the historic site is closed, so the park is well worth a visit in any case. In particular, only 500 metres beyond the camping ground the Homestead Gorge trail leads visitors to excellent examples of Aboriginal paintings and engravings. A bitumen path provides wheelchair access and a 20-minute round trip to the Thaakaltjika Mingkana site, passing traces of an Aboriginal campsite on the way. This trail winds into a small gorge to a rocky overhang with fascinating examples of the region's Aboriginal and European past. The initials WW and years LIX and LXII attest to visits to the site in 1859 and 1862 by William Wright, manager of Kinchega Station at Menindee and one of the search party for the unfortunate Burke and Wills. One of these historic graffiti lies over a painted "groonki mark", symbolising a spiritually significant area. To its left is a painting of a wand-like "yarra", made from human hair and feathers fixed to a stick, used by the "clever man", Mirikika, to beat evil spirits out of the sick. There are also tally marks, made to record the number of occurrences of significant events, hand stencils, and engravings. These include kangaroo tracks (kirripatja thina), emu tracks (kalthi thina), emu eggs (kalthi parti), and a waterhole (thumpi), delineated by a circle. For the visitor with more time and energy (and strong footwear, a bush hat and a good supply of drinking water!) the Homestead Gorge trail is an enchanting three-hour return walk past another Aboriginal art site into a majestic gorge, and after some two kilometres the rockholes loop track (30 minutes return) leads the more adventurous past a rockhole and some excellent examples of Aboriginal engravings to impressive views of the range, rockholes and gorge.

The Bynguano Range is an isolated massif surrounded by sand and gibber plains on all sides, where Australia's highest temperatures have been recorded, but semi-permanent rockholes act as an oasis in this parched desert. The rockholes have therefore long been a focus of Aboriginal occupation, and the area contains a wealth of Aboriginal sites. Within the historic site there are on record 24 rockshelters containing rock art, 15 rock engraving sites with hundreds of individual figures, 4 stone arrangements and many extensive, open campsites and scarred trees.

In many rockshelters stencils occur in long friezes along the back walls. There are numerous stencils in red, yellow and white of human hands and feet, but also less common items such as boomerangs, a club, coolamons (carrying dishes), lizards and other animals. The wide variety of stencils is a distinctive feature of the Mootwingee art. Paintings in red and yellow silhouette style appear to depict snakes, lizards, boomerangs and a club, animal tracks and abstract lines. A set of kangaroo and human footprints was interpreted by an elderly Aborigine as the story of an unsuccessful kangaroo chase.

The engravings at Mootwingee are of great importance, as they appear to have developed into a local style distinct from the similar Panaramitee style of Central and South Australia. In common with the Panaramitee style there are many bird and kangaroo tracks, but also more figurative motifs. Some areas at Mootwingee closely resemble the Panaramitee style, whereas others have far more figurative motifs. Representations of frontal static human figures abound, and other figures appear to represent kangaroos, emus and other birds, emu eggs, snakes, lizards, and men and women. Most of these engravings are fully pecked out in intaglio style rather than in outline (plates 16.4 and 16.5). Groups of figures are fairly common, including some large scenes of stick-like human figures. On one rock, 20 small men with spears are engraved, on another 12 women, some of whom are wearing plume-like forehead bands or rayed head-dresses. The age of the engravings is unknown, but to judge from the severe weathering and cracking, at least some slabs were engraved several thousands years ago.

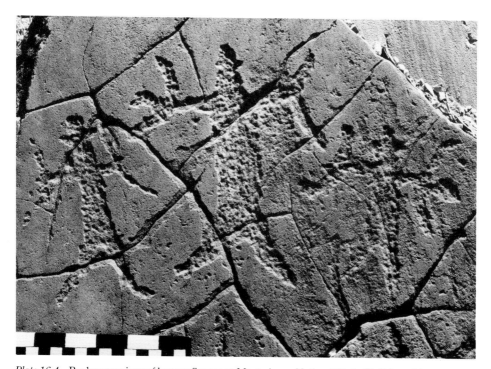

Plate 16.4   Rock engravings of human figures at Mootwingee National Park. (R. Edwards)

Plate 16.5   Engraving of an emu in Mootwingee National Park. (R. Edwards)

Mount Grenfell rock paintings, Cobar region

This historic site contains extensive and well-preserved examples of the colourful and lively "miniature" rock painting style characteristic of the northern part of the Cobar region, and is currently the only such art site open to the public. It lies some 67 kilometres north-west of Cobar, and is reached by taking the Barrier Highway for 40 kilometres to the turnoff at Springfield Tank signposted to Mount Grenfell historic site. Turn right (north) and follow this road for 27 kilometres to the carpark and picnic area. The site lies about 200 metres from the carpark, and the paintings are on the overhanging walls of rockshelters which have eroded out of the face of a low sandstone ridge which runs north-south and faces east. They cluster around a small rockhole in the adjacent creek bed.

The sheltered cave environment, arid climatic setting, remote location and care exerted by the owners of Mount Grenfell station, the Spencer family, and by the National Parks and Wildlife Service have kept the paintings in remarkably good condition, although natural weathering has also taken its toll (plate 16.6). The sites are now protected by a locked grid, and permission to visit must be obtained

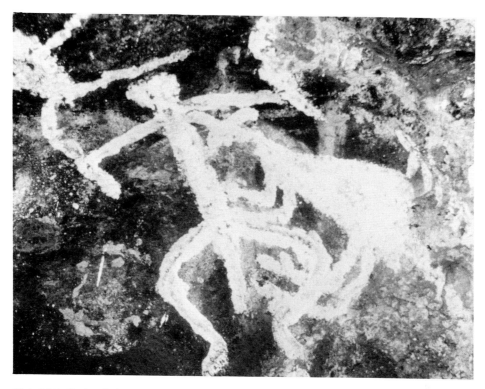

Plate 16.6   Rock painting at Mount Grenfell (National Parks and Wildlife Service)

from the landowner or the National Parks and Wildlife Service, Cobar district office (tel. 068 36 2692). There are three main decorated shelters, which present a rich array of figures in bright white, red, yellow and pink wet pigment and occasionally in black. Most were painted with a twig brush, but some with the finger tip. The art has been extensively recorded by Fred McCarthy, Ben Gunn and others. Excavations in the floor of some of the shelters revealed that occupation of these sites extended back some 1,750 years.[3]

One shelter contains one of the largest friezes of paintings found in the Cobar region. Almost the entire ceiling is covered in paintings, with many superimpositions. Figures tend to be part of compositions depicting hunting for kangaroos, emus, lizards or snakes, dancing, including two rows of small dancing men with bent arms and legs probably performing a corroboree, and a woman giving birth. Some paintings, from the period of European contact, of horses and a man riding a horse were probably painted in the middle of the last century, but the high degree of over-painting and weathering of the art indicate that much or most of it is prehistoric.

The other major shelter contains unusual paintings of a group of thin, dark red figures, a number of men wearing rayed head-dresses. In the Mount Grenfell art as a whole human figures, birds, animals and Aboriginal implements are the dominant subjects and are usually small in size, generally between 15 and 45 centimetres tall. The most common motifs are men holding boomerangs, spears or clubs, and kangaroos and emus. Bird tracks, hand stencils, other animals and scenes of men hunting kangaroos with large nets are also evident, together with rare pictures of a female figure with very long fingers and toes, and a man in a tree watching a file of six emus. One striking feature of the paintings are grids, lattices or "mazes" of wavy lines, believed to represent designs painted on carved trees at burial and ceremonial sites in areas of northern New South Wales.

The naturalistic and exuberant paintings at Mount Grenfell are the focus of this unique central western New South Wales art style, considered by rock art authority Fred McCarthy to be "the finest series of rock paintings in south-eastern Australia". They are also some of the most visually attractive of the Cobar region's sites, and can be easily visited. Other rock art sites are located on the properties of Wittagoona, Meadow Glen, Mount Doris, Mulgowan and others in the Cobar area, and on Sturts Meadow, Euriowie and elsewhere in the Broken Hill district, but permission must be received from the property owners before such sites can be visited.

Brewarrina fish traps

In the middle of the small town of Brewarrina in central western New South Wales, Aboriginal fish traps can still be seen at low water in the main stream of the Barwon River, 50 metres downstream from the weir (plate 16.7). The fish traps are constructed of rocks placed in the river bed to form a large number of circular, V-shaped or diamond-shaped enclosures. The walls are between half and one metre in height and about half a metre wide at the base. These were used to hold the fish, which were caught by spearing or with wooden, tube-shaped traps.

Plate 16.7   Fish traps at Brewarrina. (H. Creamer and National Parks and Wildlife Service)

The area of each trapping enclosure ranges from 10 to 100 square metres, and they originally extended for 1.6 kilometres downstream.

The method of trapping was observed by anthropologist R.H. Matthews in 1901.[4] When there was a fresh in the river fish travelled upstream in huge numbers and swam into the traps, which had their open ends pointing downstream. As soon as a good number were inside the trap, its opening was closed, the fish were driven into a smaller enclosure, speared, clubbed or caught by hand, and a cord was threaded through their gills to carry them to the shore. Great care was taken that no trapped fish should escape, for fear that it would swim away to warn its fellows "about the ingenuity of its enemies".

A certain amount of traditional knowledge about these fish traps has survived, including Aboriginal names for the features. Other sites in the vicinity are a group of axe-grinding grooves on a rock shelf on the southern side of the traps about 200 metres below the bend, a silcrete quarry site and ceremonial stone arrangements.[5] An Aboriginal cultural centre has recently been established at the fish trap site.

CHAPTER SEVENTEEN

New South Wales: The North

Sites particularly characteristic of northern New South Wales are ceremonial bora grounds, paintings, natural sacred sites and carved trees, examples of which are described below. Bora grounds are found throughout eastern New South Wales and south-eastern Queensland, particularly in the lands of the great nation of the Kamilaroi. The word bora is derived from the word bor or boor, the name of the fur-string belt worn by initiated Kamilaroi men.

A bora ground is a roughly circular, cleared area of some 10 to 15 metres across, enclosed by an earth bank, which was often topped by a brushwood fence. Often there were two circles, the first being larger than the other, and they were joined by a pathway of a 100 metres or more in length. This pathway would sometimes be flanked by images of totemic figures, when ceremonies were taking place, and complex designs would be made on the ground in the sand or earth.

These bora grounds were used for initiating the young men into tribal law, their obligations and privileges, duties and code of behaviour. Members of the nation would be assembled from far and near for weeks of ceremonies, usually held on summer nights when the moon was full.

Such earth-built ceremonial grounds are particularly vulnerable to destruction by plough or bulldozer, and only a few examples still survive. Likewise carved trees have been destroyed by natural and human agency at an alarming rate, and now less than 90 remain *in situ*.

Features of particular interest in the landscape of northern New South Wales are the remnants of ancient volcanoes, and some outstanding examples such as the Warrumbungles are mentioned below. The sites of central and northern New South Wales are described in a circle, commencing in the Dubbo region, then travelling north-eastwards by way of the Warrumbungles and New England to Tweed Heads and Mount Warning, and then down the coast to Sydney (see figure 17.1).

Yuranigh's grave, Molong, Bathurst region

Carved trees surround the grave of Yuranigh, who was one of Sir Thomas Mitchell's guides on his last explorations in 1845–46 and died about 1850. This is

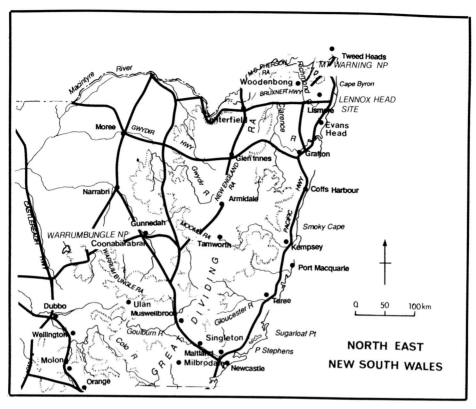

Figure 17.1   Northern New South Wales

the largest surviving group of *in situ* carved trees in Australia, and the site is open to the public. It is located south of the Mitchell Highway on Yuranigh Road, 5 kilometres south-east of Molong and 31 north-west of Orange. Travel for 1 kilometre down Yuranigh Road, and then turn left at a signpost marked Yuranigh's grave through a gate for about 500 metres to the site located on the left about 30 metres from where the track forks. There are white fences around the three carved trees and the grave and a small iron roof covering the fourth carved tree.

The carving of trees was usually associated with ceremonial grounds or burials, and as many as 120 carved trees at one time stood round ceremonial grounds such as Collymongle in New South Wales. Unfortunately such "sites" are particularly vulnerable to damage from bushfires and the like and very few such trees are now left *in situ*. At Collymongle homestead there are nine from the nearby Banarway bora ground. Over the years many carved trees have been removed to museums for safe-keeping, and a good collection is housed in the Australian Museum in Sydney, the museum in Dubbo and the Pioneer Cottage Museum in Walcha. They were originally concentrated in northern and central New South Wales and south-eastern Queensland, particularly in the traditional territory of the Wiradjuri and Kamilaroi people.

It was common practice in the Orange region for Aborigines to carve the trees round the grave of a person of high degree or repute, removing a large slab of

Plate 17.1   Carved tree at Yuranigh's grave, Molong

bark and carving the solid outer wood with designs, probably indicating the totemic or kinship affiliations of the dead person (plate 17.1). The patterns resemble those used to decorate skin cloaks and wooden artefacts, and are mainly spirals, circles, wavy lines, concentric lozenges and diamonds. Over the years regrowth of the bark tends to cover the carving, and some of the regrowth has had to be cut back by a tree surgeon so that the carvings will not be totally obscured.

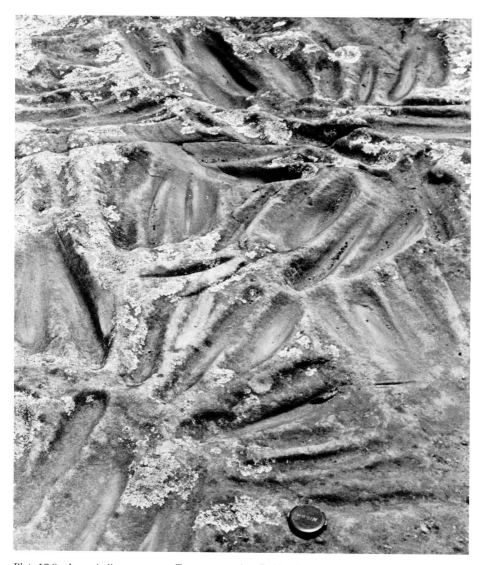

Plate 17.2   Axe grinding grooves at Terramungamine, Dubbo. (National Parks and Wildlife Service)

Four carved trees face the grave of Yuranigh. The tallest tree, a yellow box with the largest carved panel, bears a design of interconnected diamonds, each with a central slit. The other trees are eucalyptus and the two with carving visible bear similar designs of parallel wavy lines filled with concentric diamonds. On the fourth, regrowth appears to have completely covered the carving, and a fifth carved tree present in 1854 has since disappeared.

Terramungamine grinding grooves, Dubbo region

This site is a classic example of grinding grooves which have resulted from the finishing stages of the manufacture of axes and spears by the local Kamilaroi Aboriginal people. The large number of grooves at the site and their excellent state of preservation make it a particularly fine illustration of this type of Aboriginal site (plate 17.2). It is located north-west of Dubbo, and is reached by travelling north from Dubbo along the Newell Highway for about eight kilometres to a left turn at Brocklehurst for Terramungamine immediately after crossing a bridge. After proceeding west for about four kilometres a sign-post indicates the Terramungamine Reserve to the south. From the barbecue area the rubbing grooves are on an outcrop about 100 metres upstream on the northern bank of the Macquarie River.

The grooves extend over a distance of about 100 metres and there are more than 150 of them. The broader grooves result from Aboriginal men constantly rubbing their stone axes along the rock until the cutting blade was sufficiently sharp. The grooves were a by-product of this grinding process, which was used both to manufacture and re-sharpen ground-edge axes. Water was an aid to the grinding process, and was either carried up from the river in bark coolamons or the men would wet their hair and simply shake water into the grooves when required. This information comes from local Aboriginal people, for although the grooves have not been used for at least 100 years, they are still of significance to Kamilaroi people, who retain some knowledge of their traditional use. It is said that wooden implements such as the tips of spears were also sharpened here, and the numerous longer, narrower grooves are likely to have been spear-sharpening rather than axe-grinding grooves. The grooves range in length from about 15 to 45 centimetres, in width up to about 10 centimetres and in depth to 3 to 4 centimetres.

Near this site was found the grave of a woman in which there was a cache of artefacts. This included stone tools, kangaroo incisor teeth, and a long ground-edge knife-like tool made from a human shinbone.

Warrumbungle National Park, Coonabarabran district

The Warrumbungle National Park, 500 kilometres north-west of Sydney and 35 kilometres west of Coonabarabran, is dominated by spectacular pinnacles, domes and spires, the remains of violent explosions and massive lava flows between 17 and 13 million years ago. Some of the spires are formed of trachyte — molten material that solidifed in the main vent of an expiring volcano and became

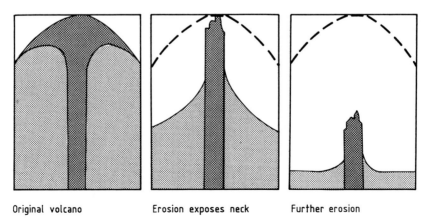

Original volcano   Erosion exposes neck   Further erosion

Figure 17.2 Formation of volcanic peaks such as the Warrumbungles. (Reproduced with permission from *Scenic Wonders of Australia*, Readers Digest (Aust.) Pty Ltd 1976, p. 167)

exposed after erosion weathered away the original cone. Other domes are dykes or sheets of magma, which hardened within the earth's crust but were exposed when the surrounding less resistant rocks wore away (figure 17.2).

The name Warrumbungle is an Aboriginal word meaning crooked mountains. Within the park are numerous Aboriginal sites, including axe grinding grooves in Tara Cave. This lies five kilometres north-west of Canyon Camp National Parks office; ask a ranger for directions (tel. 068 42 1311). The sandstone cave is very large, with good head-room, and inside there are two big boulders covered in axe grinding grooves. Aboriginal campsites abound in this landscape, and there is a rockshelter nearby where organic material is preserved. This deposit shows that the deadly macrozamia nuts were processed and detoxified here and eaten as a staple.

Mount Yarrowyck paintings, Armidale district

Aboriginal paintings are found in a small rockshelter on the western slopes of Mount Yarrowyck, about 30 kilometres west of Armidale and 25 kilometres north-west of Uralla. From Armidale follow the road to Bundarra westwards for about 29 kilometres to the junction with the Uralla-Bundarra road. Turn right and head west for one kilometre to the entry to the nature reserve on the right (north). The return walk to the art site is three kilometres, along a loop walking track. There are interesting interpretive signs, and leaflets are available from the National Parks and Wildlife Service office (tel. 067 73 7211) or on site.

The site is a small rockshelter on the western side of a large granite boulder. It is 5 metres long, 2.5 metre wide and only 1 metre high. A low fence protects the entrance and a viewing platform has been erected. The paintings cover a rock surface of about three square metres below the low overhang, and were first recorded by Isabel McBryde then of the University of New England.[1] By far the most numerous are bird tracks of the size and shape of emu feet, with over 30 being either arranged singly or combined to form patterns (figure 17.3). Also present are circles, straight lines, groups of dots and two stick figures resembling humans.

dark red
light red

0 15 30 45 cm

Figure 17.3 Rock art at Mount Yarrowyck, Armidale. (After McBryde, Sydney University Press, 1974)

Two distinct colours can be seen in the paintings: a faded red-orange and a fresher-looking rich dark red. Some of the figures are superimposed on others, and since dark red ones always occur on top, it seems that these are more recent paintings than the red-orange. Some red-orange motifs have been subsequently repainted in dark red. Such careful retouching of older figures indicates that the function of the paintings was very probably ceremonial rather than purely decorative.

The Mount Yarrowyck site is typical of a rock art style which extends over the New England Tablelands, showing the combination of circles and bird tracks in red ochre which is characteristic of the tablelands sites.

Armidale Aboriginal cultural centre and keeping place

In 1988 an Aboriginal cultural centre was opened adjacent to the New England Regional Art Gallery in Kentucky Street, on the grounds of Armidale's College of Advanced Education. The design is imaginative and the centre houses Aboriginal artefacts and arts, and is also used as an educational facility.

Tingha stone woman, Inverell district

Moving northwards, the Tingha stone woman is one of several sites of special significance to Aboriginal people in New South Wales to have been opened to the public, and interpreted with signs and leaflets, in order to increase public understanding and appreciation of Aboriginal culture. (This is largely through the work of Sharon Sullivan, Howard Creamer and Dave Lambert of the National Parks and Wildlife Service working tirelessly with Aboriginal people such as Ray Kelly, Glen Morris, Jo Gonda and Aboriginal communities, and I am grateful to them both for their efforts and the information they have supplied.)

The site is some six kilometres south of the village of Tingha on the north-western slopes of the New England Tablelands, taking the road leading south from Tingha Post Office to Sutherlands Water. It is adjacent to the property of Westrock and is well signposted, with a stile over the fence at the start of the 500 metre long access track. Visitors are asked to keep to the track and respect the rights of the adjoining private property owner. (Contact the Glen Innes District National parks office (tel. 067 32 1177) for further information.)

The young Aboriginal woman is believed to have been turned to stone for breaking the law by marrying out of her tribe, and now lies forever in the bed of the creek. She was fleeing the wrath of the tribal elders when she stopped to quench her thirst and stooped over the running waters of the creek to drink. The tribal executioner struck her down with his fearsome magic and turned her to stone. She lies there at the base of the boulders with her head in the water, her back and legs in a cleft and arms out-stretched, a vivid reminder of the perils of breaking the law.

Woolool Wooloolni Aboriginal place, Tenterfield district

Woolool Wooloolni, also known as Wellington Rock, is some 20 kilometres north-east of Tenterfield. Take the Mount Lindesay Highway, heading north for 8

Plate 17.3   Woolool Wooloolni Aboriginal place (Creamer, National Parks and Wildlife Service)

kilometres, and then the Black Swamp Road eastwards for another 8 kilometres, then left at the fork and left again 2 kilometres later, passing through a gate. Follow a gravel road for 3 kilometres, then turn right down a forest track for 2 kilometres, parking the vehicle at this point. There is a panoramic view, evoking the timeless spirit of this beautiful place (plate 17.3).

The massive, mushroom-shaped granite tors balance one on top of the other, towering 200 metres above the surrounding forest. According to Aboriginal tradition, the Dreamtime creator Woolool is associated with the rocks, and the name Woolool Wooloolni means the place of Woolool. (Repeating the name indicates the great importance of the being.) It is said that when the ancestral hero Woolool died, one of the rocks toppled over and fell into the valley below.

This site is protected as an Aboriginal place under New South Wales legislation, and is a focus of Aboriginal pride and a symbol of identity. Visitors are expected to respect the natural beauty and Aboriginal spiritual values of the place.

Tooloom Falls, Woodenbong district

Tooloom Falls is south-west of Woodenbong and three kilometres south-west of Urbenville, in the far north-east of the state close to the Queensland border.

Tooloom Falls or Dooloomi is one of the most significant sites in the country of the Gidabal, a clan of the Bundjalung, who occupy the country north of the Clarence River. It was declared an Aboriginal place in 1977, and is open to the public and signposted. Dooloom is the Gidabal word for head-lice, and Dooloomi means the place of head-lice, for it is said that these are found around the deep, dangerous pool below the falls. Spirits are believed to live in the pool, and Aboriginal children are not allowed to swim there.

A story about Dirrangun, the clever woman, explains the origins of the large hollow below the falls.

> Dirrangun quarrels with her two daughters and their husband, Balugan. Because of this feud, Dirrangun steals the only fresh water from a nearby lagoon and hides it in her

coolamon or bark dish. Balugan and his wives have a thirsty search for the water and it is not until one of Balugan's dogs, Dillilay, discovers the coolamon that they are able to find where it is hidden.

In his anger, Balugan splits the coolamon with a super-natural porcupine quill (bimburra), and this causes the water to gush out and, assisted by a big rain, the flood carries Dirrangun and the fig tree under which she was camped down towards Baryulgil and Grafton. The large hollow downstream from the falls is believed to have been created when the fig tree was uprooted and the various waterfalls along the river were formed whenever Dirrangun sat down in the flood to try and stop the torrent. Finally the entire Clarence River was created and Dirrangun and her fig tree were left on its banks somewhere downstream from Grafton.[2]

In the same wild country of the north-east, many other dramatic features such as mountain tops are Aboriginal story places. The striking cliff-topped peak of Mount Lindesay or Jalgumbun is the central landmark of the Gidabal people. It is a jurraveel or mystical site where magic to bring on sleep was performed. It is also the home of a Njimbun or hairy, little spirit man, who is a mischief-maker and at times even dangerous. Likewise Bulls Head Mountain or Balarng is the jurraveel for goannas. East of Jalgumbun is Glennies Chair or Gommorboyani. The story tells how a small boy, on his way to the sea with his grandmother, kept stopping to chew the gum from grass trees. The old woman kept calling the boy to hurry, but the Njimbun caught him and turned him into the jagged, tooth-like rock on the skyline. This tale is a strong deterrent to small children who wish to dawdle!

The north coast

Mount Warning National Park

The rocky tower of Mount Warning in the Mount Warning National Park near Murwillumbah in the Tweed Heads region is well worth a visit, and a climb. Mount Warning is the old central plug of Australia's largest volcano. This was higher than Mount Kosciusko 22 million years ago and erupted for 3 million years, but now all that is left is a distinctive peak, which was the plug of magma which set in the throat of the volcano after its final blast. The mountain can best be appreciated by a pre-dawn climb, for when the sun rises, 1,157 metre Mount Warning is the first point on mainland Australia to be struck by its rays.

Mount Warning was known by Aborigines as Wollumbin or the fighting leader, and dominates the Tweed Valley (figure 17.1). It is 15 kilometres south-west of Murwillumbah, off the Murwillumbah-Kyogle road at Dum Dum. From the park entrance a zigzag climb leads to the summit with an extremely steep final section.

Tweed Heads bora ring

The Minjungbal Aboriginal Cultural Centre has been set up within the Tweed Heads historic site, with a fine bora ring as its central feature. The centre is named after the Minjungbal people who inhabited the lower Tweed Valley. In the museum there is a well-presented display of photographs, artefacts, arts and crafts, films and slides of Aboriginal culture of the north coast. Artefacts include palm-leaf water carriers, dilly bags, stone tools, ochre, ceremonial dishes, seed beads and other ornaments. Outside, a walking track leads through forest and mangroves, with a wealth of wildlife.

Access is via Kirkwood Road east of the Pacific Highway, five kilometres south of Tweed Heads. Further information may be obtained from Minjungbal Aboriginal Cultural Centre Kirkwood Road, South Tweed Heads, NSW 2486 or the National Parks and Wildlife Service at Alstonville (066 28 1177).

Lennox Head bora ring, Ballina region

An Aboriginal ceremonial bora ring is located about 12 kilometres north of Ballina, on the western outskirts of Lennox Head township. It is approximately 700 metres west of Seven Mile Beach and 100 metres west of Gibbons Street between Foster and Lennox Streets and surrounded by a housing development; it is fenced and open to the public. The site consists of a single ring on sandy ground with an inner diameter of about 20 metres and an overall diameter of some 32 metres to the outside of the encircling raised earth bank (figure 17.4). The height of the bank varies between 40 and 60 centimetres, but would originally have been higher, and possibly topped with a brush fence. There is a gap in the bank a little west of north, through which a narrow path would have led to a smaller ring (no longer visible).

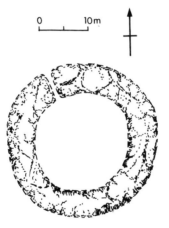

Figure 17.4   Bora ring at Lennox Head, Tweed Heads. (National Parks and Wildlife Service)

This is an unusually large bora ring, and is associated with a substantial shell midden. The site was probably an important focus of Aboriginal religious life on this part of the north coast. According to Bundjalung tradition, it was here on the beach at Lennox Head that the ancestral three brothers made one of their landings. One of them, Yarbirri, thrust a spear into the sand whereupon fresh water flowed, and when the tide is low, there is still a visible stain in that place.[3]

Tucki Tucki bora ground, Lismore region

The Tucki Tucki bora ground is well-preserved and is perhaps the finest example of this type of Aboriginal ceremonial site so far recorded in New South Wales. It is 12 kilometres by road south of Lismore, and is reached by taking the Wyrallah road out of Lismore and continuing on through Wyrallah for 4 kilometres until the Tucki Tucki cemetery on top of a small hill on the right of the road heading south. The bora ground lies on a ridge with panoramic views of the surrounding country. It is within the cemetery reserve, about 150 metres off the road along a track past a groundsman's shed.

The circle has an internal diameter of 22 metres and its earth rim, now 20 to 30 centimetres high, is about 2 metres wide. A small gap in the surrounding rim just west of south would have led downhill along a pathway to a smaller second ring, which unfortunately was destroyed by ploughing sometime before 1920, but remains of the start of the pathway are still visible. Bora rings are one of the very few Aboriginal sites which show up on aerial photographs, and the layout of this ground can clearly be seen from the air. This great bora ground was in existence in 1866, and was observed in use in 1868 and 1870 by "a very large camp of blacks".[4]

It lies on a trading route which took people as far as the Bunya Bunya mountains in Queensland, bartering for spears and other artefacts as well as the prized bunya nuts. In 1879 or 1880 John Currie witnessed a corroboree at Tucki Tucki.[5] He recounted how the Aborigines came in from all directions along a narrow path in single file, the men wearing a tabbi-tabbi, a loincloth made of possum skin. A large ring was dug, and a huge fire lit in its centre. A trench-like path was made about 100 metres long leading to a smaller ring, where the religious ceremonies took place. In preparation for the corroboree the men rubbed wild honey and charcoal into their hair to make it stand up, and painted their faces and chests with red ochre and their arms and legs with white stripes. Singing and dancing took place within the big ring where the central fire was always kept burning. The women sat on one side and the men on the other. The song-leader sang and beat time with two boomerangs, and the man and women sang and danced and the women beat time on their kangaroo skin drums. In the smaller ring a week-long initiation ceremony was held for the young men, but Currie, as a white man, was only an eyewitness to the more public ceremonies.

Goanna Headland

South of Evans Head Goanna Headland is a reserve for the conservation of Aboriginal culture and heritage, the preservation of fauna and flora and for public recreation. It is a sacred place to the Bundjalung, for the headland is believed to be a goanna turned into stone. The story tells how, when a snake was tormenting a bird, Nimbin, a Bundjalung elder with extraordinary powers, asked the goanna to come to the rescue. The goanna chased the snake hither and thither and finally to Evans Head. The snake headed out to sea and then doubled back and lay down, forming Snake Island. The goanna lay down on the shore to wait for the snake to return, thus creating Goanna Headland. The goanna's head is to the north and Schnapper Rock forms its tail.

Within the Bundjalung National Park where estuary and rainforest meet is the Gumma Garra nature walk. Archaeological evidence from middens shows that people were camping here 6,000 years ago. The major midden on this walking track contains a metre and a half of debris, mainly oyster shell, from 6,000 years of Aboriginal camping. This was traditionally an important meeting place, where local tribes exchanged seafood, salt and stone tools for bunya nuts from the north, quandong and kurrajong seeds.

Moleville Rocks axe grinding grooves, Grafton district

The Moleville Rocks Recreation Reserve, 12.5 kilometres north-west of Grafton, features a most important axe grinding groove site. As long as 6,000 years ago, Aborigines were employing the flat sandstone rocks along the banks of the Clarence River to manufacture and sharpen the blades of stone axes. The grooves are in flat sandstone slabs at the water's edge near the main picnic area. (Visitors are asked not to walk on the grooves which are easily worn, nor to mark them in any way.)

Access from Grafton is from the north on the Casino Road, and visitors turn off west onto the Old Copmanhurst Road at the 10 kilometre sign. After 5.6 kilometres a signpost points to Moleville Rocks picnic area, on the east side of a sharp bend in the Clarence River.

Scotts Head, Macksville area

According to the Gumbangirri, the three brothers landed at what is now known as Scotts Head, south of Nambucca Heads. The headlands there were said by local Aboriginal elders to have been formed when the brothers were turned to stone after they were drowned by a tidal wave induced by the younger brother taunting the sea spirits.

Nearby Yarrahapinni Mountain is another landmark on the Gumbangirri cultural landscape, marking the place where a giant koala was slaughtered in the Dreamtime.

These Aboriginal sites, and the stories associated with them, like others in this chapter, were recorded by National Parks and Wildlife Service staff during the 1970s, as part of a special survey of sites of significance to living Aboriginal people.

Stuarts Point, Macleay River Valley, Kempsey

Aboriginal shell middens are widespread along the coast, but the Stuarts Point one is remarkable for its great length (about seven kilometres) and its unusually great spread. It averages 30 metres wide and some 2 metres deep. It was in use between about 6,000 and 2,500 years ago. The shells are packed tightly together without layers of sand or earth separating them, which shows that the people camped here and discarded their refuse regularly, perhaps every year. Sand or dirt did not have a chance to accumulate before a fresh layer of shells was dumped on top of the old.

The middens are reached by heading south from Stuarts Point township along Fishermans Reach Road. Opposite Whisky Island, after about 7 kilometres, there is an interesting section of midden next to Kenjilinby homestead along the fire-break, and at the end of the road more midden is visible near Cockle Island, at a place called the Golden Hole.

The Hunter Valley

Hands on the Rock shelter, Bobadeen, Hunter region

Known locally as Hands on the Rock, the ceiling and walls of this large sandstone overhang are covered in hand stencils executed in red ochre. Some 150 to 200 hands have been stencilled over approximately 90 metres of the rock surface. Many of the hand stencils have faded with age and are difficult to make out. There are a few other motifs, such as bird tracks. Both adult and children's hands have been stencilled, and the cave was also used by Aborigines for camping.

The site is about 500 metres west of the road between Cassilis and Ulan and lies about 11 kilometres north-east of Ulan in the Goulburn River Valley. It is a popular local picnic spot and there is a sign-post to the shelter on the road. Hands on the Rock, in spite of some vandalism, is an important site to Aborigines and non-Aborigines alike. Such a plethora of hand stencils in one site is most unusual.

Milbrodale art site, Singleton, Hunter Valley

One of the most striking and unusual rock art sites in northern New South Wales is a rockshelter 48 kilometres south-west of Singleton in the Hunter Valley region. This site is accessible to the public but is on private land, and visits by large groups should be arranged in advance with the landowner of Glen Ann station, the local Aboriginal land council, or through the National Parks and Wildlife Service's Hunter district office (049 87 3108). It is just off the Putty Road which runs south from Singleton to Windsor through the spectacular Colo wilderness country. When travelling southwards, half a kilometre after the village of Milbrodale, the highway crosses Bulga Creek. Immediately west of Bulga Creek bridge a track heads off to the left, southwards across a cattle grid to Glen Ann station. The site is on the right (west) of this farm track 1.6 kilometres from here and 100 metres past another cattle grid. Steps lead up to the rockshelter, which is about 20 metres above the track and clearly visible from it. (This is a site which the disabled can see without leaving their vehicle.) Please sign the visitor's book, but do not touch the art or disturb the site in any way.

There are clear white stencils of boomerangs, an axe, hands, and other items, but dominating the site is a strange spirit figure with arms out-stretched (figure 17.5). This is believed to represent the great ancestral being Baiami (pronounced

Figure 17.5   Rock art at Milbrodale shelter, Singleton. (National Parks and Wildlife Service)

By-am-ee). He is only one metre tall, but his elongated arms span some five metres of the back wall. The figure is outlined in white, infilled with red ochre, and has two large round white eyes.

CHAPTER EIGHTEEN

New South Wales: Sydney and the South-East

The prehistoric heritage of the Sydney region and the south-east is distinguished by spectacular sandstone cliffs, sculptured into weird shapes by the elements, numerous limestone caves, and by early Aboriginal occupation and distinctive rock art. The Sydney sandstone can be seen to particular advantage in the Blue Mountains and the Morton National Park on the south coast, which both contain giant escarpments, deep-cut valleys and rocky pinnacles. Limestone caves with impressive formations can be seen at Yarrangobilly in the Kosciusko National Park, where there is also a large thermal pool, Carey's Cave at Wee Jasper, near Yass, and in the Blue Mountains region, Jenolan, Abercrombie, Wombeyan and Wellington Caves. At most of these the bones of extinct animals such as giant kangaroos and diprotodontids have been found.

The Aboriginal art of the region occurs in a more restricted region, stretching from Gosford to the Batemans Bay area (figure 18.1). Paintings and drawings tend to be large and to depict many marine creatures, but the most impressive Aboriginal legacy in south-eastern New South Wales is seen in rock engravings. These extend from the Hunter River in the north to the southern shores of Lake Illawarra in the south and the Blue Mountains in the west. More than 1,500 groups of engravings are known within this region. The content of sites ranges from one to over a hundred figures, with the average being about ten. The size of the figures ranges from a few centimetres to whales 18 metres long.

The figures are generally between half- and life-size, and depict a wide variety of subjects, such as whales, fish, emus and other birds, reptiles, kangaroos, wallabies, shields, boomerangs and clubs, men, women, human footprints or "mondoes", and animal tracks. Less common are figures resembling lyrebirds, dingoes, and sailing ships or other post-European contact motifs. A particular element of this art of the Sydney sandstone is the depiction of beyond life-size, anthropomorphic figures of roughly human form but with features of animals or birds or other non-human characteristics. Some of these figures, such as those with rayed head-dresses, may represent the sky god and culture hero of south-eastern Australia, Daramulan or Baiami — Daramulan is shown in profile and Baiami in front view, and depictions range up to 13.6 metres in height. Such

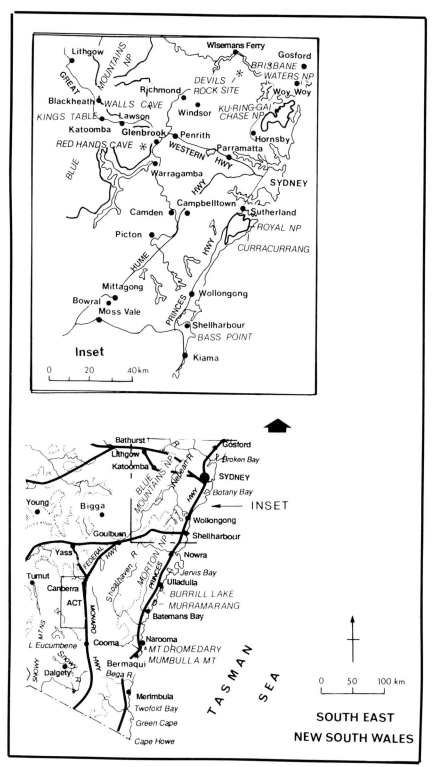

Figure 18.1 South-east New South Wales

ancestral beings wear head-dresses, whereas humans tend to have hair shown as parallel spaghetti-like strands.

Many of the human and animal figures have naturalistic proportions, and Aboriginal informants in early historic times told how these, particularly the human forms, were made by using the shadow of a model as a template.

Most engravings are on the tops of ridges of headlands, where there are horizontal exposures of Hawkesbury sandstone of up to several hectares in area. There were several steps to making an engraving. The first was probably to sketch out the outline of a figure on the rock, by scratching or with a piece of charcoal. Then the outline was engraved with a hard, pointed stone by making a series of puncture or peck marks close together along the line. In some figures, the rock between the pits was then abraded, producing a smooth groove. The average depth of the engravings is 6 millimetres, but some have weathered away through erosion and are very shallow. Engravings are best viewed early morning or late afternoon. There is an excellent field guide to Aboriginal rock engravings around Sydney by John Clegg and Peter Stanbury, with poems, capturing his reactions to each site, by the late David Campbell.

The age of the engravings is unknown, but most exposed figures are likely to be less than a thousand years old, in view of the rapid weathering rate of the Hawkesbury sandstone. Aboriginal people, however, have been in the Sydney region for more than 40,000 years, according to the evidence of the Cranebrook Terrace site, near Penrith, not open to the public.[1] Here, stone tools were found by Father Eugene Stockton associated with charcoal dated to between 40,000 and 45,000 years old. Other early rockshelters are King's Table and Burrill Lake, which is featured in an interesting display at the Australian Museum in College Street, Sydney, a good introduction to regional Aboriginal culture.

Blue Mountains region

Walls Cave, Blackheath, Blue Mountains

Walls Cave is a huge, spectacular sandstone shelter, where traces of Aboriginal occupation have been found (figure 18.1 and plate 18.1). It lies at 910 metres above sea level about 3 kilometres south-east of Blackheath, and is reached from Station Street via Evans Lookout Road, a turn right into Walls Cave Road and a walking track down to the cave.

The massive cavern was formed by an undercutting meander in the creek, and the earth floor consists of an upper and lower terrace. A small excavation in the upper terrace by Stockton revealed that Aboriginal people were camping there occasionally 12,000 years ago, using heavy hand-held stone scraping tools of what is known as the Capertian type.[2] The lower terrace was formed when increased stream activity cut down through the earth floor during a wetter period between 12,000 and 4,000 years ago. Thereafter the shelter was re-occupied by Aborigines using small tools such as Bondi points.

The importance of Walls Cave is that it shows that as long as 12,000 years ago Aborigines were not confined to the coast or large inland rivers and lakes, but

Plate 18.1 Walls Cave, Blackheath

were camping right on top of the Blue Mountains. It also provides valuable evidence of an environmental change after the end of the ice age to wetter conditions.

King's Table, Wentworth Falls, Blue Mountains

The King's Tableland lies about five kilometres south-east of Wentworth Falls, and is reached by turning south onto King's Tableland Road from the Great Western Highway about two kilometres south of Wentworth Falls, proceeding for another two kilometres to Queen Elizabeth Drive on the left and following this to the King's Table trig. The trig is on the eastern spur of the tableland and about 40 Aboriginal axe grinding grooves are to be found on the spur's rocky top. About 400 metres south-west of the trig is a western spur, which has some 84 axe grinding grooves beside shallow pools of water on the crest of the spur (plate 18.2). A walking track leads to this rocky point, from where there is a magnificent 360 degree view out over the Blue Mountains Plateau and the Sydney plains.

King's Table rockshelter faces east just below the lip of the escarpment at an elevation of 870 metres, and is 22 metres long and 8 metres high. It contains a little rock art, principally a pair of engraved emu feet, but the site's main significance is its occupation deposit, excavated by Stockton in 1972. He found that the upper part of the earth floor contained the usual Bondaian industry characterised by numerous Bondi points, but the deposit continued to a depth of 130 centimetres, where charcoal associated with a few flakes gave a date of 22,000 years.[3] Although few in number, these amorphous flakes were sufficient

Plate 18.2   Axe grinding grooves on King's Table, Wentworth Falls

to show that this area high in the Blue Mountains was visited even if only fleetingly, at the height of the last ice age.

Red Hands Cave

Red Hands Cave lies south-west of Glenbrook in the east of the Blue Mountains National Park. Leaflets on the cave are available at the Blue Mountains information centre on the south side of the Great Western Highway at Glenbrook, and on Bruce Road south of Glenbrook. The Glenbrook National Parks and Wildlife Service visitor information centre is open at weekends.

The cave is an easy ten minutes walk from Red Hands picnic area, which is at the end of the Red Hands fire trail off Oaks fire trail, about 13 kilometres south-west of Glenbrook Visitor Centre. (Four-wheel-drive is not required for this route.) Alternatively, the cave can be reached by signposted walking track from the Glenbrook Creek causeway downhill from the visitor centre. Follow Camp Fire Creek for two kilometres to the junction with Red Hands Creek, where a four kilometre circuit track leads to the cave, some axe grinding grooves, and back to the junction. (Allow six hours from the causeway for the total return trip.)

The back wall of the deeply eroded cavern of Red Hands Cave is adorned with dozens of hand stencils and prints. Many overlap and are now rather faded, so it is difficult to discern the total number, but perhaps some sixty to seventy? They are protected by a perspex screen and wooden walkways, but photographs taken through the perspex come out remarkably well. Their purpose, significance and age are unknown, but they would seem to have been the work of the Daruk tribe, who lived in the northern Blue Mountains, including the Glenbrook area.

Northern Sydney

Brisbane Waters National Park

There is an abundance of Aboriginal sites in this park in the Gosford region, the most common being rock engravings and axe grinding grooves, together with rockshelters containing drawings in charcoal or ochre. Some 250 sites have been

Figure 18.2 Engravings from various sites in Brisbane Waters National Park. (National Parks and Wildlife Service of New South Wales)

recorded in this area of Hawkesbury sandstone. Most engravings are in outline form, and subjects include ancestral beings, human figures, animals, birds, marine creatures, macropod and bird tracks and human footprints (figure 18.2).

One large engraving site, Bulgandry, has been signposted, equipped with walkways and interpretive signs and opened to visitors.[4] From the Pacific Highway Woy Woy Road is followed southwards towards Staples Lookout. Two kilometres south-west of Kariong there is a signpost to the Bulgandry Reserve. There are 28 engravings and some axe grinding grooves. Motifs resemble almost life-size kangaroos, fish, a bird, an eel, a possible canoe or large shield, an octopus, humans, a three metre long dolphin or large fish, and a tall male figure wearing an elaborate head dress and carrying a small boomerang and other objects.

Devils Rock, Maroota, Hawkesbury, Sydney

A very large and spectacular group of Aboriginal rock engravings is located on a huge flat expanse of sandstone near Wisemans Ferry on the south side of the Hawkesbury River, adjoining the extreme north-west of Marramara National Park.[5] To reach the site from the south, proceed north along the old Northern Road, turn right into Laughtondale Gully Road and after about one kilometre take an access track into the site, which has been reserved as an historic site by the National Parks and Wildlife Service of New South Wales. Access to the site is possible only by special arrangement with the Aboriginal custodians or the Parks Service.

Figure 18.3   An emu with its eggs, Devils Rock, Maroota. (J. Clegg)

Within the reserve there is a large number of Aboriginal sites, of which the engravings on the main rock platform appear to be the nucleus. Other sites include eleven other groups of engravings, a ceremonial stone arrangement, four sets of axe grinding grooves, three rockshelters with pigment or engraved art (two of them with occupation deposits), two scarred trees and an open air campsite.

The main rock platform covers an area of 58 by 25 metres, and bears 83 engravings and 54 axe grinding grooves. Virtually all the engravings have been executed by making a series of peck marks and the abrading them into a groove to depict the outline of the subject. Engraved motifs comprise 2 ancestral beings, 8 kangaroos, 2 emus and 4 other birds, 3 fish, 3 eels, 15 boomerangs, a shield and 3 other artefacts, 5 human and 5 bird tracks, 15 circles, 2 lines of pits, 5 European contact motifs, an anthropomorphous figure 2.5 metres tall and 13 unidentified motifs.

The site appears to be a planned group of engravings, and a series of compositions can be recognised, according to Fred McCarthy and Jo Macdonald, who have recorded the site. Two trails of pits run across the site; one of 98 deep pits runs roughly north-south, and the other of 179 shallow pits runs roughly east-west. At either end of the platform is a huge figure of an ancestral being. Both of these over-life-size figures are elaborately dressed; one measuring six metres is adorned with a rayed head-dress, armlets, a belt and a cicatrice design on his body, and is said to portray Daramulan, the sky god. An emu and shield close to Daramulan seem to be part of the same composition. The other figure, four and a half metres tall, is said to be Baiami, another major ancestral culture hero of south-eastern Australia.

Other compositions include an emu and its eggs (figure 18.3), a line of bird tracks, a bush turkey and "eggs", a set of running kangaroos and boomerangs, a kangaroo being struck by boomerangs and a spear, and a group of boomerangs around axe grinding grooves. At least some of the engravings were made after European settlement in 1788, for there is a sailing ship with two masts and sails, a man in a top-hat and a woman in a crinoline dress. The ship is superimposed over a kangaroo and a boomerang, and the lady over the anthropomorphous figure. The contact engravings appear to have been made with a stone rather than a metal tool. This is important evidence that the art of engraving in Aboriginal Australia continued from more than 20,000 years ago right up to historic times.

Most of the engravings of kangaroos and birds at the site are life-size or slightly larger than life-size, but several figures of birds, human tracks and a kangaroo are tiny in scale. In other words there are very small as well as "normal" sized versions of some subjects. The engraved grooves also vary greatly in depth. It is impossible at present to say whether these differences in depth were caused by a difference in either their age, the older engravings being more weathered and hence shallower, or in the technique of the engravers or by re-grooving of the deeper engravings because they were more important.

The engravings in this large and impressive group are in generally good condition, their outlines being made from deep and wide grooves, but like most engravings they only stand out clearly under the slanting light of early morning or late afternoon, which are the best times to visit the site.

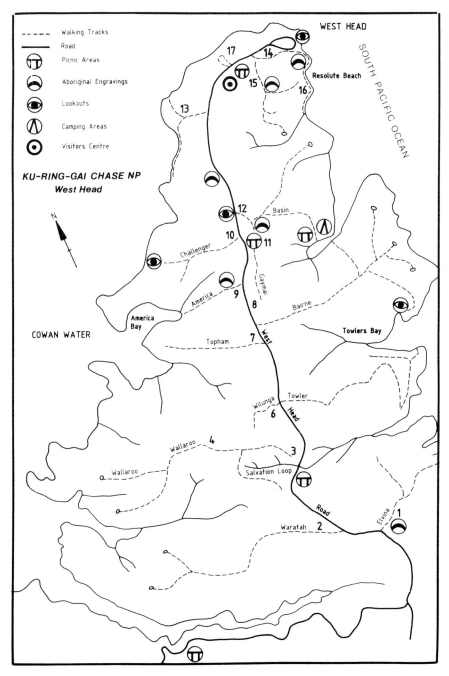

Figure 18.4 West Head area, Ku-ring-gai Chase National Park. (After National Parks and Wildlife Service of New South Wales)

Ku-ring-gai Chase National Park, Sydney

Many fine Aboriginal engravings have been carved on the sandstone of Ku-ring-gai Chase National Park 30 kilometres north of Sydney[6] (figure 18.4). The park of about 15,000 hectares is generally bounded by Broken Bay in the north, Pitt Water in the east, Sydney's northern suburbs in the south and the main north railway in the west. Car access to the western, Bobbin Head section of the park is from the Pacific Highway at Turramurra or Mount Colah. To the northern, West Head section access is from the Mona Vale Road at Terrey Hills. Visitor centres are at West Head and Bobbin Head, from where maps of the walking tracks and whereabouts of some Aboriginal engravings can be obtained.

A perfect medium for the rock engravers was provided by Hawkesbury sandstone, which is made up of sand grains and held together by a salty clay cement. The sandstone was laid down 200 million years ago as the swamps, sandbars and channels of a massive east coast delta, which became inundated by the sea and covered with sand. Some 50 million years ago the sandstone and shale formed from these sandy deposits were gradually uplifted, and the creeks and rivers cut deeper beds as the land rose. Finally about 6,000 years ago the rising post-glacial sea level flooded the valleys to form the deep channels of Cowan, Pitt and Berowra Water.

Rockshelters are formed in the sandstone because the clay cement attracts moisture and expands, making grains of sand fall from the sandstone walls. This natural weathering process gradually eats into the sandstone surface and forms an overhang or cave. Eventually, as the weathering continues, the overhang is cut so deeply that the roof will collapse.

There are some 15 rockshelters containing paintings or stencils in the park, but far more numerous are engravings on open rock pavements. More than 200 groups of engravings have been recorded on the horizontal sandstone slabs of Ku-ring-gai Chase, incorporating over 1,000 individual figures (18.5). Favourite subjects include whales, dolphins, sharks, fish, eels, kangaroos, wallabies, emus, artefacts, humans and ancestral or spirit beings. Many of the engravings are very large; there are whales up to fifteen metres long, and numerous anthropomorphs figures of four to six metres in height, which are interpreted as spirit beings from the era of creation. Foremost among these is Daramulan, the principal sky hero of Aborigines of the Sydney area.

Several groups of engravings can be found along the West Head Road, the main ones for public viewing being on the Basin track and the West Headland loop. The first group north of the start of West Head Road is near roadside guidepost number one on the right-hand side of the road just north of a rock wall on the right. The Elvina nature trail marked with a boomerang (the sign indicating rock engravings) leads after about 200 metres to a large expanse of rock on the right called a tessellated pavement, on which there are engravings, including a figure thought to be Daramulan (figure 18.6 c). This site contains a whale, large and small emus, humans and other figures as well as anthropomorphs.

The second group is on the left (west) near guidepost number 9, on the America Bay track, which leads to a lookout. When it forks after about 100 metres, the right-hand path leads down to a group of engravings including a goanna and a whale with a woman and a stingray inside it. A faint, but unusual, figure of Daramulan lies 270 metres west on a rock outcrop in a marsh (figure 18.5a).

Another 1.7 kilometres to the north, there is a signpost on the right with a white footprint and the number ten painted inside, where the Basin track leads off to the south-east. Proceed along it for about 250 metres until you see a boomerang sign on the right; the engravings lie on a group of flat slabs behind the sign, and walkways have been built and interpretive signs erected. (Leaflets on the site are available from the National Parks and Wildlife Service visitor centre at Bobbin Head.) The engravings are generally fairly clear and well-preserved, and include men with hair belts and a man and a woman with dilly bags and a carrying dish (figure 18.5 g and h), fish, a row of hopping wallabies and other figures.

North again is a group on the left-hand side of the road where there is a wheelchair sign on the road. It is an engraving site with wheelchair access. The engravings lie within 30 metres of the road, and include several fish, one more than a metre long. A long line of over 20 engraved footprints lead up a slab, and a second line leads off left up to a rare engraving of an echidna (figure 18.6).

Figure 18.5 Aboriginal engravings in Ku-ring-gai Chase National Park. (a) America Bay track. (b) and (e) Cottage Point Road. (c) and (f) tesselated pavement, Elvina track. (d) near Topham trig. (g) and (h) Basin trail. (National Parks and Wildlife Service of New South Wales)

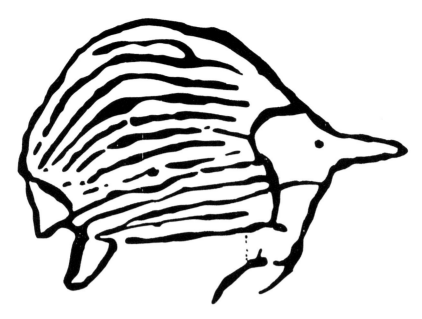

Figure 18.6   An engraved echidna, Ku-ring-gai Chase National Park. (J. Clegg)

At the Garigal picnic area just south of West Head there is an exhibition centre. From there the 100 metre long Red Hand trail leads to a rockshelter with hand stencils, and the 3.5 kilometre long Garigal Aboriginal Heritage walk leads past engravings, a rockshelter and middens on the foreshore in a loop past West Head (medium difficulty and allow three hours return). Heading south, you come after 600 metres to a rock shelf on the left with a large male figure with a club, eels and a fish. Another 600 metres brings you to the rockshelter and then down to Resolute and West Head beaches, middens and further engravings. Engravings also lie on other walking tracks around West Head such as the Waratah and Bairne tracks.

Middens may also be seen along the Sphinx track to Bobbin Head, which leaves Bobbin Head Road in North Turramurra at the Sphinx Memorial near the park entrance. Also in the Bobbin Head area engravings can be viewed on Bobbin Head track, which starts on the right-hand side of Bobbin Head Road, about 200 metres inside the North Turramurra park entrance. The track follows the ridge down to Bobbin Head, and engravings are located about 1.5 kilometres along on the left just past the powerlines.

Balls Head, Berry Island Reserve, Wollstonecraft, Sydney

On the north side of Sydney Harbour and south of Wollstonecraft is Berry Island Recreation Reserve, overlooking Balls Head Bay. Within the reserve are one site with engravings and axe grinding grooves, six shell middens and two rockshelters containing midden debris. At the engraving site, which is fenced and on the left of the road to HMAS *Waterhen*, almost the entire rock surface is covered by the pecked (and regrettably painted) outline of a whale 6.4 metres long, with a man inside, and eight other figures adjacent[7]. The man may be seeking to cure an illness, a traditional practice of some east coast Aborigines, or he may be a magician enticing the whale to become stranded for a whale feast. Access is from Waverton Station via Balls Head Road and Drive.

Quarantine Station, North Head

The grounds of the old Quarantine Station at North Head contain a number of Aboriginal sites. Hand stencils may be seen in small rockshelters on Quarantine and Store beaches, and there are engravings, mainly of fish, below an escarpment some hundred metres east of the Constitution Monument. (Enquiries should be addressed to National Parks and Wildlife Service rangers.)

The south coast

Royal National Park, Port Hacking

There are many Aboriginal sites within the Royal National Park, which is Australia's oldest national park. The park is 40 kilometres south of Sydney. Access is off the Princes Highway at Loftus or Waterfall and there is a visitor centre at Audley. Examples of shell middens may be seen on the sand dunes at Era and Garie beaches. A number of rockshelter deposits have been excavated, and the oldest site so far found is a large shelter in Curracurrang Cove, which Aboriginal people were inhabiting 7,500 years ago (plate 18.3).

A pleasant scenic walking track leads from Wattamolla Beach round the headland to Curracurrang. Several rockshelters overlook the deep lagoon and beach of Wattamolla Cove, and the public footpath to the beach leads through one of them where there are still traces of shell midden. Excavation of this shelter

Plate 18.3 Curracurrang rockshelter, Royal National Park

revealed 800-year-old occupation, with the bones of many reef fish, a few seals, muttonbirds and land mammals, seven bone points and eight crescentic fish-hooks.[8] The Wattamolla sites seem to have been specialised fishing sites of the Dharawal tribe, the women fishing with shell fish-hooks and lines of vegetable fibre from bark canoes, the men using their bone-barbed fishing spears. Fishing was frequently done at night, with a small fire being kept alight on a hearth of seaweed and clay in the centre of the canoe.

The Curracurrang area contains eight rockshelters with occupation deposits, an engraving site and a group of axe grinding grooves (plate 18.3). Four of the shelters were excavated by Vincent Megaw of Sydney University,[10] the main one being a large shelter facing out east over a grassy slope at the mouth of a well-watered gully just above the walking track and about 250 metres inland from the shore. This site contains some of the earliest occupation found on the coast, being inhabited before the sea had reached its present level about 5,000 years ago, and exhibits a change from pebble tools and large hand-held flake scrapers in the lowest levels to specialised small tools such as geometric microliths and Bondi points in the post-3,500-year layers. Over a thousand Bondi points were found.

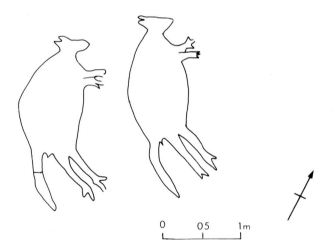

0   05   1m

Figure 18.7 Engravings of macropods in Royal National Park. (National Parks and Wildlife Service of New South Wales)

Engravings are relatively rare south of Sydney compared with the Hawkesbury area, but there are more than 80 sites around Deeban (Port Hacking). A walking track from Bundeena leads south to Marley Head, where there are engravings. A larger, superb group is on the north-west side of Jibbon Headland. From Bundeena (Neil Street) walk along to the end of the beach, and up a rough path onto low cliffs. After approximately 400 metres, turn right at a small rock step in the path and the site is on a rock slab about 50 metres long lying north-south, surrounded by bush but with a splendid view north to Cronulla, and about 30 metres from the shore. Engravings include whales more than 11 metres long, an ancestral being about 4 metres tall with upraised six-fingered arms, two very clear figures of kangaroos (one sitting), a shark, a fish and various other fainter figures.

Bass Point, Shellharbour

There is a continuous series of some 11 middens and open campsites on the north
and south sides of Bass Point. One of the larger stratified open sites on a gently
sloping hill overlooking extensive rocky foreshores on the north side at Little Bay
was excavated in 1969–70 by Sandra Bowdler.[6] Occupation went back 17,000
years, making it the oldest dated coastal campsite in New South Wales. At that
time the sea level was much lower and Bass Point was a hill about 30 kilometres
inland from the Pleistocene coast. Most Pleistocene sites were probably on the
then shoreline, so are now submerged beneath the sea, but people camped on
what is now Bass Point from time to time, and left behind them the occasional
stone tool. Then, during the last 3,500 years, after the sea had risen and the hill
had become a headland, the site became a focus for fishing, hunting and the
collecting of shellfish. A midden developed, with remains of fish, shellfish, seals,
birds, and land mammals.

Bass Point is a recreation reserve, three kilometres south-east of Shellharbour
township. The excavated site is on the north side of the point at its base, just
beyond the modern quarry. On the tip of the point is Bushrangers Bay, which
contains a rockshelter also used by Aborigines in the past.

Hidden Valley paintings, Nowra

This is a small, hard to see but characteristic example of Aboriginal rock art on
the south coast of New South Wales, located in a public recreation reserve. The
painted sandstone shelter lies one kilometre south-west of Nowra, and is reached
by travelling west along Jervis Street to the first Nowra Scout Hall and walking
about 300 metres in a south-westerly direction to the top of a small cliff
overlooking Nowra Creek. Go left and then down a small track down the cliff and
the gridded shelter will be visible on your right. It lies at a bend in the creek on the
eastern bank and faces south-west in a sheltered little valley known locally as
Hidden Valley.

Techniques used by the artists included stencilling, drawings in charcoal or dry
red ochre and bichrome paintings in a combination of white and orange-red
pigment. Most of the art is now indecipherable, but recognisable motifs are a one
metre long sinuous snake-like figure in red ochre and white wet pipe-clay and four
stencils in white of hafted stone axes about 40 by 15 centimetres in size at the
western end of the shelter.

Beecroft Peninsula, Jervis Bay

On the north-eastern side of Jervis Bay lies Beecroft Peninsula, reached via the
small town of Currarong. There a signposted walking trail leads to some
Aboriginal sites in Abrahams Bosom Reserve. A viewing platform has been built
in front of a rockshelter containing traces of past Aboriginal use.

Beecroft Peninsula is used by the Defence Forces for military bombardment, so
is not always accessible for public visits! At weekends, however, visitors may
view Jervis Bay lighthouse and the awesome cliffs around Point Perpendicular.
East of Lighthouse Road and immediately north of Crocodile Head a track leads

down to Devils Hole. This 80 metre deep abyss connects with the sea through a series of caves, which send water into the hole with great force. Devils Hole is of great significance to the Jerrinja Aboriginal people, who believe that it houses the spirit of the ancestral being, Bundoola, who drowned here. There are other Aboriginal sites on Beecroft Peninsula such as a bora ground and some small rockshelters containing paintings, and further sites lie in Jervis Bay National Park and near Wreck Bay. (Contact Aboriginal-run Wreck Bay Walkabout Tours, Jervis Bay 2540, tel. (044) 421166.)

Quiltys Mountain, Morton National Park

For the bushwalker, an excursion inland leads to one of the best-preserved Aboriginal stone arrangements in New South Wales, near the summit of Quiltys Mountain (also known as Mount Endrick) in the northern Budawang Range within Morton National Park. Access is from Newhaven Gap at Sassafras on the Braidwood-Nowra road. The track turns south off this road through a gate opposite an old farmhouse approximately 58 kilometres from Nowra and 80 kilometres from Braidwood.

From Newhaven Gap it is a pleasant full day's medium standard walk to Quiltys Mountain and back. The track wends southwards through open heath and grassy swampy country into a pocket of rainforest known as the Vines. Here the track forks; follow the left-hand branch to the top of a rise. Before the track continues downhill, a path to the right leads to a scramble up the side of Quiltys Mountain, with views to the lower Clyde Valley and Pigeon House Mountain to the south-east. At the top of the 80 metre easy climb is the Aboriginal ceremonial ground, on gently sloping sandstone rock slabs on the easternmost part of the summit plateau. Water should be carried; return by the same route.

The stone arrangement is oval in shape with a longitudinal middle line running west-east (plate 18.4). It is 17 metres long and its maximum width is 6 metres. The northern side is made of 105 stones, the southern of 105, and the median line of 98. At each end there is a low cairn of stones, the western one containing 47 stones and the eastern one 24. The space within and around the outside of the oval

Plate 18.4   Stone arrangement on Quiltys Mountain, Morton National Park

has been cleared of all loose pieces of rock. About 11 metres upslope there is a smaller oval arrangement 5 metres in length, composed of 60 stones including one very large one at the eastern end. A third stone arrangement was recorded in 1931 another 36 metres up the slope, consisting of a number of artificial piles of rock in the form of a square.[11] (Please do not disturb the stones or make any additions.) No traditional Aboriginal knowledge has survived about this stone arrangement. There used to be another stone arrangement on rock slabs on Sturgiss Mountain to the south,[12] but wind and weather have now all but destroyed it.

Pigeon House Mountain, Milton district

This dramatic peak is a prominent landmark on the south coast and was named Pigeon House by Captain Cook. Its Aboriginal name is Tytdel, and it is still of great significance to the Jerrinja people. It lies 16 kilometres west-south-west of Milton, and is signposted from the Princes Highway. About an hour is needed for the climb from the Pigeon House picnic area off Yadboro Road, the last section involving climbing steel ladders to the top. In the Pigeon House area there is a number of Aboriginal sites, but further information on them is safeguarded by their traditional owners, the Jerrinja Local Aboriginal Land Council (PO Box 110, Orient Point, NSW 2540).

Burrill Lake rockshelter, near Ulladulla

Burrill Lake is about 70 kilometres south of Nowra; the rockshelter is just south of the town and is reached through Bungalow Park (figure 18.8). But first be sure to see the fine reconstruction of the dig in the Australian Museum, Sydney! The shelter lies below a deeply overhanging ledge in the horizontally-bedded Nowra sandstone and is very large (43 metres long by 12 metres wide by 3 metres high).

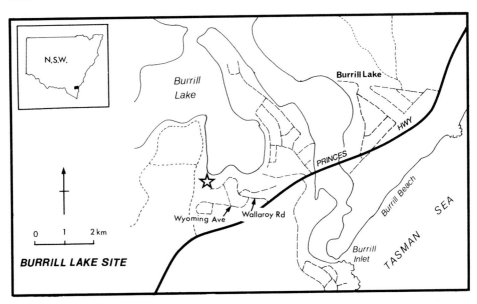

Figure 18.8 Location of Burrill Lake rockshelter

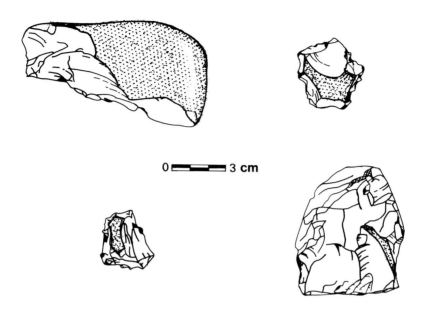

Figure 18.9   Artefacts from Burrill Lake rockshelter

It faces east and is sheltered from the onshore and prevailing southerly winds, being situated at the head of a short, densely wooded gully which leads to the estuarine Burrill Lake about 200 metres away. A semi-permanent creek runs over the southern end of the ledge which forms the shelter, and there are axe grinding grooves in its bed.

Excavation of this shelter by Ronald Lampert in 1967-68 revolutionised Australian prehistory by showing for the first time that Aborigines were present on the south-east coast of Australia during the Pleistocene period, 20,000 years ago.[13] The shelter floor is now only 3 metres above sea level, but at the height of the last ice age sea level would have been as much as 150 metres lower and the coast about 30 kilometres distant. A series of radiocarbon dates on charcoal from ancient campfires showed that this shelter had been used occasionally from 20,000 to 6,000 years ago by Aborigines, who exploited the rich food resources of the adjacent woodland and estuary. After about 6,000 years ago, the site was more constantly occupied, and marine resources were exploited; sea level stailised near the shelter at this time. The stone artefacts in the lower layers were mainly large hand-held pebble choppers, horsehoof cores and scrapers weighing 200 to 300 grams (figure 18.9). Between 5,500 and 5,000 years ago new specialised small tools such as Bondi points were added to the toolkit.

Other important evidence concerns Aboriginal burning practices. In the earliest occupation layers there is an unusually high build-up of sediments, including charred wood, washed down from surrounding hill slopes. This suggests that the first occupants of the site were firing vegetation unused to regular burning, causing massive erosion which denuded the hillsides and led to soil being washed down into the shelter. Subsequently, fire-adapted shrubs and trees became established and the slopes re-stabilised. This together with other evidence indicates that Aborigines had a considerable impact on their environment through their burning practices, effectively changing vegetation from fire-sensitive to fire-tolerant.

Murramarang Aboriginal area, Batemans Bay

Shell middens are one of the most common and visible signs of Aboriginal occupation, and they are found in their thousands along the Australian coast. The coast of New South Wales is no exception, and a particularly good characteristic example is an extensive group of middens at Murramarang Point (plates 18.5 and 18.6). This lies about 160 kilometres south of Sydney and 30 kilometres north of Batemans Bay just south of the village of Bawley Point, and is a short walk from the road between Bawley Point and Kioloa (figure 18.10).

Murramarang Point is a headland flanked by large rock platforms which are the habitat for many fish and shellfish, and across a narrow passage lies Brush Island, surrounded by similar rock platforms. Just north of the headland is a brackish lagoon which attracts many birds, so this was a remarkably rich environment for prehistoric occupants. There is abundant evidence of former Aboriginal camping over an area of about 15 hectares, with many shells and animal bones from past meals and some stone artefacts.[14] (Visitors are reminded that collection of artefacts is not permitted, and is a serious offence under New South Wales law.)

During Aboriginal occupation the land surface was a fairly stable soil developed on clay overlying the monzanite bedrock or on sand dunes, where the soil and organic matter cemented sand grains together to form a dark-brown sand-rock,

Plate 18.5   Shell midden at Murramarang. (R. Lampert)

Plate 18.6 Dingo skeleton excavated at Murramarang. (R. Lampert)

known as "coffee rock". The dune-soil was held stable by vegetation including small trees on the site, until European introduction of grazing animals led to extensive wind erosion. In a number of blowouts, including a huge one in the centre of the site, soil and sand have been stripped down to sand-rock level, and the stone artefacts and larger shells and animal bones they contained have come to rest on the sand-rock. In other parts of the site the old soil horizon is intact and the artefacts remain *in situ*, so the stratigraphy of Murramarang is extremely complex.

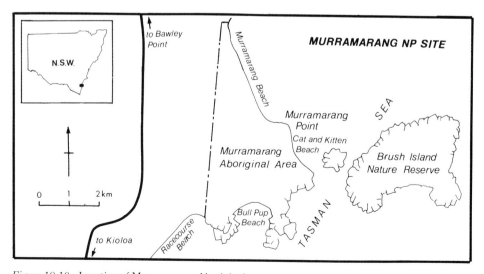

Figure 18.10 Location of Murramarang Aboriginal area

The shells are nearly all edible reef gastropods, presumably gathered from the rock platforms. Most remaining on site are the larger robust types such as the Sydney Turban; it is probable that the majority of the smaller species have disintegrated. The stone tools are usually made of chert, porphyry or silcrete, and include many varieties, with Bondi points being particularly common, and are typical of the toolkit of the east coast over the last 4,000 years.

Murramarang National Park is in three narrow strips extending down the south coast, with low dunes, flowering heaths, banksia and casuarina scrub quickly giving way to tall eucalypt forests, including some pure stands of spotted gum. Big mobs of grey kangaroos emerge from the forests at dusk to feed on dune grasses, and at Depot Beach just north of Durras they nibble at the fresh grass all day long and have become remarkably tame.

Durras North Cave, Murramarang National Park

At the northern end of a long, ocean beach at North Durras there is a small sea cave excavated by Ron Lampert,[15] which yielded important evidence about the specialised economy developed by Aborigines on the south coast over the last 500 years. The occupational deposit was full of bird bone, particularly muttonbird. Muttonbirds migrate down the south coast en route for Tasmania each October to November, and each year many collapse exhausted at sea and their bodies are swept up onto ocean beaches such as Durras North. All the prehistoric beachcombers had to do was sit in their cave and watch the rolling surf bring them their dinner. They also caught fish with spears and shell fish-hooks, and collected shellfish and burrawang *(Macrozamia)* nuts, as well, no doubt, as many other foods which have left no trace in the archaeological record.

The far south coast

Between Batemans Bay and the Victorian border there is a number of Aboriginal sites, such as coastal shell middens, scarred trees, open campsites and sites of particular significance to Aboriginal people, such as Mount Dromedary and Mumbulla Mountain, described below.[16] Examples of shell middens can be seen beside a walkway on One Tree headland immediately north of One Tree beach at Tuross Head. A large canoe tree is protected by a fence at the southern end of Broulee, adjacent to the rubbish tip and caravan park, and another overhangs the river between Moruya township and the hospital upstream.

There are also many sites around Wallaga Lake, where there is an Aboriginal reserve and community of Yuin people. In the centre of the lake is Umbarra or Merriman's Island, where King Merriman escaped from a Victorian tribe; this small island is now a sanctuary with no public access. Wallaga Lake lies between two sacred mountains, Mumbulla and Gulaga (Mount Dromedary), both of special significance to Yuin people.

Mumbulla Mountain, Bega district

Mumbulla Mountain is about 30 kilometres south-west of Wallaga Lake and 10 kilometres north-east of Bega in the Mumbulla State Forest. Its summit, where there is now a trig station and television tower, can be reached from Greendale on the Princes Highway north of Bega, via Clarkes Road and Mumbulla Trig Road. Mumbulla was the centre of Yuin ceremonial activities, and on the flanks of the mountain are an initiation ground, several sacred sites, and a waterhole used on the traditional walkabout from Wallaga Lake to Bega.[17] Thanks to the efforts of the Wallaga Lake community, notably Guboo Ted Thomas and the Penrith family, Mumbulla Mountain is now protected by both federal and state law; it is in the Register of the National Estate and has been declared under New South Wales legislation as Biamanga Aboriginal place.

Mount Dromedary (Gulaga), Narooma district

Gulaga is also in the Register of the National Estate, and lies within the Mount Dromedary Flora Reserve. This is part of the Bodalla State Forest, about 13 kilometres south-west of Narooma. The mountain is an isolated volcanic core rising 797 metres above sea level to tower over the historic village of Tilba Tilba. There are two ways of reaching the summit. The most interesting but longer route is from the east on the Tilba Tilba track, which commences from the carpark beside Pam's Store in Tilba Tilba on the Princes Highway. The return walk to the summit from here is approximately eleven kilometres and takes about five hours. (Take some water!) The alternative is the Mount Dromedary trail from the north, starting near the Narooma water supply dam, reached by following Wadonga Scenic Drive and Engine Road. This takes about four hours for the return walk of seven kilometres, from the point where non-four-wheel-drive vehicles have to be parked.

The significance of Gulaga was recorded during the last century by anthropologist A.W. Howitt, who wrote:

> Long ago Daramulun lived on the earth with his mother, Ngalalbal. Originally the earth was bare and "like the sky, as hard as a stone", and the land extended far out where the sea is now. There were no men or women, but only animals, birds and reptiles. He placed trees on the earth. After Kaboka, the thrush, had caused a great flood on the earth, which covered all of the east coast country, there were no people left, except some who crawled out of the water on to Mount Dromedary. Then Daramulun went up to the sky, where he lived and watched the actions of men. It was he who first made the Kuringal and the bull-roarer, the sound of which represents his voice. He told the Yuin what to do, and he gave them the laws which the old people have handed down from father to son to this time . . ."[18]

The Southern Tablelands

Now take a giant loop back from the south coast and look at one site on the Southern Tablelands before heading south for the Australian Capital Territory.

Bigga paintings, Crookwell, Southern Tablelands

Rock art sites are extremely rare on the Southern Tablelands and the Bigga site, although small, has an interesting range of reasonably well-preserved motifs

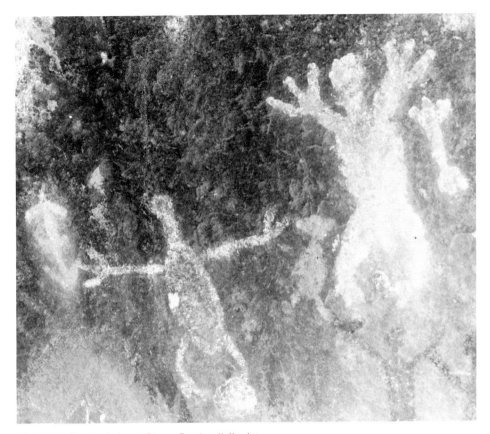

Plate 18.7   Rock painting at Bigga, Crookwell district

(plate 18.7). Bigga lies 58 kilometres north-west of Crookwell and 55 kilometres south-east of Cowra, and the site is 5 kilometres west of Bigga on the Reids Flat Road. The small granite rockshelter lies about 500 metres south of the road and faces north. The painted surface is about three metres wide by two metres high, and is now protected by a locked grid. (The key is available from the National Parks and Wildlife Service office in Queanbeyan for bona fide researchers or photographers. The site is on private land and visitors should contact the Parks Service to obtain permission from the landowner.)

The main colours used are white and light red, with some black and dark red. Across the centre of the painted panel winds a broad red line, which according to local European tradition represents a "map" of the Lachlan River and Sandy Creek, which the site overlooks. It is also suggestive of a snake, although of uneven width and without a head. The most striking figures in the frieze are two white anthropomorphs high on the wall. There are also naturalistic emus and many small animated human figures, some apparently dancing.

CHAPTER NINETEEN

The Australian Capital Territory

The Australian Capital Territory encompasses within its boundaries the northern end of the Australian Alps. Namadgi National Park covers 94,000 hectares or a third of the territory, and includes extensive areas with sub-alpine climate and significant snow cover in winter. The highest peak is Mount Bimberi, 1,911 metres above sea level and only 318 metres lower than Australia's highest peak, Mount Kosciusko. As well as magnificent wilderness country, the visitor can see an interesting range of Aboriginal sites which characterise traditional Aboriginal life in the south-eastern highlands. There are also displays on Aboriginal culture in various institutions in the nation's capital, such as the National Gallery and the National Museum.

Just as it is now, Canberra in prehistoric times was a meeting place for people from different communities and nations, speaking different languages. The Southern Tablelands was the land of the Ngunawal (the initial "ng" is pronounced like the "ng" in "sing"), whose tribal territory came as far south as Queanbeyan and Yass, where it abutted Wiradjuri country. To the south was the land of the Ngarigo, who occupied the Monaro Tablelands as far north as Canberra, and to the west were the Walgalu, who roamed the Upper Tumut Valley, the Bogong Mountains and possibly the ranges of what is now the Australian Capital Territory (figure 19.1).

The last tribal Aborigine in the region was Nellie Hamilton, who died in Queanbeyan in 1897, but there are a few Aboriginal people of mixed descent in the district, particularly from Yass, who have some links with the original local inhabitants.

Aborigines have lived in the Canberra region for at least 21,000 years, the age of the Birrigai site described below. In historic times they stayed in the area even during the cold winter months, when food supplies were scarce. Researchers do not know if this was always the case, or if in the even colder period of the last ice they wintered in warmer areas such as the coast or inland plains.[1]

The mainstays of the diet were probably possums, macropods, emus, plains turkeys, ducks and other birds, vegetable foods such as the tubers of the daisy "yam", freshwater fish, crayfish and shellfish. Possums were available all year round and were the main source of food in winter, as well as of clothing. As many

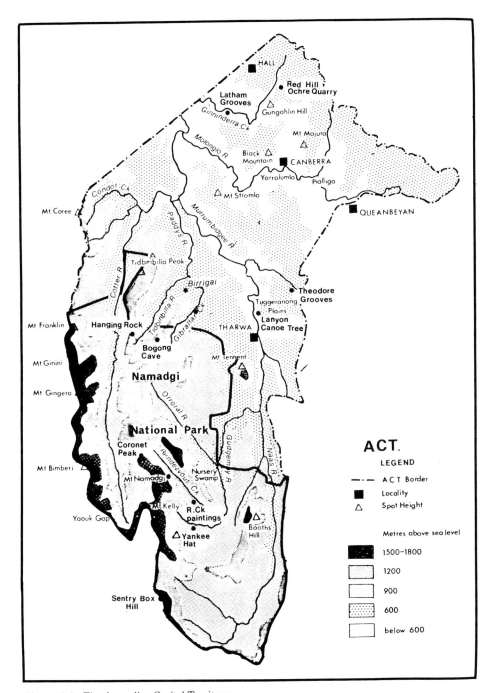

Figure 19.1 The Australian Capital Territory

as 80 possum skins were sewn together to make warm fur cloaks and rugs; sinews from a kangaroo's tail were used for thread. Belts and headbands were also made from possum skin, and ochre was used for body decoration.

Sturdy, weatherproof huts were built from large sheets of stringy bark to ward off the winter cold, but in summer simple bough shelters were used. Material equipment was kept to a minimum, as people moved camp fairly frequently to take advantage of new food supplies coming into season in other parts of the tribal territory. A man would have his spears, a stone axe, boomerang and club, a woman her digging stick and wooden carrying dishes. One distinctive implement used in the south-eastern highlands was the death spear, which was barbed with a row of jagged quartz flakes set into a groove with the gum of the grass tree. This was a deadly weapon because the stone barbs were set at an angle; when the spear head entered human or animal flesh, it could not be pulled out and usually caused a fatal loss of blood.

Traces of over 200 Aboriginal open campsites have been found in the Australian Capital Territory. Most are on the banks of the larger rivers such as the Murrumbidgee and the Molonglo, particularly near the good fishing spots. Many of these have been destroyed by urban development; the major campsite in the Canberra area was on sandhills overlooking the Molonglo River at Pialligo near the airport.[2] This has now virtually disappeared under a rubbish dump and the gardens of the government plant nursery. There were also corroboree grounds on the lower slopes of Mount Ainslie, commemorated in the name Corroboree Park in that suburb, and on Sullivans Creek near the entry to the Botanic Gardens, at the foot of Black Mountain.

A distinctive food eaten by Aborigines of the south-eastern highlands was the Bogong moth. These moths are only found in Australia and New Zealand, and in Australia they carry out a unique annual migration from their breeding grounds in the plains of western New South Wales and southern Queensland to the summits of the Australian Alps. In their millions they pass each year through Canberra around the beginning of October to spend the summer aestivating (pronounced "east-ivating" and the summer equivalent of hibernating) on the mountain tops. The migrations seem to be a mechanism to escape the summer heat of the plains, and they seek out the coolest, driest, darkest crevices on the western, windward side of the peaks.

The quantity of moths varies year by year due to natural fluctuations in population; in a "vintage year" like 1987 they were far more numerous and widespread than in other summers, when they can be difficult to find. Sometimes they are blown off course and do not reach the mountains; occasionally vast quantities of moths are washed up on Sydney beaches after being blown out to sea. And in 1988 another hazard appeared with the opening of New Parliament House in Canberra — the bright lights acted as a magnet and moths settled down there for the summer (plate 19.1)!

The moths are full of protein and provided a nutritious and easily collected traditional food for highland Aborigines. Large gatherings took place, involving as many as 500 people from different friendly tribes for initiation ceremonies, arrangement of marriages, corroborees and exchange of goods. Aboriginal people are reported to have travelled as far as 300 kilometres to such centres as Jindabyne, Blowering, Gudgenby and Omeo in the Victorian Alps. An advance party would climb up to the summits, and if the moths had arrived, would perform ceremonies with bull-roarers and then send up a smoke signal to let the others know.

During aestivation, which lasts from about October to March, the moths sit

Plate 19.1 Bogong moths on New Parliament House, Canberra, October, 1988. (Courtesy of the *Canberra Times)*

quietly on the walls of rock crevices, each with its head tucked under the wings of the one above, resembling tiles on a roof (plate 19.2). Entomologist Dr Ian Common counted 17,000 on one square metre of rock! Aborigines would scrape them off the wall with a stick and collect them in a bark coolamon or a net made from Pimelia or Kurrajong fibre. They were then roasted on a ready-prepared stone "hot plate", about a minute on each side. The moth abdomens are the size of a small peanut with an oily texture, and taste not unlike roast chestnuts.

Smooth round river cobbles were sometimes used to grind up the roasted moths into a paste to carry "moth cakes" down into the valley for the old people, women

Plate 19.2 Bogong moths aestivating on Mount Gingera. (I. Common)

and children. Such moth pestles have been found high in the Snowy Mountains and in the Namadgi National Park. One was excavated in Bogong Cave in Tidbinbilla Nature Reserve, associated with charcoal from old campfires radiocarbon-dated to 1,000 years ago. This means that moth-hunting has been going on for at least that long.

Entomologists consider that the Bogong moth migrations may have started about 10,000 years ago as a response to the increasingly warm climate after the end of the ice age. Aborigines were certainly carrying out sporadic hunting visits to the Canberra region long before that, but a more intensive use of the uplands and increased ceremonial gatherings may have been triggered when moths became available as a plentiful summer "luxury" food, enabling large numbers of people to be fed for several weeks at a time.

Although Bogong moths aestivate right along the spine of the Great Dividing Range, from the Brindabella and Tinderry Ranges near Canberra to Mount Buller at the southern end of the Victorian Alps, one of the easiest places to see them and one of the moth hunters' destinations was the Australian Capital Territory; hence their inclusion in this chapter. A number of sites which can be visited by the public are described below; they include an ochre quarry, axe grinding grooves, a canoe tree, rock paintings, rockshelters with occupational deposits, ceremonial stone arrangements and moth aestivation sites. They are arranged in four groups: those in the Gungahlin and Belconnen area, those on the east of the Murrumbidgee River in the Tuggeranong and Lanyon area, those in the Tidbinbilla area and those in the Namadgi National Park.

Previously unrecorded sites and artefacts are constantly coming to light. If you do come across something which you think may be significant, leave it as you found it, record its location as precisely as possible, and report it to the authority responsible for the Aboriginal heritage of the Australian Capital Territory (currently the Heritage Unit of the Environment and Conservation Branch, ACT Department of Environment, Land and Planning). Please note that here as elsewhere, it is against the law to collect artefacts or damage sites in any way.

Gungahlin/Belconnen

Red Hill ochre quarry, Gungahlin

In the north of the Australian Capital Territory in the Gungahlin area there is an ochre quarry and Aboriginal campsite. The whole of a small hill is made of ochre, which was crushed and mixed with water to make red and yellow ochre. Large

Plate 19.3   Red Hill ochre quarry

pits on the southern and western slopes between the road and the survey point on the hill top are evidence of ochre collecting (plate 19.3). Some 150 small stone tools have been found around and between the pits; this is clear presumptive evidence that Aborigines exploited this abundant source of excellent ochre. The ochre was also later exploited by early European settlers for lime-washing their houses, and they dug down and uncovered a source of white pipe-clay on the lower slopes of the hill, which was probably not known by the Aborigines.

Ochre deposits on this scale are extremely rare, and the Red Hill quarry is likely to have formed an important resource for the local Aboriginal community, which numbered some 500 people. The ochre was probably traded far afield, in exchange for other goods such as slabs of sandstone from the Shoalhaven River district, used as whetstones for re-sharpening tools. Stone tools found on the Red Hill site include backed blades, which in excavated sites in the district belong to the period from between about 750 and some 3,000 years ago.

Would-be visitors to this site should consult the Heritage Unit, since the situation regarding access is soon liable to change. The whole area is being developed as the new town of Gungahlin, and it is planned that the ochre quarry, which is in the Register of the National Estate, will be conserved in a hilltop reserve near the major new shopping centre. Meanwhile it is reached by taking the Federal Highway north out of Canberra, and turning left straight after the showground on Wells Station Road to Gungaderra homestead. There the road turns left again, and Red Hill is the first small hill on the right (grid ref. on ACT 1:100,000 map 954036). The quarry actually extends on both sides of this road, but the main area is on the north side. At present the land is leased out by the Commonwealth government for farming, and all care must be taken with gates, fences and stock.

Latham grinding grooves, Belconnen

Grinding grooves are usually found in sandstone, which is a relatively soft rock ideally suited to the process of manufacturing or re-sharpening the blades of tools

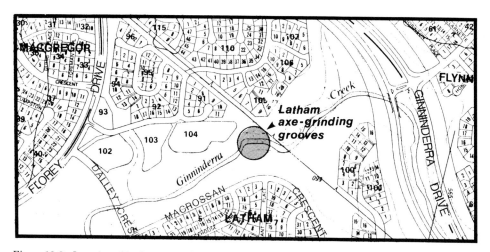

Figure 19.2 Location of Latham axe grinding grooves

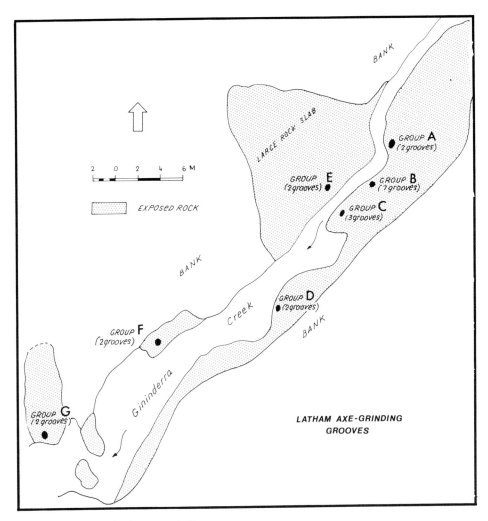

Figure 19.3   Plan of Latham axe grinding grooves

of hard volcanic rock such as ground-edge axes. There is very little sandstone in the Australian Capital Territory, and until some discoveries in the 1980s it was thought that no grooves existed there, and that Aborigines had to make do with portable sandstone slabs brought from the Nowra or Shoalhaven area. A small boy, who had lived in Sydney and was familiar with Aboriginal axe grinding grooves there, found similar grooves on rock slabs on Gininderra Creek near his home in the suburb of Latham.

There are some 18 grooves on both sides of the creek in a locality known as the rock pools, opposite Macrossan Crescent and Want Place in Latham (figures 19.2 and 19.3). Only three are easy to see, a pair on a rock on the south side and one in the bed of the creek. The rock is a hard volcanic tuff, which while not as good as sandstone, served the same purpose. Water was splashed up onto the grooves during the re-sharpening to aid the process, so grinding grooves tend to be found close to water.

Tuggeranong/Lanyon

Theodore grinding grooves, Tuggeranong

One of the very few outcrops of sandstone in the Australian Capital Territory is on the top of a low ridge in the Tuggeranong Valley, between the suburb of Theodore and the Monaro Highway. The sandstone was discovered by Aborigines thousands of years ago, and used for grinding or re-sharpening the blades of their stone axes (plate 19.4). Water was probably carried up from Tuggeranong Creek a few hundred metres north of the site, and stone tools have been found in the vicinity of the grinding grooves, indicating that people also camped there.

The site was discovered by archaeologist Rob Paton when conducting a survey prior to the development of the Tuggeranong Valley. It is the best example of axe grinding grooves yet found in the Canberra region, with some 20 generally well-preserved grooves. It is now in the Register of the National Estate, and has been set aside as a reserve for educational use. Access is from Christmas Street via

Plate 19.4   Axe grinding grooves, Tuggeranong

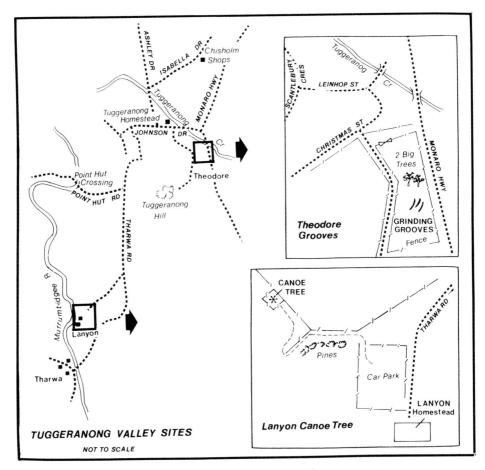

Figure 19.4 Location of Theodore axe grinding grooves site and Lanyon canoe tree

Scantlebury Crescent in the suburb of Theodore, off Johnson Drive; the grooves are on the crest of the spur a little uphill from two large trees in a fenced field of grass (figure 19.4).

Canoe tree, Lanyon

Heading further south down Tharwa Road in the Tuggeranong Valley, the suburbs are at last left behind and visitors arrive at Lanyon (figure 19.4). This not only offers a beautiful historic homestead with authentic furnishings from the nineteenth and early twentieth centuries, a Sidney Nolan art gallery, and Devonshire teas in historic surroundings, but also the only well-preserved canoe tree yet found in the territory (plate 19.5).

The canoe tree was spotted by archaeologist Jonathan Winston-Gregson, when on a lunch break from his excavations of historic remains in Lanyon's courtyard. It is only five minutes walk from the carpark, and is now protected by a small fence. The tree is a living Yellow Box (*Eucalyptus melliodora*). On the side facing the Murrumbidgee River a long scar shows where Aborigines removed a large piece of

Plate 19.5   Canoe tree at Lanyon

bark to make a canoe. The amount of regrowth around the edges of the scar suggests the scar is well over a hundred years old, and the presence of metal axe marks makes between 1820 and 1860 the most likely time.

Tidbinbilla Nature Reserve and area

Gibraltar Falls grinding grooves, Tidbinbilla area

Between Tharwa and Tidbinbilla Nature Reserve, Corin Road leads southwards off Tidbinbilla Road to Woods Reserve, Gibraltar Falls, Smokers Gap and Corin Dam. A number of Aboriginal campsites have been found in this area, and at the top of Gibraltar Falls there are also grinding grooves. The pleasant open area above the top of the falls, where there are now facilities for visitors such as toilets, a carpark and a picnic area, was once used by Aboriginal groups for camping. On flattish, granite slabs on the west (road) side of Gibraltar Creek, about 20 metres upstream from the lip of the falls, there are some grinding grooves (figure 19.5).

   This was a surprise, because granite is an exceptionally hard rock, which was not usually used by Aborigines for grinding purposes. Nevertheless there is no

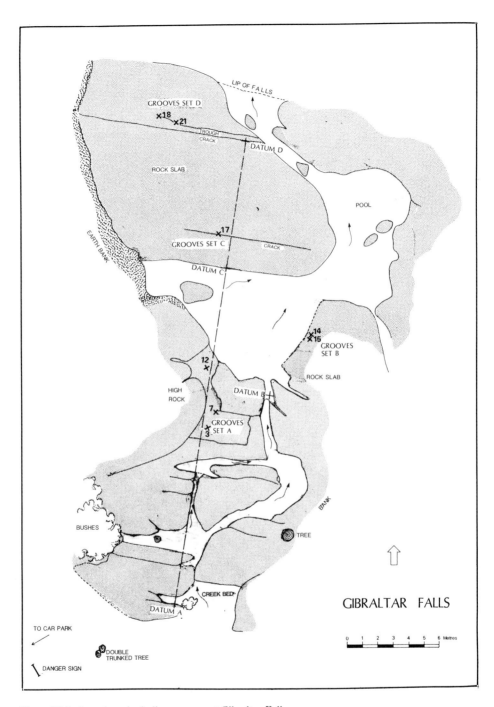

Figure 19.5   Location of grinding grooves at Gibraltar Falls

doubt that the grooves are man-made. Some are at right angles to the current, and thus cannot be natural hollows made by flowing water. One is far too deep and narrow to be natural, and some have an unnatural interior smoothness and sheen, typical of axe grinding grooves. They are all close to the water, which would have

been splashed over them to aid the grinding process. This site is in a public
reserve and can be visited safely, but visitors should not attempt to cross the
creek or go closer than 20 metres to the lip of the falls. Care should be taken on
the rock slabs, which are treacherously slippery when wet.

Birrigai rockshelter

The most exciting recent discovery in the Canberra region is the Birrigai
rockshelter, located 13 kilometres north-west of Tharwa, between the Corin Dam
Road and Tidbinbilla Nature Reserve. This was a camping place for Aboriginal
people during the last ice age, 21,000 years ago, and it was used intermittently
until the middle of the nineteenth century.[3] It lies in a group of granite boulders at
730 metres near the top of Front Hill in the grounds of Birrigai Outdoor School.
The site is protected with mesh security fencing and interpretive signs explain its
significance. (It is open to public visits but visitors must telephone Birrigai
Outdoor School (tel. 37 5191) in advance to arrange access).

The shelter's earth floor contains some tools, ochre, charcoal and a small
amount of animal bone (plate 19.6). The upper layer contains masses of charcoal

Plate 19.6   Birrigai rockshelter

Plate 19.7   Excavation in Birrigai rockshelter

and rabbit bone but very few stone tools. This probably reflects intensive use of the rockshelter in the mid-nineteenth century, when Aborigines were being pushed back into the highlands by European pastoralism. (Those who stayed in the valleys and speared cattle instead of kangaroos risked being shot.) Fragments of mussel shell in the upper layers show that the resources of the larger upland freshwater rivers were also being exploited.

The 1.5 cubic metres excavated produced only 70 stone artefacts, but these were relatively evenly spread from top to bottom in the deposit (plate 19.7). This implies that occupation was sporadic, and that only very occasional brief visits were paid to the cave. Probably these were hunting expeditions, although microscopic analysis of residues left on the working edges of stone tools shows that plants were also processed. Blood on the edge of one stone tool associated with a 16,000-year-old fireplace indicates that butchering of animal carcasses was going on at that time. Another quartz "bipolar" tool has blood on it, not on the working edge but on the side, in the exact spot where a tool-maker who mis-aimed would have hit his thumb!

The significance of this Birrigai site is that it shows that Aboriginal people were at least visiting the south-eastern highlands at the height of the last glaciation. The temperature of the Canberra region would then have felt rather like the top of Mount Kosciusko today: some 7 degrees Celsius colder on average; it was windy and snow-bound in winter. People probably came up in the summer for hunting on what were then treeless plains around Canberra and Lake George, and took refuge in the Birrigai rockshelter because of its superb weatherproof qualities. The author organised the excavation of this site. During the first season of excavation in November, 1983 there was terrible cold, wet weather and it even snowed! The shelter tended to act like a wind tunnel, with the wind whistling through from the western, windward end, but at the same time it was the driest place in the whole region. The excavators blocked off the west end of the shelter with a tarpaulin, and it became quite snug and warm.

Tidbinbilla Nature Reserve

The name Tidbinbilla is an Aboriginal word said to mean the place where boys were made men, and there is a strong local tradition that initiations were carried out on Tidbinbilla Mountain, but no traces of a ceremonial ground have yet been found there. In the valley bottom there is a large rockshelter known as Hanging Rock, which was used by Aboriginal people as a camping place over the last 400 years or longer. The huge tilted rock gives good protection against rain but little against wind and cold, which may be why occupational debris was surprisingly meagre.

A short walking trail leads to Hanging Rock. Other Aboriginal sites within the nature reserve are much harder to reach, but bushwalkers may like to climb up to Billy Billy Rocks and Bogong Cave, which is another Aboriginal occupation site and also occasionally a Bogong moth aestivation site. Billy Billy Rocks is an awesome group of granite rocks high on the ridge between the Tidbinbilla and Gibraltar Creek valleys, on the south-west rim of the nature reserve. The group can be reached from the Tidbinbilla side (ask a ranger for the best route), or from the Corin Dam Road, from Smokers Gap or further north. The easiest route, involving the least scrub-bashing, is to start where the Corin Dam Road crosses Billy Billy Creek, and to head west-south-west, keeping on the southern side of the creek for the first 1.5 kilometres. (Detailed instructions are in Graeme Barrow's book, *Exploring Namadgi and Tidbinbilla: Day Walks in Canberra's High Country* [4]).

Bogong Rocks lie at 1,433 metres above sea level a few hundred metres south-south-east of Billy Billy Rocks and 500 metres north-east of Kangaroo Flats. Bogong Cave is on the south-west side of an extensive group of huge granite boulders. The area of its earth floor is some 15 square metres, of which about 6 metres are well protected from the weather and provide an excellent dry, overnight sleeping place (plate 19.8). There is much moth debris such as wings in the floor, and moths aestivate in this cave sometimes but not every summer. Test excavations revealed no trace of past Aboriginal presence in the cave, but in the two adjacent rockshelters stone tools were found associated with charcoal dating to 1,000 years ago.

Namadgi National Park

Colourful and fairly well-preserved Aboriginal rock paintings have been found in three large and three small rockshelters in the Namadgi National Park. The best known and most easily visited site is Yankee Hat, but the other two major sites at Rendezvous Creek and Nursery Swamp are also well worth a visit (figure 19.6). On no account must the paintings be touched, dust stirred up or fires lit in the vicinity. This rock art was recorded in detail by Kelvin Officer of the Australian

Plate 19.8   Bogong Cave, Tidbinbilla Nature Reserve

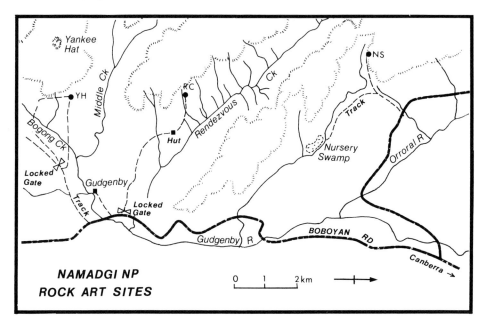

Figure 19.6   Namadgi National Park rock art sites

National University in 1989, and interpretive signs are being erected at the major sites.[7]

Yankee Hat paintings

Aboriginal rock paintings form a seven metre long frieze across the back wall of a large granite rockshelter at the foot of the beautiful, triangular peak of Yankee Hat. The fairly well-preserved, colourful paintings have been executed in red ochre and white pipe-clay (plate 19.9). The main subjects are human and animal figures, including a white long-necked tortoise, kangaroo, dogs and a red bird. At the right-hand side a white male and female human figure stand side by side, together with a strange white figure on the extreme right. At the other side of the frieze there is a scene of a kangaroo apparently being chased by two dingoes or

Plate 19.9   Paintings at Yankee Hat, Namadgi National Park

Figure 19.7   The main rock paintings at Yankee Hat 1. Possible interpretations of some motifs are: F. kangaroo; G & H. dogs; I. turtle; P. bird; S & T. anthropomorphs; V. tail-less quadruped (?koala); M. Bogong moth; N & O. crayfish (M, N & O are identified as birds by Officer).

dogs (figure 19.7). Officer has identified 138 Aboriginal marks, including 68 individual motifs or pictures, in the main shelter, and 6 white and red linear motifs on the low ceiling of the small adjacent rockshelter.

My archaeological excavation of part of the rockshelter floor revealed that Aboriginal people had been camping here over the last 700 years.[5] During this time there was a change from the use of fine-grained chert and backed blades in the earliest times to small quartz flakes more recently.

Visits to the site are possible, and leaflets with a map are available from the ACT Parks and Conservation Service in Tuggeranong or at the visitors centre on the road between Tharwa and Gudgenby, and detailed instructions and a map are also in Barrow's book.[6] Access is from the Old Boboyan Road (north), a dirt track which leads off to the right about 200 metres south of the Gudgenby River bridge. After about three kilometres there is a parking area at a pine plantation just before a locked gate. A huge boulder close to the rock paintings is visible from this carpark; it stands directly below pyramid-shaped Yankee Hat Mountain on the lower edge of the eucalypt treeline north of the Boboyan pines. A walking track heads approximately 3 kilometres in a westerly direction to the site, across a swampy area and a newly built footbridge over Bogong Creek.

The site is located at an elevation of 1,065 metres at 06/7653.60/4183 on the Yaouk 1:25,000 topographic map.

Rendezvous Creek paintings

A visit to this site involves a 14 kilometre long walk, requiring about 5 hours return. The starting point is immediately south of the bridge where the Boboyan Road crosses Rendezvous Creek. A dirt road leads off to the west through a locked gate (figure 19.6). This is followed to Rollys Hut and stockyards, where there is a visitors' book with instructions on how to locate the paintings. (Please re-close any gates you pass through.) The site is approximately 1.2 kilometres from Rollys Hut. The track is signposted to within 200 metres of the paintings near a ti tree-filled gully. Follow this gully uphill to two groups of large boulders about 50 metres apart. The well-preserved paintings are located in a deep hollow in the north-west side of a huge boulder in the left-hand group, and the site is fenced (plate 19.10). The site is located at 1,080 metres at 06/7625.60/4649 on the Rendezvous Creek 1:25,000 topographic map.)

Colours used are red, white and black and there is a wide variety of motifs. On the extreme right are two striking tall birds, thought to represent emus, which

Plate 19.10   Rendezvous Creek rockshelter, Namadgi National Park

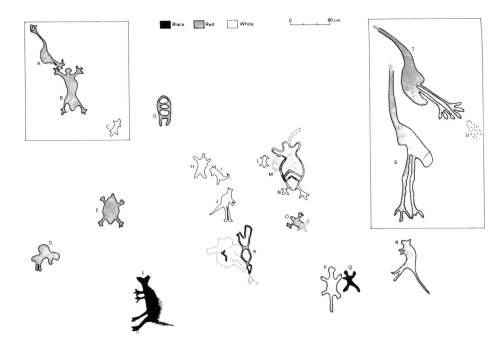

Figure 19.8 The main rock paintings at Rendezvous Creek (the insets fit on the left and right ends of the frieze respectively). Possible interpretations of some motifs are: A. bird; B,C,I,O & Q. anthropomorphs; D & M. packhorses; E. & H. echidnas; F,I,J & R. kangaroos or wallabies; N. anthropomorph (superimposed on packhorse); P. goanna (Flood), possum (Officer); S & T. emus (Officer), plains turkeys (Flood).

were common in the Canberra region at the time of the first European settlement. Other figures include 7 macropods, an echidna, a turtle, anthropomorphs, birds, and what appear to be 2 pack horses. If this identification is correct, at least some of the paintings post-date European contact, which in this region occurred in the 1820s. Some faint black paintings lie on the side of the large boulder to the right. These are thought to be of considerable age by Officer, who has identified 70 pigmented marks in this shelter, including 48 definite motifs.

Nursery Swamp art site

A visit to this site also requires a bushwalk, shorter but more uphill than that to Rendezvous Creek, and only for the moderately fit. The site is located at 1,170 metres at ACT Natmap grid reference 771505 or 06/7520.6/5154 on Rendezvous Creek 1:25,000 topographic map, on the upper reaches of Nursery Creek, where the valley is narrow and forested. The easiest access is to follow the indistinct traces of the old bridle track south from the Orroral Valley to Nursery Swamp, parking in a layby before a cattle grid and the old tracking station. After crossing a saddle the faint track winds down to Nursery Creek. It continues to Nursery Swamp, and the return trip from the Orroral Valley road to Nursery Swamp is approximately six kilometres and three hours. However, to reach the art site head up rather than down Nursery Creek, to the shelter in a group of large boulders on its north side, about 80 metres from the creek. The site is not particularly easy to find, and it may be best to wait for an organised excursion, for example in Heritage Week.

The paintings are under an overhang in the western, downslope side of a huge granite boulder. Green lichen covers much of the rock and at times grows over and obscures some of the paintings. When the site was first recorded and partially excavated in 1981 by Andree Rosenfeld of the Australian National University,[8] eight figures were identified on the wall (figure 19.9), but more are now visible due to changes in the lichen cover. (Please do not touch paintings or the lichen, or you could cause irreparable damage.) The figures are mainly what seem to be echidnas, painted in red ochre, very similar to some at the Rendezvous Creek site. Others resemble macropods, with short front and long back legs and a long tail. A white kangaroo (90 centimetres long) became visible in the mid-1980s to the left of the group of echidnas. Officer has recorded 39 marks, including 13 identifiable motifs. The excavation revealed occupation going back 3,700 years.

Namadgi stone arrangement

A well-preserved ceremonial stone arrangement survives on one of the peaks of the ACT ranges within Namadgi National Park. It lies on an unnamed peak, now known as Mount Namadgi, north of Mount Kelly, north-west of Yankee Hat and south of Creamy Flats, on the divide between the Cotter and Gudgenby valleys (Natmap grid reference 706483). It is most easily reached from the end of the Creamy Flats fire trail from the Cotter Hut, but if permission is not forthcoming from the ACT Parks and Conservation Service to approach from the west, it can also be reached from the north or east via Cotter Gap, Rendezvous Creek or Middle Creek. It is a hike of several hours from the nearest road whichever route is taken, and an overnight camp at Creamy Flats below Mount Namadgi should be planned.

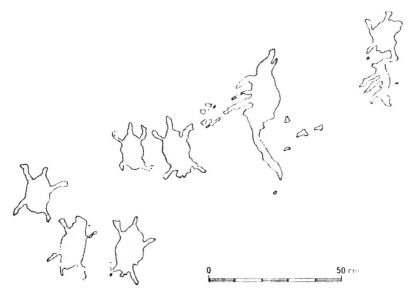

Figure 19.9 Rock paintings at Nursery Swamp (A. Rosenfeld et al. 1983). (Note: further figures have come to light since this drawing was made.)

Plate 19.11 Stone arrangement on Mount Namadgi, Namadgi National Park

The stone arrangements lie on extensive, sloping rock slabs on the northern side of the mountain, both below and close to the summit. Signs including a plan have been erected around the site. On the climb up the mountain, a 20 metre long double row of stones or "corridor" arrangement is first encountered (plate 19.11). Then there is a 50 metre long slightly curving single row, and a second corridor arrangement. A little below the summit cairn there is another single row of stones, about 20 metres in length.

This was doubtless a ceremonial site, perhaps for initiation rituals. It has a commanding view, with hills and valleys stretching out to the hazy distance in all directions. Here the tribal elders probably instructed the youths on the extent of their tribal territory, and subjected them to the rigorous rites of initiation into tribal law. Bogong moths aestivate on this and neighbouring granite peaks, providing an easily caught source of abundant food during the summer months.

Moth aestivation sites

While there are many moth aestivation sites in the south-eastern highlands, the easiest places to see Bogong moths are Mount Gingera in the Australian Capital Territory and Mount Twynam in the Snowy Mountains (not counting New Parliament House in Canberra!). On Mount Twynam the moths are found between about October and February in rock crevices on the way up to the summit from Blue Lake. At dusk they become active and fly around, emitting a weird, high-pitched humming noise.

Mount Gingera, 1,857 metres high, is on top of the Brindabella Range in the west of the territory, between Mount Bimberi and Mount Ginini. It is reached from the north via the rough, unsealed Mount Franklin Road from "Piccadilly Circus" and the Cotter. Vehicles must be left at the locked gate near Mount Ginini, unless a key has been obtained from the ACT Parks and Conservation Service. A rough track leads up Mount Gingera from where Mount Franklin Road crosses Snowy Flat Creek. A full day is needed from Canberra for this excursion, but the effort is rewarded by a panoramic view from the summit.

Bogong moths are found in summer in dry, dark crevices and small caves among the summit rocks, particularly on the windward side. Viewers need torches or time to accustom their eyes to the gloom, whereupon the moths should be visible, forming scale-like patterns on the rock walls. Visitors could try putting their hands into the crevices and feeling the rock walls, until they touch a "furry" substance under their fingers. Most moths stay quiet, but some fly around, especially when disturbed. Birds like ravens and currawongs enjoy a tasty mouthful of moth, and their cawing is a guide to moth habitats. Other traditional food items in the locality are the tubers of the yam daisy. The bright yellow, dandelion-like flowers are widespread on Mount Gingera.

CHAPTER TWENTY

Tasmania

Tasmanian prehistory has long fascinated researchers, ever since early explorers remarked in the late eighteenth and early nineteenth centuries on the distinctive physical appearance, language and lifestyle of the Aborigines they encountered. Tasmanian Aborigines' spirally curled hair and small stature contrasted markedly with the taller, straight haired people of mainland Australia, and gave rise to some wild theories about their origins. Some anthropologists believed that they had come from Pacific islands on rafts; others saw them as a last vestige of Oceanic Negritos from Papua New Guinea.

It is now established that Aboriginal people moved into Tasmania more than 35,000 years ago, during a phase of the ice age when sea level was much lower than today and Bass Strait was dry land (figures 20.1 and 20.2). The present Bass Strait islands were then simply hills on a broad land bridge which linked Tasmania to the mainland. Until recently the earliest firmly dated human occupation site in Tasmania was Cave Bay (renamed Lirevigana, meaning Island Cave) excavated by Sandra Bowdler on what is now Hunter Island.[1] In the floor of this huge sea cave a few stone tools and bone points and the smashed and burnt bones of various land animals were associated with thick layers of ash and charcoal dated to about 23,000 years old.

Then in 1988 excavation of Bluff Cave (renamed Nunamira) (figure 20.2) in the Florentine Valley by Richard Cosgrove produced a date of 30,000 years for early Aboriginal camping debris.[2] This means that people penetrated into this most southerly part of the Australian continent virtually as soon as it was possible to do so. The land bridge between the mainland and Tasmania was exposed only at times of low sea level. Entry into Tasmania could have been effected around 55,000 years ago when sea level had dropped by about 120 metres, or between 37,000 and 29,000 years ago when the land bridge was again exposed. The last glaciation caused another major drop in sea level and the disappearance of Bass Strait between about 24,000 and 8,000 years ago. The earliest occupation in Tasmania is now 35,000-year-old Warreen Cave in the Maxwell River Valley, in the south-west.

It is now clear that the Tasmanian Aborigines walked from the mainland. The physical differences between them and other mainlanders are thus most likely to be the result of genetic changes in a population numbering only some 3,000 to 5,000

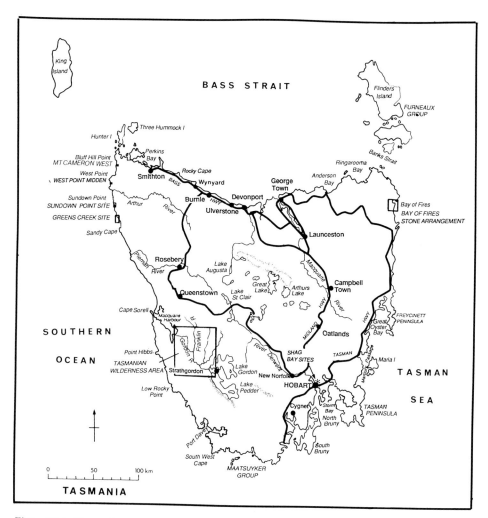

Figure 20.1 Tasmania

people, who were isolated for about 8,000 years after the rising post-glacial sea drowned their land bridge and completely cut them off from the rest of the world.

A remarkable discovery of the 1980s has been that the remote, rugged south-west of Tasmania was inhabited by at least 35,000 years ago, and there is no doubt that people were camping in caves in south-west Tasmania even at the height of the last glaciation.[3] Discoveries in the south-west first took place in the early 1980s, when the Franklin River was under threat of being dammed for hydro-electricity. The vigorous No Dams campaign and the subsequent High Court case were aided considerably by the finding in Kutikina (see below) and other caves on the Franklin of archaeological deposits of international scientific significance. The region is now on the World Heritage List, and it is hoped that there will be no further threats to the survival of the ice age sites.

The concentrated archaeological research effort in south-west Tasmania, largely funded through the Australian Heritage Commission, the Australian National University and the National Estate Grants Program and led by Rhys

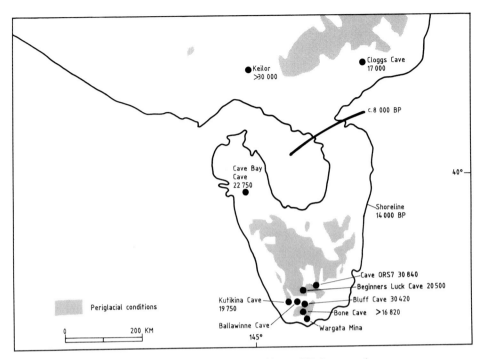

Figure 20.2 Pleistocene Tasmania, showing the land bridge and Pleistocene sites

Jones of the Australian National University, Jim Allen and Richard Cosgrove of La Trobe University, and Kevin Kiernan, Don Ranson, Steve Brown, Greg Middleton and others in association with the then Tasmanian National Parks and Wildlife Service, revealed the existence of some 20 ice age campsites in limestone caves. The greatest concentration is on the lower Franklin River, but other sites are found in the valleys of the Denison, Maxwell, Andrew, Acheron and Florentine Rivers (figure 20.3).

Nowadays this whole region is covered with dense rainforest, much of it an almost impenetrable three-dimensional maze of fallen trees and horizontal scrub, but this was not always the case. Twenty thousand years ago south-west Tasmania was in the grip of the last and most severe glaciation of the ice age. The climate was both drier and much colder, with average annual temperatures about 7 degrees Celsius lower than at present. Glaciers flowed down from mountains such as Frenchmans Cap which overlooks the Franklin Valley, and there were few trees. The landscape would have looked something like Patagonia today, with glacier-clad mountains and trees confined to the lower slopes of the river valleys.

Fossilised pollen from cores bored out of swamps in the Tasmanian highlands shows that at the height of the last glaciation, about 18,000 years ago, there were alpine herbfields and open grasslands where there is now rainforest. Rainforest was probably found then only on the valley floors and on the coast; the higher slopes were a treeless, open habitat well-suited to hunters and their prey. At Kutikina Cave (pronounced Koot-i-kine-a rhyming with miner) the ice age occupants seem to have hunted the red-necked wallaby almost exclusively. This wallaby is still common in other parts of Tasmania today, preferring relatively open habitats.

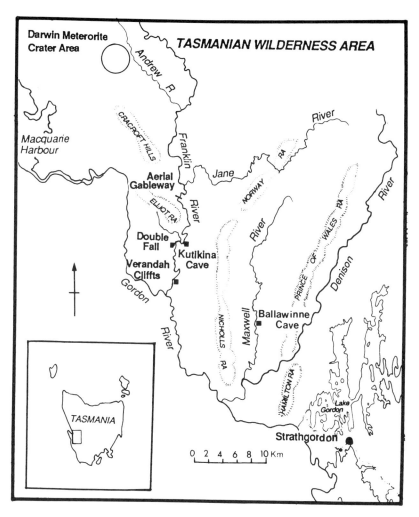

Figure 20.3 Tasmanian Wilderness Area

While much of the ice age fauna of Tasmania still exists, there were also large marsupials or megafauna which became extinct. Several bone deposits of extinct fauna have been discovered in Tasmania in places such as Mowbray Swamp near Smithton in the north-west, but in only one archaeological site so far have artefacts been found with bones of extinct animals. This is a cave named Beginners Luck, where a deposit containing a few stone tools associated with the bones of a giant kangaroo, *Macropus titan,* was radiocarbon-dated to 20,000 years ago. This limestone cave lies in the Florentine Valley, a region of dense forest but which was much more open at the height of the last ice age, and also contains 30,000-year-old occupation in Bluff Cave. The Florentine Valley is on a north-south axis, like the Franklin and Maxwell Valleys to the west, and would have provided a natural route for hunters on summer hunting excursions to the high country.

Journeying across south-west Tasmania would have been much easier during the ice age than it is now, and there is evidence that Aborigines travelled considerable distances in search of special tool-making materials. In several of the south-west Tasmanian cave deposits are tiny sharp pieces of Darwin glass, fetched from the Darwin crater, where a meteor struck, fusing rocks into natural glass (see below). The Darwin crater is 75 kilometres west of Bluff Cave, and a journey along the river valleys would have been as much as 100 kilometres.

It seems clear that ochre was fetched from distant sources, and it is present in all layers of the Kutikina Cave deposit, spanning the six millennia from about 20,000 to 14,000 years ago. This fine, high quality red ochre was ground up to make paint, which was probably used for personal adornment and warding off the cold, when mixed with animal fat and smeared on the body. (Red ochre was in historic times mixed with grease and applied by some Tasmanian Aboriginal men to their hair, faces and upper torso.)

The presence of ochre pigment in the Kutikina Cave deposit raised the exciting possibility that these ice age Tasmanians were practising art. It was not until January, 1986 that the first rock art was found in south-west Tasmania, in the Maxwell River valley which runs parallel and about 12 kilometres to the east of the Franklin. There in a dolomite cave 23 hand stencils in two groups were found in total darkness in a chamber about 20 metres from the cave entrance. Some of the hand stencils are amazingly clear, standing out in a vivid red ochre against the pale grey dolomite wall; others are quite indistinct (figure 20.4).

There are also small patches and streaks of red ochre on various parts of the ceiling and of the entry passage. These may have acted as some kind of warning marker to a special area of ritual significance. The site is now specially protected under Tasmanian legislation, and a permit is needed to visit it (from the Tasmanian Aboriginal Centre and the Archaeology Unit of the Department of Parks, Wildlife and Heritage.)

Figure 20.4 Part of the hand stencil gallery in Ballawinne Cave, south-west Tasmania. (B. Prince courtesy of the Tasmanian Aboriginal Centre)

The art of Ballawinne (pronounced Bal-a-win-ee and meaning ochre) Cave, as the Maxwell River site has now been named by Tasmanian Aborigines, proves that Tasmanian Aborigines practised painting in prehistoric times. Ironically the island which has produced the first pigmented art of indisputable, ice age antiquity in Australia has a striking lack of more recent rock art sites, with less than 20 on record. Until this find, only three stencil art sites were known in Tasmania. Their relatively fresh appearance and location in the south-east, close to early European settlement, had given rise to the belief that they might have been executed by Sydney Aborigines brought to Tasmania to help in the rounding up of the local Aborigines. No Holocene rock paintings other than stencils have yet been found, and there are only a dozen or so engraving sites on record.

Once this first ice age site had been found, the search intensified and was rewarded by the discovery in 1987 of a further 23 hand stencils and patches of red ochre in Judds Cavern in the Southern Forests. This limestone cave lies deep within rainforest in the Cracroft Valley, eight hours of hard bushwalking from Farmhouse Creek, in the heart of what is known as the Southern Forests which border on the South-West Tasmania world heritage area. It is overshadowed by three peaks which are snow-capped in winter, Mount Bobs, Mount Picton and Federation Peak.

The age of the stencils has been estimated through geomorphological evidence of the growth of stalactites and other calcium carbonate accretions over the red ochre, and they are believed to be more than 12,000 years old. Even more remarkable was the discovery that smears of red ochre plastered on the walls contain what seems to be blood.[4] The "blood" is claimed to be human and has now been dated by Tom Loy of the Australian National University (by Accelerator Mass Spectometry dating of four microns of pigment) to about 10,000 years ago. This is strong evidence of the ritual nature of this site, and Tasmanian Aboriginal people have given it the name Wargata Mina, meaning my blood (pronounced War-gar-tar Meena, war as in war and gar and tar as in bar).

While the ice age occupation of Tasmania is now well established, little is known of the succeeding period. Why were the caves of the south-west abandoned 13,000 years ago? It was at this time that the glaciers began to retreat and the world's climate to warm up. This had two major results for the ice age hunters of the south-west. The melting of the polar ice caused the sea to rise until the land link with the Australian mainland was drowned, and rainforest inexorably began to recolonise the valleys and lowlands, ruining them as hunting grounds. Evidence from pollen cores[5] indicates that the glaciers were retreating and the forests migrating upslope soon after 11,500 years ago in the Central Highlands of Tasmania. A rapid increase in temperature and rainfall continued until around 9,500 years, and an optimum period of moister and warmer conditions prevailed from about 8,000 to 3,600 years ago.

The flooding of the Bassian Plain, which now lies below 100 metres of ocean, took place between about 12,000 and 8,000 years ago. The link to the mainland would have become a narrower and narrower corridor till it finally disappeared completely.

Even if some hunters left Tasmania, others remained, completely isolated for the next 8,000 years by the 250 kilometre wide Bass Strait, one of the world's stormiest and most treacherous sea passages. No other human society on earth has ever been cut off from the rest of the world for so long or so totally.

The dingo was never introduced onto the island, although it was found all over the mainland from 4,000 years ago. The opposite is true of other animals such as the Tasmanian devil, which became extinct on the mainland, possibly because of competition for prey from the dingo, but persisted in Tasmania. Also, the Tasmanian tiger or thylacine seems to have disappeared from the mainland but survives, it is hoped, in Tasmania.

At the time Tasmania was cut off, the toolkit seems to have been similar to that of mainland Aborigines, and it was to change little for the next 8,000 years. New developments in technology on the mainland, such as the spear-thrower, stone spear points or boomerangs, never reached Tasmania. Nevertheless, a trend towards a decrease in overall size and an increase in the amount of trimming of the working edges of stone tools is apparent over the last few millennia in both Tasmania and the mainland. The main stone tools were hand-held choppers, scrapers and flakes used variously for chopping, scraping and cutting tasks. One of the main uses of stone tools was for manufacturing wooden artefacts such as spears and clubs. Bone tools existed in the ice age toolkit and are thought to have been used in the manufacture of skin rugs for clothing; in the recent past on the mainland bone points were used as awls to poke holes in kangaroo or possum skins through which animal sinew thread was then passed.

Occupation from the 12,000 to 8,000 time period in Tasmania has been found at very few sites, notably in Warragarra rockshelter in the highlands.[6] Located at 600 metres above sea level, Warragarra lies in the upper Mersey River valley in central Tasmania, some eight kilometres south of Lake Rowallon and below some of Tasmania's highest peaks, with Cradle Mountain and Mount Ossa to the west and the Central Plateau on the east. Warragarra was found by Peter Sims of Devonport when out bushwalking, and was excavated by Harry Lourandos in 1982.

The evidence suggests that the site was first occupied about 10,000 years ago, soon after the deglaciation of the area, and was probably used sporadically as a transient hunting camp. About 3,400 years ago there was an increase at Warragarra rockshelter in the numbers of artefacts, animal bones, cooking hearths and concentrations of charcoal. The stimulus for the ensuing period of expansion and development is not well understood, but over the next 1,500 years rainforests were opened up through the use of fire, trade increased, a wider variety of foods was exploited and raw materials from the west coast made their first appearance at this time at Rocky Cape (see below). Better raw materials were used for stone tools and stone tools became smaller and were used with increasing efficiency. Coastal settlements were established on the west coast, there was a flowering in the art of engraving, new ceremonial sites such as stone arrangements came into being, and there was a movement to offshore islands.

Hunter Island was re-visited, after being apparently abandoned when it was first severed from the mainland. Watercraft were needed to exploit the resources of such offshore islands, and it is thought that the distinctive Tasmanian watercraft were first developed some 2,500 years ago, in the west of the island where the need for water transport was greatest, not only to reach the islands but

Figure 20.5   Tasmanian watercraft. (Courtesy of the Tasmanian Museum and Art Gallery)

also to cross rivers, estuaries and bays, which formed considerable obstacles to travel along the coast.

The unique Tasmanian watercraft [7] were something between a canoe and a raft. Three bundles of paperbark, stringybark or reeds were tied together with a network of bark or grass string to make a sausage-shaped craft, lashed at both ends with an upcurving bow and stern and a slight hollow in the centre (figure 20.5). The side bundles acted as stabilisers and the central one provided what little buoyancy there was. Unfortunately, the bark when saturated had a density similar to water, and so after a few hours in the water the craft lost its rigidity, became waterlogged and sank. These canoe-rafts were not paddled but poled along or pushed forward by swimmers. They could hold six or seven people, but were generally not taken more than five to eight kilometres offshore. Fires were kept alight on clay hearths in the centre of the craft during these voyages. (Models of these craft are on view in the Tasmanian Museum and Art Gallery in Hobart.)

In spite of the fragility of their watercraft, prehistoric Tasmanians were outstanding mariners. Bruny Island is thought to have been re-occupied about 3,000 years ago, after having been vacated 2,000 years earlier when the final post-glacial sea rise cut it off from the mainland, and many Bass Strait Islands were visited to exploit muttonbird rookeries or colonies of seals. Even more remarkable were the voyages undertaken to the Maatsuyker Islands, off south-west Tasmania, across a strait which receives the full force of the Roaring Forties and is dangerous even for modern vessels. Maatsuyker (pronounced mat-sigh-cur) was probably reached via De Witt Island, in two stages of 10 and 7 kilometres, although no traces of Aboriginal occupation have been found on De Witt so it may even be that a direct voyage of 20 kilometres was made in these frail paperbark craft.

Visits to Tasmanian offshore islands in summer to hunt seals and collect muttonbirds from their burrows were reasonably common over the last 2,000 years, judging by the remains of prehistoric camps found on Maatsuyker. There are also substantial quantities of charcoal in middens on this and other islands. This implies that prehistoric Tasmanians could make fire, for it would have been difficult it not impossible to keep a fire burning in the watercraft all the way across to the more distant islands.

The period after 3,500 years ago was a period of expansion in prehistoric

Tasmania, but there were also some curious losses. By 3,000 years ago bone tools had dropped out of the toolkit and people had stopped eating fish. The evidence for this comes from Rocky Cape caves and a number of other archaeological sites around the island, where bone tools and fish bones are found in pre-3,000-year-old layers, but not afterwards. It is also supported by ethnographic evidence of Tasmanian Aborigines' aversion to fish when this was offered to them at first European contact.[8]

Many theories have been put forward to try to explain this "loss of useful arts", but none satisfactorily answer the questions of "Why did the Tasmanians stop using bone tools?" and "Why did the Tasmanians stop eating fish?" Certainly by the eighteenth century the Tasmanian Aboriginal material culture was the simplest of any known society in the world. It included only about two dozen items: clubs, wooden spears with fire-hardened tips, a digging stick-club-chisel used by women, wooden wedges or spatulae for prising shellfish off rocks, baskets woven from rushes or grass, water-buckets made from kelp, possum skin pouch bags, kangaroo skin cloaks, firesticks, canoe-rafts, huts, shell and other necklaces and a few hand-held stone and shell tools.

That the people who experienced the longest isolation in the world should have the world's simplest material culture is fascinating. Yet there are many uncertainties about the direction in which more recent prehistoric society was heading before its near-fatal destruction by the advent of the Europeans. It has been suggested that these few thousand people stranded on this remote, chilly island of about the size of Sri Lanka or Ireland were a doomed society, but recent archaeological evidence points on the contrary to an expansion in population, economy and cultural activity. Only further archaeological evidence can provide the answers.

Some 5,500 Aboriginal sites have been recorded in Tasmania. A sites register is held in the Department of Parks, Wildlife and Heritage in Hobart, which administers legislation protecting all Tasmanian Aboriginal sites and artefacts. The department's Archaeology Section should be contacted for information and permission to visit restricted sites. Sites described below are in most cases open to the public, but in a few cases special permission is needed. They are described in an anti-clockwise direction, beginning in the south-west where the oldest known sites occur.

South-west Tasmania

Darwin meteorite crater

Seven hundred and thirty thousand years ago a gigantic meteor blazed across the sky above south-west Tasmania and crashed into the slopes of Mount Darwin, where it blasted a crater more than a kilometre wide and 200 metres deep. So great was the heat and force with which it struck that rocks at the point of impact were melted into glass and sprayed over the surrounding country.[9]

The crater lies 26 kilometres south-south-east of Queenstown, 4 kilometres south-east of Ten Mile Hill on the Kelly Basin Road, between the Andrew River and the South Darwin Peak (figure 20.3). (AMG coordinates are 8013-895155. A track was cut into the centre of the crater, 3.5 kilometres east of the road, in 1974.) The crater can be reached by following the four-wheel-drive Kelly Basin Road for about 25 kilometres from the Lyell Highway 9 kilometres east of Queenstown, and then by rough track east to the crater. The best angle from which to view the crater is the north-west. It is rimless and filled with sediment, and is not easy to see because it lies in a valley in hilly terrain covered with dense rainforest both inside and outside the crater.

The Darwin glass was blasted from the impact point to distances of at least 22 kilometres, with the smallest pieces travelling furthest. The glass strewnfield covers at least 400 square kilometres, and was discovered by Europeans first at Ten Mile Hill on the Kelly Basin Road.

Pieces of this shiny, black "Darwin glass" had been discovered more than 20,000 years earlier by ice age Tasmanian Aborigines, who prized the obsidian-like glass for its superb cutting qualities. Mount Darwin lies about 25 kilometres north-west of Kutikina Cave, necessitating a journey of several days to reach the meteorite crater. There the small pieces of glass were collected from under up-rooted trees and stream beds and carried back to caves on the Franklin River, where they were fractured with quartzite hammerstones to make razor-sharp knives.

Kutikina Cave

Kutikina Cave is located on the east bank of the lower reaches of the Franklin River where it takes a bend to the south, some ten kilometres from its confluence with the Gordon (figure 20.3). The cave is open to the public and now has a walkway to protect the deposits, but is not easy to reach. The usual means of access is by rafting down the Franklin River from Collingwood Bridge on the Lyell Highway. This involves six or seven days of some of the toughest but most rewarding white-water rafting in Australia, down through the heart of the world heritage wilderness area. It is also possible to raft up the river from the Gordon, if visitors are prepared to carry rafts round several impassable rapids and waterfalls. The cave can be reached by a three day trek in on foot from the east, but this is only recommended for very experienced bushwalkers.

In its lower reaches the Franklin River is lined with dense walls of rainforest broken only by towering dark grey limestone cliffs. On the bend where Kutikina Cave is situated, the water is tranquil, rainforest lines the bank on the northern side and a long 30 metre high limestone cliff rises on the southern side. A gap in this cliff provides access up a slippery clay slope to the cave, which lies in bush about 35 metres back from the river's edge.

Kutikina is a major cave of 170 metres in length and features rimstone pools, stalagmites and stalactites. Its mouth is about 7 metres wide and opens directly into a large entrance chamber approximately 20 metres long, 12 metres wide and 5 metres high, with a floor area of some 100 square metres (figure 20.6). Its floor is of orange clay, and when archaeologists first came here in March 1981 hundreds of stone tools and burnt fragments of animal bones were observed protruding from the eroded face of the deposit.

This huge limestone cave was discovered by caver and geomorphologist, Kevin Kiernan, in 1977, and named Fraser Cave after the then prime minister. (Already

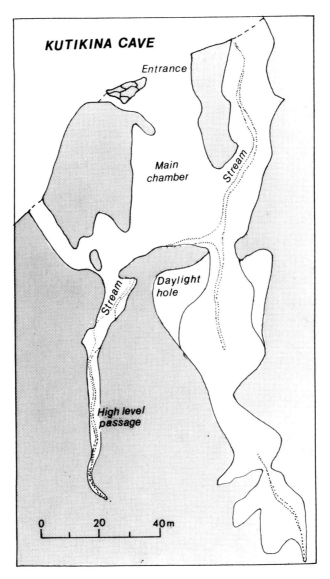

Figure 20.6   Ground plan of Kutikina Cave. (Based on Jones 1987)

the battle to save the Franklin from hydro-electricity scheme was on and it was hoped that politicians would become more conscious of the existence of the caves if they were named after them.) Its more prosaic label was F34, and in 1982 it was named by the Tasmanian Aboriginal Centre Kutikina, meaning spirit. In 1977 it was only one of 100 limestone caves on the Franklin mapped by speleologists, but in February 1981 Kiernan re-visited the site to examine the bones he had noticed in the main chamber. He found that they were wallaby bones which had been burnt and split, and that some of the pieces of stone had been fashioned into cutting tools. This was the breakthrough that archaeologists had been seeking. A joint Australian National University and Tasmanian National Parks and Wildlife

Service expedition was organised and led by Rhys Jones, and one month later the first and only excavation took place in Kutikina Cave.

This small pilot excavation into the bank of occupational deposit in the entrance chamber revealed that this is one of the richest archaeological sites ever found in Australia. The deposit is only about one metre deep, but the one cubic metre excavated contained some 40,000 stone artefacts and almost a quarter of a million fragments of animal bone, indicating that the site as a whole could hold more than 10 million artefacts. This is a more than adequate sample of the cave's contents, and the rest of the floor is being left intact for future examination (in the twenty-first century?) when even more sophisticated technology and excavation methods are developed.

It was subsequently shown that the cave had been used over more than 5,000 years, between about 20,000 and 14,000 years ago. The chronology of occupation was reconstructed from radiocarbon dates obtained from a series of hearths, ancient fireplaces where people repeatedly lit fires, leaving one set of charcoal, embers and ash on top of another. Ice age hunters began to use the cave about 20,000 years ago, just before the peak of the last glaciation. This intensely cold phase brought glaciers to mountains such as Frenchmans Cap in the upper part of the Franklin Valley, and grasslands and alpine herbfields to slopes now covered in rainforest. There the occupants of Kutikina Cave hunted the red-necked wallaby and the occasional wombat and echidna. This wallaby is now absent from the Franklin area, but may have been the most abundant, large animal species when the country was more open.

It is probable that a band of 20 or 30 people used the cave as a base camp, bringing their prey back to be butchered, roasted and eaten. Many of the wallaby bones which carpet the cave floor are charred from cooking, only certain body parts are present, and long bones have been split open to extract the marrow. Slivers from the shin bones of wallabies had been sharpened and smoothed to make bone points, probably used for pinning out skins to dry or sewing them together into rugs or garments.

Stone tools were fashioned from a wide variety of materials, including quartz, chert, chalcedony and other fine-grained rocks found in the glacial meltwater gravels and pebble banks at the river's edge. An even more exotic raw material was natural glass from the Darwin meteorite crater. The red pigment, haematite, was also present, suggesting that the art of painting was known to these early Tasmanians.

Four basic types of stone tools were found, as described by Rhys Jones[10]:

> . . . steep-edged scrapers possibly used for taking bark from trees and fat and gristle from skins; thumbnail-sized scrapers for very fine work, probably on wood; sharp flakes used for cutting, some of which may have been discarded after one use; and the stones from which the flakes were struck, used with edges sharpened for chopping and very heavy planing . . . The stone tools were in turn used to fashion wooden weapons and implements such as spears and digging sticks. The amount and type of wear on the tools indicates what they were used to work, for example wood or bone. Traces of dried blood and organic tissue on the *Kutikina* tools indicated that they were used to cut meat, scrape bone and cut skin.

At the height of the last glaciation about 17,000 years ago small, angular blocks of frost-shattered limestone fell from the roof to form rubble on the floor.

Nevertheless occupation continued, although it seems likely that caves such as Kutikina were summer hunting camps and that in winter the people retreated northwards to warmer places, perhaps as far afield as what is now mainland Australia.

Occupation of the cave was at its peak between 20,000 and 16,000 years ago, but numerous alternating layers of charcoal and burnt red clay in the upper part of the deposit show that the cave was used regularly for camping until it was abandoned about 14,000 years ago. At that time the climate was beginning to warm up. Glaciers were receding and rainforest was spreading upwards from its ice age riverside refuge. A tide of trees gradually swamped the area, and Kutikina and other caves in the south-west were vacated and never re-occupied. The charcoal, ash and burnt clay of ancient fireplaces, charred bones and stone tools were covered with a thin layer of sterile clay and then gradually sealed in under a thin layer of white calcium carbonate or "moonmilk". For the next 14,000 years no human being entered the cave.

The south-east

Shag Bay sites, Hobart area

A large number of Aboriginal occupation sites are found around Hobart, for example on the eastern shore of the lower Derwent River, directly opposite New Town Bay in the Bedlam Walls area. Between Risdon and Geilston Bay to the west of the East Derwent Highway is the only zone of natural vegetation remaining on the lower Derwent. There are more than 100 middens in this area, varying from prominent grass-covered mounds of shells and other occupational debris to sparse traces of charcoal and shell.

Three rockshelters on the shale and sandstone cliffs of Bedlam Walls south of Shag Bay contain occupational material. One has been excavated, and yielded evidence of Aboriginal occupation going back 5,000 years. There are also three sources of stone used in tool manufacture, a mudstone quarry between Porter Bay and Tommys Bight and two chalcedony-opal quarries in the Shag Bay area.

Freycinet Peninsula National Park

Many Aboriginal middens lie around Tasmania's coasts, and good, characteristic examples on the east coast may be visited on Freycinet Peninsula. In particular, the oyster-dominated middens are extensive and very exposed, and hence visible, at the northern end of Hazards Beach. They can be reached by about a two hour walk along a well-marked walking track from the Wine Glass Bay carpark in the national park.

Visitors are reminded that middens must not be disturbed in any way, such as by collecting stone artefacts or shells or by driving over them in off-road vehicles or trail bikes. Each has the potential to contribute important information towards the understanding of prehistoric Australia and they form part of the heritage of the whole community; it is also illegal to disturb Aboriginal sites, and there are heavy fines for breaking the law.

On the western side of Great Oyster Bay near Little Swanport a similar midden was excavated by Harry Lourandos.[11] It contained occupational debris such as the remains of oysters, mussels and crayfish going back almost 5,000 years. In the lowest layer there were both fish bones and shellfish, but about 3,500 years ago fish seem to have dropped out of the diet, raising again the enigma of why the Tasmanians stopped eating fish.

The north-east and the centre

Bay of Fires stone arrangements, Ansons Bay district

The only two known stone alignments in Tasmania are found beside the Bay of Fires on the far north-east coast, approximately six kilometres south-south-east from Ansons Bay (figure 20.7). The area is a coastal reserve and the sites are most easily approached by walking south along the beach for about two and a half kilometres from Policemans Point. The alignments are reached first and lie on the crest of a low grass-covered ridge above a pebble beach north of Jacks Lookout Creek (plate 20.1). Most of the ridge is covered with dense vegetation and there are many shell middens, evidence of past camping by Aboriginal groups. (Please do not disturb any of these sites.)

The main alignment extends for 56 metres in a north-south direction and is a single line of about 93 flat stones, resembling a garden path. The stones are generally rectangular (about 60 by 30 centimetres) and are set into the ground with the longest side at a right angle to the general direction of the alignment. Their surfaces are roughly flush with the surface of the ground, the stones being set into the underlying midden which caps a prehistoric sand dune. Part of this midden was excavated by Rhys Jones in the 1960s, and proved to be 30 centimetres deep, containing charcoal, stone artefacts made of white crystalline quartz and some fragments of animal bone. Below this midden was another row of stones, the remains of a second, buried stone alignment. The bases of 12 stones had been set several centimetres into sand underlying the midden, and two of them had been extensively flaked before their placement. Charcoal from the base of this midden has been radiocarbon-dated to 730 years old, which means that the lower alignment must be more than that age.[12]

It seems that a linear stone alignment was built on the surface of a sand dune. Then about 750 years ago people camped by the line of stones; shells, charcoal and discarded stone artefacts accumulated around and over the top of the original stone alignment, and eventually a new ceremonial structure was constructed. This is the only site with a buried stone arrangement yet excavated in Tasmania, and is highly significant for its testimony of the antiquity of the island's ceremonial structures.

A further stone alignment was subsequently found by archaeologist Scott Cane 115 metres to the north. It has 43 stones and extends for 6 metres in a north-south direction. The stones resemble those in the more southerly lower stratified alignment.

On the nearby pebble beach are other stone arrangements, consisting of birdnest-shaped pits, some enclosed by a rim of low stone walls, and stone cairns

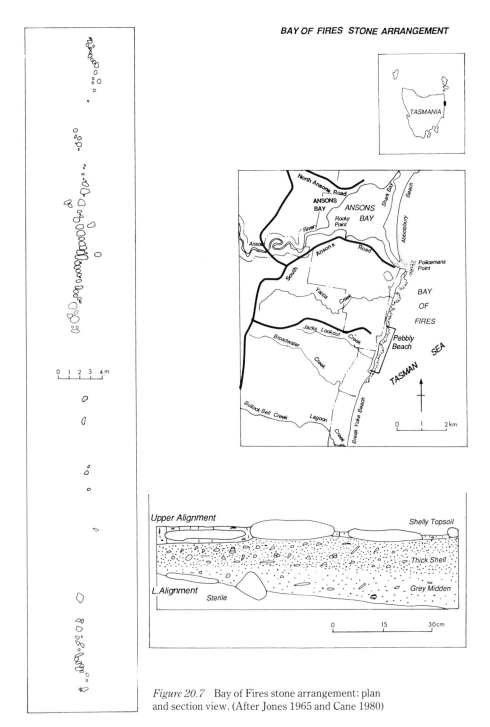

Figure 20.7   Bay of Fires stone arrangement: plan
and section view. (After Jones 1965 and Cane 1980)

made from rocks piled up into heaps. About a kilometre to the south similar stone
features are found on another pebble beach south of Jacks Lookout Creek. These
stone arrangements in fact extend intermittently for two and a half kilometres on
this stretch of coast, and include some 34 cairns and 38 pits.

Plate 20.1   Stone arrangement, Bay of Fires

Similar pits and cairns have been found on other raised pebble beaches on the north-west, west, south-west and south-east coasts of Tasmania, but their function is still uncertain. They were certainly constructed by Aboriginal people, for as well as the archaeological evidence from the Bay of Fires, there is ethnographic evidence that stone arrangements were in existence on the west coast in 1830, where George Augustus Robinson observed them whilst on his "friendly mission" to round up the remaining Aborigines of the west coast tribes. It seems most likely that they were ceremonial sites, used in the course of ritual activities, but the rapid destruction of Aboriginal society in the early nineteenth century means that information about their traditional use has been lost.

Mole Creek caves, Launceston district

The Mole Creek caves, west of Launceston, contain some of the finest examples of limestone formations in Australia. Fossils show that the limestone is Ordovician, about 350 million years old, but most of the caves are less than one million years. Two of the caves, Marakoopa and King Solomon, are open to the public. These are particularly impressive caves, as are others such as Croesus and Kubla Khan. The latter contains a 17 metre high stalagmite, the Khan, which is the tallest known stalagmite in any Australian cave. Kubla Khan Cave is generally recognised as one of the best decorated limestone caves in Australia. It may only be entered by authorised speleological or scientific parties.

Tiagarra cultural centre, Devonport

Tiagarra is an Aboriginal word meaning keep, and Tiagarra is an Aboriginal cultural museum on Mersey Bluff in Devonport. On the bluff headland Aboriginal shell middens have been found, and there are what are alleged to be Aboriginal engravings on the exposed flat surface of rocks. Most scientists, however, consider them natural stress lines in the dolerite emphasised by root action and the effects of plant acids in the grooves.[13] A visitor information centre has been built, depicting the life, customs and art of the first Tasmanians. Lifelike displays present the gathering of food, dwellings, tool-making, art and ceremonies.

Fossil Bluff, Wynyard

Fossil Bluff, which forms an attractive backdrop to the town of Wynyard, is an extremely significant Tertiary geological fossil site. It consists of Lower Miocene sediments resting on Upper Carboniferous glacigene sediments and is capped with basalt. Deposited 25 million years ago, a variety of fossils have been found in the sediments, including the fossil whale, *Prosqualodon davidis Flynn* and one of the oldest fossil marsupials in Australia, *Wynyardia*. The bluff overlooks the small bay and beach of Freestone Cove, just north of the golfcourse and river and about one kilometre north of Wynyard.

Rocky Cape caves

On the rugged north of Tasmania between Wynyard and Stanley is the 3,000 hectare Rocky Cape National Park, which contains two of the most important archaeological sites in Australia, the Rocky Cape caves. Together these caves have yielded an 8,000-year-old sequence of occupational debris, forming the longest and most complete record of the lifeways of prehistoric coastal people anywhere in Australia.

South Cave is an old sea cave cut into the sloping beds of a 60 metre high

Plate 20.2 Rocky Cape North Cave. (R. Jones)

eastward-facing cliff of preCambrian quartzite, 600 million years old. The cave floor is some 20 metres above present sea level, and is filled with a massive shell midden. The presence of Aboriginal shell midden deposits here had been known locally since the end of the last century, but the first scientific excavation of the cave was not carried out until 1965 by Rhys Jones.[14] Holes dug into the site by amateur collectors had disturbed much of the cave's contents, but the archaeologists were able to find some undisturbed parts of the deposit. The maximum depth of midden was three and a half metres; the site was first used 8,000 years ago and vacated some 4,000 years later. By 3,800 years ago the cave had become so full of refuse that the midden heap almost reached the roof.

Inside the cave, a small inner chamber had already been sealed off 6,800 years ago by midden accumulation outside its mouth. The archaeologists found these cramped living quarters just as they had been left. Piles of big abalone shells were dumped around the walls, but in the centre the floor had been swept clear for comfortable sitting round the fireplace. Here five small ashy hearths, placed close to the rock wall for maximum heat reflection, were found. Food refuse included bones of seals, fish, a few birds and small mammals, shells of rocky coast species, bracken fern stems, a lily tuber and split sections of the pith of the grass-tree. Faeces found in the rubbish dump were at first thought to be human, but analysis showed them to belong to Tasmanian devils, which no doubt scavenged there when the cave was unoccupied. Stone scrapers and a stone mortar, with pestle neatly placed on top, had been left behind by the last occupants for their next visit, a visit that never took place.[15]

North Cave, situated in a high vertical cliff facing north-west about a kilometre to the north of South Cave, has deposits which span the period from 5,500 to 500 years ago (plate 20.2). The early layers contain a series of hand-held stone tools, especially scrapers, unretouched flakes and large choppers. The choppers were used for general chopping and hammering, and to cut toeholds on trees when climbing in search of possums.

Bone tools were also present in the earlier layers, and included large, rounded tipped points or awls made from the long bones of kangaroos or wallabies, small, sharp, needle-like points but without an eye, broad spatulae, and various split slivers of bone sharpened to a point at one end. One bone tool was then being used to every two or three stone ones, but gradually bone tools dropped out of the toolkit. By 4,000 years ago only one bone tool was used for every fifteen stone ones, and by 3,500 they had disappeared from this and other sites completely, and were unknown in historic times.

Likewise there are abundant bones of scale fish of many different varieties in the early layers, but by 3,000 years ago fish seem to have dropped out of the diet all over the island. In historic times no Tasmanian Aborigines ate fish, and refused it when offered by Europeans, expressing abhorrence for it. Why? It is not a question of availability, for the waters off Rocky Cape and the other sites are teeming nowadays with the same fish that were being eaten in the earlier period at Rocky Cape. The question of why the Tasmanians stopped eating fish, and making bone points, admits no easy answers, but perhaps future research will give a solution.

Other changes took place during the eight millennia these caves were inhabited. Over time there was a steady decrease in the size of stone tools and an increase in the use of better, fine-grained raw materials. Chert, spongolite and siliceous breccia from quarries on the west coast were fetched or traded over distances of up to 100 kilometres. The tools were roughly flaked at the quarries and brought to Rocky Cape readymade.

This improvement in stone tool technology may have been accompanied by an improvement in diet, for when they dropped fish from the diet they seem to have increased the amount of seals eaten. Seals are a high fat, energy-rich food more suitable for the cold climate of Tasmania than a diet based on fish. The excavated material from the Rocky Cape caves was so rich in quantity and quality of preservation that analysis is still continuing by Sarah Colley and others, and new data coming to light. These sites are among the most significant in Australia for the unique record they have provided of the last 8,000 years of human occupation in Australia.

The north-west

Mount Cameron West Aboriginal site

This engraving site is the most well-known of some dozen petroglyph sites on the north-west coast of Tasmania. Numerous deeply sculpted circles and other motifs have been carved out of very soft calcareous sandstone, making this the most extensive of Aboriginal engraving sites in Tasmania (plate 20.3).[16] It is also the greatest surviving expression of prehistoric art in Tasmania, but unfortunately most of the site is not visible nowadays. One large rock panel of engravings was removed in 1950 to the Queen Victoria Museum and Art Gallery in Launceston where it is on display, and in the early 1960s the face of one of the most important engraved slabs was sawn off and taken to the Tasmanian Museum in Hobart where it can now be viewed. Most of the rest of the site has now had to be covered

Plate 20.3　Rock engravings at Mount Cameron West. (R. Edwards)

with sand stabilised with marram grass to protect the engravings from rapid erosion.

The site lies about 15 kilometres north of Marrawah at the northern end of a broad beach, 3 kilometres long, stretching in a shallow arc north from the 160 metre high basaltic headland of Mount Cameron West. There are two major and several minor groups of engravings, together with an extensive area of five marine middens and a stone quarry north of the engravings site. The engravings are on two outcrops 140 metres apart separated by a gully, which is partly filled with sand. The southern outcrop is now almost completely buried in mobile sand directly behind the foredune. The northern outcrop lies a few metres north of a small creek which flows into the sea and is a prominent bluff about six metres high, of calcerous sandstone called aeolianite. The engravings have been executed on both the face of the cliff and on slabs fallen from the face to form a talus slope between the present foot of the cliff and present high tide limit. Most of the blocks in the talus slope are now covered with sand, and only one engraved slab is still visible.

It is generally agreed that the site was covered with sand, which supported a thick cover of ti tree and other scrub, when George Augustus Robinson passed close by several times in the early 1830s in the course of his mission to gather together the Tasmanian Aborigines still at large. It is likely that this sand cover remained for a century until it was swept away by a storm to reveal the engravings to the eyes of a local shepherd of the Van Diemen's Land Company in 1931.

What the wind uncovered was an undercut cliff face providing an overhang under which prehistoric people camped, and a mass of engravings both on the face of the cliff and on the jumble of large blocks below it. The motifs include simple and concentric circles, barred and overlapping circles, rows of dots, crosses, trellis-like designs and bird tracks and a human track. The engravings were made by the techniques of pecking and abrasion, involving pecking a line of holes into the soft rock and then abrading the ridges between them to make a deeply incised line, giving the art a sculptural quality. Some of the motifs are five centimetres deep and range from a few centimetres to more than one metre across.

Excavation of the sheltered area behind the carved blocks produced a few large pointed artefacts of hard rock such as basalt and quartzite, which were probably chisels used by the ancient sculptors. They ate meals of mussel shells and birds and used the shelter between about 1,350 and 850 years ago. The engravings already existed at this time, but do not seem from the archaeological evidence to be more than 1,500 to 2,000 years old. By 850 years ago the shelter had become filled with a metre deep midden and the engravings were covered by wind-blown sand. The site then lay hidden for a thousand years.

Mount Cameron West is an important symbol to present day Tasmanian Aborigines of the religion, intellect and artistic achievement of their ancestors. It is the largest and most complex art site yet found in Tasmania, and is widely recognised as one of the most outstanding aesthetic achievements of any hunter-gatherer society. While it is disappointing for visitors that so much of the art lies unseen beneath their feet, perhaps it may be some consolation that conservation of the site in the same sand environment which preserved it for so long will mean that future generations can eventually once again feel awe at the artistic triumph of these prehistoric Tasmanians.

Access to this site is difficult and may only be undertaken with a Parks Service ranger or with special authority.

West Point Aboriginal site

On the north-west coast some eight kilometres south-west of Marrawah and one kilometre north of the site of West Point lighthouse (now removed) is West Point midden.[17] This is one of the largest, richest and best preserved Aboriginal occupation sites excavated in Australia (plate 20.4). It spans the period from about 1,900 to 1,300 years ago, and has made a major contribution to the understanding of the Aboriginal way of life on the west coast at that time.

The grass-covered midden rises some six metres above the surrounding country, commanding an extensive view over the rocky foreshore, bays and islets to seaward and swamps and ti tree scrub on the inland side. Formed on an ancient sand dune resting on a bank of pebbles, the midden measures 90 metres long by 40 metres wide. It is a "village midden", with seven or eight roughly circular depressions on its surface. These measure about four metres across and half a metre deep, and were the foundations of dome-shaped huts. Such huts were constructed from a framework of pliable branches such as ti tree stems, thatched with bark, grass or turf, and lined inside with skins, bark or feathers.

Many such huts, often grouped into villages, were seen by Robinson, when travelling along the west coast in the early 1830s. They were situated close to a

Plate 20.4   West Point midden. (R. Jones)

good source of water and rich foraging areas; the West Point village is situated next to a rocky platform which had an elephant seal breeding ground. The elephant seal does not now breed closer to Australia than Macquarie Island 2,000 kilometres to the south, but there are the bones of young seal calves in the midden, indicating that between 1,300 and 1,800 years ago there was a seal colony next to the village, which was inhabited in summer when the young seals were being weaned.

Seals provided about 65 per cent of the calories apparently consumed by the prehistoric inhabitants of West Point; another 25 per cent came from shellfish such as abalone, and the remainder from birds, wallabies, small marsupials and lizards. Seventy-five cubic metres of excavated deposit yielded 30,000 stone artefacts and 20,000 bones but no bone tools and only 3 fish vertebrae, which probably were transported there accidentally by birds or other agency. It seems clear that the people did not use bone tools nor eat fish, although fish are plentiful off West Point and easily speared or trapped. A preference for seals over fish makes sense in this environment, for seals are a much richer source of energy and could be captured without entering the water, which is cool in summer and icy cold in winter.

A band of about 40 people probably lived at West Point for three or four months each year, a family occupying each of the hut sites. Men did the sealing while women dived for shellfish, prising the shells off the rocks with small wooden wedges and collecting them in rush baskets suspended from their necks. Long strands of giant kelp growing up from the sea bed were used as a ''rope'' by divers to pull themselves down to depths of four metres or more to seize crayfish from under rocks and throw them up onto shore. Women also used to swim up to one or two kilometres across turbulent straits to reach offshore islands such as the Doughboys, rocky stacks a kilometre offshore from Cape Grim. There they would collect muttonbirds, which nest in burrows, making themselves easy prey to predators. Like seals, muttonbirds are an energy-rich food because of the high oil and fat content of their mutton-like flesh.

There is some tantalising evidence at West Point about prehistoric ceremonial life. Stone arrangements have been found on pebble beaches both north and south of the lighthouse.[18] Immediately south of the lighthouse are four pits (and four dry stone walls thought to be European) and there are another four pits together with four mounds directly north of the midden excavated by Jones. The pits and two of the mounds resemble other stone arrangements on the west coast, and are thought to have been ceremonial sites.

One of the most remarkable finds in the West Point midden were three cremation pits, filled with burnt and broken human bones. Two were in the middle layer and one at the base dating to 1,800 years ago. The bodies were apparently cremated, then the bones were systematically broken, collected together with the charcoal and deposited in small pits. In one cremation pit were the talons of a large hawk and the foot bones of several wallabies. In another was a necklace of 32 shells pierced with a small circular hole. These were probably personal belongings of the dead.

The human remains at West Point were fragmentary, but careful analysis showed that they were extremely similar to Australian Aborigines of the mainland. The rite of cremation is likewise found in mainland Australia as far back as 25,000 years ago at Lake Mungo; this means that ice age hunters could have brought this custom with them when they first entered Tasmania across the land bridge more than 30,000 years ago. The custom of wearing shell necklaces may similarly extend from the ice age to the present, but those found at West Point are the oldest yet found.

Sundown Point Aboriginal site

This reserve is on Tasmania's north-west coast, about 70 kilometres south-west of Smithton, 20 kilometres south of Marrawah and 8 kilometres south of the mouth of the Arthur River. Access is by gravelled tracks or along the beach from Arthur River. The main engraving site lies at the southern end of a long beach on a low outcropping headland, on the southern bank of Little Sundown Creek where it enters the sea (figure 20.8). The siltstone outcrop extends from about 70 metres inland due west almost out into the sea. It is about two metres high and ten wide. Erosion of softer rock from a bed of preCambrian laminated siltstone has left

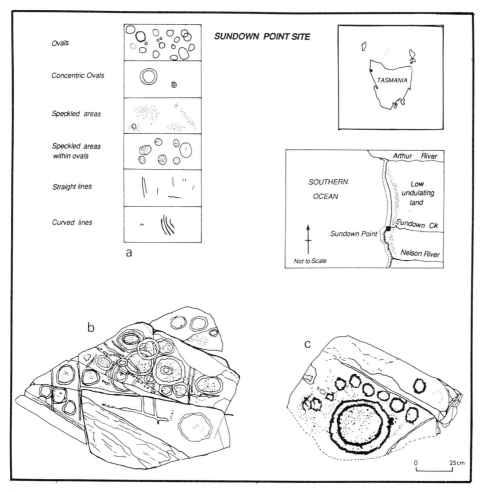

Figure 20.8   Sundown Point engraving site. (After R.G. Gunn and NPWS, 1981)

parallel rows of smooth rock slabs dipping at about 45 degrees to the north. A second, smaller site occurs about 200 metres to the south, in a small sandy beach cove bounded by jutting rock outcrops.[19]

In the main site more than 250 marks have been pecked on almost 100 individual natural panels. Many of the engravings are very shallow and weathered and can only be seen by the lateral light of late afternoon, which throws shadows into the peck marks. The motifs average about 20 to 30 centimetres in diameter, but range from 8 to 60 centimetres. Four different graphic forms occur: clusters of individual peck marks or "speckled areas", solid dots or pits (larger and deeper than the "speckles"), linear open designs (of dots in lines), and linear closed designs of dots linked together to form a solid line. The most common motifs are circles (varying in shape from circular to oval) and "speckled areas" of peck marks, but there are also concentric circles, speckled areas within circles, straight lines, curved lines either singly or in sets, sets of parallel dotted lines, simple linear designs of dots and simple dotted designs, including crosses.

One slab bears a coherent graphic composition; another such slab was removed some years ago to the Tasmanian Museum in Hobart, where it is on display. The *in situ* slab is located in the centre rear of the "gallery", and bears two large concentric circles below an arc of eight smaller circles with a scatter of speckles across the panel (figure 20.8 c). The size and conspicuous location of this panel together with its striking graphic quality make it the dominant visual element of the site.

Another large slab has a wide range of motifs superimposed on each other; circles overlap one another and enclose or are surrounded by smaller circles, and interspersed with straight lines and curved linear designs of dots (figure 20.8 b). This slab shows some of the complexity of design inherent in the engravings of Mount Cameron West further north along the coast.

The smaller engraving site to the south consists of four panels of engravings pecked onto vertical or horizontal siltstone faces. One panel on a vertical face approximately 10 metres from high tide mark has 15 pecked depressions or pounded pits (about 5 centimetres in diameter and half a centimetre deep) in a horizontal row. Two more pecked depressions occur on a panel 50 centimetres to the north-east, and the other engravings here are peck marks in clusters or lines with little formal arrangement.

Adjacent to the engravings sites are middens on or behind the foredunes. These are either the dome-shaped mound type with hut depressions visible similar to West Point midden or the doughnut variety, with a raised ring around a central hollow.

Sundown Point is an important concentration of prehistoric Aboriginal sites, with a particularly fine set of rock engravings. Such engravings are rare in Tasmanian and some of those at Sundown Point are both unusual and visually striking. The age of the engravings is unknown but the high degree of patination argues for an antiquity of several thousand years at least.

Greens Creek engravings

These rock engravings are located on the banks of the mouth of Greens Creek on the north-west coast, south of Sundown Point and immediately south of

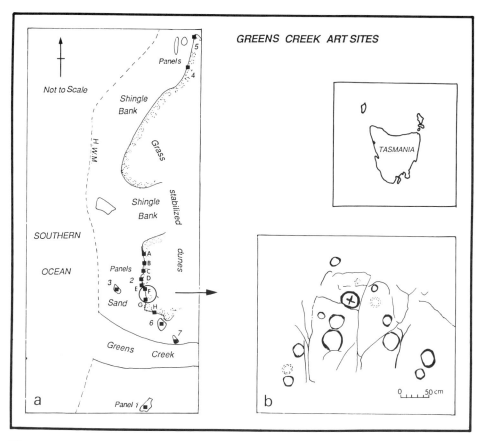

Figure 20.9 Greens Creek engraving site. (After J. Stockton and NPWS, 1983)

Ordinance Point.[20] A long sweeping beach and area of deflated dunes leads south from the site to Sandy Cape. A four-wheel-drive vehicle track leads south from Temma Harbour and crosses Greens Creek about 150 metres from the mouth. The engravings are on blocks of laminated mudstone near high water mark at the mouth of the creek; all except two of the panels are on the northern bank (figure 20.9). During storms some of the engraved panels are washed by waves.

The range of motifs is remarkably limited at Greens Creek; the motifs are all simple circles except for one circle with a cross in its centre. The circles range in size up to 90 centimetres but typical ones would be about 20 centimetres in diameter. Some 75 circles have been recorded, and there may well be more in the vicinity, as part of the site is covered by beach sand. Midden material is directly associated with one engraved panel, and several large eroded middens lie within 100 metres of the site.

Taken together, these various Aboriginal sites from all round Tasmania testify to the long-lived traditions, rich artistic and religious life and successful adaptation to a harsh environment of the first Tasmanians.

End Notes

Chapter 2 Introduction to Australian Prehistory

1. An excellent account of the changing Australian environment, flora and fauna through geological time is given in *Kadimakara: Extinct Vertebrates of Australia*, eds. P.V. Rich, G.F. van Tets and F. Knight (Melbourne: Pioneer Design Studio, 1985); See also M.E. White, *The Greening of Gondwana: The 400 Million Year Story of Australia's Plants* (Sydney: Reed Books, 1986); *Australia's Evolution,* poster by S. Hand, *Australian Geographic,* no.1, 1988; *Man in Australia,* poster by A. Alston, *Australian Geographic,* no.8, 1987.
2. K. McNamara, "Stromatolites: The ultimate living fossils", *Australian Natural History* 22(10) (1988): 476–80.
3. G. Singh, N.D. Opdyke and J.M. Bowler, "Late Cainozoic stratigraphy, palaeomagnetic chronology and vegetational history from Lake George, N.S.W.", *Journal of the Geological Society of Australia* 28(4) (1981):435–52; R. Wright, "How old is zone F at Lake George?", *Archaeology in Oceania* 21(2)(1986): 138–39.
4. J. Isaacs, ed., *Australian Dreaming: 40,000 Years of Aboriginal History.* (Sydney: Lansdowne Press, 1980).
5. K. Gollan, "Prehistoric dingo in Australia", Ph.D. thesis, Department of Prehistory, Australian National University, 1983.
6. A.G. Thorne and S.R. Wilson, "Pleistocene and recent Australians: A multivariate comparison," *Journal of Human Evolution* 6(1977): 393–402; Stephen Webb (pers. comm.).
7. P. Brown, "Pleistocene homogeneity and Holocene size reduction: The Australian human skeletal evidence", *Archaeology in Oceania* 22(1987): 41–66.
8. PP. Gorecki, R. Horton, N. Stern and R.V.S. Wright, "Coexistence of humans and megafauna in Australia: Improved stratified evidence", *Archaeology in Oceania* 19(3)(1986): 117–19.
9. J.W. Gregory, *The Dead Heart of Australia* (London: John Murray, 1906).
10. J. Flood, *Archaeology of the Dreamtime* (Sydney: Collins, 1983), pp. 200–202, 112–14.
11. L.K. Corbett, "Morphological comparisons of Australian and Thai dingoes: A reappraisal of dingo status, distribution and ancestry", *Proceedings of the Ecological Society of Australia* 13 (1985): 277–91.

Chapter 3 Introduction to Australia's Rock Art

1. D.J. Mulvaney, *The Prehistory of Australia* (Melbourne: Penguin, 1975), pp.184–88.
2. D. Dragovich, "Desert vanish as an age indicator for Aboriginal rock engravings: a review of problems and prospects", *Archaeology in Oceania*, vol. 19(2)(1984): pp.48–56.
3. M.T. Nobbs and R.I. Dorn, "Age determinations for rock varnish formation within petroglyphs: cation-ratio dating of 24 motifs from the Olary region, South Australia", *Rock Art Research*, vol.5(2)(1988): 108–45; R.I. Dorn, M. Nobbs and T. Cahill, "Cation-ratio dating of rock engravings from the Olary Province of arid South Australia", *Antiquity*, vol.62(237)(1988): 681–89.

Chapter 4   Western Australia: Perth and the South-West

1. J.E. Glover and R. Lee, "Geochemistry and provenance of chert artifacts, southwestern Australia", *Archaeology in Oceania* 19(1984):16–20.
2. C. Dortch, *Devil's Lair, a Study in Prehistory* (Perth: Western Australian Museum, 1984).
3. J. Balme, "An analysis of charred bone from Devil's Lair, Western Australia", *Archaeology and Physical Anthropology in Oceania* 15(2) (1980): 81–85.
4. M. Archer, I.M. Crawford and D. Merrilees, "Incisions, breakages and charring, probably man-made, in fossil bones from Mammoth Cave, Western Australia", *Alcheringa* 4(1–2)(1980): 115–31.
5. W.C. Ferguson, "Archaeological investigations at the Quininup Brook site complex, Western Australia", *Records of the Western Australian Museum* 8(1981):609–37.
6. W.C. Ferguson, "Mokare's domain", in *Australians to 1788,* eds D.J. Mulvaney and J.P. White (Sydney: Fairfax, Syme and Weldon Associates, 1987), pp.120–42.
7. S.J. Hallam, "Roof markings in the "Orchestra Shell" Cave, Wanneroo, near Perth, Western Australia", *Mankind* 8(1971):90–103.
8. R.H. Pearce and M. Barbetti. "A 38,000-year-old site at Upper Swan, W.A.", *Archaeology in Oceania* 16(3)(1981):173–78.
9. R.H. Pearce, "Changes in artifact assemblages during the last 8,000 years at Walyunga, Western Australia", *Journal of the Royal Society of Western Australia* 61(1978):1–10.

Chapter 5   Western Australia: the Murchison and Cue Regions

1. K. McNamara, "Stromatolites: The ultimate living fossils", *Australian Natural History* 22(10),(1988):476–80.
2. K. McNamara, *Pinnacles* (Perth: Western Australian Museum, 1983).
3. F. Bordes, C. Dortch, C. Thibault, T.P. Raynal and P. Bindon, "Walga Rock and Billibilong Spring", *Australian Archaeology* 17(1983):1–26.

Chapter 6   Western Australia: The Pilbara

1. H. Olsen, M. Durack, G. Dutton, V. Serventy and A. Bortignon, *The Land Beyond Time: A Modern Exploration of Australia's North-West Frontiers* (Melbourne: Macmillan, 1984).
2. S. Brown, *Towards a Prehistory of the Hamersley Plateau, North-West Australia* (Canberra, Australian National University, Occasional Papers in Prehistory, 1987).
3. K. Morse, "Mandu Mandu Creek rock shelter: Pleistocene human coastal occupation of North West Cape, Western Australia", *Archaeology in Oceania* 23(3)(1988): 81–88.
4. B.J. Wright, *Rock Art of the Pilbara Region, North-West Australia* (Canberra: Australian Institute of Aboriginal Studies, 1968).
5. H.P. McNickle, "An introduction to the Spear Hill Rock Art Complex, Northwestern Australia", *Rock Art Research* 2 (1) (1985): 48–64.
6. P. Vinnicombe, *Dampier Archaeological Project: Resource Document, Survey and Salvage of Aboriginal Sites, Burrup Peninsula, Western Australia* (Perth: Western Australian Museum, 1987).
7. W.C. Dix, "Facial representations in Pilbara rock engravings", in *Form in Indigenous Art: Schematisation in the Art of Aboriginal Australia and Prehistoric Europe*, ed. Peter J. Ucko (Canberra: Australian Institute of Aboriginal Studies, 1977), pp. 277–85; W. Dix, "Rock art along the stock route", *Hemisphere* 16(7) (1972): 18–25.

Chapter 7   Western Australia: The Kimberley

1. I.M. Crawford, *The Art of the Wandjina: Aboriginal Cave Paintings in Kimberley, Western Australia* (Melbourne: Oxford University Press, 1968).
2. K. McNamara, *Wolf Creek Crater* (Perth: Western Australian Museum, 1982).

Chapter 8   The Top End of the Northern Territory

1. C. Shrire, *The Alligator Rivers: Prehistory and Ecology in Western Arnhem Land* (Canberra: Australian National University, Terra Australia 7, 1982); J. Kamminga and H. Allen, "Report of the archaeological survey", *Alligator Rivers Environmental Fact-finding Study* (Canberra: 1973); R. Jones, ed., *Archaeological Research in Kakadu National Park* (Canberra: Australian National Parks and Wildlife Service, 1985); R.G. Roberts, R. Jones and M.A. Smith, "Thermoluminescence dating of a 50,000-year-old human occupation site in northern Australia", *Nature* 345 (6271) (1990):153-56.
2. Jones, *Archaeological Research,* p. 297.
3. G. Chaloupka, *From Palaeoart to Casual Paintings,* Monograph 1 (Darwin: Northern Territory Museum, 1984).
4. P. Murray and G. Chaloupka, "The Dreamtime animals: Extinct megafauna in Arnhem Land rock art", *Archaeology in Oceania* 19(3)1984: 105-16.
5. C.D. Woodruffe, J. Chappell and B.G. Thom, "Shell middens in the context of estuarine development, South Alligator River, Northern Territory", *Archaeology in Oceania* 23(3)1988: 95-103.
6. R. Edwards, *Australian Aboriginal Art: The Art of the Alligator Rivers Region, Northern Territory* (Canberra: Australian Institute of Aboriginal Studies, 1979).
7. G. Chaloupka, *Burrunguy Nourlangie Rock* (Darwin: Northart, 1986).
8. Jones, *Archaeological Research.*
9. Surveys (unpublished) have been carried out by George Chaloupka, Howard McNickle, Darrell Lewis and Ben Gunn; D. Lewis and D. Rose, *The Shape of the Dreaming* (Canberra: Australian Institute of Aboriginal Studies, 1987).
10. See the film on *Land of the Lightning Brothers* 1987, Film Australia; J. Flood, B. David and R. Frost, "Dreaming into art: Aboriginal interpretations of rock engravings, Yingalarri, Northern Territory", Proceedings of the AURA Congress (In *Rock art and ethnography* (ed. M. Morwood) in press); R. Frost, B. David and J. Flood, "Pictures in transition: discussing the interaction of visual forms and symbolic contents in Wardaman rock pictures", Proceedings of the AURA Congress (in *Rock art and ethnography* (ed. H. Morwood) in press).
11. Preliminary surveys of this rock art (unpublished) have been carried out by Ben Gunn, George Chaloupka, Howard McNickle and Conservation Commission rangers.

Chapter 9   Queensland: The North

1. P. Hiscock and P.J. Hughes, "Backed blades in northern Australia: evidence from north-west Queensland", *Australian Archaeology* 10(1980): 86-95; P.J. Hughes, "Colless Creek rock shelter archaeological site, N.W. Queensland, 18KA", in *CLIMANZ. A Symposium of Results and Discussions Concerned with Late Quaternary Climatic History of Australia, New Zealand and Surrounding Seas,* eds J.M.A. Chappell and A. Grindrod (Canberra: Australian National University, Dept. of Biogeography and Geomorphology, 1983), pp. 59-61.
2. R.A. Thulborn and M. Wade, "Dinosaur trackways in the Winton Formation (Mid-Cretaceous) of Queensland", *Memoirs of the Queensland Museum* 21(2)(1984):413-61.
3. M. Archer, S. Hand and H. Godthelp, *Riversleigh. The Story of Animals in Ancient Rainforests of Inland Australia.* (Sydney: Reed Books, 1991).
4. M. Morwood, "Facts and figures; Notes on rock art in the Mt Isa area, northwestern Queensland", *Rock Art Research* 2(2)(1985): 140-45.
5. A. Rosenfeld, D. Horton and J. Winter, *Early Man in North Queensland* (Canberra: Australian National University, Department of Prehistory, Terra Australis 6, 1981).
6. J. Flood, "Rock art of the Koolburra Plateau, north Queensland", *Rock Art Research* 4(2)(1987): 91-126.
7. P.J. Trezise, *Quinkan Country* (Sydney: Reed, 1969); P.J. Trezise, *Rock art of South-East Cape York* (Canberra: Australian Institute of Aboriginal Studies, 1971).
8. G.N. Bailey, "Shell mounds, shell middens and raised beaches in Cape York Peninsula", *Mankind* 11(1977): 132-43.
9. G. Walsh, *Australia's Greatest Rock Art* (Bathurst: E.J. Brill, Robert Brown and Associates, 1988), pp. 144-45, 246-47.
10. G. Singh, A.P. Kershaw and R.L. Clark, "Quaternary vegetation and fire history in Australia", in *Fire and the Australian Biota,* eds Gill, Groves and Noble (Canberra: Australian Academy of Science, 1981), pp. 23-54.
11. R.M.W. Dixon, *The Dyirbal Language of North Queensland* (Cambridge: Cambridge University Press, 1972).

12. B. David, "Fern Cave, rock art and social formations: rock art regionalisation and demographic models in southeastern Cape York Peninsula", *Archaeology in Oceania* 26 (1991): 41-57; B. David, "Nurrabullgin Cave: a pre-37, 170-year-old site from southeast Cape York Peninsula", *Archaeology in Oceania* (in press).
13. J.B. Campbell, "Automatic Seafood Retrieval Systems. The evidence from Hinchinbrook Island and its implications", in *Coastal Archaeology in Eastern Australia*, ed. S. Bowdler (Canberra: Australian National University, Prehistory Department, 1982), pp. 96–107.
14. Walsh, *Australia's Greatest Rock Art*, pp. 126–27.

Chapter 10   Queensland: The South-East

1. R. Neal and E. Stock, "Pleistocene occupation in the south-east Queensland coastal region", *Nature*, vol. 323, no.6089 (16 October, 1986): 618–21.
2. M.J. Morwood, "The archaeology of social complexity in south-east Queensland", *Proceedings of the Prehistoric Society* 53(1987): 337–50; J.G. Steele, *Aboriginal Pathways* (Brisbane: Queensland University Press, 1983).
3. C.C. Petrie, *Tom Petrie's Reminiscences of Early Queensland* (Brisbane: Watson, Ferguson and Co., 1904; Hawthorn, Victoria: Lloyd O'Neill, 1975).
4. P.K. Lauer, "Report of a preliminary ethnohistorical and archaeological survey on Fraser Island", in *Occasional Papers in Anthropology*, no. 8 (Brisbane: University of Queensland Anthropology Museum, 1977), pp. 1–38.
5. B. Burnum, *Burnum Burnum's Aboriginal Australia,* ed. D. Stewart (Sydney: Angus and Robertson, 1988), p. 109.
6. J. Hall and R. Robins, "A working model of Moreton Island prehistory: MRAP Stage 1", *Queensland Archaeological Research* 1 (1984): 85–94; J. Hall, "Sitting on the crop of the Bay: An historical and archaeological sketch of Aboriginal settlement and subsistence in Moreton Bay, southeast Queensland", in *Coastal Archaeology in Eastern Australia*, ed. S. Bowdler (Canberra: Australian National University, Department of Prehistory, 1982), pp. 79–95.
7. I. Walters, "The Toorbul Point Aboriginal fish trap", *Queensland Archaeological Research* 2(1985): 38–49.
8. Hall, "Sitting on the crop", p. 90.
9. J. Hall, "Exploratory excavation at Bushrangers Cave (Site LA:A11), a 6000-year-old campsite in southeast Queensland: preliminary results", *Australian Archaeology* 22(1986): 88–103.
10. D.J. Mulvaney and E.B. Joyce, "Archaeological and geomorphological investigations on Mt Moffatt Station, Queensland, Australia", *Proceedings of the Prehistoric Society* 31(1965): 147–212.
11. G. Walsh, "Composite stencil art: elemental or specialised?", *Australian Aboriginal Studies* 2(1983): 34–44.
12. M.C. Quinnell, "Schematisation and naturalism in the rock art of south central Queensland", in *Form in Indigenous Art*, ed. P. Ucko (Canberra: Australian Institute of Aboriginal Studies, 1977), pp. 414–17; G.L. Walsh, *The Roof of Queensland* (Brisbane: University of Queensland Press, 1983).
13. J.M. Beaton and G.L. Walsh, "Che-ka-ra", *Mankind* 11(1)(1977): 46–48; G.L. Walsh, *Australia's Greatest Rock Art* (Bathurst: E.J. Brill, Robert Brown and Associates, 1988), pp. 114–19, 122–25.

Chapter 11   Central Australia

1. R.A. Gould, "Puntutjarpa Rockshelter and the Australian Desert Culture", *Anthropological Papers of the American Museum of Natural History* 54 (1977).
2. S. Bowdler, "The coastal colonisation of Australia", in *Sunda and Sahul: Prehistoric Studies in Southeast Asia, Melanesia and Australia*, ed. J. Allen, J. Golson and R. Jones (London: Academic Press, 1977), pp. 205–46.
3. R.V.S. Wright, ed., *Archaeology of the Gallus Site, Koonalda Cave* (Canberra: Australian Institute of Aboriginal Studies, 1971).
4. S. Brown, *Towards a Prehistory of the Hamersley Plateau, Northwest Australia* (Canberra: Prehistory Department, Australian National University, Occasional Papers no.6, 1987).
5. R.J. Wasson, "The Cainozoic history of the Strzlecki and Simpson dunefields (Australia), and the origin of the desert dunes", *Zeitschrift fur Geomorphologie* 45 (1983): 85–115.
6. M.A. Smith, "Pleistocene occupation in arid Central Australia", *Nature* 328 (1987): 710–11; Rhys Jones, "Pleistocene life in the dead heart of Australia", *Nature* 328 (1987): 666; G. Walsh, "Cleland Hills: Heritage Site Investigation", unpublished report, Australian Heritage

Commission, 1987; M.A. Smith, "The case for a resident human population in the Central Australian Ranges during full glacial aridity", *Archaeology in Oceania* 24(3) 1989: 93–105.

7. R. Edwards, "Prehistoric rock engravings at Thomas Reservoir, Cleland Hills, Western Central Australia", *Records of the South Australian Museum* 15(4) (1968): 647–70.

8. M.A. Smith, "The antiquity of seedgrinding in arid Australia", *Archaeology in Oceania* 21(1) (1986): 29–39.

9. M.A. Smith, "A revised chronology for Intirtekwerle (James Range East) Rockshelter, Central Australia", *The Beagle, Occasional Papers of the Northern Territory Museum of Arts and Sciences* 3 (1)(1986): 123–30.

10. M. Smith "The antiquity of seedgrinding".

11. R.G. Kimber, pers. comm.

12. R.G. Kimber, "Resource use and management in central Australia", *Australian Aboriginal Studies* 2 (1984): 12–23; C.P. Mountford, *Nomads of the Australian Desert* (Adelaide: Rigby, 1976); M.J. Meggitt, *Desert People: A Study of the Walbiri Aborigines of Central Australia* (Sydney: Angus and Robertson, 1962); Ian Dunlop, Director film *Desert People* (Sydney: Film Australia, 1966).

13. L.K. Napton and E.A. Greathouse, "Archaeological investigations at Pine Gap (Kuyunba), Northern Territory", *Australian Archaeology* 20 (1985): 90–108.

14. S. Forbes, "Aboriginal rock engravings at N'Dhala gorge, Northern Territory", in *Archaeology at Anzaas 1983,* ed. Moya Smith (Perth: W.A. Museum, 1983), pp. 199–213.

15. Conservation Commission of the Northern Territory, *Chambers Pillar Historical Reserve* (Alice Springs: 1981).

16. S. Wyche and M.J. Freeman, *Astro-geological features of Central Australia* (Alice Springs: Northern Territory Geological Survey, Department of Mines and Energy, 1980).

17. Ibid.

18. Australian National Parks and Wildlife Service, *Uluru (Ayers Rock–Mount Olga) National Park Plan of Management* (Canberra: Australian National Parks and Wildlife Service, 1986).

19. D. Roff, *Ayers Rock and the Olgas* (Sydney: Ure Smith, 1979); Charles P. Mountford, *Ayers Rock* (Adelaide: Rigby, 1965); W.E. Harney, *The Significance of Ayers Rock for Aborigines* (Alice Springs: Conservation Commission of the Northern Territory, 1960); R. Layton, *Uluru: An Aboriginal History of Ayers Rock* (Canberra: Australian Institute of Aboriginal Studies, 1986).

20. Australian National Parks and Wildlife Service, *Uluru.*

21. A.M. Fox, "Uluru (Ayers Rock and Mount Olga)", in *The Heritage of Australia* (Canberra: Australian Heritage Commission, 1981), pp. 8/42–8/45.

Chapter 12   South Australia: The North

1. M. Nobbs, "Rock Art in Olary Province, South Australia", *Rock Art Research* 1(2)(1984): 91–118.

2. R. Lampert, "Archaeological reconnaissance on a field trip to Dalhousie Springs", *Australian Archaeology* 21 (1985): 57–62.

3. D. Tunbridge, *Flinders Ranges Dreaming* (Canberra: Aboriginal Studies Press, 1988).

4. Ibid., pp. 135–37; G. Walsh, *Australia's Greatest Rock Art* (Bathurst: E.J. Brill, Robert Brown and Associates, 1988), pp. 158–59.

5. Tunbridge, *Flinders Ranges,* pp. 141–45.

6. Ibid., pp. 120–21: Walsh, *Greatest Rock Art,* pp. 62–63.

7. C.P. Mountford and R. Edwards, "Rock engravings in the Red Gorge, Deception Creek, Northern South Australia", *Anthropos* 59 (1964): 849-59.

8. D.M. Bates, *The Passing of the Aborigines* (London: John Murray, 1938) pp. 132-34; *Australasian* 20 August 1921.

9. R.V. S. Wright, ed., *Archaeology of the Gallus Site, Koonalda Cave* (Canberra: Australian Institute of Aboriginal Studies, 1971).

Chapter 13   South Australia: The South

1. R.G. Gunn, "The Aboriginal Rock Art of the Mount Lofty Ranges, South Australia: Preliminary analysis and other observations", unpublished report, Adelaide Department for Environment and Planning 1981.

2. R. Edwards, *Aboriginal Bark Canoes of the Murray Valley* (Adelaide: Rigby, 1972).

3. H.M. Hale and N.B. Tindale, "Notes on some human remains in the lower Murray Valley, South Australia", *Records of the South Australian Museum* 4(1930): 145–218.

4. R.G. Bednarik, "Parietal finger markings in Europe and Australia", *Rock Art Research* 3(1)(1986): 30–61; G.C. Aslin and R.G. Bednarik, "Karlie-Ngoinpool Cave: A Preliminary Report", *Rock Art Research* 1(1)(1984): 36–45.
5. J. Flood, *Archaeology of the Dreamtime* (Sydney: Collins, 1983) pp. 111–20.

Chapter 14   Victoria: The Grampians and the West

1. M.C.S. Godfrey, "Seasonality and shellfishing at Discovery Bay, Victoria, unpublished M.A. thesis, Division of Prehistory, La Trobe University, 1984; "Shell midden chronology in southwestern Victoria: Reflections of change in prehistoric population and subsistence?", *Archaeology in Oceania* 24(1989):65–69.
2. H. Lourandos, "Intensification: a late Pleistocene-Holocene archaeological sequence from southwestern Victoria", *Archaeology in Oceania* 18(2)(1983): 81–94.
3. P.J.F. Coutts, R.K. Frank and P. Hughes, *Aboriginal Engineers of the Western District, Victoria* (Melbourne: Victoria Archaeological Survey, 1978).
4. R.G. Gunn, "Aboriginal rock art in Victoria. Second catalogue of Victorian rock art sites", unpublished report to the Victoria Archaeological Survey, Melbourne, 1987; T.T. Thomas, *Fifty Walks in the Grampians* (Melbourne: Hill of Content, 1986; J. Calder, *The Grampians: A Noble Range* (Melbourne: Victorian National Parks Association, 1987).
5. R.G. Gunn, *The Prehistoric Rock Art Sites of Victoria: A Catalogue* (Melbourne: Victoria Archaeological Survey, 1981), pp. 48–51.
6. Ibid., pp. 36–47.
7. Ibid., pp. 11–35; R.G. Gunn, "Black Range 2 and the art of the Black Range, Western Grampians", unpublished report to the Victoria Archaeological Survey, Melbourne, 1987.
8. Gunn, *Prehistoric Rock Art Sites*, pp. 87–99; R.G. Gunn, *Aboriginal Rock Art in the Grampians* (Melbourne: Victoria Archaeological Survey, 1983), pp. 94–123.
9. Gunn, *Prehistoric Rock Art Sites*, pp. 138–45.
10. Ibid., pp. 115–37.
11. P.J.F. Coutts and M. Lorblanchet, *Aboriginals and Rock Art in the Grampians, Victoria, Australia* (Melbourne: Victoria Archaeological Survey, 1982), pp. 14, 87.
12. Gunn, *Aboriginal Rock Art*, pp. 78–85.
13. Ibid., pp. 71–77.
14. Gunn, *Prehistoric Rock Art Sites*, pp. 215–28.
15. R.G. Gunn, *Bunjil's Cave: Aboriginal Rock Art Site* (Melbourne: Victoria Archaeological Survey, 1983).

Chapter 15   Victoria: The Centre and the East

1. P.J.F. Coutts and R.M. Cochrane, *The Keilor Archaeological Area* (Melbourne: Victoria Archaeological Survey, 1977).
2. I. McBryde, "Kulin greenstone quarries: The social contexts of production and distribution for the Mt William site", *World Archaeology* 16(2)(1984): 267–85.
3. Ibid.
4. H. Lourandos, "Intensification: a Late Pleistocene-Holocene archaeological sequence from south western Victoria", *Archaeology in Oceania* 18(2)(1983): 81–94.
5. D.J. Mulvaney, "Archaeological excavations on the Aire River, Otway Peninsula, Victoria", *Proceedings Royal Society of Victoria* 75(1)(1962): 1–15.
6. P.J.F. Coutts, *The Archaeology of Wilsons Promontory* (Canberra: Australian Institute of Aboriginal Studies, 1970).
7. J. Flood, *The Moth Hunters: Aboriginal Prehistory of the Australian Alps* (Canberra: Australian Institute of Aboriginal Studies, 1980).
8. R.G. Gunn, *Mt Pilot 1 Aboriginal Rock Art Site* (Melbourne: Victoria Archaeological Survey, 1983).

Chapter 16   New South Wales: The West

1. J.M. Bowler, R. Jones, H.R. Allen and A.G. Thorne, "Pleistocene human remains from Australia. A living site and human cremation from Lake Mungo", *World Archaeology* 2(1970): 39–60.
2. F.D. McCarthy, *Rock Art of the Cobar Pediplain* (Canberra: Australian Institute of Aboriginal Studies, 1976); John Gerritsen, *Mootwingee — The Rockholes* (Tibooburra: Tibooburra Press, 1976).
3. McCarthy, *Rock Art.*
4. P. Dargin, *Aboriginal Fisheries of the Darling-Barwon Rivers* (Brewarrina: Brewarrina Historical Society, 1976), pp. 32–49.
5. I. McBryde, "Stone arrangements and a quartzite quarry site at Brewarrina", *Mankind* 9(2)(1973): 118–21.

Chapter 17   New South Wales: The North

1. I. McBryde, *Aboriginal Prehistory in New England* (Sydney: Sydney University Press, 1974), pp. 105–7.
2. C. Haigh and W. Goldstein, *The Aborigines of New South Wales* (Sydney: National Parks and Wildlife Service, 1980), p. 96.
3. Burnum Burnum, *Burnum Burnum's Aboriginal Australia: A Traveller's Guide* (Sydney: Angus and Robertson, 1988), p.84.
4. McBryde, *Aboriginal Prehistory*, chapter 2 and p. 56.
5. Account by kind permission of Mrs Myrtle Larrescy of Tucki Tucki, courtesy of National Parks and Wildlife Service of New South Wales.

Chapter 18   New South Wales: Sydney and the South-East

1. G.C. Nanson, R.W. Young and E.D. Stockton, "Chronology and palaeoenvironment of the Cranebrook Terrace (near Sydney) containing artefacts more than 40,000 years old", *Archaeology in Oceania* 22(2)(1987): 72–78.
2. E.D. Stockton and W.N. Holland, "Cultural sites and their environment in the Blue Mountains", *Archaeology and Physical Anthropology in Oceania* 9(1)(1974): 38–39, 52–60.
3. Ibid., 42, 52–60.
4. J.V.S. Megaw, ed., *The Recent Archaeology of the Sydney District: Excavations 1964-67* (Canberra: Australian Institute of Aboriginal Studies, 1974), pp. 1-12; P. Stanbury and J. Clegg, *A Field Guide to Aboriginal Rock Engravings with special reference to those around Sydney* (Sydney University Press, 1990), 85-89.
5. Ibid., 96-101.
6. Ibid., 48-74.
7. Ibid., 22-24.
8. J.V.S. Megaw, ed., *The Recent Archaeology of the Sydney District: Excavations 1964-67* (Canberra: Australian Institute of Aboriginal Studies, 1974), pp. 1-12.
9. J.V.S. Megaw, "A dated culture sequence for the South Sydney Region of New South Wales", *Current Anthropology* 9(1968): 325-29.
10. S. Bowdler, "Hook, line and dillybag; an interpretation of an Australian coastal shell midden", *Mankind* 10(4)(1976): 248-58.
11. C.C. Towle, "Oval arrangement of stones, Endrick Mountain", *Oceania* 3(1)(1932): 40-45.
12. J. Flood, *The Moth Hunters: Aboriginal Prehistory of the Australian Alps* (Canberra: Australian Institute of Aboriginal Studies, 1980), pp. 144-46.
13. R.J. Lampert, *Burrill Lake and Currarong* (Canberra: Australian National University, Department of Prehistory, Terra Australis 6, 1971).
14. R.J. Lampert, "Coastal Aborigines of South-eastern Australia", in *Aboriginal Man and Environment in Australia*, ed. D.J. Mulvaney and J. Golson (Canberra: Australian National University Press, 1971), pp. 114-32.
15. R.J. Lampert, "An excavation at Durras North, N.S.W.", *Archaeology and Physical Anthropology in Oceania* 1(1966): 83-118.
16. D. Byrne, *The Mountains Call Me Back: A History of the Aborigines and the Forests of the Far South Coast of New South Wales* (Sydney: National Parks and Wildlife Service, 1984); video film, *Sites We Want To Keep* (Canberra: Australian Heritage Commission and Emu Productions, 1988).
17. B. Egloff, *Mumbulla Mountain: An Anthropological and Archaeological Investigation* (Sydney: National Parks and Wildlife Service, 1979).
18. A.W. Howitt, *The Native Tribes of South-East Australia* (London: Macmillan, 1904).

Chapter 19 The Australian Capital Territory

1. J. Flood, *The Moth Hunters: Aboriginal Prehistory of the Australian Alps* (Canberra: Australian Institute of Aboriginal Studies, 1980).
2. P. Bindon, "Surface campsite collections from the ACT", *Australian Institute of Aboriginal Studies Newsletter* 3(6)(1973): 4–11.
3. J. Flood, B. David, J. Magee and B. English, "Birrigai: A Pleistocene site in the south-eastern highlands", *Archaeology in Oceania* 22(1987): 9–26.
4. G. Barrow, *Exploring Namadgi and Tidbinbilla: Day Walks in Canberra's High Country* (Canberra: Dagraja Press, 1987), pp. 15–17.
5. Flood, *The Moth Hunters,* pp. 130–36, 235–39, 330–34.
6. Barrow, *Exploring Namadgi,* pp. 30–34.
7. K. Officer, "Namadgi Pictures. The Aboriginal Rock Art Sites within the Namadgi National Park, ACT: Their recording, significance, analysis and conservation," unpublished report to ACT Administration, Heritage Unit, and the ACT Parks and Conservation Service, 1989.
8. A. Rosenfeld, J. Winston-Gregson and K. Maskell, "Excavations at Nursery Swamp 2, Gudgenby Nature Reserve, Australian Capital Territory", *Australian Archaeology* 17(1983): 48–58.

Chapter 20 Tasmania

1. S. Bowdler, *Hunter Hill, Hunter Island* (Canberra: Department of Prehistory, Australian National University, *Terra Australis* 8, 1984).
2. R. Cosgrove, "Thirty thousand years of human colonisation in Tasmania — new Pleistocene dates", *Science* 243(1989): 1706–08.
3. K. Kiernan, R. Jones and D. Ranson, "New evidence from Fraser Cave for glacial age man in southwest Tasmania", *Nature* 301(1983): 28–32; R. Jones, "Ice Age hunters of the Tasmanian Wilderness", *Australian Geographic* 8(1987):26–45; J. Allen, R. Cosgrove and S. Brown, "New archaeological data from the Southern Forests region, Tasmania: A preliminary statement", *Australian Archaeology* 27(1988):75–88.
4. R. Jones, R. Cosgrove, J. Allen, S. Cane, K. Kiernan, S. Webb, T. Loy, D. West and E. Stadler, "An archaeological reconnaissance of karst caves within the Southern Forests region of Tasmania, September 1987", *Australian Archaeology* 26(1988): 1-23; T.H. Loy, R. Jones and D.E. Nelson, "Radiocarbon dating of human blood proteins in Australia", *Antiquity* 64 (1990): 110-16.
5. M. MacPhail and J. Peterson, "New deglaciation dates from Tasmania", *Search* 6 (1975): 127–30; E.A. Colhoun, "The late Quaternary environment of Tasmania as a backdrop to man's occupance", *Records of the Queen Victoria Museum* 61(1978): 1–12.
6. H. Lourandos, "10,000 years in the Tasmanian Highlands", *Australian Archaeology* 16(1983): 39–47.
7. R. Jones, "Tasmania: aquatic machines and offshore islands", in *Problems in Economic and Social Anthropology*, eds G. de G. Sieveking, I.H. Longworth and K.E. Wilson (London: Duckworth, 1976), pp. 235–63.
8. R. Jones, "Why did the Tasmanians stop eating fish?", in *Explorations in Ethnoarchaeology,* ed. R. Gould (Santa Fe: University of New Mexico Press, 1978), pp. 11–47.
9. R.J. Fudali and R.J. Ford, "Darwin glass and Darwin crater: A progress report", *Meteoritics* 14(3)(1979): 283–96.
10. Jones "Ice Age hunters", 40–41.
11. H. Lourandos, "Dispersal of activities — the east Tasmanian Aboriginal sites", *Papers and Records of the Royal Society of Tasmania* 2(1968): 41–46; H. Lourandos, "Stone tools, settlement, adaptation: a Tasmanian example", in *Stone Tools as Cultural Markers*, ed. R.V.S. Wright (Canberra: Australian Institute of Aboriginal Studies, 1977), pp. 219–24.
12. S. Cane, "Stone features in Tasmania", M.A. Qualifying thesis, Australian National University, Canberra, 1980; R. Jones, "Archaeological reconnaissance in Tasmania", *Oceania* 35 (1965): 191–201.
13. P.C. Sims, "Variations in Tasmanian petroglyphs", in *Form in Indigenous Art: Schematisation in the Art of Aboriginal Australia and Prehistoric Europe*, ed. P.J. Ucko (Canberra: Australian Institute of Aboriginal Studies, 1977), pp. 429–38.
14. R. Jones, "Rocky Cape, West Point and Mount Cameron West, north-west Tasmania", in *The Heritage of Australia* (Canberra: Australian Heritage Commission, 1980), pp. 7/86–90; R. Jones, "Different strokes for different folks: Sites, scale and strategy", in *Holier than Thou*, ed. I. Johnson (Canberra: Prehistory Department, Australian National University, 1980), pp. 161–67.
15. J. Flood, *Archaeology of the Dreamtime* (Sydney: Collins, 1983), pp. 164–65.

16. R. Jones, "Rocky Cape, West Point".
17. Ibid.
18. S. Cane, "Stone features in Tasmania", pp. 83–91.
19. R. Cosgrove, *Tasmanian West Coast Aboriginal Rock Art Survey* (Hobart: Tasmanian National Parks and Wildlife Service Occasional Paper no. 5, 1983); R.C. Gunn, "The petroglyphs of Sundown Point, northwest Tasmania", unpublished Report to the National Parks and Wildlife Service, Tasmania, 1981.
20. J. Stockton, *Greens Creek Aboriginal Engraving Site.* (Hobart: Tasmanian National Parks and Wildlife Service Occasional Paper No. 1, 1977).

Glossary

abraded groove   A continuous linear groove made by rubbing a stone, bone or wooden tool to and fro across a rock surface.

adze   A stone tool used as a wood-working chisel, usually mounted in a handle.

anthropology   The study of the human species.

anthropomorph   A human-like figure with some non-natural characteristics.

archaeology   The study of the material traces of the human past.

artefact   An object modified by human agency.

awl   A small pointed tool, usually made of bone, used for puncturing or pricking, particularly hides.

axe   Hafted stone hatchet head.

backed blade   A stone blade with the margin opposite the worked edge deliberately blunted by flaking to form a back.

blade   A parallel-sided stone flake, at least twice as long as it is wide.

blank   A roughly shaped but unfinished stone tool.

Bondi point   An asymmetric backed blade, first identified at Bondi Beach.

bora ground   A ceremonial site with one or more roughly circular enclosures, surrounded by raised banks.

BP   Before the Present ("Present" is 1950, the beginning of radiocarbon dating).

cairn   A pile of stones.

calcarenite   Dune limestone.

calcrete   Superficial gravels cemented by deposits of calcium carbonate formed from solutions of calcium bicarbonate.

caldera   An enlarged volcanic crater which is bounded by a low rim of lava fragments and rock debris.

campsite   An area in the open air showing a concentration of debris associated with human occupation.

canoe tree   A tree scarred by the removal of a large sheet of bark to make a canoe.

carved tree　　A tree from which a slab of bark has been removed and the exposed wood carved in geometric or curvilinear designs. Other carved trees have designs or figures carved into the bark or outer wood. Carved trees are generally associated with ceremonial sites, bora grounds or burials.

cation ratio dating (CR)　　The CR dating method for dating rock varnish within petroglyphs depends on determination of the ratio of calcium and potassium to titanium — (K + Ca)/Ti — concentrations within the rock varnish. The calcium and potassium ions are more mobile than titanium and are more readily leached from the surface; from this reaction the older the varnish, the closer the ratio approaches 1:1. The ion concentrations are determined by chemical analysis. Calibration is effected by accelerator mass spectrometry (AMS) dating of the varnish of a limited range of samples from the same area. Cation ratios in rock varnishes on surfaces of known numerical age such as historic graffiti are compared to the CRs of rock engravings. Systematic changes which occur in the ratio of the cations in varnish over time are utilised in estimating ages.

cheniers　　Shelly beach ridges parallel to one another.

chert　　A fairly pure, siliceous, fine-grained rock.

clan　　A local, land-owning group whose membership was fixed by birth.

conchoidal fracture　　A shell-like, curved surface with ripple marks formed in certain types of rock fracture.

coolamon　　Aboriginal carrying dish, usually made of wood or bark.

core　　A lump or nodule of stone from which flakes have been removed by striking it with another stone.

cycads　　Woody, cone-bearing plants, "living fossils" with many primitive characteristics; the poisonous seeds were detoxified and used as food by Aborigines.

desert varnish　　A surface coating, usually brownish-black and glossy, consisting mainly of clays and oxides of iron and manganese, which builds up over the millennia on stable rock surfaces, particularly in arid environments.

dilly bag　　A woven bag used by Aboriginal people, especially women, for collecting food.

dingo　　The wild dog of Australia *(Canis familiaris dingo).*

direct percussion　　Percussion by a hand-held hammer.

doline　　A conical depression in limestone, characteristic of karst landscape.

drawings　　Pictographs or freehand rock art made with dry pigment, often charcoal.

Dreamtime　　The era of creation; the time when ancestral beings travelled across the country creating the form of the landscape.

Dreaming track/ songline	A route taken by a Dreaming or ancestral being, along which track a series of events occurred which are part of Aboriginal oral tradition and are marked by a series of sites.
engraving/ petroglyph	A way of making marks on rock, whereby the engraver removes some of the rock surface by pecking, pounding, abrasion or scratching.
ethnography	Writings about local indigenous people.
fault	A fracture in the Earth's crust, along which the rocks on one side have been displaced in relation to the other side.
figurative	Rock art motifs which resemble objects familiar to the observer; representational or naturalistic.
findspot	The place where a single artefact was found.
firestick	A smouldering stick traditionally carried by Aboriginal groups when travelling.
flake	A piece of stone detached by striking a core with another piece of stone.
fossils	The remains and traces of animals and plants which are found naturally incorporated in rocks. They comprise both the actual remains of organisms, casts and impressions thereof, and footprints of animals and humans.
geology	The science involving the study of the whole evolution of the Earth.
geometric microlith	A backed blade which is generally geometric in shape (e.g. triangular, trapezoidal, crescentic) and usually less than twice as long as it is wide.
geomorphology	The study of present day landscapes, and the elucidation and explanation of their histories.
glaciation	The covering of an area, or the action on that area, by an ice sheet or glacier.
gracile	Lightly built and thin-boned human physique.
greenstone	Altered volcanic rocks of Cambrian age, predominantly amphibole hornfels in south-eastern Australia.
grinding groove	A tool-sharpening groove produced by manual rubbing of an artefact to and fro to grind or re-sharpen its surface.
ground-edge tool	Tool with a sharp cutting edge at one end produced by grinding rather than flaking.
haematite	Hydrated form of high grade ferric oxide yielding a red pigment.
hafting	The process of mounting an artefact in a handle or onto another artefact.
hearth	The site of a campfire, represented by ash, charcoal, discoloration, and possibly hearth stones around it.
Holocene period	The last 10,000 years.
horsehoof core	High-backed, steep-edged stone core, resembling a horse's hoof in shape, typical of the old Australian core tool and scraper tradition.
ice age	The period during which ice sheets and glaciers covered large areas of the northern hemisphere.

igneous rock   All rocks of magmatic and plutonic origin. Igneous rocks
                          are formed from the consolidation of magma, which are
                          molten fluids highly charged with gases and vapours
                          generated in the depths of the Earth.

indirect   Percussion by the hammer and chisel method.
percussion

in situ   Undisturbed in its original position.

karst   Landscape which shows a pattern of denudation in
                          limestone and dolomitic rocks. This topography is produced
                          by percolating ground waters and underground streams.

limonite   Hydrated form of ferrous oxide yielding a yellow pigment.

lithic scatter   A small number of stone artefacts lying on the surface of the
                          ground.

macropod   Macropod means "long foot", and these animals of the
                          family Macropodidae are essentially herbivorous
                          marsupials with enlarged hind limbs and apparently
                          reduced forelimbs.

mammals   Hairy vertebrates, whose young are nourished on milk.

manuport   An unmodified object transported by human agency.

marsupials   Mammals characterised by having a pouch to carry and
                          nourish their young.

material culture   The tangible objects produced by a society.

megafauna   Large, extinct animals.

mesa   A flat-topped, table-like mountain which falls away steeply
                          on at least three sides, and is formed from a plateau in arid
                          regions.

metamorphic   Rock formed by the structural alteration of igneous or
rock   sedimentary rock by natural agencies of pressure or heat.

microlith   A small stone artefact, less than 3 centimetres in its
                          maximum dimension.

micron   One millionth of a metre.

midden   A refuse heap, often composed largely of shells.

motif   A mark, or combination of marks, of human origin which
                          can reasonably be interpreted to have made up an individual
                          or separate picture or design.

mound   Artificial elevations formed by the deliberate heaping up of
                          earth from the surrounding plain. Many such mounds have
                          occupational debris in the surface layers and some have
                          evidence that wooden huts were formerly built on top of
ochre   them.
                          oxide, used to make red, yellow, or brown pigment.

oven,   A shallow depression in the ground, containing ash and
ground-oven   charcoal and often lined with stones or lumps of baked clay.

painting   Freehand art, whereby an artist mixes pigment with water
                          and then manually paints the rock surface.

palaeontology   The study of the fossil remains of animals.

palynology   The study of fossil pollen and spoors.

pecking	A method of engraving involving making precise deep nicks, peck marks or pits in the rock surface.
pigmented art/pictographs	Pictures in which pigment has been added to the rock surface, comprising paintings, drawings, stencils and prints.
Pleistocene	Glacial epoch preceding the Holocene, extending back from 10,000 to about two million years ago.
prehistory	The story of human development before the time of written records.
pressure-flaking	Shaping a stone by pressing off small thin flakes with a bone or wooden tool.
print	A positive impression of a hand or other object on a rock surface, made by dipping it in wet pigment and pressing it against the rock surface.
quarry	A place where a source of raw material has been exploited, often consisting of pits and hollows where material has been dug out of the ground, and identifiable by a dense scatter of broken stone, flakes, chips, and roughly shaped artefacts.
quartz	A common white rock with naturally sharp edges.
quartzite	A granulose metamorphic rock, representing a re-crystallised sandstone, consisting predominantly of quartz, an excellent tool-making raw material.
Quaternary	The last two million years, including both the Pleistocene and Holocene periods.
radiocarbon dating	A scientific method of dating organic fossil remains such as charcoal, bone and shell, based on the content of carbon 14.
robust	Strongly built, thick-boned human physique.
rock art	Marks or pictures painted, drawn, stencilled, imprinted or engraved on a rock surface.
rockshelter	A naturally-formed overhang in a cliff, outcrop or boulder, sheltering a floor area.
sacred site	Dreaming, mythological, traditional, ethnographic, story or living site, of particular significance to contemporary Aborigines; places where ancestral creative beings made things the way they are.
scarred tree	A tree showing a scar caused by the removal of bark by Aborigines for making artefacts such as canoes, shields, or containers.
scoria	A rock formed from lava, containing empty cavities.
scraper	Stone tool made on a flake, with one or more working edges, generally used for chiselling, cutting, gouging or planing.
sedimentary rock	Rocks formed of sediment, usually deposited in water.
seed-grinding patches	Patches of rock worn smooth by grinding by Aboriginal people, usually women, grinding acacia or grass seeds into flour.
silcrete	A fine-grained rock with good conchoidal fracture.

site (archaeological)	A place where past human activity is identifiable.
stencil	A negative silhouette of a hand or other item outlined by splattered paint on the rock face. The paint is usually pigment mixed with water and sprayed from the mouth.
stone arrangement	A man-made alignment of stones, consisting of a circle, line, pile or other design, used for ceremonial or ritual purposes.
stratified site	A site with successive layers of occupational debris and/or sediments.
stromatolite	An organo-sedimentary structure produced by the sediment-trapping binding and precipitation activity of micro-organisms.
tally marks	A series of short, parallel strokes, usually in horizontal rows, painted or engraved by Aborigines on rock.
talus slope	The slope at the foot of a cliff or below a rockshelter, often covered with scree (rock debris).
tessellated pavement	The result of weathering of rock forming a regular, chequered pattern.
thermo-luminescence dating	A scientific method of dating objects, such as those of baked clay, which have been heated to more than 400 to 500 degrees C in the past, by measurement of their thermoluminescent (TL) glow.
tool, implement	An artefact manufactured for use or showing clear signs of use.
totem	An animal, plant or other natural object used as the emblem or token of an individual or group, in a system of relationships (totemism) that provides spiritual linkages between people and the natural and physical universe.
tribe	A major Aboriginal social and kinship group, possessing a common language, identity, culture and territory.
type/diagnostic artefact	An artefact with a wide distribution in space but a restricted one in time, useful for correlating cultural sequences over large areas and for cross-dating.
type site	A site containing artefacts typical of a particular prehistoric phase.
use-wear	Wear produced on the working edge of a tool from use.
waste flake	A piece of stone detached from a core by striking the core with another stone, but subsequently unmodified.
weathering	The alteration and decay of rocks as far down as the depth to which atmospheric agencies can penetrate.

Further Reading

Australian Heritage Commission. *The Heritage of Australia*. Melbourne: Macmillan, 1981.

——. *The Heritage of South Australia and Northern Territory*. Melbourne: Macmillan, 1985.

——. *The Heritage of Tasmania*. Melbourne: Macmillan, 1983.

——. *The Heritage of Victoria*. Melbourne: Macmillan, 1983.

——. *The Heritage of Western Australia*. Melbourne: Macmillan, 1989.

Australian National Advisory Committee for UNESCO. *Australian Aboriginal Culture*. Canberra: Australian Government Publishing Service, 1973.

Berndt, R.M. and C.H. Berndt. *Aborigines of the West: Their Past and Their Present*. Perth: University of Western Australia Press, 1979 (revised edition 1980).

——. *The Speaking Land: Myth and Story in Aboriginal Australia*. Melbourne: Penguin, 1988.

——. *The World of the First Australians: Aboriginal Traditional Life: Past and Present*. Canberra: Aboriginal Studies Press, 1988.

Berndt, R.M., and E.S. Phillips. *The Australian Aboriginal Heritage*. Sydney: Ure Smith, 1973.

Blainey, G. *Triumph of the Nomads: A History of Ancient Australia*. Melbourne: Sun Books, 1975.

Burnum Burnum. *Burnum Burnum's Australia*. Sydney: Angus and Robertson, 1988.

Corke, D. *The First Australians*. Melbourne: Nelson (Young Australia series), 1985.

Cowan, J. *Mysteries of the Dreaming: The Spiritual Life of Australian Aborigines*. Sydney: Prism Unity Press, 1992 (new edition). (And other works)

Dixon, R.M.W. *The Languages of Australia*. Melbourne: Cambridge University Press, 1980.

Edwards, R. *Australian Aboriginal Art: The Art of the Alligator Rivers Region, Northern Territory*. Canberra: Australian Institute of Aboriginal Studies, 1979.

Elkin, A.P. *The Australian Aborigines: How to Understand Them*. Sydney: Angus and Robertson, 1964.

Flood, J.M. *Archaeology of the Dreamtime*. Sydney: William Collins, 1983 (new edition 1989).

Frankel, D. *Remains to be Seen: Archaeological Insights into Australian Prehistory.* Melbourne: Longman Cheshire, 1991.

Gibbs, R.M. *The Aborigines.* Hawthorn: Longman, 1974.

Godden, E., and J. Malnic. *Rock Paintings of Aboriginal Australia.* Sydney: Reed (new edition 1988).

Haigh, C., and W. Goldstein. (eds). *The Aborigines of New South Wales.* Sydney: New South Wales National Parks and Wildlife Service, 1980.

Hallam, S.J. *Fire and Hearth.* Canberra: Australian Studies, 1975.

Horton, D. *Recovering the Tracks: The Story of Australian Archaeology.* Canberra: Aboriginal Studies Press, 1991.

Isaacs, J. (ed.) *Australian Dreaming: 40,000 Years of Aboriginal History.* Sydney: Lansdowne Press, 1980.

Layton, R. *Australian Rock Art. A New Synthesis.* Melbourne: Cambridge University Press, 1992.

Maddock, K. *The Australian Aborigines.* Ringwood: Penguin, 1982 (second edition).

McBryde, I. *Aboriginal Prehistory of New England.* Sydney: Sydney University Press, 1974.

McCarthy, F.D. *Australian Aboriginal Rock Art.* Sydney: Australian Museum, 1979.

——. *Australian Aboriginal Stone Implements.* Sydney: Australian Museum, 1979.

Meehan, B. and R. Jones (eds). *Archaeology with Ethnography.* Canberra: Prehistory Department, Australian National University, 1988.

Mulvaney, D.J. *Prehistory and Heritage: The Writings of John Mulvaney.* Canberra: Prehistory Department, Australian National University, 1990.

——. *The Prehistory of Australia.* Ringwood: Penguin, 1975.

——. *Encounters in Place: Outsiders and Aboriginal Australians 1606-1985.* Brisbane: University of Queensland Press, 1989.

Mulvaney, D.J., and J.P. White, (eds). *Australians: A Historical Library: Australians to 1788.* Sydney: Fairfax, Syme and Weldon Associates, 1987.

Presland, G. *Land of the Kulin.* Melbourne: McPhee Gribble/Penguin, 1985.

Roberts, A., and C.P. Mountford. *The Dreamtime.* Adelaide: Rigby, 1965.

——. *The Dawn of Time.* Adelaide: Rigby, 1969.

——. *The First Sunrise.* Adelaide: Rigby, 1971.

Ryan, L. *The Aboriginal Tasmanians.* Brisbane: University of Queensland Press, 1981.

Stanbury, P. (ed.) *10,000 Years of Sydney Life: A Guide to Archaeological Discovery.* Sydney: Macleay Museum, University of Sydney, 1979.

Stanbury, P., and J. Clegg. *A Field Guide to Aboriginal Rock Engravings with Special Reference to Those Around Sydney.* Sydney: Sydney University Press, 1990.

Thorne, A., and R. Raymond. *Man on the Rim.* Sydney: Angus and Robertson, 1989.

Tindale, N.B. *Aboriginal Tribes of Australia.* Canberra: Australian National University Press, 1974.

Walsh, G. *Australia's Greatest Rock Art.* Bathurst: E.J. Brill, Robert Brown and Associates (Aust.) Pty Ltd, 1988.

White, J.P., and J. O'Connell. *A Prehistory of Australia, New Guinea and Sahul.* London: Academic Press, 1982.

List of Contacts

National

Australian Heritage Commission
(53 Blackall Street)
GPO Box 1567
CANBERRA, ACT 2601

Tel. (06) 271 2111

Australian Institute of Aboriginal and Torres Strait Islander Studies
(Acton House, Acton)
GPO Box 553
CANBERRA, ACT 2601

Tel. (06) 246 1111

Federation of Aboriginal Land Councils
PO Box 3321
ALICE SPRINGS NT 0871

Tel. (089) 52 3800

Australian Capital Territory

* Heritage Unit
  ACT Environment and Conservation
  Department of Environment, Land and Planning
  PO Box 1119
  Tuggeranong
  CANBERRA, ACT 2901

Tel. (06) 246 2714

New South Wales

* Division of Cultural Resources
  and Information Services
  National Parks and Wildlife Service
  (43 Bridge Street)
  PO Box 1967
  HURSTVILLE NSW 2220

  Tel. (02) 585 6444

Northern Territory

* Museums and Art Galleries of the NT
  (Conacher Street, Bullocky Point)
  GPO Box 4646
  DARWIN NT 0801

  Tel. (089) 82 4211

* Aboriginal Areas Protection Authority
  (MLC Building, Smith Street)
  GPO Box 1890
  DARWIN NT 0801

  Tel. (089) 81 4700

  Conservation Commission of the Northern Territory
  PO Box 486, Palmerston
  DARWIN NT 0831

  Tel. (089) 89 4411

Queensland

  Cultural Heritage Branch
  Division of Conservation
  Department of Environment and Heritage
  (160 Ann Street)
  PO Box 155, North Quay
  BRISBANE QLD 4002

  Tel. (07) 227 6492

South Australia

* Aboriginal Heritage Branch
Department of Environment and Planning
(55 Grenfell Street)
GPO Box 667
ADELAIDE SA 5001

Tel. (08) 216 7777

National Parks and Wildlife Service address and phone number as above.

Tasmania

* Archaeology Section
Department of Parks, Wildlife and Heritage
(134 Macquarie Street)
GPO Box 44A
HOBART Tas. 7001

Tel. (002) 30 6679

Victoria

* Victoria Archaeological Survey
Department of Conservation and Environment
(29-31 Victoria Ave)
PO Box 262
ALBERT PARK Vic. 3206

Tel. (03) 690 5322

Department of Conservation, Forests and Lands
(240–250 Victoria Pde
East Melbourne)
PO Box 41
EAST MELBOURNE Vic. 3002

Tel. (03) 412 4011

Western Australia

* Aboriginal Sites Department
WA Museum
3rd Floor, Construction House
35 Havelock Street
WEST PERTH WA 6005

Department of Conservation
and Land Management
(50 Hayman Road, Como)
PO Box 104
COMO WA 6152

Tel. (09) 386 8811

*State/territory bodies with statutory responsibility for Aboriginal sites.

Index